THE QUIET POWER OF INDICATORS

Using a power-knowledge framework, this volume critically investigates how major global indicators of national legal governance are produced, disseminated, and used, and to what effect. Original case studies include Freedom House's Freedom in the World indicator, the Global Reporting Initiative's structure for measuring and reporting on corporate social responsibility, the World Justice Project's measurement of the rule of law, the World Bank's Doing Business index, the World Bank–supported Worldwide Governance Indicators, the World Bank's Country Performance Institutional Assessment, and the Transparency International Corruption (Perceptions) index. Also examined is the use of performance indicators by the European Union for accession countries and by the U.S. Millennium Challenge Corporation in allocating U.S. aid funds.

Sally Engle Merry is Silver Professor of Anthropology at New York University.

Kevin E. Davis is Beller Family Professor of Business Law and Vice Dean at New York University School of Law.

Benedict Kingsbury is Murry and Ida Becker Professor of Law and director of the Institute for International Law and Justice at New York University School of Law.

CAMBRIDGE STUDIES IN LAW AND SOCIETY

Cambridge Studies in Law and Society aims to publish the best scholarly work on legal discourse and practice in its social and institutional contexts, combining theoretical insights and empirical research.

The fields that it covers are: studies of law in action; the sociology of law; the anthropology of law; cultural studies of law, including the role of legal discourses in social formations; law and economics; law and politics; and studies of governance. The books consider all forms of legal discourse across societies, rather than being limited to lawyers' discourses alone.

The series editors come from a range of disciplines: academic law, sociolegal studies, sociology, and anthropology. All have been actively involved in teaching and writing about law in context.

Series Editors

Chris Arup, *Monash University, Victoria*
Sally Engle Merry, *New York University*
Susan Silbey, *Massachusetts Institute of Technology*

A list of books in the series can be found at the back of this book.

The Quiet Power of Indicators

MEASURING GOVERNANCE, CORRUPTION, AND RULE OF LAW

Edited by

SALLY ENGLE MERRY

New York University

KEVIN E. DAVIS

New York University

BENEDICT KINGSBURY

New York University

CAMBRIDGE
UNIVERSITY PRESS

CAMBRIDGE
UNIVERSITY PRESS

32 Avenue of the Americas, New York, NY 10013-2473, USA

Cambridge University Press is part of the University of Cambridge.

It furthers the University's mission by disseminating knowledge in the pursuit of
education, learning, and research at the highest international levels of excellence.

www.cambridge.org
Information on this title: www.cambridge.org/9781107427877

© Cambridge University Press 2015

First published 2015

Printed and bound in Great Britain by Clays Ltd, St Ives plc

A catalog record for this publication is available from the British Library.

Library of Congress Cataloging in Publication Data
The quiet power of indicators: measuring governance, corruption, and the rule of law /
edited by Sally Engle Merry, Kevin E. Davis, Benedict Kingsbury.
    pages   cm. – (Cambridge studies in law and society)
Includes bibliographical references and index.
ISBN 978-1-107-07520-7 (hardback) – ISBN 978-1-107-42787-7 (paperback)
1. Public administration – Evaluation.   2. Rule of law.   3. Law and economic development.
4. Political indicators.   5. Ranking and selection (Statistics) – Political aspects.   I. Merry, Sally
Engle, 1944– editor.   II. Davis, Kevin E. editor.   III. Kingsbury, Benedict, editor.
JA71.7.Q54   2015
340'.11–dc23   2014049551

ISBN 978-1-107-07520-7 Hardback
ISBN 978-1-107-42787-7 Paperback

Contents

PART II   INDICATORS IN LOCAL CONTEXTS

Notes on Contributors

Migai Akech is a legal scholar based in Nairobi, Kenya. He teaches at the University of Nairobi's School of Law, where he is an associate professor. He is a graduate of the University of Nairobi, Cambridge University, and New York University School of Law, where he was a Hauser Global Scholar. He has published widely on legal and public policy issues. He is the author of "Constraining Government Power in Africa" (*Journal of Democracy* 2011) and *Privatization and Democracy in East Africa: The Promise of Administrative Law* (East African Educational Publishers, 2009), among others. He was a Reagan-Fascell Democracy Fellow at the National Endowment for Democracy (Washington, DC) between October 2009 and February 2010. He consults for local and international organizations. His research interests are democracy, governance, public law (constitutional and administrative law), public procurement, sports law, security, and international trade and development.

Paul Benjamin is a labor and public lawyer based in Johannesburg, South Africa. He has held academic positions at the University of Cape Town and the University of the Witwatersrand, where he is currently a visiting associate professor in the School of Governance. He combines legal practice with academic life and during the apartheid years was involved in major human rights and trade union litigation. Since the advent of democracy in South Africa, he has focused on legislative policy development and drafting.

Christopher G. Bradley holds a JD, magna cum laude, from New York University School of Law; an LLM in International Law from New York University School of Law; a doctorate in English Literature from the University of Oxford; and a bachelor's degree, summa cum laude, from Princeton University. He has served as law clerk to the Hon. Patrick E. Higginbotham of the United States Court of

Appeals for the Fifth Circuit; practiced commercial and bankruptcy litigation with the law firm of Weil, Gotshal & Manges; and served as postgraduate research Fellow at the University of Texas at Austin.

Debbie Collier is an associate professor in the Department of Commercial Law at the University of Cape Town and a member of the Institute of Development of Labour Law at the University of Cape Town. Debbie is involved in teaching various aspects of employment law; her current research projects are in the field of workplace discrimination and equality law with a particular, comparative, focus on regulatory approaches and the limitations of the law, in a globalized context, in regulating behavior in this field of study.

Kevin E. Davis is Beller Family Professor of Business Law and Vice Dean at New York University School of Law. He has written extensively about anticorruption law as well as the relationship between law and economic development in such journals as the *American Journal of Comparative Law, Law and Society Review*, and the *New York University Law Review*.

Nikhil K. Dutta is an attorney advisor with the Office of Legal Adviser at the US Department of State. His contribution to this volume is published in his personal capacity and the views expressed do not necessarily reflect those of the United States government. Nikhil received his AB from Harvard College, his MPA from Princeton University, and his JD from New York University School of Law.

Benedict Kingsbury is Murry and Ida Becker Professor of Law and director of the Institute for International Law and Justice at New York University School of Law. In addition to being coeditor-in-chief of the *American Journal of International Law* he is the editor and coeditor of more than fifteen books, including *International Financial Institutions and Global Legal Governance* (2011).

Sally Engle Merry is Silver Professor of Anthropology at New York University. She is the author or editor of nine books, including the J. Willard Hurst Prize–winning *Colonizing Hawai'i: The Cultural Power of Law* (2000) and *Governance by Indicators* (2012, coedited with Kevin Davis, Angelina Fisher, and Benedict Kingsbury).

Smoki Musaraj is Assistant Professor of Anthropology at Ohio University and Faculty Affiliate at the Center for Law, Justice, and Culture at Ohio University. She holds a PhD in anthropology from the New School for Social Research and was recently a Postdoctoral Scholar at the Institute of Money, Technology, and Financial Inclusion at the University of California, Irvine. Her research focuses on money, value, and economic transformations as well as corruption and the rule of law in postsocialist contexts.

David Nelken is Professor of Comparative and Transnational Law and Head of Research at the Dickson Poon Law School at King's College, London, UK; Visiting Professor of Criminology at Oxford University's Centre of Criminology; and Distinguished Professor of Legal Institutions and Social Change at the University of Macerata in Italy. Widely published, David received a Distinguished Scholar award from the American Sociological Association in 1985. In 2009 he was given the Sellin-Glueck international career award by the American Society of Criminology and was made an Academician of the UK Academy of the Social Sciences. In 2011 he gained the biannual senior Podgorecki career prize from the International Sociological Association. In 2013 the (US) Law and Society Association gave him its International Scholar Award, and Cambridge University awarded him an LLD degree as an authority in his subject(s). He is the independent board member responsible for evaluating all law journals for the Scopus Web site (Elsevier).

Galit A. Sarfaty is Canada Research Chair in Global Economic Governance and an assistant professor in the Faculty of Law at the University of British Columbia. She holds a JD from Yale Law School, a PhD and MA in anthropology from the University of Chicago, and an AB summa cum laude from Harvard University. She previously served as an assistant professor in the Department of Legal Studies and Business Ethics at the Wharton School of the University of Pennsylvania. Prior to her position at Wharton, Galit was a Fellow at Harvard Law School's Program on the Legal Profession and Human Rights Program, a graduate Fellow at Harvard's Center for Ethics, and a visiting scholar at the American Academy of Arts and Sciences. Her scholarship offers an anthropological perspective to the study of international law and regulatory governance. In particular, she studies the convergence of economic globalization with public law values, such as human rights. Galit's research has focused on major international economic organizations such as the World Bank, and she recently published a book on the subject entitled *Values in Translation: Human Rights and the Culture of the World Bank* (2012).

Mihaela Serban is an assistant professor of law and society at Ramapo College of New Jersey. Mia's teaching and research interests include law and society in Eastern Europe, law and culture, human rights and women's rights, comparative law, and constitutional law. Her most recent publication on sociolegal issues in Central and Eastern Europe is "Surviving Property: Resistance against Urban Housing Nationalization during the Transition to Communism (Romania, 1950–1965)," in *Special Issue: Interdisciplinary Legal Studies: The Next Generation, Studies in Law, Politics, and Society*, Volume 51 (2010), ed. Austin Sarat. She is currently working on a book manuscript provisionally entitled *Law, Property and Subjectivity in Early Communist Romania (1945–1965)*.

María Angélica Prada Uribe is a research Fellow and coordinator of the International Law Master at Universidad de los Andes. She holds a master's degree in international law from Universidad de los Andes. She is also professor of the International Economic Law course at the same university. She has been a teaching assistant for the Legislation and Public Policy, Public International Law, International Economic Law, and Comparative Law courses. She is currently a researcher for the first component of the "Global Administrative Law Network" Project, funded by the International Development Research Centre. She has also worked as an intern at the International Legal Office of the Colombian Ministry of Commerce.

René Urueña is an associate professor and director of the International Law Program at Universidad de Los Andes (Bogota, Colombia). He also belongs to its Global Justice and Human Rights Clinic, working in its human rights and foreign investment practice. He earned his doctorate in law at the University of Helsinki (eximia cum laude) and holds a postgraduate degree in economics from the Universidad de Los Andes. He has published extensively on international law and currently leads a project on Inter-Institutional Evaluation through the Use of Indicators, which brings together young scholars from Latin American and Africa exploring the use of indicators in global governance.

Acknowledgments

From the beginning, this was a very collaborative project. Generous support from the National Science Foundation and from New York University's Institute for International Law and Justice (IILJ) enabled us to bring together for regular meetings a group of scholars working directly on indicators and measurement in relation to rule of law, corruption, and good governance (the contributors to this volume), together with several other young scholars doing very interesting work on other data and indicators issues focused in particular on developing countries: Yamini Aiyar, Jane Anderson, Paola Bergallo, Nehal Bhuta, Rene Gerrets, and Luciana Gross Cunha. All of us in this research collective were greatly enriched in our thinking by the intellectual contributions of other scholars who attended some of our workshops and conferences. These included Christian Arndt, Sabino Cassese, Lorenzo Casini, Wendy Espeland, Marianne Fourcade, Tom Ginsburg, Terrence Halliday, Bronwen Morgan, David Nelken, Catherine Powell, Jothie Rajah, Annelise Riles, Maira Rocha Machado, Meg Satterthwaite, Greg Shaffer, and Horatia Muir Watt. Terry Halliday went far beyond the call of duty in preparing written comments on draft contributions by many of the participants, and David Nelken kindly made numerous comments and wrote the concluding chapter.

The Law and Society Association at its annual meetings very helpfully provided a setting for this work, as did more specialized conferences at New York University Law School and the Aspen Institute in Rome. This project grew out of the long-term collaboration of Kevin E. Davis, Benedict Kingsbury, and Sally Engle Merry. We have been mightily aided in all of this by Angelina Fisher, IILJ Program Director, who has throughout been a creative intellectual participant and interlocutor, a key person in orchestration of IILJ funding, and a superb organizer. We are immensely grateful to her. We also appreciate the help of Mayuri Anupindi in putting the book together.

Finally, we could not have carried through this project without the support of the Law and Social Sciences Program of the National Science Foundation. The conferences and workshops that formed the book were made possible by two grants from the National Science Foundation, #SES-1023717 and #SES-1123290. The latter was a RCN grant, designed to facilitate the creation of a Research Collaboration Network.

Introduction

The Local-Global Life of Indicators:
Law, Power, and Resistance

Kevin E. Davis, Benedict Kingsbury, and Sally Engle Merry

This book is about the quiet exercise of power through indicators. With the turn to evidence-based governance, reliance on statistical data along with its synthesis into the kinds of scales, ranks, and composite indexes we refer to as indicators has become essential for policy formation and political decision making. The use of indicators in governance has expanded from economic and sector-specific quantitative data to measurement of almost every phenomenon. This book focuses on indicators of governance itself, specifically governance through law: indicators purporting to measure practices or perceptions of good governance, rule of law, corruption, regulatory quality, and related matters.

This volume presents nine original case studies that investigate how leading indicators of legal governance produced with global or transnational scope or aims are created, disseminated, and used, and with what effects. The indicators studied include Freedom House's Freedom in the World indicator, the Global Reporting Initiative's structure for measuring and reporting on corporate social responsibility, the World Justice Project's measurement of the rule of law, the Doing Business index of the International Finance Corporation of the World Bank, the World Bank–supported Worldwide Governance Indicators, the World Bank's Country Performance Institutional Assessment (CPIA), the Transparency International Corruption (Perceptions) index, and several indicators (including some of these) used by the U.S. Millennium Challenge Corporation in determining which countries are eligible to receive certain US aid funds.

The underlying theoretical framework of this volume is the linkage between knowledge and power. Indicators are both a form of knowledge and a technology for governance. Like other forms of knowledge, indicators influence governance when they form the basis for political decision making, public awareness, and the terms in which problems are conceptualized and solutions imagined. Conversely, the kinds of information embodied in indicators, the forms in which they are produced and disseminated, and how they function as knowledge are all influenced by governance

1

practices. The production of indicators is itself a political process, shaped by the power to categorize, count, analyze, and promote a system of knowledge that has effects beyond the producers. In these respects indicators are comparable to law. Law as a technology of governance can have very substantial effects on knowledge – the legal processes and legal forms of trials, investigations, inquests, legislative hearings, statutes, and treaties, for instance, can all be important sources of information that shape wider understandings of the world. Like law, indicators order the buzzing array of actual behavior into categories that can be understood in more universalistic terms. Like law, indicators not only make sense of the messy social world but also help to manage and govern it.

Some of the case studies examine the conceptualization, production, use, and contestation of prominent global indicators. Others focus on the impact of global indicators in specific local contexts. They are designed to shed light on issues such as: Which actors produce indicators? What kinds of expertise and resources do they draw on? How are they affected by law? How do forms of knowledge and technologies of governance from "global" and "local" sources interact in particular contexts? The case studies are innovative in posing many questions about indicators that are parallel to those more routinely asked about law as a form of global governance (other work with a comparable orientation includes Frydman and van Waeyenberge (2014) and Bhuta (2015)).

This inquiry into indicators of national legal governance brings two separate areas of scholarship together into a productive collaboration. The first area is the sociology of knowledge. One strand of this focuses on the technologies of knowledge production and adoption by a variety of publics, in some cases informed by ideas of *governmentality* (e.g., Foucault 1991; Valverde 1998; Rose 1999). Another strand focuses on technologies and cultures of specific practices in public and private organizations, such as audit (Power 1997; Strathern 2000; Kipnis 2008). Technologies of quantification and commensuration have been studied in important work by scholars such as Desrosières (1998, 2008), Porter (1995), Bowker and Star (1999), and Espeland and Stevens (1998, 2008), work that has extended to the study of specific indicators, including many indicators of legal governance (Espeland and Stevens 1998, 2008; Davis and Kruse 2007; Davis, Fisher, Kingsbury, and Merry 2012; Davis 2014). Several scholars have examined the important roles played by social science techniques in creating this form of governance, and the use of quantification to provide more apparently objective and nonpolitical forms of knowledge (Hacking 1990; Porter 1995; Poovey 1998). Work on the sociology of knowledge, including work in science and technology studies (STS) discussed later, has established a theoretical framework shedding much light on the centrality of forms of knowledge to practices of governance as well as the socially constructed nature of knowledge (Foucault 1980a, 1980b; Asdal, Brenna, and Moser 2007; Frydman and van Waeyenberge 2014).

The second area of scholarship is concerned with regulation and governance. Some of this work compares the uses and effects of different approaches to regulation, including choices among normative instruments that are more and less formal, and strategic or haphazard mixes among contracts, "soft law," administrative practices, pragmatic problem solving, self-regulation, fiscal or market incentives, and command-and-control regulations. Much of this scholarship has been premised on rational-actor political economy models, but other scholars have constructivist or postmodern orientations. A significant strand for present purposes is addressing the place that law plays in systems of global regulation, including relations involving international and domestic law as well as actions of international administrative agencies (Dezalay and Garth 2002; Kingsbury, Stewart, and Krisch 2005). Roles of information in global regulatory governance have been studied from the perspective of information economics, but increasingly are receiving attention from political science scholars (Buthe 2012; Kelley and Simmons 2015; Cooley and Snyder 2015) as well as lawyers (Davis, Fisher, Kingsbury, and Merry 2012; Frydman and Van Waeyenberge 2014). Ethnographic work that traces the role of actors and organizations provides insights into the interpretive, cultural work of indicators and its temporality (Merry 2014; Merry and Coutin 2014).

We do not seek to contribute directly to debates among statisticians, mathematical economists, social science survey designers, and other experts about specific techniques for making certain indicators more robust. A substantial literature in this vein focuses on measurement error, comparability, weighting of factors, and gathering reliable data, with the general objective of helping to develop specific, effective, reliable, and valid measures. In contrast, this collection examines the institutional contexts and theoretical frameworks that underlie indicators, and investigates whether and how they are used and contested.

In the next section of this introduction we define the scope of this research project, explain the methodology and the principles of case selection used, and summarize each of the chapters. In the following section we set out some of the key lessons learned from our case studies about the conceptualization, production, use, and contestation of indicators. We conclude with remarks on future research directions.

PROJECT OVERVIEW

Indicators Defined

In earlier work, we have proposed that the category of "indicator" has distinct *knowledge* effects as a means of constructing understandings and the terrain of classification and contestation, and distinct *power* effects insofar as the conceptualization, production, and use of indicators change the nature of governance and of power interactions and can indeed in some cases constitute a form of governance. In that work as well as the present project we define "indicator" as follows:

> An indicator is a named collection of rank-ordered data that purports to represent the past or projected performance of different units. The data are generated through a process that simplifies raw data about a complex social phenomenon. The data, in this simplified and processed form, are capable of being used to compare particular units of analysis (such as countries or institutions or corporations), synchronically or over time, and to evaluate their performance by reference to one or more standards.

This definition includes composite or mash-up indicators that are themselves compiled by aggregating and weighting other indicators (Davis, Kingsbury, and Merry 2012, 73–74). Some indicators are numerical, some qualitative (producing information that may or may not be rendered numerically), and some mix quantitative and qualitative information. They all involve cultural work, however: practices of category construction, counting strategies, measurement decisions, forms of presentation, and the basic decision about what to measure and what to call it. Their operation in the world involves cognitive processes, usually among users and consumers as well as producers (Lampland 2010).

Increasingly indicators are built into sets of prescriptive standards of behavior. In some cases this is to enable local flexibility or to allow different regulated entities to pursue different pathways toward the same goals. In others it is more bluntly to measure performance or compliance (see Rosga and Satterthwaite 2009). In many of the cases studied in this volume, indicators are incorporated into a legally orchestrated evaluation or decision process. Although indicators may thus be closely connected with legal-type norms or processes, indicators are not (usually) framed as laws. Instead, they are typically presented simply as summaries of information that may be useful. Their conceptualization, production, and use are governed by few if any of the constitutional or procedural requirements typically prescribed for the making of laws or of authoritative policies. Yet indicators in the fields studied here are concerned with elements of national governance that are closely connected with law. Many of these indicators, or at least components of them, might be termed indicators of legal governance, although this simplification requires much qualification and elaboration in particular cases.

Methodology

Given the relative novelty of the field of inquiry, and the emphasis we suspected was required on fine-grained context to elucidate dynamics of knowledge and power/ governance, in designing this collaborative study we determined that a series of rich case studies of institutional processes and local effects would produce the most insight and illumination. This ruled out not only research designs using large-*n* quantitative studies, but also the use of a highly prescriptive template for case studies. Instead the authors met regularly as a group with us and a superb set of co-participants and interlocutors, in three annual meetings and several smaller meetings, facilitated by two grants to us from the U.S. National Science Foundation. This process enabled the building of a research network on indicators and the mentoring and development of promising younger scholars. Five of the contributors to this volume are based in developing countries (Kenya, South Africa, Colombia), and three others have very substantial research experience and accompanying linguistic expertise in Central Europe. Almost all the authors in the collection are qualified lawyers, and the others are social scientists who have close familiarity with legal institutions and practices as objects of study.

Case selection was an iterative process, premised on an initial view among the editors of what was needed to cover a reasonable proportion of leading indicators and institutions, and a reasonable selection of local contexts, within the framework proposed for the project. Authors were invited based in part on existing expertise on cases judged by the editors as likely to contribute significantly to understanding of particular institutions and their processes or particular local contexts and dynamics. The editors took account also of other parallel research, particularly the drafts now finalized and published in the Cooley and Snyder volume (2015). The availability of that volume and other work obviated the need to pursue exact symmetry between the institutional indicators studied in Part I, and the local contexts for such indicators studied in Part II. In particular, significant work is available on the institutions and production of leading anticorruption indicators (e.g., Bukovansky 2015), and on the institutional production, some local contextual effects, and dynamics between local contexts and indicator producers, with regard to several leading indicators of democracy and democratization (Tsygankov 2015; Cooley and Snyder 2015).

Through the collaborative process the authors participating in this project have come largely to share a science and technology studies (STS) sensibility (although without the insignia of membership). They identify in indicators and their alternatives the world-making processes of experts, in which networks of people, ideas, and technologies gradually build up a technology of measuring and knowing the world, some of which takes on a "black box" quality, as does a thermometer or barometer (e.g., Latour 1987). They trace roles of actors, institutions, and theories in the creation of instruments that provide new forms of knowledge (cf. Latour 2005), but extend this to integrate the study of governance and the interactions between knowledge and governance. The ways in which the various authors do this are partly influenced by discipline and training layered onto basic legal and political methods for the study of regulation and governance: thus Musaraj, Serban, and Sarfaty use ethnographic and anthropological methods, Bradley draws on his skills as an archival historian, Dutta uses analytical methods drawn from public policy training, Akech, Urueña and to some extent Prada use techniques combining interviews and legal analysis developed in doctoral work on law, Collier and Benjamin draw on media and political sources and policy debates in which they have been directly involved as participant-observers.

Overview of the Collection

The five case studies in Part I examine the processes of conceptualization, promulgation, use, and contestation of influential governance-related indicators by six prominent organizations. Three of the organizations are nongovernmental – Freedom House, the World Justice Project, and the Global Reporting Initiative – although in some cases they have close connections to government or intergovernmental agencies, as with Freedom House's links to the US government. The World Bank, the European Union, and the U.S. Millennium Challenge Corporation are major intergovernmental or governmental producers or users of indicators. Each case study makes a particular argument about the knowledge and power/governance effects of the institutional processes of indicator conceptualization, production, use, and contestation.

Christopher G. Bradley's history of the creation and development of Freedom House and its Freedom in the World indicator, starting in the late 1930s, offers a fascinating study of an entity that has remade itself over time as the world has changed. Beginning from a campaign against Nazism, it changed to a series of other issues concerning civil and political liberties. Although its goals changed somewhat over time as the anti-Nazi movement gave way to the Cold War and its aftermath, it continued to promote the same overarching ideology. It has survived and been an unusually successful and long-lived indicator in a crowded field. Bradley argues that to understand this indicator, it is important to examine the institution that created it. It generates a great deal of media and attention for its premier indicator, Freedom in the World, yet its methodology for calculating country rankings is rough and it does not make a significant investment of resources in data collection.

Rene Urueña examines the rule of law indicator produced by the World Justice Project (WJP), an independent organization generously supported by foundation funding. Multiple rule of law indices are now in existence, as good governance has become an important goal in the third phase of law and development work. The index constructs a theory of the rule of law and promotes it through its measurements. Although the idea of the rule of law is deeply contested, Urueña argues that the indicator creates a space for that contestation. Moreover, given the multiplicity of indices and legal regimes for rule of law ideas, both domestic and international, the indicator provides a common language that helps groups communicate with each other. Urueña also shows that the WJP index establishes a normative system through quantification: it creates an understanding of the rule of law and promotes this legal consciousness. The indicator's technical role is essential to its credibility but at the same time its use is inevitably political, possibly in ways that differ from what the creators intended.

One of the areas of considerable interest in the use of governance indicators is corporate social responsibility. Galit A. Sarfaty examines one of the prominent global indicators of corporate sustainability reporting, the Global Reporting Initiative (GRI), a private organization that focuses on human rights and environmental performance. She traces the development of this indicator over time, the way its measurements are created, and the organizations that promote it. At first it sought to increase corporate accountability to consumers and NGOs, but has shifted to facilitating reporting from companies about their human rights and environmental records. Sarfaty raises questions about the effects of this indicator, pointing to the way that the measures are developed through consultations among business, labor, NGOs, and other organizations such as accounting and consulting firms and governments, a process dominated by business and international consulting firms. She describes the appeal of numerical measures for improving corporate social responsibility at the same time as she points to the drawbacks of this turn to numbers, such as a tendency for superficial compliance and ticking boxes rather than rethinking business strategies. Even though it has made significant efforts to publicize its work, consumers are relatively unaware of its rankings, and the audience for the GRI's work is increasingly businesses themselves and the accounting firms who certify the data.

Indicators are widely used in economic development work as well as in the good governance fields. María Angélica Prada Uribe examines the genealogy of development indicators, focusing in particular on those created by the World Bank. The chapter provides a valuable history of development indicators and their underlying theories, showing the differences among them and the way some indicators nevertheless achieve hegemonic status. As is the case for rule of law indicators, there is a struggle among indicators for acceptance and credibility. Those produced by powerful institutions such as the World Bank have an institutional advantage. She exposes the theories of development embedded in development indicators by comparing different indicators and the way they articulate standards for development. For example, the World Bank, a major promoter and user of indicators, uses a neoliberal, economics-based frame of reference and theory of growth. In contrast, the United Nations Development Programme (UNDP) promotes the Human Development Index, which is more focused on human rights and human well-being. Because of the power and influence of the World Bank, its indicators are globally dominant among some epistemic networks. The World Bank's development indicators reinforce its theory of development. As these indicators become widely accepted standards of development, governance becomes a matter of fostering compliance with established norms, what Prada Uribe, following Nicolas Rose, calls "government at a distance."

The four case studies in Part II focus on the impact of legal governance indicators and examine specific local contexts in which such indicators have been invoked. These case studies cover rule of law indicators in Romania, anticorruption indicators in Albania and in Kenya, and international labor indicators such as the World Bank's Employing Workers Indicator (part of the Doing Business indicators) in South Africa.

Nikhil Dutta's chapter compares two mechanisms for assessing country performance, one based on quantitative data, the Millennium Challenge Corporation (MCC), and one on qualitative data, the EU accession process. Both are conditionality arrangements, in which the transfer of benefits to recipients depends on their compliance with the terms specified by the grantors. However, the MCC, a mechanism for distributing US foreign aid, relies on quantitative measures while the EU accession process relies on qualitative narrative reports and discussions. A comparison between the effects of the two methods shows that they have quite different implications for accountability. The quantitative method is more legible than the qualitative one, but the quantitative method is not as transparent as it claims, because, despite the public availability of its standards and metrics, it sometimes fails to explain its discretionary decisions. This comparison shows that even though qualitative processes appear more participatory than quantitative ones, in this case, given the sharp imbalance of power between the EU and states that wish to join, the qualitative process lacks significant opportunities for flexibility and participation. Thus, the comparison between two specific methods shows how these technologies of knowledge shape decision making. The quantitative approach does not necessarily enhance accountability or provide a transparent, legible, and understandable process either to the public or to those who are being managed.

Mihaela Serban's analysis of rule of law indicators in contemporary Romania shifts the focus from the genealogy of indicators to their effects in particular contexts. The chapter describes the reception of indicators in a country that is measured and governed through indicators, yet has relatively little control over these measuring techniques. It examines reactions to rule of law indicators in Romania where they serve both as a mode of governance, as the EU seeks to pressure Romania to conform to a conception of the rule of law, and as a mode of reform by civil society and the state to diminish corruption and improve governance. Serban argues that there is skepticism and resistance vis-à-vis rule of law indicators when they appear to be mechanisms for outside actors to control a country, or when they are mobilized by inside actors to promote goals such as eliminating corruption when these actors are themselves seen as corrupt. Central to their power is their promise of objectivity and impartiality. Their credibility depends on being able to deliver on these promises. Some are seen as more vulnerable to politics and pressure, while others seem more based on "hard data" and more credible in the national sphere, where there is considerable competition among indicators promoted by very different actors and organizations.

Smoki Musaraj's chapter examines the national reactions to globally created indicators, focusing again on the way they are mobilized within local political struggles. It examines the production and circulation of a corruption survey in Albania in 2008 and its political uses in a power struggle within the Albanian leadership. It highlights how this form of knowledge becomes a powerful actor within national politics. She also shows how the indicator itself is the product of global as well as national actors as it is developed, implemented, and then used politically. Sponsored by the United States Agency for International Development (USAID), the indicator was used by the American ambassador to Albania to criticize some members of the government. Musaraj argues that the use of indicators is a turn to a corporate form of producing and that using such forms of knowledge is a shift toward the use of this kind of expertise in decision making. Her analysis highlights the interconnections of private and public actors and global/local relationships for understanding the effects of indicators.

Migai Akech examines the mobilization of corruption indicators in Kenya, where similar tensions between public/private control and global/local power emerge. He describes the efforts of Transparency International to measure corruption in Kenya and notes the difficulty of measuring it at all. He points to the inadequacy of it's measurements in Kenya that fail to tap into the widespread practices of corruption among political and economic elites. He locates the Kenyan Transparency International survey in the context of the global organization, offering a careful analysis of the national survey. He notes that corruption is a systemic problem yet measurement mechanisms do not count it that way. They focus on whether individuals have to pay bribes to get services but not on corruption within systems. He describes a promising approach being developed in Kenya: the use of performance indicators for situations such as public procurement and service delivery which, he thinks, can contribute to reducing corruption in public procurement and service delivery. His chapter emphasizes the role of the constitution and major institutions in controlling corruption and shows the value of more local approaches to indicator construction over more global ones.

Debbie Collier and Paul Benjamin consider the effects of labor market indicators, including those produced by the International Finance Corporation of the World Bank Group, for South Africa. They find that there are several labor market indicators in use globally, but South Africa's ranking on these indicators varies greatly. Its score depends on how each indicator values either a flexible labor market or the social welfare of workers. Some focus on flexible labor while others measure decent work. The former articulate a free market, neoliberal ideology favored by the World Bank Group's Doing Business indicator, while the latter express the concerns with quality of work of the International Labor Organization. South Africa's affirmative action and labor protection laws lead it to rank poorly in the Doing Business indicator but well when the indicator measures decent work. These indicators shape public opinion and policy formation in South Africa along with their underlying ideologies and theories of economic growth. Although indicators are commonly challenged by alternative indicators, it is relatively rare for an indicator to change because of external pressure. However, this chapter discusses the successful effort to change one of the World Bank's indicators that equates ease of doing business with a lack of protection for workers.

THE TRAJECTORY OF INDICATOR DEVELOPMENT

The case studies show the value of viewing the development and crystallization of indicators over time, a process Halliday and Shaffer refer to as "normative settling" in their analysis of transnational legal orders (2015). In this section we highlight observations from our case studies about the knowledge and governance effects of indicators by distinguishing four phases of the trajectory of development and use of indicators over time. These four phases can be presented in a stylized way as initially chronological, but once an indicator is established in pilot form or is finalized and put into use, there is likely to be reflexivity between the phases, particularly if there are proposals for revision. The first three phases are conceptualization, production, and use. The fourth phase is the impact or effect of the indicator, both in extranational institutions and – especially important in this book – in local contexts.

Conceptualization

The first phase is the conceptualization of the indicator. The indicator is named and its underlying theory of social change established. This requires a theoretical position, the development of categories for measurement, and modes of analyzing the data (see Bowker and Star 1999; Lampland and Star 2009). Every one of the global indicators examined in this book is predicated on an initial set of theoretical views. When an indicator is formulated and labeled as measuring, for example, rule of law or corruption, it builds on a theory of what constitutes a good society, or what constitutes a problem or pathology to overcome in the course of improving the national society and polity. A complex indicator further specifies a series of measures that constitute its organizing concept (e.g., rule of law), with good performance on these measures implicitly treated as steps on a pathway to attaining the good described in the organizing concept. The indicator effectively defines its organizing concept by the package of specific criteria and measurements it identifies. Thus, indicators translate broad standards into specific actions. This translation is itself based on a theory of causation or steps or at least correlations, as it implicitly specifies which actions produce what kinds of results. This process of specification may incidentally produce indicator creep: the gradual expansion of obligations as new measurements are created to operationalize standards that extend beyond the initial standards.

Influences on the conceptualization of indicators can be analyzed under four headings: actors and institutions, expertise, temporality, and resources. First, the actors and institutions who develop an indicator determine which concepts are being deployed, for what purposes, and with which theoretical orientation. For example, the World Bank labor indicator Collier and Benjamin studied relies on a neoliberal theory of economic growth and embodies a World Bank model of development. Freedom House expresses its ideology about liberty in its Freedom in the World indicator, as Bradley describes. Sarfaty describes the process of developing the Global Reporting Initiative as a complex negotiation among a variety of stakeholders including business, NGOs, and governments that produced a measure of more interest to business than consumers. It matters who the actors and institutions are that create an indicator.

There is not necessarily a straightforward connection between the theory informing a particular indicator and the underlying purpose and theoretical orientation of the institution that creates it. The degree of alignment between the indicator and the mission of its creator depends on factors such as the degree of centralization or factional divergence within the institution, and the importance of the indicator to the institution as a whole. A close alignment with a theoretical orientation that has remained largely steady over time is traced in Chris Bradley's study of Freedom House. The World Bank group has embraced different theoretical approaches to its development agenda over time, and these have been manifested by the addition of new sets of indicators; some, such as the Doing Business indicators, are viewed quite critically in other sections of the Bank, whereas the CPIA, which is a central determinant of which countries receive funding, has been quite steady and much less buffeted by tides of new theory or by controversy. Galit Sarfaty's study of the GRI shows that its indicators have remained relatively steady, although moving somewhat toward corporate box-checking and further away from evaluating on-the-ground justice and societal impacts. But the institution itself has changed, shifting its constituencies and audience and reflecting their objectives and concerns;

the GRI has turned, Sarfaty suggests, from a concern with an audience of NGOs and consumers to a concern with the corporations that are being measured.

A second feature of indicator conceptualization is the relevant expertise. As Bradley shows, Freedom House began with the work of an academic with political science expertise, whereas many of the development indicators Prada discusses were developed by economists.

A third feature is the temporality of the process. Many of the successful indicators have been many years in the making and have acquired visibility based on their past reputations as well as their ability to adapt as situations changed. For example, Bradley describes how Freedom House was born in the era of anti-Nazi activism of the 1930s, shifted to a Cold War orientation, and emphasized civil and political rights. The shift in development indicators and increasing concern with corruption and the rule of law is the product of a long-term shift in the way development is conceived and a growing concern that the reason for the failure of development is poor governance, as Prada shows. Indicators follow this path, but also strengthen it.

A fourth feature is resources. Conceptualizing indicators and linking them to data, even if there is no additional data collection process, can be an expensive and time-consuming process. It requires significant input from governments, international organizations, wealthy advocacy groups, businesses hoping to turn a profit, or academics using existing data sets. Which indicators are formed and what they measure depends in large part on where the financial support for the initiative comes from. Again, the case studies highlight questions of sponsorship and funding and show how the nature of the indicator is a product of these factors.

Production

The second phase of an indicator's trajectory is production, in which the conceptualization of the indicator is married to available or created data. During this phase, those who know about available data search for appropriate or useful databases that either measure the desired phenomenon or serve as a proxy. A key element of production is the promulgation of an indicator: its presentation, packaging, and dissemination. This involves developing modes of presenting the information that are tailored to the imagined prospective users. If an indicator is intended for a wide audience, there is likely to be a premium on formats that are clear and easy to use, conceptually simple, and visually attractive (see Espeland and Stevens 2008). One such standard technique is the use of interactive maps with countries coded in different colors depending on their performance (Bhuta 2012).

Indicators depend on data, so the book also considers sources of data and the significance of using one or another source. Several of the indicators studied in this book depend on substantial collection of primary data, or on conducting opinion surveys. Where the supply of data depends on widely dispersed individuals or entities to collect and supply it, indicator production depends on a degree of buy-in from these participants, many of whom may have incentives to under- or overreport or to reconstruct categories. Many indicators are crafted from already existing data. Some existing data are provided by national or international mechanisms of counting such as census data or demographic and health surveys, while others are cobbled together from other indicators or smaller data collection efforts. Inherent in these processes is contestation over the data, particularly between national and international sources. The chapters explore how these debates take place and how they are managed in different countries and for different kinds of data.

Conceptualizing an indicator entails defining categories of analysis, naming what is being measured, and in many cases building on an existing legal standard. Producing an already conceptualized indicator typically involves compromises and the use of proxies when the desired data are not available. The technical challenges of production may of course operate as a constraint on conceptualization, as the concepts to be measured must be related to the data that is available. Some of the entities studied here, including the World Bank and the WJP, are unusual in having the resources to elicit and gather significant data to instantiate concepts they themselves defined, such as the WJP's definition of the rule of law. Most private indicator-producing institutions in global governance, however, do not have large data-origination capacities, leading them to resort to more simple data collection, and to search for available data that can be used as a proxy for what they wish to measure. Indicator producers grapple with the problem of measuring the same thing in very different historical and cultural contexts, requiring frames of measurement that can cross national and cultural borders and remain relatively constant over time. One strategy, used, for example, by Freedom House, is to interpose a layer of staff assessment between raw data and the data that are actually used to make the indicator, raising concerns among skeptics about how "expert" and "objective" the staff are who play this important and difficult-to-scrutinize role. The World Bank builds in subjective expert opinion in a contained way in its CPIA, incorporating the assessments of its field staff as one scored component.

Production is often depicted as a pragmatic process: the statistician does the best she can with the data available, despite challenges and slippages. It is not typically understood or announced as a political, conceptual, or interpretive process, even though it requires politics and interpretation. It focuses on where data is available, who collects it for what purposes, who pays for it, how it is categorized, and who owns it. For example, much of the household-level data for developing countries comes from demographic and health surveys conducted by Macro International and paid for by USAID or from the Multiple Indicator Cluster Survey carried out by UNICEF in collaboration with national governments and paid for by governments or UNICEF. In each case, there is some collaboration with national governments over the scope and nature of the survey.

As with the earlier discussion of conceptualization, production can also be analyzed in terms of actors and institutions, expertise, temporality, and resources. The key actors are statisticians, either from governments or in private settings such as survey companies. Both national and international organizations are engaged in data collection, sometimes leading to conflicts when there are discrepancies in the data. The dominant expertise is statistical and technical. Official statisticians' fundamental principles emphasize professionalism and noninterference by politicians. Temporality is important, since there is often inertia and resistance to change. Tried and established models are generally preferred for data collection while changing previous techniques of gathering data undermines long-term comparisons. Resources matter, since data collection is very expensive. Some forms are less expensive, such as expert opinion surveys, while indicators that can use administrative data already collected by state agencies such as the police or the courts are clearly less expensive. New questions of ownership of data, particularly data held in the private sector, are changing the availability of data. Relatively few private organizations can afford their own data collection, and most use proxies. As Akech shows, Transparency International does its own data collection, but uses primarily perception data by experts, clearly a limited kind of data. Expert opinion surveys are far less expensive than surveys of all potential victims or all top level officials who might have bribed or been bribed. In the absence of independent data gathering, the collection of data can become deeply problematic, as it is for the GRI that Sarfaty discusses in which corporations are responsible for collecting their own data on their compliance with GRI standards.

The interaction between conceptualization and data collection is critically important, since each shapes the other. In each case, one must ask, which comes first – the data availability or the problem to be measured? Does one look at what the data are and decide how to use them, or does one conceptualize the measures and then look for data to plug in? Or does one search for funds to collect new data? Statisticians tend to start with data and derive indicators, while advocates tend to begin with concepts and look for data. The order matters. If the indicator must rely on existing data, its definition is limited to what has already been measured or what can be interpreted from it. To move into new territory, it may be necessary to develop new data, which requires funding to collect it and even more funding to collect it over time.

Uses of Indicators

The third phase in the trajectory of an indicator is the one in which the indicator is treated as a source of knowledge, meaning that it is used to form background beliefs or understandings, develop or test scientific hypotheses, and to form conclusions that provide a basis for decision and action. For instance, the Freedom in the World Index might be used in forming general impressions about the importance of promoting liberty, in statistical tests of theories of the relationship between political institutions and economic development, in deciding whether to donate to Freedom House, or in deciding whether to provide aid to Ghana. An indicator, especially if highly authoritative and stable over time, can also provide a focal point around which to align expectations. The World Bank Group's Doing Business indicators, Freedom House's Freedom in the World indicator, the World Economic Forum's Global Competitiveness Index, and the U.S. State Department's Trafficking in Persons indicator each seem to have operated as a focal point aligning expectations and influencing behavior, as have the *U.S. News & World Report* rankings of law schools within the United States. The influence of a focal point on behavior is heightened if use of the indicator becomes sufficiently embedded that network effects result. The system of letter-graded credit ratings for sovereign bonds is so embedded in legal rules and market practices (including requirements that some entities invest only in bonds rated as "investment grade") that network effects result, making major changes to the system more costly and less likely.

Some or all of the uses may be entirely foreign to the intentions of the original conceptualizing and producing institution or individuals. The set of people whose knowledge is shaped by any given indicator – for example, government officials, NGO leaders, journalists, or the educated public – will depend in part on how the indicator circulates through news media, government speeches, action plans, NGO and social movement activity, and political debate.

Effects and Impacts of Indicators

Assessing the causal effects of indicators is almost impossible to do with any precision, as their influence can seldom be isolated from a myriad of other confounding causes or distortionary factors. The effects of indicators within individual organizations are the easiest to track, especially when those organizations are committed to transparency in decision making. For example, it is not that difficult to understand the role of the CPIA in determining which countries receive development aid or World Bank loans.

Macro knowledge effects are more difficult to isolate, but there have been some notable efforts. For example, case studies show that there is significant indicator-influenced acceptance, fostered by the news media, that the concept of "development" is well articulated by the UNDP's Human Development Index (Davis, Kingsbury, and Merry 2012), that political "freedom" is distributed much as Freedom House says it is (Cooley and Snyder 2015), and that countries ranking very low on the Transparency International CPI are indeed among the most corrupt. Case studies in this volume suggest that the Doing Business Employing Workers Indicator did initially have some effects on understandings by some South Africans of what constitutes good labor regulation, and that Transparency International's indicators did help convince Kenyans that corruption was both severe and a problem that ought to be addressed. Bradley shows clearly that Freedom House provides knowledge to a wide public even though the indicator is not used directly in any decision making. Despite these studies, many of the less direct but still potentially significant impacts of indicators remain to be explored. These include the effects of indicators on foreign investors' assessments, on the decisions of activist-minded tourists, or on the efforts of international humanitarian organizations or election monitoring organizations to pinpoint sites for intervention.

Indicators vary in their influence. Some become well established and remain influential while others receive little uptake or decline in importance. We have not sought in this research systematically to inquire into reasons why some indicators are more influential than others, although some of the case studies provide incidental evidence for analyses and hypotheses about supply and demand for indicators (Buthe 2012), indicator ecology (Halliday 2012), status and influence of institutions espousing particular indicators (Bhuta 2012, 2015; Cooley and Snyder 2015), or indicator quality (Davis 2004; Kaufmann, Kraay, and Mastruzzi 2010; Lampland 2010; Symposium 2011; Davis, Kingsbury, and Merry 2012). For instance, Migai Akech shows that some indicators have less impact because they are perceived as failing to measure the phenomenon they seek to understand. This occurred with the Transparency International measure of corruption in Kenya, which was regarded as not counting systemic corruption among political and economic elites but instead as focusing only on bribes paid by people in the course of their everyday lives.

Contestation

Once an indicator is created, it is difficult to challenge it and force it to change its categories. Indicators are established over time and gradually become more resistant to change. Yet, there are some examples of contestation. A dramatic example is that described by Collier and Benjamin, when the World Bank was persuaded to give up using its Employing Workers Indicator in its then-existing form (see also Benjamin and Theron 2009). There are more subtle examples of resistance in Akech's paper on Kenya and Serban's on Romania. These are relatively powerless countries subjected to measurement and management by more powerful ones. In a sense, the participation of corporate actors in the regular reformulation of the GRI is a form of contestation from within: they shape what gets measured and what does not and therefore are able to channel the way they are regulated.

Contestation occurs at the level of conceptualization, as people/countries fight about what is the best measure for poverty, development, or violence against women, but it also happens at the level of data as countries or organizations chose what to measure and what to ignore. In meetings of the UN Statistical Commission, representatives of developing countries regularly insist that if the developed world wants them to measure something, they will need more resources to do so. Developing countries sometimes object to international data that contradicts national data and demand that their national data should be taken more seriously. Data collection itself can become politicized, of course, as can the project of developing indicators and categories.

INTERACTION BETWEEN GLOBAL INDICATORS AND LOCAL KNOWLEDGE AND GOVERNANCE PRACTICES

One of the main purposes of this volume is to analyze the relationship between global systems of knowledge production, such as indicators, and the local meanings, uses, and effects of these global systems. The case studies demonstrate that these global measurement systems acquire their own political and cultural meanings in particular local situations. There are several dimensions to this interaction.

First, indicators produced in global contexts use universalizing categories to measure phenomena such as rule of law or good governance, yet these apparently universal categories are based on particular local or national models which define certain social forms as indicative of rule of law or good governance. These definitions are often based on the political and economic theories of those who create the indicators. In cases such as Freedom House, Transparency International, or the Doing Business indicators, those who produce and use the indicators are usually in prosperous countries while those being measured are frequently in impoverished developing countries. This situation raises the possibility that powerful actors will use indicators as technologies of governance. However, the magnitude of this governance effect may depend on broader power dynamics. For instance, Romania took seriously the indicator components of EU accession requirements when seeking to become a member of the EU. However, once Romania's membership was complete, EU monitoring had less bite, and the direct governance effects of externally defined rule of law indicators have waned. In the case studies of Albania and Kenya the governance effects of the global indicators also tended to decline over time, and to end up being modest.

Second, the meanings of global indicators depend on the local political and cultural situations within which they are interpreted, producing effects that sometimes differ from what their creators imagined. They may become part of local political struggles or manipulated through "gaming" the indicator. Some encounter resistance, resentment, or rejection. They may be contested locally, particularly when the global categories misread local practices. Despite this localization of meaning, global indicators are not fully transformed but retain their inspiration and sustenance from the broad drivers of global indicators. Rule of law, political freedom, corruption, and good governance are central public issues in struggles for reform in many developing countries. Global indicators produced by extranational institutions are used in local political struggles by reformers. Such uses are discussed by Musaraj, Akech, and Serban in their studies of Albania, Kenya, and Romania respectively; and a much more public contestation about reform of South African labor law linked to global indicators is discussed by Collier and Benjamin. A major complication for such reformers is that invoking a global indicator tends to cast them as aligned with an extranational institution that may be viewed with skepticism by local political actors, and that may be pursuing, including through the indicator, a different set of political interests or ideological commitments than those the local reformers wish to embrace. All four of these case studies suggest that the invocation and effects in the local politics of the pertinent global indicators have tended to decrease, with other more locally specific quantifications and techniques coming to the fore instead.

Third, contestation of the terms of global indicators by local or national organizations is difficult but does occur under certain conditions. An initiative of one or more developing countries seldom influences global indicators directly, even if the indicator is incongruent or misaligned. However, the story of the Employing Workers Indicator suggests that when a powerful constituency within the institution producing the indicator challenges its terms or develops an alternative, there can be change or innovation.

INDICATORS AND THE LAW

Indicators and law both embody standards, and for this reason both can operate as an expression of values and political commitments. Some of the pathways through which indicators can influence expectations, social categories, status relations, behavior, and even identities are similar to those applicable to international legal instruments. These include naming, shaming, praising/blaming, emulation, acculturation, information changing beliefs or strategic calculations, behavioral or identity adaptations of the indicated, empowerment or redefinition of the indicators promulgator, altering external power structures, altering distributions of power within an entity, and building or intensifying networks. In these respects global indicators are comparable to international legal norms. Indicators are distinctive, however, in that (typically) the indicator simultaneously articulates the standard and applies it. The flow of costs and benefits as incentives to perform better on an indicator may be greater or less than the flows attached to legally binding instruments.

Our case studies hint at several possible similarities, differences, and forms of interaction between law and indicators. The differences between law and indicators are particularly apparent at the production stage. These differences may reflect in part the different actors involved in producing law and indicators. Sarfaty's study of the GRI hints at the possibility that accountants gravitate toward producing indicators while lawyers prefer to generate standards. Generally speaking the production of indicators appears to be subject to less regulation and constraint than is the production of formal legal standards. This is not to say that the production and use of indicators are wholly lawless. Our case studies reveal several instances in which indicators have been produced or used at the behest of legal actors. Urueña describes Colombian judicial decisions that demand the production of human rights indicators and Serban describes an EU instrument, the Cooperation and Verification Mechanism, which has indirectly stimulated the production of rule of law and corruption indicators in Romania. US legislation demands the use of indicators in allocating the Millennium Challenge Corporation grants discussed in Dutta's study. An investigation undertaken by the World Bank's Independent Evaluation Group, a review mechanism within a partially juridified process, led to abandonment of the Employing Workers Indicator discussed in Collier and Benjamin's study. Nonetheless, it is evident that the production of global indicators is much less formal and constrained than the production of global legal norms. Negotiation, adoption, and ratification of multilateral treaties is slow and complex, and "soft law" instruments such as World Bank policies or Basel Committee bank supervisory standards are increasingly subject to extended negotiation and consultation processes before adoption. Participation in these lawmaking processes is often much broader and political contestation much stronger, than in processes to create and promulgate an indicator.

At the same time, the motivations for producing law and indicators may not be that different. Musaraj's study suggests that public actors are willing to contract out the production of indicators to private actors, paralleling a trend that has been observed in the production of legal norms.

It is also fruitful to compare global indicators and international legal norms in terms of their reach and pathways of impact. Indicators are increasingly used in efforts to overcome the limits of the traditional intergovernmental "Foreign Office model" of international law in achieving direct international regulation of private persons. First, indicators can be used to measure, evaluate, and seek to influence

behavior of private entities. This is a central feature of efforts to construct effective
regimes of corporate responsibility, with certification at different levels by the UN
Global Compact, and layered structures of reporting and audit superintended by
organizations such as the GRI. Second, indicators can be used to measure and report
the nature and levels of the private conduct that an international legal regime seeks
to curb or promote. Third, indicators can be used to assess the degree to which a
state is in fact successfully controlling private actors, or to monitor the level of effort a
state is making to regulate private conduct. This may be done by intergovernmental
monitoring organizations such as the Financial Action Task Force (monitoring state
regulation of banks and other financial entities to control money laundering) and the
UN Security Council's Counter-Terrorism Committee (monitoring state measures
against nonstate terrorism measures), by single governments monitoring other
governments, or by private entities. Fourth, indicators can be used to help define and
quantify a state's duties in relation to private persons or conduct in markets.

Interactions between laws and indicators merit further attention. For instance,
indicators may serve either to promote or to undercut the objectives of existing
law. The potential for complementarity is especially clear when indicators are
incorporated by reference into a legal rule, or are used to extend, elaborate on the
scope of, or give added specificity to a legal rule. Urueña provides the example
of domestic and international tribunals using indicators to assess compliance with
social or economic rights (also Rodriguez-Garavito 2011). By contrast, indicators that
provide a competing standard and bypass existing law can create a more pluralistic
legal environment and undercut the standards embodied in the law. On one view
the International Finance Corporation (IFC)'s Doing Business project tried to do
this through the Employing Workers Indicator, which in favoring national legal
arrangements that made it easier to fire workers appeared to undercut applicable
International Labor Organization (ILO) Conventions. Over time, these kinds of
tensions between law and indicators may create pressure for law reform.

Another way of examining interactions between law and indicators is to ask how
law affects the impact of indicators. Preliminary research in Central Europe suggests
that indicators of democracy or rule of law or good governance have the most
demonstrable influence where an authoritarian regime is weakening or where a
new democratic regime has just been established, in much the same way as human
rights treaties have differential effects (Simmons 2009).

CONCLUSION AND AREAS FOR FURTHER RESEARCH

Taken together, these chapters highlight the fact that indicators exist in a complicated
ecology characterized by relations of symbiosis, coexistence, or competition and
in environments that may change rapidly. In several chapters, different indicators

that express divergent theories compete in the same social field. Those that prevail are often sponsored by powerful organizations such as the World Bank. However, some acquire visibility through their simplicity and the appeal of their underlying theory, such as Freedom House and Transparency International, an effect proponents of other ideas may seek to emulate through new indicators (Bell and Mo 2013). Indicators have knowledge effects by increasing awareness and specificity of standards. They smuggle theories of corruption, rule of law, and development into apparently neutral systems of measurement. Some achieve such hegemonic worldwide acceptance that they shape legal consciousness while others are ignored. Indicators and theories work together: an indicator is more acceptable if its implicit theory is accepted, while a theory may receive wider support if it is expressed in a clear and widely used indicator.

Effects on governance are inextricably related to effects on knowledge. The underlying theories affect how decisions are made: indicators that become dominant persuade decision makers to follow their models. Indicators also affect governance when they specify a standard such that decision making becomes an assessment of performance with relation to the metrics of that standard. Effects are direct when an indicator is used to make a decision and indirect when they shape modes of thinking and analysis that provide the information on which decisions are made. The chapters in the book, together with other work, establish that the turn to quantitative knowledge is having subtle but powerful effects on the way the world is understood and governed.

From this platform, it is possible to identify four areas in which further research can be expected to be highly fruitful. First, our observation that local indicators tend to be relatively influential in comparison to global indicators calls for further examination of the conceptualization, production, use, and impact of local indicators.

Second, our studies of the conceptualization and production of indicators focus on individual indicators, ignoring other features of the crowded landscape in which those indicators exist. New indicators of good governance, rule of law, development, and corruption jostle for attention with one another as well as with older, more established, indicators of economic production and mortality. Some indicator producers invite technical suggestions and contestation and make underlying data and weightings freely available; others do not. Whether these strategies impact the demand for and credibility and influence of the indicator has not, however, been systematically tested. Nor is it known whether there is variance on these issues according to whether the indicator addresses matters that obviously involve political choices, such as the indicators of national legal governance discussed in the present volume. Further attention should be devoted to how choices made in the course of producing indicators affect their use and impact. This will require careful comparisons across indicators and their alternatives.

Third, our analysis here focused on indicators of legal governance, but only incidentally on law. A study designed to understand the interactions between indicators and law would devote more attention to law. A study of this kind might make considerable progress on questions such as: Will indicators become law-like, in terms of their influence and perceived legitimacy? Will law become more indicator-like, with more legal instruments specifying their goals in numerical terms?

Fourth, the analysis should be extended beyond indicators and law to other practices that might have similar effects on both knowledge and governance. The leading example is "big data," the practice of compiling large amounts of data on behavior such as movements, consumption patterns, and social interactions. Computers can use these compilations to observe patterns and draw inferences that would otherwise be invisible. The collection of such data is a way of both shaping knowledge and exercising power. Studies of law and indicators can and should be expanded to include big data.

REFERENCES

Asdal, Kristin, Brita Brenna, and Ingunn Moser (eds.) 2007. *Technoscience: The Politics of Interventions*. Oslo: Oslo Academic Press.

Bell, Daniel, and Yingchuan Mo. 2013. "Harmony in the World 2013: The Ideal and the Reality." *Social Indicators Research*.

Benjamin, Paul, and Jan Theron. 2009. "Costing, Comparing and Competing: The World Bank's *Doing Business* Survey and the Benchmarking of Labour Regulation." In Hugh Corder (ed.), *Global Administrative Law: Innovation and Development*, 204–234. Cape Town: Juta.

Bhuta, Nehal. 2012. "Governmentalizing Sovereignty: Indexes of State Fragility and the Calculability of Political Order." In Kevin Davis, Angelina Fisher, Benedict Kingsbury, and Sally Engle Merry (eds.), *Governance by Indicators: Global Power through Classification and Rankings*, 132–162. Oxford: Oxford University Press.

　　2015. "Measuring Stateness, Ranking Political Orders: Indexes of State Fragility and State Failure." In Alexander Cooley and Jack Snyder (eds.), *Ranking the World: Grading States as a Tool of Global Governance*. Cambridge: Cambridge University Press.

Bowker, Geoffrey C., and Susan Leigh Star. 1999. *Sorting Things Out: Classification and Its Consequences*. Cambridge, MA: MIT Press.

Bukovansky, Mlada. 2015. "Corruption Rankings: Constructing and Contesting the Global Anti-Corruption Agenda." In Alexander Cooley and Jack Snyder (eds.), *Ranking the World: Grading States as a Tool of Global Governance*. Cambridge: Cambridge University Press.

Buthe, Tim. 2012. "Beyond Supply and Demand: A *Political*-Economic Conceptual Model." In Kevin Davis, Angelina Fisher, Benedict Kingsbury, and Sally Engle Merry (eds.), *Governance by Indicators: Global Power through Classification and Rankings*, 29–51. Oxford: Oxford University Press.

Cooley, Alexander, and Jack Snyder. 2015. *Ranking the World: Grading States as a Tool of Global Governance*. Cambridge: Cambridge University Press.

Davis, Kevin E. 2004. "What Can the Rule of Law Variable Tell Us about Rule of Law Reforms?" *Michigan Journal of International Law* 26: 141–161.

2014. "Legal Indicators: The Power of Quantitative Measures of Law." *Annual Review of Law and Social Science* 10: 37–52.

Davis, Kevin E., and Michael B. Kruse. 2007. "Taking the Measure of Law: The Case of the Doing Business Project." *Law and Social Inquiry* 32(4): 1095–1120.

Davis, Kevin, Benedict Kingsbury, and Sally Engle Merry. 2012. "Indicators as a Technology of Global Governance." *Law and Society Review* 46(1): 71–104.

Davis, Kevin, Angelina Fisher, Benedict Kingsbury, and Sally Engle Merry (eds.), 2012. *Governance by Indicators: Global Power through Classification and Rankings.* Oxford: Oxford University Press.

Desrosières, Alain. 1998. *The Politics of Large Numbers: A History of Statistical Reasoning.* Translated by Camille Naish. Cambridge, MA: Harvard University Press.

2008. *L'Argument statistique. Pour une sociologie historique de la quantification (tome I) et Gouverner par les nombres (tome II)*. Paris: Presses de l'école des Mines,

Dezalay, Yves, and Bryant G. Garth. 2002. *The Internationalization of Palace Wars: Lawyers, Economists, and the Contest to Transform the Latin American State.* Chicago: University of Chicago Press.

Espeland, Wendy Nelson, and Mitchell L. Stevens. 1998. "Commensuration as a Social Process." *Annual Review of Sociology* 24: 313–343.

2008. "A Sociology of Quantification." *European Journal of Sociology* XLIX(3): 401–436.

Foucault, Michel. 1980a. "Truth and Power." In Colin Gordon (ed.), *Power/Knowledge: Selected Interviews and Other Writings 1972–1977*, 109–126. New York: Pantheon.

1980b. "Two Lectures." In Colin Gordon (ed.), *Power/Knowledge: Selected Interviews and Other Writings 1972–1977*, 78–108 New York: Pantheon.

1991. "Governmentality." In Graham Burchell, Colin Gordon, and Peter Miller (eds.), *The Foucault Effect: Studies in Governmentality*, 87–105 Chicago: University of Chicago Press.

Frydman, Benôit, and Arnaud van Waeyenberge (eds.). 2014. *Gouverner par les standards et les indicateurs: De Hume aux rankings.* Brussels: Bruylant.

Hacking, Ian. 1990. *The Taming of Chance.* Cambridge: Cambridge Univ. Press.

Halliday, Terrence C. 2012. "Legal Yardsticks: International Financial Institutions as Diagnosticians and Designers of the Laws of Nations." In Kevin Davis, Angelina Fisher, Benedict Kingsbury, and Sally Engle Merry (eds.), *Governance by Indicators: Global Power through Classification and Rankings,* 180–217. Oxford: Oxford University Press.

Halliday, Terrence C., and Gregory Shaffer (eds.). 2015. *Transnational Legal Orders.* Cambridge Series in Law and Society, Cambridge: Cambridge University Press.

Kaufmann, Daniel, Aart Kraay, and Massimo Mastruzzi. 1990. "The Worldwide Governance Indicators: Methodology and Analytical Issues." World Bank Policy Research Working Paper No. 5430. Washington, DC: World Bank.

Kelley, Judith, and Beth Simmons. 2015. "Politics by Number: Indicators as Social Pressure in International Relations." *American Journal of Political Science* 59(1): 55–70.

Kingsbury, Benedict, Richard B. Stewart, and N. Kirsch. 2005. "The Emergence of Global Administrative Law." *Law and Contemporary Problems* 68(3–4): 15–61, http://www.iilj .org/GAL/documents/TheEmergenceofGlobalAdministrativeLaw.pdf

Kipnis, Andrew B. 2008. "Audit cultures: Neoliberal governmentality, socialist legacy, or technologies of governing?" *American Ethnologist* 35(2): 275–289.

Lampland, Martha. 2010. "False Numbers as Formalizing Practices." *Social Studies of Science* 40(2010): 377–404.

Lampland, Martha, and Susan Leigh Star (eds.). 2009. *Standards and Their Stories: How Quantifying, Classifying, and Formalizing Practices Shape Everyday Life*. Ithaca and London: Cornell University Press.

Latour, Bruno. 1987. *Science in Action: How to Follow Scientists and Engineers through Society*. Cambridge, MA: Harvard University Press.

    2005. *Reassembling the Social*. Oxford: Oxford University Press.

Merry, Sally Engle. 2011. "Measuring the World: Indicators, Human Rights, and Global Governance." In Damani Partridge, Marina Welker, and Rebecca Hardin (eds.), *Corporate Lives: New Perspectives on the Social Life of the Corporate Form*. Wenner-Gren Symposium Series. *Current Anthropology*, 52, Supplementary Issue 3: S83–S95.

    2014. "Global Legal Pluralism and the Temporality of Soft Law." Special Issue on Temporalities of Law, *Journal of Legal Pluralism and Unofficial Law* 46(1): 108–122.

Merry, Sally Engle, and Susan Coutin. 2014. "Technologies of Truth in the Anthropology of Conflict." Co-authored with Susan Coutin. *American Ethnologist* 41(1): 1–16.

Poovey, Mary. 1998. *A History of the Modern Fact: Problems of Knowledge in the Sciences of Wealth and Society*. Chicago: University of Chicago Press.

Porter, Theodore M. 1995. *Trust in Numbers: The Pursuit of Objectivity in Science and Public Life*. Princeton, NJ: Princeton University Press.

Power, Michael. 1997. *The Audit Society: Rituals of Verification*. Oxford: Oxford University Press.

Rodríguez-Garavito, César. 2011. "Beyond the Courtroom: The Impact of Judicial Activism on Socio-Economic Rights in Latin America." *Texas Law Review* 89: 669.

Rose, Nikolas. 1999. *Predicaments of Freedom*. Cambridge: Cambridge University Press.

Rosga, AnnJanette, and Margaret L. Satterthwaite. 2009. "The Trust in Indicators: Measuring Human Rights." *Berkeley Journal of International Law* 27(2): 253–315.

Simmons, Beth A. 2009. *Mobilizing for Human Rights: International Law in Domestic Politics*. Cambridge: Cambridge University Press.

Strathern, Marilyn (ed.). 2000. *Audit Cultures: Anthropological Studies in Accountability, Ethics, and the Academy*. London and New York: Routledge.

Symposium 2011. "Indices and Indicators of Justice, Governance, and the Rule of Law: An Overview." In Juan Carlos Botero, Robert L. Nelson, and Christine Pratt (eds.), *Hague Journal on the Rule of Law* 3: 2.

Tsygankov, Andrei. 2015. "The Securitization of Democracy: The Politics of Special Interests and the Freedom House Ratings of Russia." *European Security* 31(1): 77–100.

Valverde, Mariana. 1998. *Diseases of the Will*. Cambridge: Cambridge University Press.

PART I

Global Indicators of Governance, Corruption, and Rule of Law

1

International Organizations and the Production of Indicators

The Case of Freedom House

Christopher G. Bradley

WHY ARE INDICATORS PRODUCED?

Global indicators, which purport to render characteristics of states measurable and comparable across national borders, have become ubiquitous in news reports and public policy discussions. Global indicators assess and rank states on every basis: medical care, education, and business regulatory environment, as well as more abstract concepts such as "freedom." Some indicators, for instance, gross domestic product, have long served as foundations of policy analysis (despite known limitations; see Stiglitz et al. 2009a, 21–40, 85–142), while newer indicators, such as "state fragility," have achieved prominence only recently (Bhuta 2012).

Initially, scholarly attention lagged behind the policy influence and public prominence of indicators, but research into indicators has developed significantly in recent years, including in the form of numerous books, articles, and policy

This project depended on the vision and commitment of Benedict Kingsbury, Kevin Davis, and Sally Engle Merry, as well as the support of Angelina Fisher, the Institute for International Law & Justice at the New York University School of Law, and the National Science Foundation. Portions of this chapter were presented at the Law & Society Association Annual Meeting in San Francisco, June 2–5, 2011. I thank the participants and respondents in the workshops in which this chapter took shape (including Tom Ginsburg, Terence Halliday, and Catherine Powell), as well as Jaremey McMullin, for helpful criticism and comments. Work was eased by the prompt and accurate aid provided by the staff at Princeton's Mudd Manuscript Library, and I am grateful to University Archivist Daniel J. Linke for generous consultations on locating related materials, and, later, on turning my notes into scholarship. John and Jan Logan offered their New Jersey hospitality over the course of numerous visits to the archives over the years.

Finally, I am grateful to Freedom House and its leadership, especially its longtime executive director, Leonard Sussman. Although I have never met Mr. Sussman or any of the current or past Freedom House leadership, I am grateful they made the laudable decision to make their archives available to researchers. We who are interested in the workings of international organizations – and the implications of that work for our world – are deeply in their debt.

reports (e.g., Morse 2004; Arndt 2008; Davis et al. 2012b; Cooley and Snyder, forthcoming). Nonetheless, as the editors of this volume observed in a previous article (Davis et al. 2012a, 4), "little attention has been paid to questions such as: What social processes surround the creation and use of indicators? How do the conditions of production influence the kinds of knowledge that indicators provide?" They noted that "the answers to these questions all have significant normative, theoretical and practical implications" (Davis et al. 2012a, 4; see also Halliday 2012; Pistor 2012).

Using the prominent indicator producer Freedom House as a case study, this chapter proposes some answers to these questions and sketches some normative, theoretical, and practical implications. The historical evidence from Freedom House's archives suggests that its indicator production was motivated predominately by the goal of strengthening Freedom House's own institutional identity and reputation. Among other things, the indicator appealingly defined Freedom House's "brand," which in turn enhanced its ability to raise funds (including most importantly from the United States government), which in turn allowed the organization to engage in widespread "pro-freedom" activist efforts around the world. The indicator also served as the basis for policy advocacy and impact in directions aligned with Freedom House's institutional commitments.

The case of Freedom House confirms that indicators are profoundly shaped by the interests of the indicator producer and the context of indicator production. Freedom House's indicator cannot be understood if denuded of the circumstances of its creation and production.

Further, it is likely that adjusting the shape or scope of indicators will require consideration of how to alter or accommodate the motivations of the indicator producer. The chapter closes by proposing adjustments that could be integrated into the work of Freedom House without compromising its organizational commitments. It is hoped that similar adjustments might be workable and beneficial for other indicator producers.

The Range of Motivations of Indicator Producers

There are a number of possible motivators of indicator production, each of which has found some support in the available scholarship (see, e.g., Arndt 2008; Dutta 2010; Halliday 2012; Pistor 2012). Motivations fall into a few major categories, several of which may apply to any given indicator producer:

- **Money**. Indicator producers may reap a financial profit from their indicator by charging fees to those who use it or those who would like to be measured by it (Pistor 2012, 167–169). For other organizations, indicators generate website traffic or demand for the organization's consultancy services. Even without a direct profit motive, there may be indirect financial motivations in the form of easier fund-raising, employment for indicator staff, and so on.

- **Reputation, "Brand," Institutional Identity.** Indicators may yield reputational benefits. An indicator helps build a brand and facilitates other projects of the producer. The prominence and influence of organizations may depend on the indicators they produce (e.g., Espeland and Sauder 2012).
- **Ideology.** Ideological or altruistic motives may drive a producer and its staff, directors, and donors, who intend to promote preferred policy outcomes (e.g., Pintér et al. 2005; Rosga and Satterthwaite 2009; Stiglitz et al. 2009a).
- **Research.** Indicators may be produced for the sake of research, to contribute to knowledge about chosen issues, states, or regions (e.g., Bollen 1979, 2009).

Even based on these generalities, it can readily be seen that the motivations of a producer will affect an indicator's design, implementation, and promulgation. This is particularly true given the lack of any accepted standards for indicator production – an absence that those observing the rapid rise of indicators as tools of public policy have noted with alarm. Understanding what motivates indicator producers and how those motivations affect the resulting indicators is therefore a useful – even urgent – project.

This Study of Freedom House and Its Archives

This chapter analyzes the historical conditions of production of one well-known indicator, the *Freedom in the World* indicator of Freedom House. *Freedom in the World* is one of the most prominent and established global indicators. For decades, its results have been relied on in news articles, policy analysis, and scholarship. Even so, although its methodology has been subjected to sporadic criticism, the factors that have motivated its production remain unexplored. This chapter begins to fill that gap in understanding of this important indicator.

The case of Freedom House is particularly revealing because extensive records from Freedom House's history are available in public archives, unlike the records of other comparable indicator producers. This trove of documentation allows for the development of a uniquely detailed institutional history of this important indicator producer. As a result, this study provides a fine-grained view of the dynamics of indicator production in a prominent nongovernmental organization (NGO), and it demonstrates the value of close analysis of the organizational dynamics that underlie the production of any complex policy instrument such as the *Freedom in the World* indicator.

Research Materials and Methods

This study relies primarily on data drawn from Freedom House's archives. Based on evidence from Freedom House's records – dating from the 1950s when the first iteration of the indicator was produced, through 2007 – this chapter probes Freedom House's motivations in designing, producing, and adjusting its indicator over the course of several decades.

Because this chapter presents evidence from the Freedom House archives, it focuses on the perspective of Freedom House actors. The records are most useful in reconstructing historical motivations: the correspondence, board meeting materials, and other documents show with surprising precision what Freedom House's staff and board considered as they made crucial decisions. The chapter largely leaves to the side other important questions – for instance, concerning how Freedom House's product might be critiqued or defended on methodological grounds. Methodological questions have been treated to some extent in other studies (Bollen 1886, 1993; Gastil 1986, 1990; Giannone 2010; Steiner forthcoming), and they are considered here only when relevant to Freedom House's driving motivations and internal discussions concerning the indicator.

Research for this chapter was conducted in the Freedom House Records archives at Princeton University.[1] The archives contain 182 boxes, including hundreds of items of correspondence, minutes from frequent meetings of the Freedom House Board of Trustees and Executive Committee, notes and memos by staff and officers, and various sorts of published materials. The records cover the sweep of Freedom House's history, from the lead-up to American involvement in World War II through 2007. Research included detailed examination of every box and folder in the archives as well as relevant materials in related archives.

How reliable are the records? This question is fundamental to any archival study. At a few points, the records are incomplete (pages missing, correspondence incomplete, photocopies illegible), and the more recent acquisitions have not been fully processed by Princeton's archivists, which occasionally hinders the usefulness of the records. But the archives are as complete as can be expected given that they were accumulated over a long period of time by a nonprofit NGO with limited resources and little to no legal recordkeeping requirements. Although the records are somewhat informal and disorganized, in the course of my extended and fine-grained study I saw no indication of manipulation, fabrication, or censorship.

In fact, the records are surprisingly complete in some ways, as they include documentation of several potentially embarrassing personal and organizational conflicts.[2] For instance, the records include extensive evidence of a financial and regulatory crisis in the mid- to late 1980s, when the organization's finances were extremely strained. Auditors allegedly failed to conduct suitable audits of Freedom

House's books for several years, and there was concern that US government funding for Freedom House's activist efforts had been insufficiently accounted for, raising risk of legal sanction and public embarrassment. In addition, the records include evidence of power struggles and back-biting among Freedom House officials. Frank expressions of doubt about some of Freedom House's endeavors also appear in the records.[3] Although there is no way to rule out entirely the possibility that "culling" of documents took place before the records were transmitted to the archives, there is no evidence of selective preservation. In sum, the records appear reliable, in the sense that they have not been intentionally manipulated to project any particular image of Freedom House.

Of course, just because archives are rich and reliable does not mean they are straightforward. Letters, memorandums, board minutes, and even balance sheets can hardly be taken at face value; their authors will make mistakes and will pursue various individual and institutional goals (often hidden or unexpressed) as they compose the documents. But these problems of interpretation are hardly specific to archival documents. Such concerns must be addressed by careful, contextualized investigation.

Overview

This chapter has four parts.

After this introductory part, the second part provides an overview of Freedom House and its indicator. Using both archival and published materials, it surveys Freedom House's history, its indicators, its funding and finances, and its overall political viewpoint.

The third part explores the motivations behind Freedom House's production of the indicator. In general terms, the chapter concludes that Freedom House's production of its indicator has been motivated primarily by the benefits to reputation and institutional identity that have accrued to the organization as a result of its indicator's prominence and credibility. This account of Freedom House's motivations should not be taken as a denial of the range of perspectives and relationships that contributed to Freedom House's development. Overarching organizational motivations rely on all sorts of complex and even conflicting aspirations on the part of all the human actors involved. For instance, the indicator's first major author, Raymond Gastil, also had aspirations for the indicator to contribute to policy research, but particularly after he left in the late 1980s, such motivations had no real force in the organization.

In the fourth part, this chapter turns from the descriptive to the normative. It suggests implications of this study for indicator producers and for policymakers seeking to accurately evaluate, and fruitfully make use of, indicators. It identifies several ways in which the existing motivations of this organization (and other similarly situated indicator producers) could be harnessed to foster the production of more useful indicators. Most importantly, indicator producers should be encouraged to highlight – rather than obscure or understate – the contingent and contestable nature of their measurements, as a way of sparking active, inclusive, and locally informed policy dialogue. Such a move might begin to close persistent and deeply problematic gaps between the measurers and the measured. Freedom House, for example, could use its platform as an indicator producer to provoke policy dialogue, spark social organization, encourage local involvement, and educate communities, all with the goal of contributing to durable progress on otherwise intractable policy difficulties. This chapter suggests that openness to more critical approaches – including allowing for greater contestation concerning indicator production and use – might actually aid indicator producers in attaining their various goals, rather than hindering them.

FREEDOM HOUSE, ITS "FLAGSHIP" INDICATOR, AND ITS ARCHIVES

The Beginnings of Freedom House and Its Indicator

Freedom House took shape in New York in the 1930s, in response to perceived apathy on the part of the American populace toward the encroachments on freedom portended by the rise of Hitler. The name "Freedom House" was intended as an answer to the "Braunes Haus," the Munich headquarters of the Nazi Party (Sussman 2002, 14–15).[4] A number of well-connected Americans supported Freedom House at its inception, including First Lady Eleanor Roosevelt. The organization coalesced out of a welter of other pro-intervention groups with names such as Warhawks, Committee to Defend America, and Fight for Freedom, and actually came into formal existence in late October of 1941, barely a month before the surprise attack on Pearl Harbor on December 7, and the United States' declaration of war on Japan (Sussman 2002, 9–16).

After World War II, Freedom House continued to advocate for vigilance against perceived encroachments on liberal democratic values. Concerned about the threat of communism, it called for stern, interventionist policies in Korea and Vietnam (though its support for the conflict in Vietnam eventually waned). At the same time, it protested prejudice and red-baiting in the United States (Freedom House [FH] 1965). Consistent with its stance on these domestic social issues, its midtown Manhattan headquarters helped house such groups as the National Association for the Advancement of Colored People (NAACP) and Anti-Defamation League (Sussman 2002, 24).

To promote its positions in the postwar years, beginning in 1955 its executive director George Field and his staff put together an annual *Balance Sheet of Freedom*.[5]

The *Balance Sheet* – the first incarnation of what ultimately became the *Freedom in the World* indicator – was given prominent placement in the "Freedom House News Letter and Year-end Review" (FH 1955). In describing the *Balance Sheet* project to his board in 1957, Field explained (FH 1957): "In several years past we have prepared a study entitled 'The *Balance Sheet* of Freedom' for year-end release. Such a balance sheet might become a factor in puncturing some of the current complacency, and, if our past experience is repeated, it should receive considerable press attention." Each *Balance Sheet* was a summary account of the previous year's "gains" and "losses" in freedom worldwide. Board members and insiders weighed in on its text (e.g., Roper 1959; Stout 1957), but it was largely an in-house, informal production dominated by Field's vision. It included no numerical ratings, although a nascent quantitative impulse is apparent in its dominant metaphor – a "balance sheet" used to "chalk up" the gains and losses, or "credits" and "debits," of freedom across the world.

The early balance sheets include criticism of deficiencies in the United States, especially relating to racial discrimination. But the main themes are the need for vigilance against Soviet encroachments, dictatorships, and other perceived injustices abroad. The *Balance Sheets*, updated and released annually until they were transformed into the *Comparative Survey* (the immediate predecessor of *Freedom in the World*) in the 1970s, were produced by the Public Affairs Committee of Freedom House. Meeting minutes (FH 1959) show that press attention to the *Balance Sheets* was energetically solicited and carefully tracked.[6]

This embryonic indicator-research arm of Freedom House was secondary to other organizational priorities. In these early years, the prime goal of Freedom House was providing support – moral support and, as years went on, financial support, often through funds originating with US government agencies – to activists in "not free" countries. Freedom House's energies were also directed to giving awards to promoters of freedom, placing editorials in newspapers and magazines, and lobbying and testifying in front of political officials.

From its early days, Freedom House's operations were (as they have remained) roughly tripartite (Windsor 2005). The three focus areas are research, advocacy, and activism: (1) *research* in the form of indicators, analyses to accompany indicators, and other various reports; (2) *advocacy* in op-eds, award banquets, lobbying, and congressional testimony; and (3) *activism* in supporting Freedom House employees and contractors and funding third-party initiatives. Importantly, although research, primarily in the form of indicators, is what the organization is best known for, the archives suggest that it has never been the primary focus of the organization's resources or staff.

Initially, advocacy was the primary focus of Freedom House's small staff, and even its limited advocacy activities stretched the staff thin. Throughout most of its history, Freedom House has been smaller than its reputation might suggest, its ambitions limited by a perpetual lack of funding. In 1967, for instance, Freedom House's "core staff" consisted of "the executive director, two secretaries, and a receptionist for the building" (Sussman 2002, 52).

Freedom House's activism was even more limited than its advocacy – until the organization began to accept more government funding in the 1980s and 1990s. Over time, dramatic increases in funding and the corresponding capacity to exercise influence more directly led to activism becoming more important – as well as more controversial – than the other parts of Freedom House's operation. Currently, Freedom House is headquartered in Washington, DC, and maintains a New York office; its other offices are in locations where its activist activities are pursued: Kyrgyzstan, Jordan, Mexico, and South Africa (FH 2013a).

The Freedom House records demonstrate that its far-flung interventions were both very important and very risky to the organization. To take one example, at a January 2000 board meeting, in discussing pro-democracy efforts in Cuba, the executive director noted (FH 2000a) to the board that "most likely Castro is unaware [of Freedom House activities], and that we want to keep it that way." Soon after, Cuba and other often-criticized "not free" countries lodged a complaint against Freedom House with the United Nations, alleging that it was not an independent NGO but an instrumentality of the US government (see FH 2001).

Research did not take anything like a defining role in the organization at least until the 1970s, and even then, the prominence of Freedom House research was arguably more apparent than actual. Funding of activist and advocacy activities, as discussed later, has far outstripped research funding over Freedom House's history. But despite the rise, and by many measures the predominance, of activism, the *Freedom in the World* indicator became the organization's primary public face, at least in the United States and Western Europe (Windsor 2006). Both inside and outside of the organization, the *Freedom in the World* indicator has been referred to as the organization's "flagship" (FH 1998a; Sussman 2002, 119; Puddington 2006).

The *Balance Sheet of Freedom*, which is not a fully-formed indicator, took a formalized and quantitative turn with the *Comparative Survey of Freedom* in the early 1970s. Transforming the *Balance Sheet* into the *Survey* was the idea of Freedom House's second executive director, Leonard Sussman. The *Survey* initially emerged as an ancillary product to support another big idea of Sussman's – a twenty-foot-long, ten-foot-high "Map of Freedom" blazoned across the lobby of Freedom House's downtown New York headquarters (Sussman 2002, 25, 61). The Map color-coded every country in the world according to its status as "free," "not free," or "partly free," as determined by Freedom House. The hitch to this plan was that Freedom House had not produced such a comprehensive and public analysis of each and every state in the world – nor did it then have the capacity to update such an analysis frequently enough to prevent the Map from instantly becoming an outdated (and perhaps embarrassing) curiosity. Until then, the *Balance Sheet* had been little more than a hobby for the executive director and his knowledgeable but unpaid board. A broader, more rigorous project was now required.

The Map and the *Comparative Survey* debuted in 1972 (Sussman 2002, 61; 1972b). An academic named Raymond Gastil was tasked with constructing the *Survey*, initially on a part-time basis. Gastil had conducted research on what he called "social indicators," assessing state and regional differences within the United States. Correspondence in the archives indicates that Gastil found the *Survey* both an ideologically and intellectually rewarding opportunity, although he felt stymied by the limitations of Freedom House's funding. He wistfully wrote (1972b) to Sussman: "Sometimes I wish Freedom House were a foundation and not just another struggling institution; one could make a project like this a vocation and be at least as useful as the other things I do." (Gastil's academic career left him without satisfactory institutional support independent of Freedom House.[7]) Especially in light of the modest support he required, Gastil contributed enormously to Freedom House. The Map and *Survey* were considered runaway successes, and Freedom House reveled in the coverage its new projects received in the press. After the initial release of the *Survey* and Map, Sussman (1973a) reported to Gastil that "[t]he world-wide response has been phenomenal" (while also noting that "I think your checklist [the basis for indicator scoring] needs to be more extensive"). An unsigned, undated essay (FH n.d.) that appears to date from the mid-1970s trumpeted it as an "Overnight Success." A few years later, Sussman (1976b) reported that the survey of that year (which appeared in the Freedom House magazine *Freedom at Issue*) "was completely sold out in ten days and has been republished and is still in high demand." In other correspondence, Sussman (1976a) noted that after a "highly publicized address" at the United Nations relied upon the Survey, "[f]or two weeks, correspondents of foreign press agencies, foreign diplomats and the American press inquired day-long about the Survey and Freedom House. Shortly thereafter, our latest Survey appeared and attracted the widest attention it has yet received." These are not isolated remarks; from the start, Freedom House carefully noted, and warmly welcomed, the attention the indicator received.

The Indicator and Its Methodology

After it replaced the *Balance Sheet of Freedom* in 1972, the *Comparative Survey of Freedom* was itself reborn as the *Freedom in the World* indicator in 1978. The *Comparative Survey* and *Freedom in the World* shared the basic approach of annually rating each state in the world as "free," "not free," or "partly free." Today, these three labels continue to be applied to each state in the world annually by the *Freedom in the World* indicator.

In recent years, some of the intermediate levels of the indicator's ratings have also been released, and the methodology used to determine them has become somewhat more transparent in the last several decades. But change has been gradual and, as discussed later, the methodology remains very far from fully transparent.

Moves toward transparency began in 1989. Bruce McColm took over the executive director position in 1988, and after Gastil departed in July of 1989, the organization moved to address perceived inadequacies in its methodology. The prior executive director Leonard Sussman (1989), who remained deeply involved with the organization, told the staff: "We are examining all of the criteria employed in the Survey, as well as academic critiques of its methodology. We plan to state our criteria clearly to indicate what they do and do not convey. Data on each country will be enlarged. Reasons will be given for each country's rating. Changes will be clearly stated whether they reflect a new status within the country or an adjustment of the analysis." McColm, in an internal memo to Sussman, offered a more pointed assessment:

> Freedom House and I am in a difficult position concerning defending the past Surveys. The emperor has no clothes from an academic point of view, even though, ironically, if he [Gastil] had worked at it, it would. We can not sustain a fraud or cloak the Survey in academic obscurantism. This year's Survey should have an open methodology, which for the sake of the reading public we are putting at the end of the book. We will clearly state our assumptions as well as "subjective elements" in the criteria and what criteria are weighted more than others. The past Surveys gave greater weight to free and fair elections and freedom of expression, even though that was never explicitly stated. (In fact, the Survey was never really developed beyond the first 4 items on the Checklist.) (McColm 1989a)

McColm's criticism is revealing. It is true that early *Comparative Surveys* provide little to no methodological discussion, a contrast with later years. After leaving Freedom House, Gastil published an article (1990, 25) in which he conceded that his indicator used only a "loose, intuitive rating system," and that the "original intention was to produce, with relatively few man-hours, an orienting discussion of variation in levels of freedom." Gastil emphasized (26) that he received "little or no staff support" (a fact that the archives confirm), and that he relied significantly on "hunches and impressions" as well as reference books. Materials from the early years of the *Comparative Survey* reflect that only particularly difficult decisions (e.g., assessing South Africa in light of Apartheid) received specific or significant discussion. The methodology appears to have been: Adjust as necessary but otherwise leave well enough alone.

After Gastil labored essentially alone for more than fifteen years, the indicator's staff came to include several staff members and numerous consultant experts.[8]

Based on information in the archive and in Freedom House publications, the actual roles and responsibilities of these individuals remain unclear. The influence of the many listed consultant experts, in particular, has not been evident, either historically or in the indicator as it is produced today. The material that was found in the archives suggests that the experts' role consisted of commenting on drafts circulated each year and engaging in serious but unstructured discussion on points that they felt merited comment (FH 1999). Empirical research based on interviews with these experts might better reveal how they conceived their role and what influence they had. Archive materials suggest that experts contributed significantly to the qualitative, narrative discussions produced by Freedom House to accompany the indicator but added little to the quantitative ratings and scorings that constitute the actual indicator. The reason for the limited involvement of external experts on scoring may be that the scoring methodology has been idiosyncratic, distinctive to Freedom House, and not easily susceptible to intervention by outsiders.

The indicator scores are currently derived as follows. (Freedom House's methodology has remained roughly consistent throughout the history of the indicator, but because it has been spelled out in greater detail in recent years, this explanation is based on those later years. Thus, although most of this chapter is historical in focus, this section on methodology briefly moves closer to the present.) A country's status as "free," "not free," or "partly free" is determined by reference to an average of subscores for civil liberties and political rights. As discussed later, other categories of rights, such as economic, social, and cultural rights, or freedom from intervention, are not included. The averages are given on a scale of 1 through 7, with 1 (oddly) as the best and 7 as the worst. Countries with average ratings of 1.0 to 2.5 are classified as "free," 3.0 to 5.0 as "partly free," and 5.5 to 7.0 as "not free" (FH 2011b). Thus, a very high subscore on civil liberties and a very low subscore on political rights could balance out to a comfortable overall score of "partly free." Such an outcome is uncommon in practice; in most instances, the two scores are very similar. Whether this derives from cognitive bias among the scorers, flawed survey design, or accurate perception of on-the-ground realities, is an open question.[9]

The civil liberties and political rights ratings are each derived by reference to a series of questions that yield subscores of 0 to 40 for political rights and 0 to 60 for civil liberties; those figures are then mapped onto the 0 to 7 scale. For these political rights and civil liberties subscores, higher scores are better (the higher the score, the more "free" the country). The subscores are derived from answers given by scorers to fifteen main questions under civil liberties and ten main questions (as well as two additional, discretionary questions) under political rights. Each main question is fleshed out in subquestions to guide scorers, although even these subquestions are highly general and subjective in nature. In 2011, for instance, a main question for "Functioning of Government" included "Is the government free from pervasive corruption?" and the subquestions included "Is the government free from excessive bureaucratic regulations, registration requirements, or other controls that increase opportunities for corruption?" and "Has the government implemented effective anticorruption laws or programs to prevent, detect, and punish corruption among public officials, including conflict of interest?" (FH 2011a). The subquestions illuminate some aspects of the main question but are hardly designed to lead to comprehensive or verifiable results. On the basis of their answers to the main and subquestions, scorers are to award each state a sub-subscore of 0 to 4 points for each main question. (In addition, for political rights, one discretionary question gives the scorer a chance to deduct points, while another discretionary question allows the scorer to add points.)

Freedom House has made the subscores available for all countries and territories since 2003, and certain sub-subscores have been available for all countries and territories since 2006 (FH 2006c, 2013b, 2013c). These steps purport to make the indicator less of a black box. But even the sub-subscores cover remarkably broad ranges of topics.

In addition, the actual, question-by-question breakdown of data – not to mention the scorers' identities, scorecards, or rationales – is not publicly available. The lack of this information greatly limits the indicator's transparency. Although it is useful at least to know what sort of questions are guiding each score, it remains difficult at best to understand, critique, or falsify any of the survey's "findings" without more detailed information about the precise basis for the "findings." In a sense, the supposedly increased transparency amounts simply to one black box being replaced by several layers of smaller black boxes. The smaller boxes still hold their secrets well sealed inside; it still remains virtually impossible to understand the actual basis of, or assess the accuracy of, any rating.

In fact, it is difficult even to *use* the ratings for many common purposes. For instance, consider a scholar or journalist interested in using Freedom House's assessment of "personal social freedoms, including gender equality, choice of marriage partners, and size of family," in, for example, China. Freedom House's rating of this topic was available only as part of *Freedom in the World*'s general Civil Liberties score until 2006, and even after 2006, it remains incorporated in a Civil Liberties subcategory of "Personal Autonomy and Civil Rights," where the score is available only in aggregation with scores concerning "freedom of travel or residence, employment, or institution of higher education," property ownership rights, rights to operate private business without "undu[e] influence" from the government, and rights to freedom from "economic exploitation" (FH 2011a). There is no breakdown of how any particular "Personal Autonomy and Civil Rights" score was arrived at, despite this broad range of underlying questions that scorers were supposed to consider.

Freedom House's viewpoint becomes only somewhat clearer in the narrative "country report" that accompanies each year's indicator results. Freedom House's "country report" on China stretches to approximately 4,200 words in 2011 and 4,400 words in 2013. About 1,500 words of the 2011 description are shared with (i.e., repeated in) the 2013 description. Perhaps 250 to 400 words of each narrative could be seen as addressing "personal social freedoms," and the hypothetical researcher could look there for information, where Freedom House provides a sentence or two of some arguable relevance to "personal social freedoms, including gender equality, choice of marriage partners, and size of family." But, of course, there is no effort to tie the narrative to particular indicator scores. Although the "country report" narratives are reasonably useful discussions in and of themselves, they do little to bolster the usefulness or reliability of the indicator.

These gaps in what the indicator conveys about the bases for its "measurements" have not gone unrecognized, even from within Freedom House. Many of the difficulties with Freedom House's indicator were present from the beginning, which Gastil readily acknowledged. Although Gastil deeply believed in the worth of his task, he held no illusions about the challenges he faced – in fact, he exhibited a startling degree of intellectual honesty about the limitations of his project.

Gastil acknowledged at an academic conference in 1986 that he arrived at his ratings "by going through the flow of essentially journalistic information that comes to the *Comparative Survey*" and simply picking out what he deemed relevant based on checklists of general topic areas and issues (Gastil 1986). He took information from public sources and arrived at his ratings using his checklists, although no evidence of systematic scoring survives, and the checklists were only loose guides (Gastil 1974a, 14, 16). Records confirm that on crucial, difficult questions – e.g., the rating for South Africa under Apartheid or the ratings of certain US territories and allies – Sussman, Gastil, and other individuals connected with Freedom House considered the ratings carefully. Aside from these "problem areas," there is, historically, little evidence of thorough consideration of scores in the archives.

Although financial resources were always in short supply, the problem was less one of resources than of research design and methodology. The problem is succinctly presented in a letter of April of 1973 that Sussman wrote to Gastil, as the *Comparative Survey* was just beginning to take shape:

> I have had a chance to go through country evaluation checklists and find them very helpful ... There is still one question remaining (in my mind, at least): how do you derive the ratings from the checklist? I assume each rating is the result of a computation that goes on inside your head (unless you have some specially programed computer that I don't know about). It is at that point, I suppose, that judgment takes over but if you have some weighting for the several factors in the evaluation – a weighting that leads to the bottom line – I would appreciate seeing that too. (Sussman 1973c)

No direct response to this request could be located in the archives, nor is there any evidence that a satisfying answer was available. In Freedom House's magazine, *Freedom at Issue*, in which the *Comparative Survey* was published in the years before it appeared as a volume on its own, Gastil acknowledged his doubts about the defensibility of his ratings. In response to "readers [who] have objected to the procedure of placing numerical values on judgments that are necessarily qualitative," he informed them that they "should be assured that there is actually no quantitative process occurring. We are always interested in overall judgment" – that is, he ranked states with respect to other states and not (despite appearances) on any absolute scale of "freedom." Gastil wrote: "There is not, and never has been, subratings that are somehow added up to make the reported ratings. I do not use an organized checklist in this fashion because of lack of data, and because in comparing apples and oranges I think the overall determination must depend on holistic judgment."

In his remarkably forthright article, Gastil explicitly disclaimed a contribution to the science of indicators, on methodological grounds: "The *Comparative Survey* is not, and never was proposed as, an exercise in developing a new level of social indicators... Social indicators, it seems to me, are most useful if they are statistical measures of measurable quantities. The more doubtful the basis of the measurement, the less useful the indicator." As noted previously, Gastil's pre–Freedom House scholarly work dealt with social indicators within the United States, so he spoke from a position of some authority. He added: "Indicators that combine a number of basic statistics into a higher level 'statistic' generally confuse more than they enlighten, and the more so to the degree that the statistics brought together are themselves of doubtful validity." These statements, which echo the remarks Gastil published in Freedom House's magazine *Freedom at Issue* in 1974 (Gastil 1974a), are remarkable in light of the claims that have been made in subsequent years for Freedom House's indicators, which retain most or all of the weaknesses Gastil identified here. The indicator involves more formal consideration of each individual element than it did in Gastil's time, which probably adds some reliability at the margins (see Steiner forthcoming). Still, it remains basically as it was – a high-level indicator of perceptions, filtered through the loosely guided assessments of the staff and consultants of Freedom House. However finely the perceptions are sliced, the fundamental determinants of results will remain perceptions, and are not supported by any more tangible or telling (or falsifiable) form of data. In essence, it is still "tortoises all the way down."

Since its earliest days, the Freedom House indicator attracted attention, largely credulous and positive, from journalists. In addition, the indicator has been an object of scholarly curiosity, including sharp criticism.[10] Despite an undercurrent of methodological criticism from scholars, the indicator has been employed frequently in research.[11] Although few academics may trust the indicator for refined analysis, it provides them a convenient aggregation of mainstream opinion over a lengthy time frame.

As far as what the indicator measures, *Freedom in the World* is more properly called "liberal democracy in the world." It focuses on "negative rights" as well as the political institutions and legal predicates of liberal democracy.[12] The freedoms largely track the rights outlined in the International Covenant on Civil and Political Rights. Freedom House generally ignores other types of "freedom," including those outlined in the International Covenant on Social, Economic, and Cultural Rights. This myopic focus accords with the long-dominant emphases of human rights discourse in the United States and Europe (e.g., Mutua 2001) – a problematic fact for which Freedom House does not bear responsibility. But Freedom House's failure to broaden conceptions of freedom over the years in light of new developments in human rights is noteworthy.

To take an example, the restrictions on freedom that are wrought by class immobility or lack of access to healthcare and education are ignored in the *Freedom in the World* indicators. The last question of the four questions (FH 2011a) in the Personal Autonomy and Individual Rights category of Civil Liberties could in theory measure such rights: "Is there equality of opportunity and the absence of economic exploitation?" But that question is fleshed out in a way that orients it away from such concerns. The category is in fact about free markets; the first subquestion is "Does the government exert tight control over the economy ... ?" This is an example of how important it is to get down to the level of what an indicator is actually measuring, rather than trusting to the generalities in which an indicator's conclusions are often couched.

Freedom House's indicator measures not just formal protections of rights – law on the books – but the actual extent of freedom as lived by citizens. This decision, although defensible, may have the effect of hindering the indicator's usefulness as a measure of effective *governance*, because factors beyond the control of governments – natural disasters, resource constraints, or regional instabilities – can severely impact the scores. That said, a close read of recent editions of *Freedom in the World* suggests that the indicator typically focuses more on government actions, so the distortive effect of this stated policy may, in practice, be muted, notwithstanding the stated methodology.

While *Freedom in the World* is Freedom House's oldest and most visible indicator, the organization produces other indicators as well. The long-time executive director of Freedom House, Leonard Sussman, who advocated strongly for press freedoms during and after his years at Freedom House, proposed a "social indicator" of press freedom in his first year on the job, in 1967, and succeeded in introducing the survey of press freedom in 1979. This survey eventually developed into a quantitative indicator, with a map of press freedom, in 1994 (Sussman 2002, 57–59, 61–62, 113). Another indicator, titled *Nations in Transit*, began in 1995 to provide a "comprehensive, comparative study of political and economic change" in post-communist states (Sussman 2002, 62). Although discussion of these indicators is largely beyond the scope of this chapter, all are in Freedom House's "research" branch.[13] Arguably, Freedom House's capacities and contributions are better suited for these narrower policy arenas, where indicators can more effectively exhibit analytical depth and build awareness of particular problems. The freedom indicator, by contrast, though very prominent, is a "mashup" indicator (Ravallion 2010) that suffers from the same vague and imprecise boundaries as other broadly framed measurements of "failed" or "fragile" states (Davis and Kingsbury 2011, 11; Bhuta 2012, 134), or of "governance" or "rule of law" (Pistor 2012).

Funding the Organization and Its Indicators

The Freedom House archives shed much light on how Freedom House's activities, including its indicator production, have been funded. The two key insights are that Freedom House's indicator production has cost relatively little, and that a steep rise in government funding of Freedom House's operations has presented a long-lasting and persistent threat to the indicator's claim to impartiality.

How Much Does an Indicator Cost?

The first important insight that the archives yield is that the Freedom House indicator has been surprisingly inexpensive given its prominence. In terms of the resources it has consumed and the organizational benefits it has conferred, the *Freedom in the World* indicator has been a bargain. In the early days, research was covered by a small academic-level stipend to Gastil, with modest amounts for administrative and research assistance (FH 1976b, 1977). The remaining costs of the indicator were publication costs, mostly printing.[14] In correspondence, Gastil (1974b) referred to the survey, with apparent regret, as a "weekend and evening activity" only, due to the paltry funding at that time. The fact that Gastil – the only Freedom House employee specifically tasked with producing the survey – was not paid on a full-time basis until late 1976 demonstrates how excellent a bargain the survey was for the organization, excellent publicity purchased very cheaply.

The budget remained modest in later years, as the annual volume stretched to several hundred pages and solidified its status as the institution's main public face. Although budgets in the archives are not detailed enough to tally the cost of the indicator exactly, the total 2005 budget for the indicator was $360,000 (Puddington 2006, Annex A), much of it apparently printing costs. Staff included only one full-time and one part-time employee, in addition to four Freedom House officers as supervisors (Puddington 2006, Annex A). Other Freedom House budgets over the years show that the indicator never required more than 10 percent of the organization's annual expenditures, and the entire "research and publications" budget of Freedom House, which includes numerous global indicators and other projects, generally consumed less than 20 percent of the organization's total budget (e.g., FH 2000). Although promoted as crucially important to the organization, the truth is that the indicator was not a primary focus of its spending (or, as discussed later, its operations and management). It is no surprise that although research endeavors (including indicators) are occasionally mentioned in Sussman's institutional history (2002, 61–62), they are far from a major focus.

Fund-Raising Difficulties, Government Funding, and the Appearance of Bias

By the mid-1990s, Freedom House had come to rely heavily on US government funding. The appearance of bias due to government funding was recognized as a problem, not just by outside critics but also within the walls of Freedom House. It was ultimately accepted as a necessary evil; Freedom House took repeated opportunities to accept government funds and thereby hugely increased the organization's global impact. But it accepted funds reluctantly, only after deliberation, and it recognized the risks that government funding posed to its actual and perceived independence. The records do not support Freedom House's claims that its main indicator remained completely independent. The organization was no doubt influenced by its biggest donor, the US government, at least indirectly. At the same time, the archives provide no support for allegations that the US government used funding or other means of direct control to determine the outcome of Freedom House's indicators.

While pleas to the board of directors for greater devotion to fund-raising recur throughout the archives, they became more urgent as government funding rose over the years, particularly after the Cold War, when Freedom House became involved in extensive pro-democracy activism in former communist states. Board members were exhorted to increase their giving and new sources of funding were brainstormed and discussed, but despite all of these efforts, the organization continued to accept large amounts of government funding. Freedom House's finances were tenuous at a number of points, and the archives reflect frequent money worries. Government funding helped the organization remain active through lean times, and then to grow as it engaged in extensive, activist interventions.[15] The necessity of accepting the funding was remarked on with frustration, and its potential dangers continued to be lamented.[16] This is a major theme in the archives, particularly in the board minutes.[17] By the 1990s, Freedom House appears to have accepted dependence on government funding as a necessary evil. Increasingly through the end of the period of archived materials in 2007, government funding supplied the lion's share of Freedom House's operating budget.

The core operating budget of Freedom House in 1994 was approximately US$1.2 million (20 percent of which was funded by the US government); a separate program budget of US$700,000, half of it directly financed by the US government, covered specified activist endeavors abroad. These figures affirm the importance of the activist programs, and of US government support, for the organization. In the years afterwards, the budget rose remarkably, such that government funding alone was almost US$10 million by 2004, a large majority of the overall budget of the organization.[18] In a 2003 document titled "Freedom House Fundraising Strategy," which was presented to the board, the organization's leadership sought to spur the board to fundraising action. The document notes with alarm that the ratio of private to government funding was 28:72 in fiscal year 2000, and had dropped further, to 16:84, by fiscal 2003. It argues that in light of this ever more lopsided funding situation, "[w]e are at a critical juncture in maintaining a perception of organizational autonomy, given our dependence on governmental revenue."

Freedom House's receipt of significant government funding drew criticism from, among others, countries taken to task by Freedom House in its indicators or other writings and those aggrieved in some way by Freedom House's activist efforts. Critics alleged that the organization could not plausibly claim independence given its reliance on the US government and that Freedom House was essentially a "front" for a sort of "laundering" of US government funds, allowing the government to do or say indirectly what it could not do or say directly.

A more extreme criticism came in the form of a rumor that the US Central Intelligence Agency actually funded or directed the activities of Freedom House. Although the financial information included in the archives does not allow for a thorough or decisive assessment of this charge, no support for it was found in the archives. And it seems unlikely that influence was or is exerted in so direct a manner – particularly given the numerous opportunities for powerful indirect influence.[19]

Freedom House's basic responses to accusations of bias were, first, that it kept funding for the *Freedom in the World* indicator separate from government funds, to guarantee the indicator's autonomy; and, second, that the organization's track record of criticizing the US government demonstrated its independence. A 2006 memo titled "FH Publications: Yesterday, Today and Tomorrow," written by Freedom House's Director of Research, Arch Puddington, to the board, offers these responses to the problem of alleged "capture" by the US government. First, Puddington noted that "[i]n 2005, Freedom House produced four annual surveys, two of which are exclusively funded by private sources (*Freedom in the World* and *Freedom of the Press*), and two exclusively by the US government (*Nations in Transit* and *Countries at a Crossroads*)." Second, he stated that the research staff was preparing a special report to deal with freedom in the United States, and he observed that one advantage of this plan was that "[a] special report on the US will also help to answer critics who feel that Freedom House is not independent of the US government."

The problem presented by Freedom House's reliance on government funding is difficult to assess. On the one hand, the organization made real efforts to segregate funding for most of its research activities, including *Freedom in the World*. It did so by earmarking private funding for the indicator. And it is true – as Freedom House has been happy to proclaim – that the organization was critical of the United States at numerous junctures in history, for instance, recently with respect to aspects of the "War on Terror." (The criticisms appear never to have been so extreme as to risk alienation from mainstream American sentiments, but that might be because those producing the indicators and other materials largely held those roughly mainstream views themselves, not because of a fear of losing government funding.)

On the other hand, Freedom House's activities – including its indicator production – were undertaken in the shadow of its largest sponsor, without whom many of its activities would simply not be possible. Government money was a boon to Freedom House, enlarging its operations and boosting its profile considerably. It could not escape the notice of Freedom House's staff and leadership that the tap of government money could run dry if they were not at least somewhat solicitous of US government views and positions. And, unsurprisingly in a small organization like Freedom House, the indicator production does not appear to have been completely separated from all other activities, even if it received some independent funding. At a minimum, there appears to have been substantial overlap of staff, management, and facilities.

As far as Freedom House's criticism of US policy, a more cynical view would be that it might have been allowed in service of the government's own goals. The argument would run that the US government's aims were served by allowing Freedom House the room to make limited criticisms. The US government benefits from allowing the organization to show it is not a "puppet" – even if, in fact, it may be – by offering some light criticism. This study does not allow for a decisive assessment of that possibility, though if there was such an understanding between Freedom House and its government "minders," there was absolutely no evidence of it in the archives.

The more likely scenario appears to be that the views of those involved with an organization like Freedom House, which has been so strongly associated with mainstream neoliberal American views, have overlapped in large part with the views of those in the US government who make the funding decisions that affect Freedom House. Freedom House's strong association with these views has attracted more like-minded individuals (including some from government itself) to Freedom House, in a self-reinforcing process: ideological convergence, but without any conspiracy.

In sum, it seems implausible, based on the relatively comprehensive materials in the Freedom House archives, that there was any government conspiracy to control Freedom House and its indicators directly, but there is some reason to think that Freedom House's reliance on US government funds weakened its independence.

Freedom House's Political Viewpoint

In keeping with its position as an arbiter of mainstream liberal opinion from the earliest days onward, Freedom House's directors and officers have been well-connected, largely middle-of-the-road figures, drawn from US and international policy, journalistic, and philanthropic circles. For instance, Republicans Donald Rumsfeld and Paul Wolfowitz served on the board before their service in the George W. Bush Administration, but numerous Democratic figures served during the same general time period. There is no evidence from the archived materials, including in board minutes or correspondence, that any one particular set of partisan views was systematically privileged as a matter of organization policy (Sussman 2002, 67, 73, 80). Based on both its public activities and its archives, the organization's positions have accorded generally with mainstream American political views, with a particular emphasis on civil and political human rights and a propensity to encourage intervention in favor of such freedoms abroad.

The leadership of the organization consistently stressed the need to preserve, as Sussman terms it, "US freedom of action" in foreign affairs (e.g., Sussman 2002, 127). Its overall pro-intervention stance of course resonated with the organization's founding as an anti-isolationist group encouraging entry into World War II and might now be cast as "neo-conservative." At the same time, Freedom House's strident support for human rights and for deeper involvement in international organizations such as the UN could be interpreted as left-leaning. Most often, the organization has tacked right and left slightly, but always more or less along with mainstream opinion, hewing fairly close to the center line.

An academic critic of Freedom House recently claimed (Giannone 2010, 69) that *Freedom in the World* has "suffered … the effects and influence of the dominant paradigm" with respect to its definitions of a "free" society. This statement is more or less undeniable. Less clear is whether this accusation is surprising in any way. In fact, Freedom House has emphasized that its concept of freedom accords with generally accepted views. Freedom House has not purported to be beyond the "influence of the dominant paradigm." Indeed, Freedom House would more likely state its goal as spurring the world to act on the reality or truth (as it sees it) of the "dominant paradigm" – giving a call to action.

What may in fact provoke critics of Freedom House is its refusal to acknowledge how multifaceted and contested the concept of freedom is – a refusal to acknowledge the worth of any paradigm aside from the "dominant" one. Freedom House has drawn criticism by making claims to precision and universality beyond what is realistically attainable in its relatively cursory analysis of freedom across the globe.

As noted previously, Freedom House's indicator omits what are considered fundamental aspects of freedom through much of the world, among them economic, social, and cultural rights. Even aside from these notable omissions, freedom is a normatively and ideologically charged concept that defies easy specification or measurement,[20] and Freedom House has largely ignored this fact. More concretely, Freedom House's ratings have offered little adjustment for the drastically differing cultural or political contexts of different countries. Problems of concept validity in measurements of ideas such as "freedom," "governance," and "democracy" have been pointed out repeatedly by scholars (e.g., Bollen 1990; Bollen and Paxton 2000; de Vries 2001; Davis 2004; Morse 2004; Arndt 2008; Ravallion 2010; Thomas 2010), but these critiques appear to have had little impact on the shape or scope of indicators, including Freedom House's.

Thus, while Freedom House has not been "partisan" in any narrow sense throughout its history, and while Freedom House's concept of freedom has included certain aspects identified with both the right and the left of American politics, critics have understandably attacked the limitations of Freedom House's analysis – most notably, its omission of important aspects of globally accepted concepts of freedom and of the diverse local contexts in which freedom is actually lived.

MOTIVATIONS OF AN INDICATOR PRODUCER

The previous section gave a historical overview of Freedom House as an organization and of the *Freedom in the World* indicator. This part turns to questions of motivation: What motivated Freedom House's production of its "flagship" indicator? How have those associated with Freedom House viewed its activities? What has actually driven the organization's decision makers? What influenced their deliberations? What were their goals (and their fears) for the organization? How did the indicator fit into their view of the organization?

The archives provide revealing, contemporaneous data concerning these questions, although they cannot provide complete answers. The archive-based analysis offered here complements other studies concerning the motivations and strategies of NGOs, many of which have been based primarily on interviews (e.g., Halliday 2012). Archival methods are useful in reconstructing historical motivations that would be difficult to identify otherwise, in light of faded memories and limited lifespans. Of course, despite the excellent data underlying it, this historical account, which is based on the prominence of considerations with the archive, cannot purport to be anything other than suggestive and impressionistic. Moreover, Freedom House's various motivations overlap significantly and cannot be completely disaggregated, as discussed in the text that follows.

Indicator producers may be motivated to (1) have an effect on other actors (such as targets of measurement, donors of aid, or investors); (2) bring benefits to the organization (for instance, through reputation-building or fund-raising); and (3) construct an accurate, useful, refined tool of measurement (whether to help with factors 1 or 2, or simply for the sake of research).

For Freedom House, the results are fairly clear among these three broad categories: the predominant consideration in production of the indicator over the years was building Freedom House's reputation, its institutional identity; the focus was on the indicator's usefulness to the organization itself. In addition, to a lesser degree, the organization sought to impact aid, investment, and policy decisions based on indicator ratings. Very little attention was paid to accuracy of measurement, aside from its impact on reputation; nor, relatedly, were the potentially harmful side effects of the indicator's use in aid, investment, or policy decisions considered in any depth.

As will emerge, however, this picture is complicated somewhat because there is an interrelationship between categories 1 and 2 – that is, between the outward-looking, mission-regarding factors and the self-regarding factors. The archives show that Freedom House's concern with reputation has been connected with the goals of influencing government officials and giving cover to Freedom House's own activist projects. The reputational capital built up from being a producer of a "respected," "objective" indicator has been spent in support of more controversial interventions that may be, to many involved with the organization, the most compelling aspects of Freedom House's mission. Freedom House's good name has been its entrée into funding and policy circles that might be closed to it, were it not considered a "respectable" producer of knowledge and "scholarly" analysis by virtue of its indicators. This "objective" reputation has provided cover to the organization's more controversial activism and advocacy activities, which are arguably the primary (if less-heralded) focuses of the organization's efforts and expenditures.

Financial motivations have been enmeshed with these reputational and institutional identity concerns as well; fund-raising is a perpetual concern of most nonprofit organizations, and as discussed previously, Freedom House has been no exception (Gastil 1974b). The indicator has been seen as a useful tool of sharpening institutional identity, carving out space in a competitive field, and attracting donors, including perhaps the US government itself.

Benefits to Reputation and Institutional Identity

For decades, Freedom House's staff and board were extremely attentive to the reputational benefits the indicator provided to Freedom House. Based on extensive materials from the archives, press coverage emerges as the most commonly and carefully examined gauge of Freedom House's own reputation, with citation of the indicator by government officials and scholars as the next most important. Maintaining Freedom House's reputation and building its desired institutional identity emerge as the highest priorities of the staff and board when they received reports or made decisions relating to the indicator.

Freedom House's staff and board have paid careful attention to the pervasiveness and thrust of press coverage of the indicator. For decades, discussion and analysis of press coverage were consistent features of Freedom House's board meetings. (In later years, in addition to collecting traditional press clippings, the organization monitored digital impact and coverage, Web traffic, and so on [e.g., Puddington 2006, Annex B].) Regular updates on press coverage were prepared for the board and staff. The archives are stuffed with many hundreds of press clippings of stories reporting the indicator scores (not to mention op-eds by Freedom House staff). Mostly the clips are of the "Freedom in [Country] Rose/Dropped This Year Due to [Prominent News Event/Issue]" variety, from newspapers all across the United States and around the world.

Coverage of the 1991 *Freedom in the World* indicator serves as an example (Box 126, Folders 1–2, *Freedom House Records*). This set of clippings is not unusual either in number or in type of coverage reflected. The tally is as follows. Fifty-six individual sources published articles on aspects of the 1991 indicator results.[21] Twenty-seven of these include quotes either from the report itself or from Freedom House leadership. Six include a map or a chart conveying survey results in visual format. Sources range from prominent national dailies such as *The Washington Post* and *Boston Globe* to local papers such as the *Lufkin* (Texas) *News*. The vast majority of the clippings were drawn at least partially from wire services, and many resemble one another, often containing identical language. Some are syndicated opinion columns. Many of the articles reference Freedom House's long history and describe Freedom House as a "respected," "independent," or "non-partisan" "human rights organization" that "monitors" or "tracks" democracy or human rights or freedom.

The 1991 publicity is entirely positive. There is no questioning of Freedom House's approach or results in any of the stories.[22] In addition to this direct coverage, there are thirty clippings covering the "Human Suffering Index," an indicator produced by a different NGO partially on the basis of Freedom House's indicator. The clippings based on this derivative use of Freedom House's work all name Freedom House as the source of underlying data. Again, no critical attention is paid to the production of Freedom House, its indicator, or the Human Suffering Index indicator.

A later collection of clippings was accompanied by a memo (FH 2006b), dated May 25, 2006, titled "Freedom House Press Update," from the Freedom House Communications Officer addressed to the Board of Trustees. This memo canvasses the coverage for the preceding year and gives an indication of how well the published indicator was considered to have performed: "This was one of the best years for press coverage of the report." The report notes that the "most common way that the organization is mentioned in the news" was in "[a]rticles that use *Freedom in the World* and other survey data to substantiate a point or give general background information." Although Freedom House might have preferred stories to use its indicator as the primary source rather than making fleeting mention of it as background, the latter was still considered a success. This makes good sense in light of the organization's broader goals. The widespread use of the indicator as a sort of neutral, background assessment has associated the organization with objective and even-handed analysis, reinforced its desired identity as arbiter of "freedom in the world," and portrayed the organization as trusted, established, noncontroversial, and "cerebral." In addition to the monitoring of press coverage, use of the indicator by scholars and policymakers was also monitored. But whereas the records of press coverage evince constant, pervasive interest (e.g., FH 2000a, remarks of Arch Puddington and Larry Diamond), scholarly citations were followed less carefully.

This 2006 "Freedom House Press Update" served, in essence, as an indicator of the success of that year's indicator. For the research staff within the organization, the press clippings were a tangible demonstration that their indicator was being widely noticed. Such reports (some less formal than this) are included throughout the archives. Reports to the board and officers appear to have been the primary way in which the indicator was formally considered and assessed within the organization. Aside from these press impact assessments and occasional budgetary discussions, the indicator received rare attention by the Freedom House board over its long history. Of course, some Freedom House staff devoted considerable time to the indicator, but the fact that it held so little of the board's attention compared to other projects is telling. This supports the theory that the indicator was a cost-effective means of enhancing the organization's "brand" and giving cover to the organization's more controversial activist endeavors, which occupied more of the board's time and required more of the organization's money.

The archives include another representative report on the indicator, this one delivered in a board meeting in February of 2006. The report (FH 2006a) asserts that "Freedom House's publications have helped increase respect for Freedom House over the past few years, and these results are reflected by" many op-eds and other press sources "using Freedom House publications for background information about countries." The report notes that, thanks to this increased respect, Freedom House officers received a number of invitations to policy and advocacy events. The report celebrates the fact that both the targets of measurement (foreign governments) and a key audience (aid providers) showed signs of paying attention to Freedom House's opinions: "Increasing number of foreign government officials are making the effort to convince Freedom House that their ratings are flawed as more companies and foreign aid groups rely upon Freedom House publications to decide where aid should be sent first." These facts are all chalked up as positive outcomes, despite the fact that the report acknowledges that some of the attention has been critical – concerning particular indicator scores considered unfair and concerning the organization as a whole, its US government ties, its alleged bias, and so on. Some of the motivations present in this report – that of provoking responses from foreign governments and aid providers – are discussed in further detail in the following sections. But it bears noting that even when the organization has been criticized for particular indicator scores, the reputational benefits of being a "force to be reckoned with," of having an opinion worth noting (even if the opinion is contradicted or challenged) apparently relieved most of the sting of criticism. This is somewhat in tension with the "objective" or "cerebral" reputation that Freedom House coveted, and that tension appears to have remained unresolved. This demonstrates how what appears to be a singular focus on building reputation actually involved several competing types of reputational motivation.

The February 2006 report assures Freedom House leadership that scholars have "begun to cite Freedom House on an ever increasing basis as a reliable source of information."[23] The discussion for the board includes various steps that could be used to bolster publicity for the indicator; but tellingly, it includes no comments on methodology, on efforts to deepen or sharpen the analysis, or on responsiveness to any criticism. In sum, and in a sense true to form, an indicator that is based on perception relied largely on the perception of others to judge how it is doing.

The most important threats to Freedom House's reputation as a result of the indicator have come in two main varieties: (1) critiques based on the indicator's methodology and (2) critiques based on alleged pro-US bias, especially as a result of the organization's reliance on government funding. Within Freedom House, both of these threats have been treated with little concern as long as they have no clear effect on *outcomes* – as measured by press coverage and comment from policymakers (and to a lesser degree academics). Methodological critiques, in particular, have been leveled at the indicator since it formally took on characteristics of an indicator – that is, since it became a country-by-country numerical rating – in 1972. On some rare occasions, the organization has responded to such criticisms (see, e.g., the section "Direct Impact on the Targets of Measurement," later in this chapter), but the reality is that the archives show very little internal hand-wringing over such critiques.

An example of a reputation-centered response to a critique of the indicator's methodology comes from Freedom House's then-Director of Research, Arch Puddington (2006), who wrote in a report to the board: "As the surveys are taken more seriously and their findings used both as a diagnostic and a decision making tool, we have *felt pressure* to enhance and ensure the rigor of our product" (emphasis added). What is notable is that the criticism was seen as *pressure* being *felt* from *outside*. What was *not* said is: Because so many lives the world over may be affected by the imperfections or unconsidered presuppositions of this increasingly prominent indicator, our indicator-producing organization has a deep responsibility to refine its methodology. The latter might seem a more natural response given the fact that this same document discusses the use of Freedom House's indicator as one of the sources of evaluation of countries for eligibility for funds from the Millennium Challenge Corporation. This was a "real-world" application that might have given pause to an indicator producer, which might (and should) be skeptical about its effectiveness as a forward-looking prescriptive tool for inducing change (that is, rather than as a descriptive analysis of current states). Yet such doubts simply do not appear to have arisen from within the organization. Instead, a response was provoked only when "pressure" was "felt."

Further, even though some criticisms of Freedom House may have had some minor impact on indicator design and execution, the changes that have been made to the indicator over the years should not be overstated. The archives reflect more consistency than change. The most important adjustment in the indicator methodology since the 1970s was the regularization of scoring. The increase of detailed attention may have forced more thorough consideration of each factor in each category and diminished somewhat the subjective judgments of scorers who might otherwise, consciously or not, have tended to emphasize one or two prominent elements and disregard others. One scholarly analysis suggests that the shifts may have had this effect (Steiner forthcoming). Another change was Freedom House's increased disclosure of subscores and factors. This move enhanced the transparency of the indicator, but still left it in a woefully limited state, as noted earlier. These changes were real, but did not change the product in any fundamental way or justify its use in the policy contexts into which it has been inserted, as discussed later in this chapter.

In addition to methodological critique, the second major critique faced by the organization is that it is too closely tied to US government interests, and that because of funding or personnel overlap, the organization is "captured," acting as essentially a servant of the US government. As discussed previously, the organization has shown sensitivity to this attack, with its concern mostly involving the risks to institutional identity and reputation. Over the years, Freedom House officers and board members expressed concern over the degree of the organization's dependence on US government funding, and took some steps to address the criticism – while still accepting huge amounts of funding.

In any case, regardless of whether these particular arguments are convincing, they affirm that the organization has been keenly aware of challenges to its reputation, and it has been willing to act to meet them as well as it can – given its financial and other constraints. That said, judging by the organization's few concrete discussions of critiques, and their minor impact on Freedom House's actual activities, their importance has been limited.

Impact on Investment and Development Aid

As shown in the previous section, the dominant set of motivations for indicator support and decision making has been building Freedom House's reputation and bolstering its institutional identity. As this section discusses, using the indicator to have direct effects on world affairs has also been considered desirable. Specifically, influencing the flow of investment and aid money to countries based on their "not free" or "partly free" indicator scores has been an explicit pursuit of Freedom House.

In early 2000, it was reported that the massive Wisconsin and California state pension funds were considering restricting their investments to countries disapproved on "freedom" bases by Freedom House. In a report to the board, the chair of Freedom House noted (FH 2000b) that California was also considering using Heritage Foundation indicators instead of Freedom House. He noted that if the fund were to choose Freedom House, it "would be a very exciting development for Freedom House." This discussion – that is, the mere consideration of use by large pension funds – is summarized prominently in the first page of this set of board meeting minutes, in the "Overview" section, and further discussion of the situation appears later in the board minutes. In other words, it was a very important topic of discussion.

The minutes from this meeting discuss the Wisconsin pension plan's intention not to invest in "not free" countries and assert that Freedom House "convinced TIAA-CREF and other major pension funds to withdraw investments from companies that have direct business relations with Sudan." Pleased with this development, Freedom House's leadership embraced the effects that it believed such direct reliance on its indicator would have:

> We are not generally advocates of negative sanctions, but now *our studies are being increasingly used as a way of linking values to value.* In the midst of this debate that is emerging, *an argument is being made that political openness and transparency guarantees a greater economic stability*; that democracy leads to greater political stability and that emerging markets, which have more features of political openness *are, therefore, safer havens for investment.* (FH 2000b, emphasis added)

If Freedom House's logic holds, then, for reasons of economic good sense, sophisticated investors such as CalPERS (California Public Employees' Retirement System) should seek to invest in countries that facilitate greater freedoms. However, just because an "argument is being made" that robust civil liberties and political rights guarantee economic development and stability does not mean that "argument" is on solid factual ground. What Freedom House here describes as its "studies" certainly do not prove such a causal link. In fact, scholars of growth and development have long been unsure about the relationship between government policies, economic growth, and security of investment (e.g., Barro 1997). At best, Freedom House's "argument" was simplistic and unsupported. At worst, the policies endorsed could be detrimental: serious harm could result if, on the basis of a pseudo-scientific caricature of the means and causes of political and economic stability and development, Freedom House restricted or guided the flow of aid or investment. A well-intentioned doctor, wielding a blunt instrument, can do much harm. Despite these dangers, Freedom House evinced little or no interest in the complex links between economic development and whatever it is that Freedom House's indicator measures. Freedom House simply encouraged direct policy interventions on the basis of its indicator. The goal of having direct impact on real-world funding decisions has overshadowed any substantive concern about possible deleterious, unintended effects. Sudanese government policies were inarguably damaging many Sudanese citizens, but it does not necessarily follow that a broad disinvestment strategy was helpful. For instance, is it clearly right for large pension funds to "withdraw investments" from medical companies that had "direct business relations" in the form of supplying needed medicines or emergency equipment? What of companies providing the sort of jobs that can build a civil society and, perhaps, empower a challenge to the governing elite? What of companies providing technological infrastructure that might well allow Sudanese citizens to organize more effective advocacy networks? Development policy experts are deeply divided on these issues (e.g., Eyler 2007). The point is that Freedom House's indicators' effects were simply assumed to be positive – in part, one suspects, because if Freedom House's indicators were not used, another organization's indicators might be. In an increasingly competitive environment of indicator producers, the choice to pursue direct influence seems motivated in part by the institution's compelling need to lead – to have clear impact – or risk being supplanted by others in a crowded field (Espeland and Sauder 2012; Halliday 2012).

Another instance of policy analysis being disregarded in favor of "overselling" the indicator can be found in a December 2000 press release that accompanied the *Freedom in the World* indicator for that year. The release (FH 2000c) is entitled "Global Democracy Continues Forward March," and states that "[i]n a major study released today, Freedom House concludes that democracy and human rights made major gains over the past year." The "major study" is none other than the *Freedom in the World* indicator, which is said to support the conclusion that "[e]conomic growth is accelerated in an environment where the rule of law is respected, property rights are enforced, citizenry is actively engaged in the political process, and investigative media serve to expose, and thus reduce corruption." The release repeatedly calls the indicator a "study," and focuses on the indicator's supposed causal demonstration that the acceleration of economic growth results from rule of law reforms. But this claim – whether true or not, as a matter of empirical reality – is at a minimum unsupported by any of the "findings" of the indicator materials, which do not engage in any analysis of causation, much less one that could carry the burdens of demonstrating the broad principles that Freedom House claimed.

These statements concerning causation are dangerous. They mislead as to how development happens, and they invite policy intervention on an inadequate basis. As other studies of indicators have shown (e.g., Zaloznaya and Hagan 2012), even well-constructed indicators can be deployed for a range of purposes, good and bad. At a minimum, indicators are powerful instruments for setting agendas, including distorted agendas (Morse 2004; Grindle 2007; Arndt 2008, 280–284). When promoted or used without sufficient reflection, indicators can become abusive and unaccountable instruments of governance at a distance (see generally Rose and Miller 1992; Espeland and Sauder 2007; Sauder and Espeland 2009). Used without adequate care, an indicator of "freedom" may well serve a freedom-dampening role. The danger is most acute where, as in this example from Freedom House, there is a mismatch between the policy recommendations and what the data actually show (see de Vries 2001; Davis 2004; Grindle 2007). Direct interventions into policy should be predicated on causal understanding that goes beyond the expert description and perception-based assessment that an indicator such as Freedom House's can provide.

Of course, if a connection between Freedom House's indicator and successful policy outcomes did exist, it would enhance Freedom House's status and shore up the basis of Freedom House's activism and advocacy. Thus the exaggerated view of the indicator's policy import served institutional interests and has been unlikely to be challenged from within.

In addition, it may be that Freedom House presupposed a causal connection between good performance on its indicators and successful economic development because of the ideology of those who have chosen to be associated with it. The president of Freedom House provided support for this view when he stated at a board meeting that Freedom House "has always envisioned the Freedom Survey as an objective document, but it is also an implicit argument for what should be the priority areas of foreign policy, what are the areas of opportunity in which we should invest in foreign aid resources, and what are the markers of successful transitions" (FH 2000a). It is hard to see how the indicator can be an "objective document" and yet also, from the start, be structured to make an "implicit argument" concerning what "priority areas of foreign policy" should be. There appears to have been no discussion of alternative "priority areas" that Freedom House's presupposed priorities might be displacing, for better or worse.

In sum, although the emphasis on direct impact through aid and investment appears to have waxed and waned in the course of Freedom House's history, the moments where it was most prominent were not the organization's finest moments; they were moments where organizational self-interest and individual ideological presuppositions eclipsed a commitment to shaping beneficial policy based on careful study.

Direct Impact on the Targets of Measurement

A final motivator for Freedom House has been the possibility of having a direct impact on the countries that it has measured. Reports to the board have made reference to reactions of various countries, often through their ambassadors, to the Freedom House ratings – usually to a rating perceived as unfair (FH 1975a).[24] These were somewhat isolated instances, perhaps because, owing to the nontransparent nature of Freedom House's rating system, it is difficult to produce specific objections even if one thinks the indicator's rating is wrong. (By contrast, indicators based on more clear and specific factors are easier for experts within the country to answer or falsify [e.g., Arruñada 2007; Benjamin and Theron 2009].)

As noted previously, when the Map of Freedom in the lobby of the Freedom House building was first unveiled, it received significant media coverage. The organization gloried in the press – as well as in high-level rejoinders to the judgments portrayed on the Map. The government of Sweden, for instance, reacted to its surprisingly low rating in light of its high reputation for quality of life, social order, and freedom. An internal document (FH, n.d.) reported that "[t]he Swedes sent a television camera crew to the Map and had us spell out in a 15-minute program precisely why we warned about the trend [toward 'bureaucratization'] in Sweden and perhaps other free but highly bureaucratized countries. Ultimately, the Prime Minister of Sweden directed the Embassy in Washington to phone us and secure further background on the history of Freedom House and this project." Here as in the previous section, there is an overlap of Freedom House's desire for reputational benefit and its desire for direct impact.

Freedom House appears to have viewed reactions and complaints from countries as positive signs that the indicator was making a difference. In correspondence, Sussman (1979) stated that "[o]ne of the important values of the Survey, in fact, is to encourage the leaders of countries to want to do better. Many ambassadors and others query us about the ratings of their countries. Often they argue for better judgments." These reactions form another way for the indicator's success to be measured, from within the organization. Sussman (1980) reported, soon after the publication of the 1980 edition of *Freedom in the World*, that "[s]ome eight governments have already responded by questioning our assessments of their political and civil systems. We are gratified by this expressed interest in our criteria and judgments." (He expressed no interest in whether those governments were right.[25])

Aside from these reactions, the archives reveal little effort by Freedom House to use the indicator to impact foreign governments more aggressively or on specific policy points. The organization appears to have accepted that the indirect routes of publicity and of foreign aid/investment were its most effective routes to policy impact. If anything, direct approaches to countries on the basis of the indicator might have represented dangerous ground, mixing what is supposed to be the objective research component of Freedom House's operations with its advocacy and activist endeavors, and thus eroding the reputation of neutrality Freedom House wished to preserve – a reputation that was extremely useful to its more controversial activist and advocacy interventions. The importance of this "unbiased" reputation has been acknowledged often – and recognized as vulnerable in light of the close relationship of the organization to the government – at Freedom House board meetings (see, e.g., FH 2004).

SOME IMPLICATIONS: INDICATOR PRODUCERS AND THEIR (DANGEROUSLY) POTENT TOOLS

As the preceding account of Freedom House's archives shows, Freedom House has produced and promoted its indicator for several interrelated reasons. Most importantly, the indicator has advanced the desired image of the organization and thus facilitated Freedom House's other activities – its advocacy and activism. In addition, to a lesser degree, Freedom House has sought to bring about what it considers positive policy advancements by seeking to tether investment and aid decisions to indicator performance and by directly impacting policy in the countries that are criticized by the indicator, especially in the developing world. The pursuit of what Freedom House considers policy advancement has been driven by the priorities and principles embedded in the indicator itself, and by the ideological convictions of the organization's members, with little regard for nuances of development policy realities.

As discussed in the section "Organizations, Their Indicators, and Their Ecosystems," this Freedom House research confirms the broad principle that *the entity by whom, and the context in which, an indicator is produced strongly influences the direction that indicator takes.* One crucial implication is that indicators should not and cannot be studied in isolation from the context within which they are generated. This research also confirms other studies' suggestion that international organizations strive to differentiate their "brands" and "products" from potential competitors, and that organizations are motivated by a mix of ideological and more practical factors such as fund-raising and publicity.

The section "Indicators, Opinion, and Reality" explores some other normative implications that arise from this research. It argues that embedded within current discourse about indicators are possible directions for more productive development of indicators as tools of social change – and as servants of their host organizations.

Rather than outside-looking-in measurements, indicators could be deployed to spur discussion and deeper involvement of both the measurer and the measured. They could be tools of social organization, mobilization, and education. A shift to what could be termed a more "open" indicator culture could not only serve "target" populations better but would also magnify the impact of indicator producers. Seeds of this different approach have been present within Freedom House's walls, though they have been obscured by other, arguably less productive, approaches.

Organizations, Their Indicators, and Their Ecosystems

The research in this chapter supports the view that international organizations are competitive players who must keep up their reputations and promote their products, and whose identity and product will tend to take forms that maintain their advantages in their competitive fields, their ecosystems.[26] Some factors that may require organizations to pursue competitive advantages are the need for funding, the desire of individuals associated with the organization for prominence and influence, and simply a wish to have impact for ideological or altruistic reasons. The example of Freedom House is particularly fascinating. Its lengthy history and considerable success in attaining the goals of prominence and influence show that it successfully competed in a crowded NGO environment.[27]

The archival research suggests that important factors in Freedom House's success included (1) its historical pedigree, with early connections with very powerful people and core ideals of post–World War II mainstream America; (2) its commitment to Central and Eastern Europe in the 1980s and 1990s, where it engaged in prominent pro-democracy initiatives; and (3) its emphasis, beginning in the early 1970s, on the technology of indicators as a means of attracting US and international attention to its favored issues. As the Freedom House example shows, demand for an indicator need not be driven by commercial interests or by a specific demand for a useful measure of a particular phenomenon. Rather, an indicator may arise from an organization's own entrepreneurial energies, as a tool to support the organization and its mission by speaking to (and ultimately shaping) existing public sentiments along desired lines.

The reliance of Freedom House's institutional identity on its indicator is not unusual. Scholars have shown that when *US News & World Report* began producing its rankings of higher education programs, it did so in a preliminary and exploratory fashion and was surprised by the huge demand for the rankings (Espeland and Sauder 2012, 35). *US News* recognized in this demand an opportunity to distinguish itself – in fact, to survive against the odds. The turn was dramatic, leading to redefinition of the organization away from news publication and toward rankings and research (Espeland and Sauder 2012, 90). "Rankings, it seems, would no longer 'save the franchise.' Instead, they have become the franchise" (Espeland and Sauder 2012, 90).

Freedom House's indicators emerged similarly to *US News*' rankings. They were a venture that gained surprising traction. They became a useful way to reorient the organizational identity: for *US News*, away from news and toward rankings; for Freedom House, away from activist "opinion" and toward objective "research." And in both cases, these developments served other organizational goals: for *US News*, profit; for Freedom House, reputational prominence and a "credibility cover" for more activist goals. But while indicators may have been at the *reputational core* of Freedom House, they were never at its financial core, which was advocacy and activism. Based on its budgets and activities, Freedom House's rankings did not "become the franchise" – although Freedom House seemed in some ways to foster that impression. They merely served as a useful, appealing public face.

A crucial lesson emerging from this analysis of an indicator's emergence, and of the ongoing motivations of its production, is that the sources of an indicator matter. *Freedom in the World* has been a crucial part of Freedom House's identity. This fact motivated Freedom House to make the indicator acceptable to a wide audience, but it may also have led Freedom House to be less inclined to face or admit the faults and limitations of its indicator.

It may seem obvious that the institution cannot be understood apart from its important product, the indicator. It is less obvious, but equally true, that the indicator cannot be understood apart from its producer, the organization. The source of the indicator is important because institutional goals will shape the way the indicator is constructed and promoted.

Indicators, Opinion, and Reality

Early on, Freedom House's indicator was conceived (Gastil 1986) as a way of focusing public attention where it might otherwise be lacking: "The Survey brings into consciousness the often forgotten fact that the countries most often accused of repression are generally not the most repressive. There is simply too little news from the most repressive states ... for the world to give them the sustained attention received by states with a more moderate level of repression, such as Chile or Nicaragua." This capacity to "bring into consciousness" certain facts is a crucial feature of how policy and public opinion are shaped.

The great care with which Freedom House for decades followed media coverage of its indicator demonstrates further the importance of media coverage even to the organization's self-assessment. Useful studies could be conducted on the impact of news coverage on indicator producers, or, to state it differently, the symbiotic and recursive relationship between the two. Scholars have explained already that indicators' shaping of consciousness is also a shaping of reality, precisely because it can so effectively transmit opinion or perception as if it is fact. René Urueña (2012, 271) put it thus: "The connection between indicators and the news media is crucial to understand the former's role as technologies of global governance. Indicators become relevant and influential as news media begin to quote them and use them as evidence of a social reality."[28] This accords with the findings in this chapter, in which an indicator based on perceptions generated further perceptions, and ultimately interventions. The processes by which opinions, perceptions, or analyses become social realities (including through indicators) merits more fine-grained attention.

Perhaps precisely because indicators draw their power from their impact in the public square, the *non*-public face of indicators – their backgrounds, their histories, their sources, their contexts – has a way of fading into the background, unquestioned but implicitly trusted. Indicators have a way of appearing transparent and objective, whether or not they are. While "indicators have the apparent virtue of permitting relatively transparent decision-making – at least at first glance," the "transparency of decision-making based on indicators is merely superficial ... if the process of producing the indicator is opaque" (Davis and Kingsbury 2011, 45–46). A lack of transparency in policy decision making can be transformed silently into a lack of transparency regarding indicator production (Arndt 2008, 285), and in the process, be hidden or forgotten. Quantification is often a crucial part of this transfer; reliance on the "objective" tools of quantification – such as those deployed by indicator producers – eases and masks an accumulation of influence and control (e.g., Porter 1995; Rosga and Satterthwaite 2009). The trust in quantification is unearned, however, without a transparent methodology that can be challenged by those outside the indicator-producing organization.

Aside from a few narrow exceptions – for instance, the need to protect confidential sources, or if scores could be used to "game" the indicator – it is hard to imagine legitimate justifications for nonprofit indicator producers to refuse to disclose virtually everything about their processes, their underlying scores, and their contributors. This is particularly true when (as is usually the case) indicators are being promulgated with a view toward having direct, real-world impact. If an indicator is to be used to make a public policy decision, then the making of the indicator merits all the scrutiny that the decision would have merited in the absence of the indicator. The fact that a judgment is made by an indicator producer instead of a policymaker should not, in itself, provide any comfort unless the scrutiny that would have been applied to the policy decision can be applied to the indicator.

Dialogue, Contestation, Participation

In the case of Freedom House, the desired "impact" of the indicator has been, almost without exception, one-directional, from indicator producer to indicator target: the indicator producer measures – and intends to influence, through various means – the target of the measurement.

But this need not be the only way for indicators to function. "Discussions of indicators need not be technical conversations devoid of political contestation. Nor must they be conversations in which participants are seeking to submerge difficult questions of judgment in the abstract language of numbers" (Rosga and Satterthwaite 2009, 315). There are other possibilities, particularly for perception-based indicators such as Freedom House's. "Indicators can influence action by mobilizing actors around either constructing or contesting them"; they can be "a means for social organizing and community education" (Davis and Kingsbury 2011, 7). Indicators reoriented around the goals of participation, contestation, and organization could increase their impact while also increasing the accuracy of their outputs – their measurements and their policy proposals.

Kevin Davis and Benedict Kingsbury have predicted that "the growing emergence of user-generated information that actively involves beneficiaries in the collection, production, and assessment of data will likely significantly shape the next generation of indicators" (Davis and Kingsbury 2011, 5). Development is complicated and full of trade-offs that implicate not only analytical complexities but also competing values, rights, and priorities (Sen 1999; Grindle 2007). Rather than ignoring or minimizing these complicated realities, "the next generation of indicators" (and their producers) can seize a productive role by "promot[ing] locally-initiated experimentation at numerous sites" (Davis and Kingsbury 2011, 49) and developing locally tailored development policy initiatives with the goals of "social organizing and community education." "Sustainable development" indicators and "experimentalist" efforts have demonstrated the potential (as well as the difficulties) of such an approach (Hardi and Zdan 1997; Pinter et al. 2005; Rust 2008; De Burca 2010; Davis and Kingsbury 2011, 7–8; Stone 2012). Experimentalist, locally engaged indicators may provide the opportunities for open dialogue and nuanced problem solving that have been too often lacking in the discourse around indicators.

These comments are particularly salient in considering "freedom," the concept measured by Freedom House's indicator. While broad aspirational principles in favor of "freedom" are easy to state, the specific steps appropriate to the development of "freedom" within a region will differ significantly based on history, on existing social and political structures, and on available resources. Assessment of "freedom," therefore – even if based on "universal" ideals (which themselves may be more problematic than they first appear) – should be contextually nuanced and constantly evolving based on facts on the ground. The promotion of "locally initiated experimentation at numerous sites" is one way of making freedom a reality in actual circumstances. The indicator should help empower rather than ignore the actors whose "freedom" it purports to care for. Although they have rarely done so up to this point, indicator producers could and should help with this sort of local involvement in the ever-evolving process of knowledge production and policy experimentation.

Allowing for contestation of and participation in the development of indicators by "targets" of measurement might seem radical. But in fact, some seeds of more active engagement are already evident in the activities of indicator producers – although finding them requires close observation. Three examples from the Freedom House archives demonstrate some paths that this different sort of engagement might take.

The first example is from the writings of Raymond Gastil, the first researcher responsible for the *Comparative Survey of Freedom*, the predecessor to today's *Freedom in the World* indicator. As noted already, Gastil was open about what he saw as the challenges inherent in the task that Freedom House had undertaken. A couple of years after the *Survey*'s debut, Gastil wrote an article, "A Survey of Freedom," for *Worldview* (September 1, 1974), introducing the indicator and describing some of the findings from its first several editions. Although the article trumpets the insights of the *Survey*, Gastil is far from strident. Taking a reflective, academic stance with respect to the *Survey*, he tallies its "admitted weaknesses," including that many of its results are "marginal" and depend on "arbitrary category boundaries"; he concedes that the *Survey* "remains on the philosophical surface of its subject," and even acknowledges that has "a long way to go before it achieves even the basic purpose of reliably comparing in simple terms the status of freedom in the states of the world." (In an illuminating article published just after he left Freedom House, Gastil [1990] strikes a similar tone, emphasizing the lack of reliably available information that would be required to produce a more substantial, fine-grained analysis, and explaining his decisions for how to construct the indicator given the resource and institutional constraints he faced.)

A few months later, *Worldview* (November 1, 1974) published two critiques of Gastil, as well as Gastil's response. The critiques were harsh and went to core aspects of the project. In "'Miss Freedom' Awards Are, at Best, Irrelevant," Thomas E. Quigley described Gastil's work as "painfully pretentious puffery." In "Freedom Does Not Exist in a Vacuum," Denis Goulet confessed that Gastil's work ultimately leaves him "skeptical, with a sense of unreality." Both critiques attacked what they considered Gastil's cramped view of "freedom's" scope and lamented the lack of consideration of social and economic factors. Gastil's response was again measured. He defended his methodology from the critics, but with striking modesty he added that he "hope[d] to develop the seriousness of the Survey by careful explication and continual reevaluation." He described the project as merely an "exploration of the meaning and institutionalization of freedom," and he closed the article by inviting contributions to the field from critics.

In the forty years since his writing, and despite Gastil's early aspirations, his methodology has been tinkered with at the margins – and never thoroughly "reevaluat[ed]." Gastil's early recognition that his aspiration should be for "continual reevaluation" and not immediate use as an instrument of great "seriousness" contrasts with the defensive positions that were later taken by Freedom House. Other writings confirm that Gastil's original goal was for greater openness; in fact, Gastil apparently believed that his "league table" presentation of findings would make contestation *more* likely (rather than making the results seem unassailable and "purely" scientific). As the indicator was initially being produced, Gastil wrote, in a letter to the executive director, Leonard Sussman:

> I see a comparative table that allows easy comparisons in space and time, as the primary output. By forcing comparative judgments on the author the result is *more open to criticism*, and therefore *improvement* [sic] either in the definitions or the labeling of the countries. (1971a, emphasis added)

Gastil viewed his project as one involving criticism and improvement, a dialogue or a research project designed to take account of the views of others on the way to a more refined understanding. But his aspiration for refinement and development of the indicator has not been realized. It is worth asking, why not? The very success of the indicator may have raised the stakes too high to allow for experimentation, and thus stunted its development. Also, resource constraints may have limited changes to those attainable with minimal year-to-year investment.

But Gastil's goal remains laudable – one to which Freedom House might be well advised to return. Is there a way to shift the indicator from a fundamentally combative stance based on strict division of measurer and measured, and toward a more open one, intended to foster dialogue? The problem might be, of course, that as the *Worldview* articles from long ago demonstrated, such a shift might invite critics who would attack core aspects of the indicator – including its limitation to political and civil rights. But these challenge too might ultimately lead to productive results (see, e.g., Hardi and Zdan 1997; Pintér et al. 2005; Stiglitz et al. 2009a, 2009b).

A second example of a potential reorientation of Freedom House's approach to indicators comes from 1986, when Freedom House produced an educational curriculum based on its indicator (FH 1986). The curriculum was distributed to New York high schools for a pilot program. At first glance, this might seem to be another example of the indicator being presented as knowledge imparted from the measurer-on-high to those below, in this case the schoolchildren. Indeed, the educational materials located in the archives suggest the project (which soon lapsed) was exactly that. But the nascent connection of indicators with education might be worth reviving. For instance, students could be called on to analyze, reconstruct, or reconceive ratings – to "check the experts" – and thus to use indicators as tools for sparking dialogue and contestation. At a theoretical level, in fact, debates over indicators are profoundly related to debates over education – over the relative importance of imparting universal, established knowledge on the one hand or empowering critical thought and invention on the other. An educational venture based on indicators as spurs to dialogue would require indicator producers to view their task as one of promoting dialogue and development of knowledge, rather than the simple implementation of one-size-fits-all analytical templates onto every target of measurement.[29] To foster this open model would, of course, be to forsake some aspects of the *US News & World Report* rankings model, but it might serve Freedom House's broader goals (not to mention "target" populations) better than that model.

A third avenue of change is to focus on measuring more concrete aspects of freedom. Again, this suggestion actually comes from a "road not taken" in Freedom House's own history. In a set of notes apparently intended to guide internal discussions of Freedom House's initiative "Launching a Global Dialogue on Freedom" (FH 2006c, emphasis added), Freedom House staff members argued that "Freedom House should focus on those freedoms that are *concrete to people*: rule of law, freedom of express, freedom of worship, and protection for property rights. These are universally accepted freedoms, and *easier to discuss* in difficult environments." The very fact that an indicator producer took cognizance of the fact that certain rights might be more "concrete to people" and therefore "easier to discuss" represents a significant departure from the norm – from a conception of an indicator as some sort of pristine, universal, objective measurement toward a conception of an indicator as a spark for local discussion and social change.

In the same document, the Freedom House writers note that while they are seeking to make some methodological improvements in their indicator, they "do not want the discussion to descend into quibbling about Freedom House methodology than [sic] using it as a springboard for discussions within the country as to where the core issues related to freedom exist." There were no records in the archives showing that this suggestion – of using the indicator as the basis for local discussions – actually occurred. But the idea is an attractive one, in part because implementing it might require more care to be taken with the indicator, shifting output toward a more detailed, defensible, and public set of ratings.

As these examples show, there may be multiple visions for an indicator even within one organization, or within an organization over time. On the one hand, at times there have been unjustified, presupposition-driven claims about what Freedom House's indicator can "demonstrate"; on the other hand there have been aspirations simply to spur dialogue on issues that may be broadly relatable and clear some expressive space for individuals who need it. These aspirations to dialogue should be honored. With a commitment to local engagement and an openness to contestation and experimentation, the very aspects of indicators that have been the biggest weaknesses – their need for engagement with the "targets" of measurement and with practical realities above ill-fitting universals – all could be turned into strengths.

NOTES

1 Freedom House Records; 1933–2007, Public Policy Papers, Department of Rare Books and Special Collections, Princeton University Library. For some background on Freedom House's decision to archive at Princeton, see documents contained in Box 180 of the Freedom House Records, in the folder labeled "Board of Trustees Meeting, Washington, D.C. 1995 January 17."

2 The fact that potentially damaging incidents transpired is not the point. For more than seven decades – far longer than most organizations even survive – Freedom House has been an effective organization. The important point is that the organization was willing to make its "dirty laundry" public. From the perspective of a researcher, the fact that these records were archived and made publicly available is admirable.

3 Several folders in Box 183 illustrate these points, including "Grant Thornton, 1996–1997," "Various Memos on Finances/Fundraising," as well as the folder "Freedom House Publication and By-Laws Correspondence, 2001–2007" in Box 180. The details of these disputes and controversies are largely irrelevant, and only limited discussion is provided in the text that follows.

4 Freedom House's history is sketched in anecdotal form in Sussman (2002), which was published by Freedom House and written by a long-time executive director of Freedom House. Although it is not an objective history, the archives confirm that the book is factually reliable, and it usefully articulates the policy viewpoints of the organization's leadership over time.

5 Although the concept is in evidence in some rudimentary materials from earlier years, this is the earliest *Balance Sheet* that could be located in the archives.

6 One Balance Sheet (FH 1959) includes the following, amid notes on progress in nuclear disarmament (gain) and the ongoing Berlin standoff (loss): "The gains for freedom were evidenced by: [...] More refrigerators, televisions sets and other consumer amenities in the Communist countries."

7 Gastil's graduate work was at Harvard, and he was for a time associated with the Batelle Institute in Seattle (Gastil 1990, 25). He was also at least at one point associated with the Hudson Institute (Gastil 1971b; Sussman 1972a). He noted that Batelle "occasionally had negative feelings about" (Gastil 1976) his Freedom House work, although he did not explain why. He requested (Gastil 1972a) that Sussman not identify him as a "Batelle employee," but rather "as a Hudson consultant or employee, or simply independent," because "I have never cleared it [the Freedom House work] with the people here [at Batelle]."

8 Sussman's book lauds the 2001 *Freedom in the World* as stretching to 600 pages and being informed by the work of seventeen regional specialists and twelve experts (Sussman 2002,

119–120). The 2012 *Freedom in the World* lists twenty academic advisors and almost sixty "Contributing Authors" whose contributions are categorized at a general regional level but with no further detail (FH 2012).

9   Freedom House has acknowledged this fact but appears to contend that these outcomes reflect a universal reality rather than a quirk of the survey methodology. "Countries and territories generally have ratings in political rights and civil liberties that are within two ratings numbers of each other. For example, without a well-developed civil society, it is difficult, if not impossible, to have an atmosphere supportive of political rights" (FH 2011b; see also Gastil 1990, 28–29).

10   Critiques of the *Comparative Survey* and *Freedom in the World* indicator are presented (or answered) in Bollen (1986, 1993), Gastil (1986, 1990), Fedderke et al. (2001), Giannone (2010), and Steiner (forthcoming). For broader discussion of methodological limitations of indicators such as Freedom House's, see Bollen (1990, 1993), Bollen and Paxton (2000), Morse (2004), Arndt and Oman (2006), Arndt (2008), Rosga and Satterthwaite (2009), Bhuta (2012), and Pistor (2012).

11   Pistor (2012, 168) states that "[t]he Freedom House data had some impact on academic writings in political sciences, where they were frequently criticized but nonetheless often used given the lack of alternative data." This is borne out by academic papers citing Freedom House – although the critiques are fewer and less detailed than might be expected. Examples of academic papers using Freedom House indicators are Wilson (2006), MacCulloch and Pezzini (2010), and Sobel and Coyne (2011). All rely on Freedom House indicators in empirical analysis but offer no critique of or investigation into the bases of Freedom House scores. By contrast, Burke-White (2001, 2004) uses Freedom House's indicators merely in confirmation of an independent analysis and shows an awareness of the dangers of putting more weight on the indicator than it can bear.

12   In an early letter to Gastil, Sussman (1973b) noted that "[o]ne of the questions which arises with regularity as I discuss the Comparative Survey is: Suppose a communist analyst were to undertake a study like ours from the Marxist point of view; would not the black become white and vice versa?" He asked Sussman to address the issue, which may have resulted in Gastil (n.d.), which discusses this "relativistic" position at some length, and which appears in modified form in "A Survey of Freedom," for *Worldview* (September 1, 1974). The *Worldview* article is discussed more in the text that follows.

13   It is also worth noting that even when Freedom House does not itself produce indicators, it has played a role in the growth of other indicators: Freedom House encouraged Congress to produce annual human rights reports on all countries, as well as country-by-country reports on religious freedom (FH 1975b, 1976a; Sussman 2002, 70, 113–114). Freedom House's motivations for these efforts are beyond the scope of this chapter, although they all appear to have enhanced Freedom House's connection with government officials in the human rights arena and promoted Freedom House's role as a producer of indicators. The US reports do not directly compete with Freedom House because they do not produce similar quantitative ratings.

14   A number of useful financial records can be found in Box 76 of the archives, as well as in the other budget documents referenced in this chapter.

15   See, e.g., Box 69, Folder 3 for extensive material from the late 1980s and early 1990s on democratization activities around the time of the fall of the Berlin Wall, with the clear expectation of US government support.

16 The records are replete with decades of examples. "Everyone on the Board has to pitch in to make FH more independent of the federal government" (FH 2005). "Mr. O'Rourke ... stressed that the political situation in the US and around the world is and will continue to be volatile, and Freedom House cannot simply act as a conduit for government money in this situation" (FH 2004b). Other board members had expressed concerns: "Mr. Roper expressed concern about the fact that approximately one third of FH's budget comes from US government monies. He asked whether this was a 'dangerous' percentage to have" (FH 1995). Public funding of Freedom House rose from approximately two million dollars in fiscal year 1997 to almost ten million in fiscal year 2004 (FH 2004b, section heading "Funding Trends").

17 This is one of the most frequently expressed comments in the board records, from the mid-1990s onward. See, for instance, the various board minutes in Boxes 180 and 183 of the Freedom House Records, as well as the folder in Box 183 titled "Various Memos on Finances/Fundraising"; Puddington (2006). In his book, Sussman (2002, 116–117) mentions US Agency for International Development (USAID) funding, although the proportion of it relative to other funding sources is not emphasized.

18 At a meeting in early 2004 (FH 2004a), a board member "expressed concern that over 80% of Freedom House's funding now comes from the US government." A document (FH 2004b) titled "Funding Trends" provides numbers demonstrating the trend. For fiscal year 1999, the overall budget (FH 1998b) broke down to 67 percent government and 33 percent private funding. Sussman (2002, 111) states that staff "more than doubled" in 1990s, under the tenure of Bette Bao Lord as chairperson; it can hardly have been lost on anyone that this increased capacity directly corresponded with dramatic increases in government funding.

19 Freedom House staff addressed this rumor directly. See, for instance, the correspondence in Box 6, Folder 6 of the archives. It is discussed in Sussman's history (2002, 71, 106–107). In a 1976 memo from Sussman (1976b) as executive director, he noted that "[t]he CIA incident is apparently closed. The Board received copies of a letter from [then-CIA director] George [H. W.] Bush stating categorically that the CIA had never funded Freedom House directly or indirectly." The rumors apparently stemmed from the involvement of some Freedom House–associated figures with *Encounter* and other covertly CIA-funded anti-communist activities and publications; Sussman (2002, 107) states that after the CIA funding of *Encounter* was revealed, and the magazine began to rely on "private" funding, Freedom House provided a "major share" of the budget. Given that a "major share" of Freedom House's own budget was provided by US government sources, it is understandable that critics were not completely convinced of the organization's independence. The switch in *Encounter*'s funding from covert-US government to US government-via-Freedom House might seem like a cynical shell game. Although there is no evidence the organization was directly influenced by the CIA or any other government agency, its funding might have given an appearance of impropriety, as several of its board members worried over the years.

20 As the then-president of the African-American Institute wrote (Cotter 1970) to Freedom House's executive director Leonard Sussman, explaining why he could not contribute to that year's *"Balance Sheet of Freedom"*: "Quite frankly I think it would be impossible to do justice to the very complicated question of the status of 'Freedom' during 1970 in Africa. The very definition of freedom itself is, of course, troublesome. It is open to widely divergent interpretations[.]" Fedderke et al. (2001, 108) also focus on South Africa and

argue that "that the definition, specification and measurement of political liberties is inherently problematic."

21 There are also clippings of pieces written by Freedom House staff and clippings related to Freedom House's other indicators. These are not included in this count.

22 Only one article, from the *Poughkeepsie* (New York) *Journal*, gave any indication of methodological consideration. The article compares Freedom House's measurement with a similar measure produced by Human Rights Watch, criticizing neither measure but noting their differences by way of explaining some relatively minor differences in results.

23 It bears emphasizing that these assessments were made by Freedom House, and specifically by Freedom House's staff, and therefore may or may not reflect reality. What they do reflect, however, and what this chapter seeks to show, is how Freedom House's staff portrayed the organization to its board. The document conveys an informed view of what the board wanted to know about the organization, what it looked to, and how it measured success.

24 In answering a question regarding the impact of human rights efforts, Sussman (1976c) wrote: "I gave you several quick examples of the manner in which our *Comparative Survey of Freedom* is received by some governments abroad. I cited the examples of Sweden, India, and Guyana, all of which dissented from the negative aspects of our judgments about them. The fact that they listened at all was, we believe, noteworthy." Noteworthy because it might lead to policy changes, or because it shows Freedom House's prominence – or both?

25 Not that Sussman himself did not care about this question. His correspondence – extensively represented in the archives – reveals Sussman to have been knowledgeable and engaged in policy discussions, and "getting it right" was one of his concerns. The point here is that the impulse to "get it right" appears barely to have registered at all on an *organizational* level, in terms of indicator design, decision making, or development. In other words, it was not much of a motivator for the indicator-producing organization.

26 Halliday (2012, 180–216) provides trenchant analysis of the competitive ecosystem of indicators. Dutta (2010) usefully compares the roles of different indicators for different indicator-producing organizations. Fisher (2012, 224) shows that the World Health Organization's focus on developing an expertise in health statistics was fueled by the demand for "measurable" outcomes and easily comparable information; the expertise then became part of WHO's business model and helped shape the organization's identity in the face of the growing number of actors in the arena of global public health.

27 This is more or less explicit throughout much of the archived materials. For instance, an internal memo from a Freedom House executive director (McColm 1989b) explicitly pushes for an earlier publication of the indicator "[b]ecause of my general feeling that this year there will be competitors in the bushes."

28 Urueña (ibid.) goes on to describe indicators as participating a two-level game and forming part of "an important circle" by which "one indicator produced domestically is entered into a process of transformation by being cited by an international report, and then cited back by domestic media. Once the indicator 'bounces' back, it acquires a new form, as if it had been produced by a different entity and a different method, and gains renewed authority in the domestic political debate."

29 Interestingly, this more open approach seems largely to be the approach Freedom House has taken toward its assessments of the United States. Perhaps familiarity makes nuanced policy analyses more readily available? This observation would further support the need for locally driven indicator data collection and analysis.

REFERENCES

The Freedom House records present several citation challenges. Some folders have not been fully processed by archivists and are labeled by description rather than number; although cumbersome, that convention is followed in this bibliography. Some sources in the archives are technically "published" but remain difficult to locate even in the digital age; both standard citations and an archive location are included here.

Arndt, Christiane. 2008. "The Politics of Governance Ratings." *International Public Management Journal* 11(3): 275–297.

Arndt, Christiane, and Charles Oman. 2006. *Uses and Abuses of Governance Indicators.* Paris: OECD Development Center.

Arruñada, Benito. 2007. "Pitfalls to Avoid When Measuring Institutions: Is Doing Business Damaging Business?" *Journal of Comparative Economics* 35(4): 729–747.

Barro, Robert J. 1997. *Determinants of Economic Growth: A Cross-Country Empirical Study.* Cambridge, MA: MIT Press.

Benjamin, Paul, and Jan Theron. 2009. "Costing, Comparing and Competing: The World Bank's Doing Business Survey and the Bench-Marking of Labour Regulation." In Corder, Hugh, ed., *Global Administrative Law: Innovation and Development,* 205–236. Cape Town: Juta, 2009.

Bergman, Marcelo. 2012. "The Rule, the Law, and the Rule of Law: Improving Measurements and Content Validity." *Justice System Journal* 33: 174–193.

Bhuta, Nehal. 2012. "Governmentalizing Sovereignty: Indexes of State Fragility and the Calculability of Political Order." In Davis, Kevin E., Angelina Fisher, Benedict Kingsbury, and Sally Engle Merry, eds., *Governance by Indicators: Global Power Through Quantification and Rankings,* 132–164. Oxford: Oxford University Press.

Bollen, Kenneth A. 1986. "Political Rights and Political Liberties in Nations: An Evaluation of Human Rights Measures, 1950 to 1984." *Human Rights Quarterly* 8(4): 567–591.

    1990. "Political Democracy: Conceptual and Measurement Traps." *Studies in Comparative International Development* 25: 7–50.

    1993. "Liberal Democracy: Validity and Method Factors in Cross-National Measures." *American Journal of Political Science* 37(4): 1207–1230.

    2009. "Liberal Democracy Series I, 1972–1988: Definition, Measurement, and Trajectories." *Electoral Studies* 28: 268–274.

Bollen, Kenneth A., and Pamela Paxton. 2000. "Subjective Measures of Liberal Democracy." *Comparative Political Studies* 33(1): 58–86.

Burke-White, William W. 2001. "Reframing Impunity: Applying Liberal International Law Theory to an Analysis of Amnesty Legislation." *Harvard International Law Journal* 42: 467–533.

    2004. "Human Rights and National Security: The Strategic Correlation." *Harvard Human Rights Journal* 17: 249–280.

Cooley, Alexander, and Jack Snyder. Forthcoming. *Ranking the World: The Politics of International Rankings and Ratings*. Cambridge: Cambridge University Press.

Cotter, William R. 1970. Letter to Leonard Sussman, Nov. 4. Box 27, Folder 8. In *Freedom House Records*.

Davis, Kevin E. 2004. "What Can the Rule of Law Variable Tell Us About Rule of Law Reforms?" *Michigan Journal of International Law* 26: 141–161.

Davis, Kevin E., and Benedict Kingsbury. 2011. *Indicators as Interventions: Pitfalls and Prospects in Supporting Development Initiatives*. New York: Rockefeller Foundation. http://www.rockefellerfoundation.org/blog/indicators-interventions.

Davis, Kevin E., Benedict Kingsbury, and Sally Engle Merry. 2012a. "Introduction: Global Governance by Indicators." In Davis, Kevin E., Angelina Fisher, Benedict Kingsbury, and Sally Engle Merry, eds., *Governance by Indicators: Global Power Through Quantification and Rankings*, 3–28. Oxford: Oxford University Press.

Davis, Kevin E., Angelina Fisher, Benedict Kingsbury, and Sally Engle Merry, eds. 2012b. *Governance by Indicators: Global Power Through Quantification and Rankings*. Oxford: Oxford University Press.

De Burca, Grainne. 2010. "Stumbling into Experimentalism: The EU Anti-Discrimination Regime." In Charles Sabel and Jonathan Zeitlin, eds., *Experimentalist Governance in the European Union*, 215–236. New York: Oxford University Press.

Denton, James. 1998. Letter to Therese Lyons, Apr. 9, Re: Fundraising. Box 183, Folder "Various Memos on Finances/Fundraising." In *Freedom House Records*.

De Vries, Willem F.M. 2001. "Meaningful Measures: Indicators on Progress, Progress on Indicators." *International Statistical Review* 69(2): 313–331.

Dutta, Nikhil K. 2010. "Accountability in the Generation of Governance Indicators." *Florida Journal of International Law* 22: 403–465.

Espeland, Wendy Nelson, and Michael Sauder. 2007. "Rankings and Reactivity: How Public Measures Recreate Social Worlds." *American Journal of Sociology* 113(1): 1–40.

Espeland, Wendy, and Michael Sauder. 2012. "The Dynamism of Indicators." In Davis, Kevin E., Angelina Fisher, Benedict Kingsbury, and Sally Engle Merry, eds., *Governance by Indicators: Global Power Through Quantification and Rankings*, 86–109. Oxford: Oxford University Press.

Eyler, Robert. 2007. *Economic Sanctions: International Policy and Political Economy at Work*. New York: Palgrave Macmillan.

Fedderke, J.W., R.H.J. de Kadt, and J.M. Luiz. 2001. "Indicators of Political Liberty, Property Rights and Political Instability in South Africa: 1935–97." *International Review of Law & Economics* 21: 103–134.

Fisher, Angelina. "From Diagnosing Under-Immunization to Evaluating Health Care Systems: Immunization Coverage Indicators as a Technology of Global Governance." In Davis, Kevin E., Angelina Fisher, Benedict Kingsbury, and Sally Engle Merry, eds., *Governance by Indicators: Global Power Through Quantification and Rankings*, 217–246. Oxford: Oxford University Press.

Freedom House (FH). 1955. "Freedom House News Letter and Year-end Review." Box 126, Folder 4. In *Freedom House Records*.

    1957. "September 25, 1957 Board Meeting." Box 1, Folder 15. In *Freedom House Records*.

    1959. "*1959 Balance Sheet of Freedom*, Annual Freedom House Report, From: The Public Affairs Committee." Box 126, Folder 6. In *Freedom House Records*.

    1965. Balance Sheet of Freedom. Box 126, Folder 6. In *Freedom House Records*.

1975a. "January 14, 1975 Board Meeting." Box 3, Folder 7. In *Freedom House Records*.

1975b. "December 1, 1975 Executive Committee Meeting." Box 3, Folder 7. In *Freedom House Records*.

1976a. "June 21, 1976 Board Meeting." Box 3, Folder 7. In *Freedom House Records*.

1976b. "October 6, 1976 Board Meeting." Box 3, Folder 7. In *Freedom House Records*.

1977. "January 31, 1977 Executive Committee Meeting." Box 2, Folder 8. In *Freedom House Records*.

1986. "June 23, 1986 Board Meeting." Box 2, Folder 17. In *Freedom House Records*.

1995. "January 17, 1995 Board Meeting." Box 180, Folder "Board of Trustees Meeting, Washington, D.C., 1995 Jan 17." In *Freedom House Records*.

1998a. "January 20, 1998 Board Meeting." Box 180, Folder "Board of Trustees, Washington, D.C. 1998 Jan 20." In *Freedom House Records*.

1998b. "September 24, 1998 Board Meeting." Box 180, Folder "Board of Trustees Meeting, Washington, D.C. 1999 Jan 28." In *Freedom House Records*.

1999. "January 28, 1998 Board Meeting." Box 180, Folder "Board of Trustees Meeting, Washington, D.C. 1999 Jan 28." In *Freedom House Records*.

2000a. "February 10, 2000 Board Meeting." Box 180, Folder "Board of Trustees Meeting, Washington, D.C. 2000 Feb 10." In *Freedom House Records*.

2000b. "May 17, 2000 Board Meeting." Box 183, Folder "Willkie Memorial Annual Board of Trustees Meeting, New York, NY 2000 Sept 28." In *Freedom House Records*.

2000c. "Global Democracy Continues Forward March." Press Release dated Dec 20, 2000. Box 173, Folder "Press Releases 2001." In *Freedom House Records*.

2001. "May 22, 2011 Board Meeting." Box 181, Folder "Board of Trustees Meeting Washington, D.C., 2001 May 22." In *Freedom House Records*.

2003. "Freedom House Fundraising Strategy." Box 181, Folder "Board of Trustees Meeting New York, N.Y., 2003 October 21." In *Freedom House Records*.

2004a. "Jan. 27, 2004 Board Meeting." Box 181, Folder "Board of Trustees Meeting, Washington, D.C., 2004 January 27." In *Freedom House Records*.

2004b. "Oct. 20, 2004 Board Meeting." Box 181, Folder "Board of Trustees Meeting, Washington, D.C., 2005 February 23." In *Freedom House Records*.

2005. "Feb. 23, 2005 Board Meeting." Box 181, Folder "Board of Trustees Meeting, Washington, D.C., 2005 February 23." In *Freedom House Records*.

2006a. "Feb. 21, 2006 Board Meeting." Box 181, Folder "Board of Trustees Meeting, Washington DC, 2006 February 21." In *Freedom House Records*.

2006b. "Freedom House Press Update." Box 181, Folder "Board of Trustees Meeting, Washington, D.C., 2006 June 21." In *Freedom House Records*.

2006c. "Launching a Global Dialogue on Freedom." Box 181, Folder "Executive Committee Meeting 2006 Sept 21." In *Freedom House Records*.

2011a. "Checklist Questions." *Freedom in the World 2011*. http://www.freedomhouse.org /report/freedom-world-2011/checklist-questions.

2011b. "Methodology." *Freedom in the World 2011*. http://www.freedomhouse.org/report /freedom-world-2011/methodology.

2012. "Survey Team." *Freedom in the World 2012*. http://www.freedomhouse.org/report /freedom-world-2012/survey-team.

2013a. "Our Offices." http://www.freedomhouse.org/content/our-offices.

2013b. "Freedom in the World: Aggregate Scores, 2003–2013." http://www.freedomhouse .org/sites/default/files/AggregateScores_FIW2003-2013%20%28final%29.xls.

2013c. "Freedom in the World: Aggregate and Subcategory Scores." http://www .freedomhouse.org/report/freedom-world-aggregate-and-subcategory-scores# .UoyurKot6U4.

n.d. "Maintaining and Developing the Map of Freedom and the *Comparative Survey*." Undated. Box 40, Folder 11. In *Freedom House Records*.

Freedom House Records: 1933–2007, Public Policy Papers, Department of Rare Books and Special Collections, Princeton University Library.

Gastil, Raymond. 1971a. Letter to Leonard Sussman, Sept. 2. Box 40, Folder 11. In *Freedom House Records*.

1971b. Letter to Leonard Sussman, Oct. 15. Box 40, Folder 11. In *Freedom House Records*.

1972a. Letter to Leonard Sussman, Oct. 12. Box 40, Folder 11. In *Freedom House Records*.

1972b. Letter to Leonard Sussman, Nov. 19. Box 40, Folder 11. In *Freedom House Records*.

1974a. "Comparative Survey of Freedom IV." *Freedom at Issue*, No. 26, July-Aug. 1974. Box 129, Folder 4. In *Freedom House Records*.

1974b. Letter to Ralph T. Fisher, Dec. 29. Box 40, Folder 11. In *Freedom House Records*.

1976. Letter to Leonard Sussman, Oct. 6. Box 3, Folder 7. In *Freedom House Records*.

1986. "The *Comparative Survey* & Human Rights Indicators." May 27, 1986, Paper presented at "A Review and Assessment of Human Rights Statistics and Indicators," Symposium at 1986 Annual Meeting of American Association for the Advancement of Science, Philadelphia, May 27. In *Freedom House Records*.

1990. "The Comparative Survey of Freedom: Experiences and Suggestions." *Studies in Comparative International Development* 25(1): 25–50.

n.d. "A Survey of Freedom." Box 40, Folder 11. In *Freedom House Records*.

Giannone, Diego. 2010. "Political and Ideological Aspects in the Measurement of Democracy: The Freedom House Case." *Democratization* 17(1): 68–97.

Grindle, Merilee S. 2007. "Good Enough Governance Revisited." *Development Policy Review* 25(5): 553–574.

Halliday, Terence C. 2012. "Legal Yardsticks: International Financial Institutions as Diagnosticians and Designers of the Laws of Nations." In Davis, Kevin E., Angelina Fisher, Benedict Kingsbury, and Sally Engle Merry, eds., *Governance by Indicators: Global Power Through Quantification and Rankings*, 180–216. Oxford: Oxford University Press.

Hardi, Peter, and Terrence Zdan. 1997. *Assessing Sustainable Development: Principles in Practice*. Winnipeg: International Institute for Sustainable Development and the Assembly of Manitoba Chiefs.

MacCulloch, Robert, and Silvia Pezzini. 2010. "The Roles of Freedom, Growth, and Religion in the Taste for Revolution." *Journal of Law & Economics* 53: 329–358.

McColm, Bruce. 1989a. Memo to Leonard R. Sussman, July 23. Box 8, Folder 11. In *Freedom House Records*.

1989b. Memo to "the Survey Team, August 8. Box 153, Folder "Comparative Survey." In *Freedom House Records*.

Morse, Stephen. 2004. *Indices and Indicators in Development: An Unhealthy Obsession with Numbers*. Sterling, VA: Earthscan.

Mutua, Makau W. 2001. "Savages, Victims, and Saviors: The Metaphor of Human Rights." *Harvard International Law Journal* 42: 201–245.

Pintér, László, Peter Hardi, and Peter Bartelmus. 2005. *Sustainable Development Indicators: Proposals for a Way Forward*. Winnipeg: International Institute for Sustainable Development.

Pistor, Katharina. 2012. "Re-Construction of Private Indicators for Public Purposes." In Davis, Kevin E., Angelina Fisher, Benedict Kingsbury, and Sally Engle Merry, eds., *Governance by Indicators: Global Power Through Quantification and Rankings*, 165–179. Oxford: Oxford University Press.

Porter, Theodore. 1995. *Trust in Numbers: The Pursuit of Objectivity in Science and Public Life*. Princeton, NJ: Princeton University Press.

Przeworski, Adam. 2003. "Freedom to Choose and Democracy." *Economics and Philosophy* 19: 265–279.

Puddington, Arch. 2006. "FH Publications: Yesterday, Today and Tomorrow, Memorandum to Board of Trustees." Box 181, Folder "Board of Trustees Meeting, Washington, D.C., 2006 February 21." In *Freedom House Records*.

Ravallion, Martin. 2010. "Mashup Indices of Development." Policy Research Paper No. 5432. Washington, DC: The World Bank.

Roper, Elmo. 1959. Letter to George Field, December 18. Box 27, Folder 8. In *Freedom House Records*.

Rose, Nikolas, and Peter Miller. 1992. "Political Power Beyond the State: Problematics of Government." *British Journal of Sociology* 43(2): 173–205.

Rosga, AnnJanette, and Margaret Satterthwaite. 2009. "The Trust in Indicators: Measuring Human Rights." *Berkeley Journal of International Law* 27(2): 253–315.

Rust, Christa. 2008. *Developing a Sustainability Indicators System to Measure the Well-being of Winnipeg's First Nations Community: Framework Development and the Community Engagement Process*. Winnipeg: International Institute for Sustainable Development and the Assembly of Manitoba Chiefs.

Sauder, Michael, and Wendy Nelson Espeland. 2009. "The Discipline of Rankings: Tight Coupling and Organizational Change." *American Sociological Review* 74: 63–82.

Sen, Amartya. 1999. *Development as Freedom*. New York: Knopf.

Sobel, Russell S., and Christopher J. Coyne. 2011. "Cointegrating Institutions: The Time-Series Properties of Country Institutional Measures." *Journal of Law & Economics* 54: 111–134.

Steiner, Nils. Forthcoming. "Comparing Freedom House Democracy Scores to Alternative Indices and Testing for Political Bias: Are US Allies Rated as More Democratic by Freedom House?" *Journal of Comparative Policy Analysis*. Draft titled "Testing for a Political Bias in Freedom House Democracy Scores: Are U.S. Friendly States Judged to be More Democratic?" available at http://papers.ssrn.com/sol3/papers.cfm?abstract_id=1919870.

Stiglitz, Joseph, Amartya Sen, and Jean-Paul Fitoussi. 2009a. *Report of the Commission on the Measurement of Economic Performance and Social Progress*. http://www.stiglitz-sen-fitoussi.fr/documents/rapport_anglais.pdf.

2009b. *The Measurement of Economic Performance and Social Progress Revisited: Reflections and Overview*. http://www.stiglitz-sen-fitoussi.fr/documents/overview-eng.pdf.

Stone, Christopher. 2012. "Problems of Power in the Design of Indicators of Safety and Justice in the Global South." In Davis, Kevin E., Angelina Fisher, Benedict Kingsbury, and Sally Engle Merry, eds., *Governance by Indicators: Global Power Through Quantification and Rankings*, 281–294. Oxford: Oxford University Press.

Stout, Rex. 1957. Letter to George Field, 19 December. Box 27, Folder 8. In *Freedom House Records*.

Sussman, Leonard. 1972a. Memo to Contributors to 1973 Balance Sheet of Freedom and Others, Oct. 16. Box 40, Folder 11. In *Freedom House Records*.

1972b. Letter to Raymond Gastil, 3 May. Box 40, Folder 11. In *Freedom House Records*.

1973a. Letter to Raymond Gastil, 11 January. Box 40, Folder 11. In *Freedom House Records*.

1973b. Letter to Raymond Gastil, 13 March. Box 40, Folder 11. In *Freedom House Records*.

1973c. Letter to Raymond Gastil, 12 April. Box 40, Folder 11. In *Freedom House Records*.

1976a. Memo to Gerald Steibel, 21 January. Box 40, Folder 12. In *Freedom House Records*.

1976b. Memo to Richard Gambino and Aaron Levenstein, 21 April. Box 40, Folder 12. In *Freedom House Records*.

1976c. Letter to William Evan, 7 April. Box 40, Folder 12. In *Freedom House Records*.

1979. Letter to Ned Bandler, 5 February. Box 41, Folder 1. In *Freedom House Records*.

1980. Letter to Board of Trustees and Advisory Council, 8 September 1980, Box 7, Folder 5. In *Freedom House Records*.

1989. Letter to Paul Seabury, 24 July. Box 153, Folder "Comparative Survey." In *Freedom House Records*.

2002. *Democracy's Advocate: The Story of Freedom House*. New York: Freedom House.

Thomas, M.A. 2010. "What Do the Worldwide Governance Indicators Measure?" *European Journal of Development Research* 22: 31–54.

Urueña, René. 2012. "Internally Displaced Population in Colombia: A Case Study on the Domestic Aspects of Indicators as Technologies of Global Governance." In Davis, Kevin E., Angelina Fisher, Benedict Kingsbury, and Sally Engle Merry, eds., *Governance by Indicators: Global Power Through Quantification and Rankings*, 249–280. Oxford: Oxford University Press.

Wilson, Jeremy M. 2006. "Law & Order in an Emerging Democracy: Lessons from the Reconstruction of Kosovo's Police & Justice Systems." *Annals of the American Academy of Political and Social Science*, 605: 152–177.

Windsor, Jennifer. 2005. Speech, "The Promotion of Freedom in U.S. Foreign Policy: Opportunities and Challenges." Box 182, Folder "Democracy and Human Rights, 2002–2003." In *Freedom House Records*.

2006. "Presentation to Aspen Institute." Box 182, Folder "Democracy and Human Rights, 2002–2003." In *Freedom House Records*.

Zaloznaya, Marina, and John Hagan. 2012. "Fighting Human Trafficking or Instituting Authoritarian Control? The Political Co-optation of Human Rights Protection in Belarus." In Davis, Kevin E., Angelina Fisher, Benedict Kingsbury, and Sally Engle Merry, eds., *Governance by Indicators: Global Power Through Quantification and Rankings*, 344–364. Oxford: Oxford University Press.

2

Indicators and the Law

A Case Study of the Rule of Law Index

René Urueña

INTRODUCTION

This chapter explores some of the ways in which indicators interact with law. Accordingly, it studies the Rule of Law Index, an indicator developed and applied by the World Justice Project to measure the adherence of almost 200 countries to the rule of law. Such quantitative technologies of measurement, this chapter argues, are here to stay in the law and development agenda. They create a community of practice and provide normative criteria for the evaluation of whether a country adheres to their particular idea of what the rule of law is (and is not). Because of their origin in multilateral financial institutions, the Index and other rule of law indicators tend to be seen by some as implausible neoliberal simplifications that simply should be dismissed. This chapter takes a different perspective. Irrespective of the Index's origins, the genie is out of the bottle. Rule of law indicators are veritable technologies of global governance, and it is therefore important to engage with them, as they open a space for contestation, intervention, and policy debate on what it means to encourage the rule of law in the developing world.

The chapter is organized in three parts. The first one puts the Index in context and argues that it can be read as an expression of a post-neoliberal moment of the law and development agenda. The second part unpacks the Index itself – its added-value and methodology – and proposes a characterization of the notion of rule of law that underlies it. According to this section, the "rule of law" of the Index is substantive, noninstrumental, and features a certain realist sensibility. Building on these premises, in the third part I rethink the role that the Index, and other rule of law indicators like it, play in global governance. The fourth part concludes the chapter.

SITUATING INDICATORS IN THE LAW AND DEVELOPMENT AGENDA

The idea of measuring quality of governance has gained increased notoriety in the last two decades. Although it is difficult to know the exact number of governance indicators currently in use (some proponents say there are more than 100 out there) (Botero, Ponce, and Pratt 2012), it seems rather clear that reliance on such quantitative technologies of measurement is increasing at both the international and domestic levels (Oman and Arndt 2006).

However, as Katharina Pistor has shown, governance indicators are hardly something new. Ever since the early 1970s, private firms have compiled governance indicators to provide business decision makers with tools to assess risk: for example, the Business Environment Risk Intelligence (BERI) was first compiled in 1972 and the International Country Risk Guide (ICRG) in 1980 (Pistor 2012). Until the 1990s, these indicators were mostly unconcerned with law. Of course, a crucial part of providing information on risk involved "law and order" variables; for example, the ICRG has included since its beginning the "law and order tradition" as part of its political risk rating (ICRG 2012). Nevertheless, these legal variables were not concerned specifically with legal reform. Despite the fact that these indicators were *about* governance, they were not intended to be used *for* governance. Instead, the idea was to provide foreign investors with information that would complement other sources of data about their target countries (Pistor 2012).

Indicators in the First Law and Development Movement

How did we go from that point to the current expansion of rule of law indicators? To understand this change, it seems useful to start by noting that, while these private indicators were being produced, a different group of people, other than investors, were interested in law and order in foreign lands. That group was the development community. As is well known, the idea that law and development are connected gained momentum and became a "movement" in the 1960s (Merryman 1977). From its emergence in US academia, it was then put into operation in Africa and Latin America through projects funded by the Ford Foundation and the United States Agency for International Development (USAID).[1] This is what Trubek and Santos call the "first moment" of law and development: the moment when law was understood as an instrument for effective state intervention in the economy (Santos and Trubek 2006). It was built around the economic commonsense of the time that prescribed state intervention in the economy, import substitution, and the development of domestic markets. For these reformers, though, law in developing countries was not up to the task of being a useful instrument for the policymakers, as it was too "formalistic" and thus unable to provide practical solutions for the people who needed them (Trubek 2006). The answer was a change in the "legal culture" of countries, which meant in practice that an important component of this agenda was the transformation of legal education in developing countries, specifically by funding training of local legal professionals (Prado and Trebilcock 2011).

Legal indicators were of little use in this context. No data were available, and funding priorities seemed to be directed toward programs that would transform legal education. More importantly, though, was that the law and development movement had an instrumental approach to law for which quantitative data on legal issues were not particularly relevant. If anything was worth measuring, it was the results of legal rules: economic growth, reduction of poverty, and the like. Of course, it was not that law and development reformers were indifferent to the importance of "the rule of law" in the sense of providing equal access to justice – even democracy or human rights. It was that there was an implicit faith in a spillover effect from "an effective and instrumental economic law to 'democracy values' like access to justice and protection of civil rights" (Trubek 2006, 77).

Moreover, by the 1960s quantitative measurement in developing countries was perceived as the province of economists and statisticians. For example, part of the development agenda of the 1950s in Latin America was the creation of specialized institutes of statistics, proposed first by the Inter-American Statistical Institute (IASI) (established in 1940 and a proponent one decade later of the Census of the Americas), and then by the Inter-American Conference on Statistics (established in 1950 by the Organization of American States) (CEPAL 2009). This trend was joined in its early years by the World Bank, which sent special missions to the region to provide advice on the creation and maintenance of national statistics services; crucially, these missions were manned by economists and statisticians – not lawyers.[2]

This first wave of scholarship and reform was short lived. Its approach was criticized as the "model of liberal legalism" by some of the scholars who originally proposed it (Trubek and Galanter 1974). Those who participated in this first moment faced two kinds of failure. One was a failure as defined in their own instrumentalist terms: even when they were successful at getting developing countries to adopt legal reform, such reform often failed to take root and remained a dead letter (Trubek 2006). The second was a failure as defined in political terms. Even in the few cases when reforms did take root and were implemented, they were susceptible to being co-opted by domestic elites and the desired spillover effect seldom occurred. Such was the case of the Ford Foundation's "Chile Law Project" in 1965, which was captured by conservative elites and, as was evident by the early 1970s, had very little impact in transforming the country.[3] Hence, in Trubek's words, "[the] chastened reformers found themselves facing the frightening possibility that legalism, instrumentalism, and authoritarianism might form a stable amalgam so that their efforts to improve economic law and lawyering could strengthen authoritarian rule" (Trubek 2006, 79). Ultimately, the first law and development Movement never had an impact in mainstream policymaking, and law fell off the radar of reformers and the development community for the next few decades.

Indicators in the Second Law and Development Moment: Doing Business

The situation changed in the 1990s. As is well known, the Washington Consensus triggered a new developmental commonsense that favored liberalization and market-based solutions.[4] In this context, law was perceived to play two different roles. On the one hand, law was part of the *institutions* of society, which, together with "the standard constraints of economics (. . .) define the choice set and therefore determine transaction and production costs and hence the profitability and feasibility of engaging in economic activity" (North 1991, 97) (generally, see North 1990). In a manner close to the instrumental view of the first law and development movement, this perspective saw law as a means of achieving economic development – this time, though, by keeping out of the way of investors and private transactions and being successful in forcing the state to do the same (Kennedy 2006).

From this perspective, there was a connection between the hurdles that entrepreneurs had to face to establish business and economic development. Peruvian economist Hernando de Soto famously argued at the time that red tape in the South led people to informality, where lack of proper title and enforceable contracts led to underdevelopment (de Soto 1989). Quoting the dominating paradigm of the day, "institutions mattered"; hence, development could be achieved through institutional (and legal) reform.

This approach became influential at multilateral financial institutions. However, as Davis and Trebilcock report, skeptics were as numerous as optimists in the debate on whether legal reform could foster development (Davis and Trebilcock 2008). Yet, optimists had a crucial devise that skeptics lacked: indicators (Davis 2004). Indeed, the notion that law was relevant for development was this time accompanied by a wealth of cross-country research seeking correlations between the rule of law and economic development, or between the latter and certain characteristics of legal systems (e.g., their legal tradition, the time taken to enforce a contract, etc.). These studies seemed methodologically sophisticated to nonspecialists and managed to accumulate a wealth of innovative variables to measure abstract concepts such as the rule of law. From that point, indicators seem to have been the logical next step: if the variables were developed and the data were gathered, it was a marginal effort to organize the information and present the results in the form of indicators.

Doing Business (DB) is a good example of the role indicators play in this instrumentalist view of the connection between law and development. DB is a product of the International Finance Corporation (IFC), which is part of the World

Bank Group, and seeks to measure the cost to firms of business regulation – most recently in 185 countries around the world (World Bank – IFC 2013). The first DB Report was published in 2004 (World Bank – IFC 2004) and mirrored much of De Soto's views. It used indicators to argue an inverse relation between red tape and development, as "poor countries regulate business the most" (World Bank – IFC 2004) and "heavier regulation is generally associated with more inefficiency in public institutions – longer delays and higher cost [. . .] – and more unemployed people, corruption, less productivity and investment, but not with better quality of private or public goods" (World Bank – IFC 2004, xiv). From this point of view, legal reform was instrumental to development, mostly in the form of deregulation.

Revealing its policy importance, DB's premises were criticized from different fronts. One example is the controversy around DB's index of labor market regulation, known as "Employing Workers."[5] This indicator was contested in a campaign of a transnational group of workers' representatives (spearheaded by the International Trade Union Confederation), together with the International Labor Organization and several academics, for whom countries that have less protective labor legislation seemed to score better on the index, thus bypassing International Labor Organization (ILO) conventions[6] and possibly encouraging labor market deregulation – particularly if the index was used as a guide for determining loans by international financial institutions (Berg and Cazes 2007). Facing such criticism, the World Bank – IFC adopted certain changes in the indicator for its 2010 Report (published in 2009), convened an "Employing Workers Consultative Group" in the same year (Doing Business Employing Workers Consultative Group 2011), and ultimately suspended use of the indicator in its 2013 DB Report.

Much of the criticism directed toward DB was, in fact, a symptom of the *Zeitgeist* that was emerging at the time, as the failures of the Washington Consensus became more evident in different contexts (Kennedy 2006). As the controversy about DB grew, the Bank – IFC requested an independent evaluation of the project, which was published in 2008 (World Bank Independent Evaluation Group 2008). The report deals in detail with several of the challenges in DB's methodology; the central point of the assessment, though, is clear enough: following closely the instrumental consensus of the second law and development moment, the Bank – IFC's methodology presumes that less regulation is better than more regulation, in every case, everywhere. This premise, the report concludes, obscures the fact that some regulation may be appropriate; that is, "DB measures the costs but not the benefits of regulation" (World Bank Independent Evaluation Group 2008, xvii). The Report remains instrumental in its view of the law and subscribes to the idea that less burdensome business regulation is associated with better private sector performance (World Bank Independent Evaluation Group 2008); however, it seems to reject the DB's strict neoliberal view and recognizes some virtues in regulation.

The Independent Report is an example of how governance indicators are able to outgrow their neoliberal cradle and remain influential in development circles, even when the developmental commonsense has changed. As the original underlying premises of DB were subject to critique, the Independent Report triggered a change in the rhetoric surrounding the Index. In fact, in 2013, the World Bank – IFC was speaking of "Smart Regulation": "the economies that rank highest on the ease of doing business are not those where there is no regulation – but those where governments have managed to create rules that facilitate interactions in the marketplace without needlessly hindering the development of the private sector. In essence, *Doing Business* is about smart business regulations, not necessarily fewer regulations" (World Bank – IFC 2013, 16). This is not say that the actual DB methodology has changed in the sense suggested by this statement[7]; however, it does go to show that DB sought to respond to a new developmental commonsense, where De Soto's views are not taken for granted, and it is not necessarily true that less regulation is always better.

Indicators in the Third Law and Development Moment

DB's transformation can be read as a transition toward what has been called the third moment of law and development. Although the rule of law is still seen as instrumental for development, a new view seems to be emerging, according to which legal institutions are parts of development in themselves: law is, in this context, a developmental goal for its own sake (Santos and Trubek 2006). And, following the lessons learned from the use of indicators in the instrumental view of law, it became clear that indicators could also be a useful platform to implement this new developmental commonsense, in which the rule of law could be measured as a value, regardless of its direct impact on other variables of development.

Enter thus the Rule of Law Index. The Index seeks to provide a comprehensive picture of the extent to which a state adheres to the rule of law in its multiple dimensions, as defined in the Index's methodology. It is an expression of the third law and development moment, in that it focuses on the rule of law in itself: not as a proxy for other values, and not as a platform for economic development. The following section explores the Index in more detail: it first gives a brief description of its origins and methodology, and then situates the idea of "rule of law" underlying it.

THE RULE OF LAW INDEX

The Rule of Law Index (RoLI) is published by the World Justice Project (WJP), an organization that first emerged in 2006 as an initiative of the American Bar Association under the presidency of William H. Neukom, former general counsel of Microsoft Corp. The initiative was first led by Mark D. Agrast (Podgers 2007), an American lawyer who then went to work at the Center for American Progress and the Obama administration, at the Department of Justice (US Department of Justice 2009).

Original funding for the program came in 2007 with a two-year, US$1.75 million, grant from the Bill & Melinda Gates Foundation to the American Bar Association (ABA 2007). Since then, WJP has become an independent nonprofit organization under US law, and is supported financially by multiple organizations, corporations, and individuals. According to its IRS Form 990 for year 2010, its revenue in 2009 was US$4.590.937, and US$ 1.321.740 in 2010, all of which comes from grants, gifts, and contributions (Form 990 available at http://www.guidestar.org/). As of early 2013, WJP's Executive Director was Juan Carlos Botero, a Colombian Harvard-trained lawyer who, before holding that post, had been responsible for the Index.

When first published, the Index entered a fairly crowded ecosystem. At least seven other rule of law indicators were available in 2006 (Skaaning 2010). Among others, the Bertelsmann Transformation Index, a German initiative of important dimensions that evaluates whether developing countries and countries in transition are steering social change toward democracy and a market economy, which features a rule of law component since 2003 (Hillenbrand 2006). Also available in 2006 were the Worldwide Governance Indicators, an initiative headed by Daniel Kaufmann, Aart Kraay, and Massimo Mastruzzi, affiliated with the World Bank Institute and the Development Research Group of the World Bank, which has included a rule of law variable since 1996 (Worldwide Governance Indicators 2014). Freedom House, in turn, also had at the time three rule of law–related indicators: one in its Freedom in the World ranking (Freedom House [FH] 2006a), another in its Countries at the Crossroads (FH 2006b), and one connected with Judicial Framework and Independence in its Nations in Transit Index (FH 2005).

The United Nations also developed its own Rule of Law initiative, which included indicators. It was launched in 2008 as a joint initiative of the United Nations Department of Peacekeeping Operations and the Office of the United Nations High Commissioner for Human Rights, and was developed in cooperation with the Vera Institute of Justice. The Vera Institute of Justice is a nonprofit organization based in the United States. It was founded in 1961 and focuses on different justice reform projects, mostly in the United States and increasingly in other countries. Despite the fact that Vera is a larger organization than the World Justice Project (according to Vera's IRS Form 990, its revenue in 2009 was US$24.388.128, and US$28.612.706 in 2010) it had joined the latter in developing the Vera–Altus Indicators Project, which sought to complement the Rule of Law Index by adapting its de jure standards to *de facto* measures (Parson et al. 2008). The first six-month pilot of the Vera–Altus Indicators Project was applied in four cities (Chandigarh, India; Lagos, Nigeria;

Santiago, Chile; and New York City) and the results were published in 2008. The UN project was also developed by the Vera Institute (yet seemingly without the World Justice Project), and resulted in a toolkit of UN-backed Guide for Rule of Law Indicators, launched in 2011, which is currently tested in Haiti, Liberia, and South Sudan.[8]

What was the added value of yet another rule of law indicator? Two points stand out: specialization and independent data collection. All of the aforementioned indicators use the rule of law to measure something else (e.g., social transformation or freedom), and use only certain aspects of the concept to that effect. The WPS's Rule of Law Index presented itself as the first indicator to focus on the rule of law in itself, with the ambition to measure the notion comprehensively (Agrast, Botero, and Ponce 2009, 9). Moreover, the Rule of Law Index was one of the few indicators to independently collect data from stakeholders – adding to that a unique general poll, described in the methodology that follows, which limited the indicator's dependence on experts. Funding plays a key role here: gathering data independently (and not relying on other sources) is an expensive undertaking that is available only to well-funded organizations. These two aspects helped differentiate the WJP's initiative from those of its competitors, and carved out a niche for it in the market.

Methodology

For the Index's purposes, the "rule of law" is defined by four guiding principles, presented in Table 2.1, each of which provides the basis for certain "factors" that are measured in each country. Each factor is in turn subdivided into subfactors. Table 2.1 shows the basic architecture of the Rule of Law Index, and its changes since the first Index Report was published in 2009, to the most recent, in 2012. For the sake of brevity, the table excludes the subfactor level of the indicator.

The Index measures each of these factors from two perspectives: (1) a general population poll, conducted by local polling companies using a sample of 1,000 respondents in the three largest cities of each country (run every three years); and (b) a Qualified Respondents questionnaire, completed by in-country experts in civil and commercial law, criminal justice, labor law, and public health (run yearly) (Agrast, Botero, and Ponce 2009, 26–28); (Agrast, Botero, and Ponce 2010, 10); (Agrast, Botero, and Ponce 2011, 14–15); (Agrast et al. 2012, 18–19, 186–188).

In each of these instruments, a set of questions is posed to the respondent (lay person, in the case of the polls, or expert, in the case of the qualified respondent) and a score is given to their answers. The score resulting in each question is then linked to one (or several) subfactors of the Rule of Law, and the average of such scores is calculated, with a weight of 50 percent for the expert answers and 50 percent for the poll results. The average is the score of the country for the subfactor. The subfactors

TABLE 2.1. *The Changing Architecture of the Rule of Law Index*

Principles	Factors 2009	Factors 2010	Factors 2011	Factors 2012
I. The government and its officials and agents are accountable under the law.	1. Government powers limited by constitution	1. Limited Government Powers	1. Limited Government Powers	1. Limited Government Powers
	2. Governmental and nongovernmental checks	2. Absence of Corruption	2. Absence of Corruption	2. Absence of Corruption
	3. Accountable government officials and agents			
	4. Accountable military, police, and prison officials			
	5. Compliance with international law			
II. The laws are clear, publicized, stable and fair, and protect fundamental rights, including the security of persons and property;	6. Laws are clear, publicized, and stable	3. Clear, Publicized and Stable Laws	3. Fundamental Rights	3. Fundamental Rights
	7. Laws protect fundamental rights	4. Fundamental Rights	4. Order and Security	4. Order and Security
	8. Laws protect security of the person	5. Order and Security		
	9. Laws protect security of Property			
III. The process by which the laws are enacted, administered and enforced is accessible, fair and efficient	10. Accessible process	6. Open Government	5. Open Government	5. Open Government
	11. Fair and efficient Administration	7. Regulatory Enforcement	6. Effective Regulatory Enforcement	6. Effective Regulatory Enforcement

RULE OF LAW

(continued)

83

TABLE 2.1 (continued)

Principles	Factors 2009	Factors 2010	Factors 2011	Factors 2012
IV. Access to justice is provided by competent, independent, and ethical adjudicators, attorneys or representatives, and judicial officers who are of sufficient number, have adequate resources, and reflect the makeup of the communities they serve.	12. Impartial and accountable judicial system	8. Access to Civil Justice	7. Access to Civil Justice	7. Access to Civil Justice
	13. Efficient, accessible and effective judicial system	9. Effective Criminal Justice	8. Effective Criminal Justice	8. Effective Criminal Justice
	14. Competent and independent attorneys or representatives			
	15. Fair and efficient alternative dispute resolution	10. Informal Justice	9. Informal Justice	9. Informal Justice
	16. Fair and efficient traditional justice			

Sources: Principles: Agrast, Botero, and Ponce (2009, 7–8; 2010, 8; 2011, 9); Agrast et al. (2012, 9). Factors 2009: Agrast, Botero, and Ponce (2009, 15–25). Factors 2010: Agrast, Botero, and Ponce (2010, 9–12). Factors 2011: Agrast, Botero, and Ponce (2011, 10–14). Factors 2012: Agrast et al. (2012, 10–17).

are then aggregated to form a score for each factor, which are in turn aggregated to create scores for each principle. The scores are then ordered, rankings established, and color maps drawn to compare countries (Botero and Ponce 2010, 17–26, 39–54; Agrast et al. 2012, 188–190).

For example, in 2012, Principle I (Accountability) is the basis Factor 1 (Limited Government Powers), one of whose subfactors (1.2) is "government powers are effectively limited by the legislature." To measure that subfactor, WJP asked experts, among many other things, whether "in practice, the chief executive (President, Prime Minister, etc.) of [their Country] rules without regard to legislative checks," and asked them to state whether they strongly agree, agree, disagree, or strongly disagree with that statement. This answer is then given a score (in this example, o for "strongly agree," 1 for "strongly disagree," and mid scores for answers in between). In turn, WJP's polling company asked a lay person, again among many other things, to "assume that one day the President decides to adopt a policy that is clearly against the [their Country's] Constitution: How likely is the National Congress/Parliament to be able to stop the President's illegal actions?" The answer is again given a score (here, o for "very unlikely," 1 for "very likely," and intermediate scores). The questionnaires include several questions such as these, each giving a score that is then weighted and averaged to calculate a score for the respective subfactor, and then aggregated to create a country score for the relevant factor, and then for each of the principles.

Situating the "Rule of Law" of Rule of Law Index

RoLI's underlying notion of the rule of law has three characteristics.

- It is *substantive*.

The Index is not concerned with the formal pedigree of the law, but rather that the law enshrines certain characteristics that coincide with the Index's factors and subfactors. WJP seems to have been aware since the first pilots of the division of what they call "thick" and "think" definitions of the rule of law (Agrast, Botero, and Ponce 2009, 12), and tried to navigate between the extremes: if the definition was too "thick" (i.e., requiring substantive characteristics such as respect for self-government and fundamental rights) the Index would seem too provincial (most likely, Western-centric) and would have limited universal appeal. However, if the definition was too "thin" (requiring only certain formal characteristics of the law without normative criteria to evaluate it), the Index would risk falling into a formalist apology of totalitarian regimes justified through the "rule by law" (Daniels and Trebilcock 2008, 12–36).

The compromise between these two extremes was the four principles described in Table 2.1, which according to the Index's architects, "rotate around the principles that political power must be exercised in accordance with law rather than in an arbitrary or self-interested manner, and that disputes among private individuals and between them and the Sovereign must be subject to independent adjudication" (Botero and Ponce 2010, 5).

This is, though, hardly a real compromise, as the four principles reflect an understanding of the relation between law and society that seems close to some aspects of what Trubek called, in the middle of the crisis of the first law and development moment, "liberal legalism" (Trubek and Galanter 1974, 1071–1081); that is, the idea that "a legal system is an integrated purposive entity which draws on the power of the state but disciplines that power by its own autonomous and internally derived norms. With some slippage and friction, social behavior is aligned with and guided by legal rules. Moreover, that behavior can be consciously modified by appropriate alternations of these rules" (Trubek and Galanter 1974, 1072). In that sense, despite its rhetoric, the RoLI's view of the rule of law is aligned with a substantively liberal view of the rule of law.

- It is *noninstrumental*.

The Index does not subscribe to the other aspect of legal liberalism as defined by Trubek, namely, the underlying theory of a relationship between law and development (Trubek and Galanter 1974, 1073–1074). RoLI appears to consider the rule of law as important in and of itself, and not as a means to an (economic) end (Tamanaha 2007, 6–12). As may be gleamed from its methodology, it is not primarily concerned with the effects that adhering to the rule of law may have on development, thus reflecting a different mindset from the instrumental view of the Washington Consensus (as exemplified by Doing Business).

Rule of Law scores may be comparatively stronger or weaker (Chile, with a score of 0.61, may have a more effective criminal investigation system than Argentina, with a score of 0.30), but such information will not be specific enough to establish the causal relations between factors that may explain the score. Marking a stark difference with indicators in the neoliberal moment of law and development, RoLI has explicitly rejected prescriptions since its first Report (Agrast, Botero, and Ponce 2009, 30; Botero and Ponce 2010, 26). As such, then, the Index is not simply a one-size-fits-all laundry list for institutional reform: even if a country wanted to "game" the indicator to get a better score, it would require that the reform it adopted is perceived by its general public and its own experts as contributing to one of the factor or subfactors. Therefore, the reform that is perceived as contributing to, say, a more effective criminal investigation system in Argentina may not be perceived that way in Chile.

This approach is coherent with the Index's substantive inclination. It understands its factors and subfactors as criteria whose pull to normativity derives from the factors themselves, and not from an external source such as "development," "efficiency," or "justice." This deontological perspective allows the Index to have a claim to universality in its definition of the rule of law, without the self-conscious doubts triggered by the connection between cultural diversity and the rule of law, that were at the heart of the abandonment of the first moment law and development.

- It has a *realist sensibility*.

The Index is keen on showing that it seeks to measure "law in action," as opposed to "law on books" (Agrast, Botero, and Ponce 2009, 12, 2011, 15; Botero and Ponce 2010, 108; 2011; Agrast et al. 2012, 17). To be sure, this idea immediately calls to mind the distinction as captured by Roscoe Pound (Pound 1910) and the American Realist tradition. The point, though, goes beyond a mere linguistic coincidence. First, the Index is an expression of the old realist dream that quantitative studies could provide a valuable input for understanding legal outcomes (Llewellyn 1930, 1243–1244). The turn to empirical legal studies has led to talk of a "new legal realism" in the United States (Miles and Sunstein 2008), and the Rule of Law Index seems to be a contribution to that body of scholarship.

More important, though, is the fact that, just as the early Realists, RoLI reacted to the perceived rule-formalism of other legal indicators, which are satisfied with measuring the existence of certain rules "on the books," without measuring its effects in reality. The "reality" of the Index, though, is one of perception: the facts of the Index are opinions by laymen and experts. Indeed, the Index's approach is not to trust formal expression of the rule of law ("law on the books"), and neither is it to gather data describing how the justice system actually works (e.g., number of courts, judges, prosecutors, or number of days to have a conviction), but rather to measure the perception of the public of the justice system. This perception is both "expert" and "popular" (each weighting 50 percent of the score). The Index's approach to the rule of law is, thus, twofold: first, for the Index, the rule of law is a factual phenomenon that exists beyond formal rules. Instead, it is a set of facts that can be observed in reality, measured, and then ranked. Second, this factual phenomenon is the perception of the public, not the underlying conditions that trigger such perception. This approach is presented as a step beyond "paper rules" and into reality, a move parallel to that encouraged by the Realists (Feldman 2000, 112–113).

Of course, one could argue that the perception of a phenomenon is not the actual phenomenon. Following RoLI's approach, a health indicator would not measure infant mortality, but rather the perception mothers have of the attention their babies received at the hospital. However, that point is moot with regard to the rule of law.

Observer ▭▭▭▭▭⟶ Fact (e.g., a judicial decision)
Law on the books

FIGURE 2.1. Traditional realism.

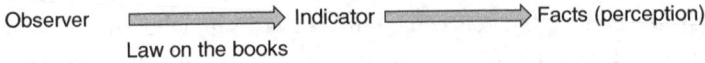

Observer ▭▭▭▭▭⟶ Indicator ▭▭▭⟶ Facts (perception)
Law on the books

FIGURE 2.2. Rule of Law Index.

The Index's premise is that the "reality" of the rule of law is the experience of those living (or not living) under it. In that sense, it would be wrong to accuse WJP of mistaking perception with reality, when it is arguable that there is no reality beyond such perception. In the case of the rule of law, the indicator allows the WJP to see reality – in this very restricted sense, reality is being constructed by the indicator.

For traditional Realists (those focused on law in action), this was a nonissue: from their perspective, the dichotomy between the "rule of law" and "the rule of men" was not as sharp as one expected (Tamanaha 2004, 79), and through this insight, posed a formidable challenge to the notion that formal law actually constrains adjudication – a challenge that remains relevant today (Schauer 2012). As is shown in Figure 2.1, in traditional realism the observer understands that law in the books has very little power for predicting outcomes, and thus overlooks it to search for law in action (the facts, which would often be the judicial decision).

Of course, this move is not available for the Rule of Law Index, whose very existence is justified by the premise that the rule of law is different (and better) than the rule of men. Thus, the Index has to recur to a different strategy: as is illustrated in Figure 2.2, in the Rule of Law Index the observer (i.e., the WJP) also understand that law in the books has very little power for describing reality, and thus overlooks it to search for law in action. However, the facts that the WJP looks for are not readily available (as would be, e.g., the Realist's judicial decision): not all the facts are relevant, they need to be found, chosen, organized, and classified. And, because the criterion that guides that choice and classification cannot be derived from the facts themselves, the observer needs a normative criterion to create its reality. Enter thus the indicator, which serves as a mediator between the WJP and facts (in this case, a perception held by a group of people).

The indicator's mediation is both a descriptive and a normative exercise – even if it is not openly prescriptive as other indicators such as Doing Business. It is descriptive, because it allows the WJP to *see* what the respondents think of their own country's performance under each principle, factor, and subfactor. But it is also normative, as it reflects WJP's set of deontological choices (the principles, factors, and subfactors) about what it means to adhere to the rule of law. The Rule of Law Index therefore can be read as *both* a technology of observation that facilitates the Realist ideal of going beyond "law on the books" (and is akin to statistics or demography) and a new layer that injects normative judgment where only disorganized facts existed. The Index thus embodies a particular way of defining the rule of law normatively and a theory about what the rule of law is. The Index then acts, in effect, to promote this theory.

RETHINKING THE FUNCTIONS OF THE RULE OF LAW INDEX IN GLOBAL GOVERNANCE

Governance indicators have been subject to some sharp critique, ranging from statistical issues to transparency (Oman and Arndt 2006; Langbein and Knack 2008). Most relevant for the Rule of Law Index, though, seems to be one specific line of critique: the problem of definition. According to this line, the rule of law is inherently difficult to define. In Judith Shklar's words:

> It would not be very difficult to show that the phrase "the Rule of Law" has become meaningless thanks to ideological abuse and general over-use. It may well have become just another one of those self-congratulatory rhetorical devices that grace the public utterances of Anglo-American politicians. No intellectual effort need therefore be wasted on this bit of ruling-class chatter. (Shklar 1987, 1; quoted in Waldron 2002, 139)

The problem here is that it is hard to reach a significant agreement on what the rule of law actually means. And if it is impossible to define the notion with any analytical clarity, it becomes impossible to measure – or, at the very least, any measurement always will be open to this definitional challenge: Why this definition, and not that one? Why include this aspect of the rule of law and not this other? (Ginsburg 2011, 270–274)

This concern misses the point. Although it is certainly true that no clear-cut, generally accepted, definition of the rule of law is forthcoming, arguing that this eliminates the uses of the concept (or its measurement) overlooks some of its most important dimensions. Indicators do not (indeed, cannot) measure reality objectively, in the way a thermometer would measure temperature. Rather, they inject, as we have seen, a normative analysis to the reality they measure, and constitute it. That is the case of the Rule of Law Index. Despite the conceptual approach of the Index, the rule of law is not a checklist but rather, as Jeremy Waldron has suggested, an essentially contested concept (Waldron 2002). The rest of this chapter will build upon this insight and consider its implications for the Rule of Law Index, and its use in global governance.

Now, let us be clear from the outset that proposing that the rule of law is an essentially contested concept does not mean that all definitions are irrelevant, and neither does it imply some sort of conceptual relativism in which all definitions are acceptable and none is final.

The idea of essentially contested concepts refers to two levels of dispute (Waldron 2002, 148–153). First is its *location*: the debate on the meaning of the rule of law is not restricted to the borderlines of "hard cases" (e.g., whether the protection of property should be part of the rule of law), but occurs at its core: those advancing the arguments disagree on the *essence* of concept, and disagree on paradigmatic cases that may exemplify such essence (e.g., is the United States a paradigmatic example of adherence to the rule of law?).

That the debate refers to the core of the concept makes the rule of law a *complex* notion. However, complexity is not enough for essential contestedness. There is a further *normative* dimension to it: the rule of law is a desirable outcome, and all participants of the discussion on its meaning agree on that. In Waldron's words, "everyone says that the achievement is valued as a whole, even though they disagree about the parts" (Waldron 2002, 150). The rule of law is, at the same time, the issue being discussed and the benchmark against which the conclusions are evaluated.

This combination of complexity and normativity saves us from cynicism. If the rule of law were merely a *complex* concept, then the debate would be pointless: each definition would be as valid as any other, and only power or influence would decide which definition succeeds. However, the normative dimension of the concept, "the sense that *somewhere* in the midst of this contestation there is an important ideal that social and political systems should aspire to" (Waldron 2002, 151), engages all the participants in proposing a definition that is bound to be controversial and contested, but that is judged against the benchmark of the ideal of rule of law. This ideal, though, is not at all established: it is horizon that all participants share, which justifies the fact that they are engaged in this debate, and not just quit. Over time, through this process, some of the outlines of the achievement come into focus (e.g., the rule of law requires general laws). However, a final definition will never be reached – as further elements of the rule of law become clear, other definitions appear that will in turn be contested, and so on and so forth.

The rule of law is not a checklist, but a space for contestation. Far from condemning us to cynicism and immobility, the idea of the rule of law as an essentially contested concept implies that there is an active community engaged in discussing it. The Rule of Law Index is able to play a crucial rule in this community. For that purpose, it is able to draw on the two dimensions of the indicator discussed earlier: descriptive and normative, as we now turn to see.

The Rule of Law Index as an Instrument: Communities of Practice and Interaction among Regimes

As may be recalled, the Index is an *instrument,* in the sense that it is a technology that the WJP uses to see reality. Others also use this technology: sometimes approvingly, as policymakers or academics who refer to the Index, and sometimes to contest it, as is the case of scholars who question the Index's definitions, or other suppliers of indicators who seek to undermine its credibility. The point, though, is that the Rule of Law Index becomes a platform where this community of users meets, interacts, and debates. The instrument creates the community: the Index creates a space where this community of practice, all participants of the debate on a rule law, is able to interact (Emanuel Adler 2005, 11).[9]

There are, however, multiple communities of practice in global governance. In this sense, indicators not only create a community, but are also able to serve as a platform for the interaction between that community and other communities of practice, created around a specific problem, or a specific legal regime. Although the Rule of Law Index has not yet proved particularly useful in this second function, other examples of law-related indicators show the potential in this sense. Indeed, many of the debates taking place these days on the structure of the international legal system can be usefully understood as problems derived from the interaction among regimes. Climate change, investment protection, humanitarian intervention – all these problems imply the interaction of different legal regimes (domestic, international, or transnational) whose outcomes and effectiveness depend not only on their own "internal" characteristics (i.e., intra-regime), but also on the way in which they interact with each other – sometimes bolstering each other's effectiveness, sometimes annulling the very limited results they achieve.

In this context, legal indicators such as the Index not only create a community around them, but also work as a hinge between communities. In a world where each regime seems to derive its legitimacy from closed communities of experts (Kennedy 2005), legal indicators work as a common language for communication among regimes (Koskenniemi 2012; Teubner and Korth 2012). With their claim to technical neutrality, their well-organized and easily understood bits of information, and their transnational, non-culturally based terminology, indicators are well placed to help communities communicate with each other, outside their own narrowly defined area of expertise.

Consider the case of human rights. Here we have one of the most important areas of international legal regulation, and we also have one area where indicators have been developed in more detail. In this case, quantitative measurement is instrumental for experts and activists acting within the human rights regime to communicate with people and institutions acting outside that regime. For example, indicators play a role in the interaction between development experts and human rights lawyers, as is made clear by the World Bank's recent report on Human Rights Indicators and Development (Sano and McInerney-Lankford 2010), by the role of indicators in monitoring the UN Millennium Development Goals (UN Secretary General 2010), and by efforts of the United Nations Development Programme (UNDP) to use indicators in its evaluations of development (UNDP 2000).

Law-related indicators are also a platform for the interaction between international and domestic communities of practice. Here, indicators play two different roles. First, they frame the way in which compliance with international legal norms is understood. This is particularly truth with regard to economic, social, and cultural rights where, perhaps in an attempt to balance the inherent indeterminacy of these kinds of rights, indicators constitute the preferred technique to assess compliance (Perez 2010), thus facilitating the communication between international and domestic stakeholders. For example, Article 19 of the San Salvador Protocol of the Inter-American Convention of Human Rights orders State Parties to report on advancements toward compliance with the Protocol, which is to be done in the form of indicators. What is more, in 2000 the UN's Committee on Economic, Social and Cultural Rights adopted a General Comment on the Right to Health in which it suggested that a state party lacking indicators to measure advancement could, because of this fact in itself, be in breach of the Covenant.

Moreover, indicators also play crucial role in the way in which international law is applied by domestic courts. Recent scholarship has explored the role of domestic courts in the international legal system, focusing mainly on the role of domestic courts as enforcers and interpreters of international rules (Knop 1999; Knop, Michaels, and Riles 2009; Nollkaemper 2011). Legal indicators are an important part of this process. International institutions are increasingly adopting quantitative mechanisms of monitoring that are then adopted by domestic courts as part of an "international legal compact" of sorts, which is then used in domestic adjudication. Here, again, human rights law provides a useful example. Following Article 19 of the San Salvador Protocol, mentioned earlier, the Inter-American Commission of Human Rights adopted in 2008 a set of guidelines for developing indicators of social and economic rights, which go into a pretty impressive degree of detail (Inter-American Commission of Human Rights 2008). I can report that the Colombian Constitutional Court has adopted these guidelines to the last detail (Corte Constitucional Colombia 2011, 12–14). It domestically enforces international legal standards, whose international binding status remains doubtful (such as the Deng Principles of Internal Displacement, or the Committee's General Comments) through the domestic deployment of indicators.

Finally, law-related indicators developed by international institutions also frame the way in which domestic communities of practice interact with each other. Water indicators, for example, are a platform that communicates regulators of water as a public utility at independent agencies, with judicial institutions deciding structural injunctions related to the human right to water (Uruena 2012).

The Rule of Law Index as Norm: Communities of Practice and Inherent Normativity

In its descriptive dimension, the Rule of Law Index is able to foster a community of practice and to facilitate interaction between different communities. In its normative dimension, the Index is able to play a similarly crucial role. Such a role is triggered by the particular kind of community of practice fostered by the rule of law. As we have seen, as an essentially contested concept, the rule of law has two levels of debate: its complexity and its normativity. The community that emerges around the Index exists in these same two dimensions:

1. It is engaged in a particular practice that consists of debating a complex concept (and as such, the community converges around the Index and also interacts with other communities through the indicator).
2. The community is engaged in a normative undertaking, where the debate occurs with the purpose of achieving a goal shared by the community (the rule of law) that provides the normative criterion to evaluate the proposals.

In this process, WJP puts forward a (contestable) definition of the rule of law, the Index, which is a reflection of its deontological choices (the principles, factors, and subfactors). It is, in that sense, one proposal more in the debate on this essentially contested concept, and competes with other proposals coming from other quarters (Worldwide Governance Indicators or the Bertelsmann Transformation Index). However, if the Rule of Law Index is permanent and consistent enough, it stops being one more voice in the debate: the expectations of the other participants of the community of practice become influenced by it, and so certain elements of the WJP's proposal become part of the benchmark against which other possible answers are measured.

We have seen this happening before: by being stable and widely cited over time, DB became the benchmark against which other possible answers to the relation between regulation and development would be assessed. To be sure, as we have seen, DB is a product of a certain intellectual moment, and its answer is one of several other possible alternatives. However, it succeeded in its transformation from being one more currency to becoming the gold standard against which all other currencies are measured.

To become the accepted standards, the indicator's funding and institutional backing could be relevant, as they contribute to its diffusion and trustworthiness, making it more influential. In that sense, the Rule of Law Index is exceptional, as it is not directly backed by a formal international organization such as the World Bank. Up to now, it has grown to be influential, mainly because (as we have discussed earlier) it is the only show in town that specializes in the rule of law. However, as the UN continues developing its Rule of Law Indicators Initiative, with the aid of the Vera Institute of Justice, an interesting competition may emerge between different initiatives to become the gold standard in rule of law indicators.

In this process, the Index (or some other rule of law indicator) could become the standard by which other proposed definitions of the rule of law are assessed. What does this possibility mean? The implications of the normative function of the Index can be explored in two different contexts: law and development and the international rule of law. The final paragraphs of this chapter consider each.

- *Law and development*

While the first law and development moment held antiformalism as its standard to evaluate legal systems in developing countries, and the second turned its attention toward efficiency, the third law and development moment may find in the Index its normative criteria. To be sure, one could say that this is actually happening right now: the Index is applied to legal systems around the world, and they are judged on that basis. The normative implications being discussed here, though, refers to a wider possibility. There seem to be three levels in which the Index, and other similar rule of law indicators, may exert influence in the context of law and development.

The first one is the most directly causal level of influence, in which a country changes its behavior to achieve better scores. As was mentioned before, at least in the case of the Index, this possibility is unclear, as the indicator is hard to "game" because it is based on local perceptions. This level of influence, though, should not be underestimated, as is shown by the DB example.

The second level refers to the construction of a deeper sense of what is appropriate in the law and development community – its legal consciousness. Just as antiformalism and efficiency, the rule of law indicators can permeate the legal consciousness of this new moment, and contribute to a new emerging sense of what is appropriate for a legal system. This move is novel, in the sense that the Index, and other similar indicators, could be read as useful platforms to promote the ontological choices made by WJP about what the rule of law is. Thus, just as the early waves of law and development used field missions in Chile and scholarships in elite American law schools to promote their set of ontological choices, this third moment could be read as using indicators as a conveyor belt to propagate a certain way of understanding the rule of law.

The Index and other similar indicators seem keen on measuring their own influence by applying a yardstick situated in a middle point between the first and second levels mentioned previously. More often than not, the Index will quote a head of state, a minister of justice, or a high-level judge, praising the Index and its possibilities. This move allows the Index to show that it is "action oriented" (in the sense that it changes reality, it changes the way decision makers think and understand the rule of law), but not exactly prescriptive – like DB, or a conditionality-based pack of reforms. It is worth noting, though, that there is currently no research available on the actual influence of the Rule of Law Index on decision making; and, as far as I have been able to gather, there are no plans to develop a methodology to test a pilot of such study. The WJP does publish media coverage of the Index in its webpage by country; however, most of the coverage is only marginally concerned with the rule of law and the Index, and makes passing references to it. No more data are available on the first and second levels of influence.

The third level of influence refers to the technology itself. This expansion of a certain set of values is performed through a technology of quantitative measurement. This fact, on the one hand, bolsters the Index's influence in the first and second levels described previously, as it facilitates the expression of complex normative concepts, allows for the supervision of compliance with its chosen values, and facilitates the propagation of those values through domestic and international bureaucracies, and across the boundaries of different communities of practice. Moreover, the fact that a quantitative technology is used to create and propagate normative standards may have an impact in the way we think about those very standards. What is the role of measurement in the construction of our normative ideals? In the perpetual process of drawing the outline of an essentially contested concept, should "measurability" be added to the ideal of the rule of law that the community is trying to achieve?

- *The international rule of law*

Finally, the implications of the normative function of the Index can also be explored in the context of the international rule of law. To get there, it seems important to situate this potential in the more general debate of the role of law in global governance. Indeed, there is a general instrumental view of the legal language that permeates our understanding of global governance. This approach suggests that law in general (and international law in particular) is just one of many regulatory alternatives to achieve a given goal. This view, then, submits that there is no inherent normative value in law that needs to justify its relevance in instrumental terms (Tamanaha 2007, 2). It follows from such a view that law is, by no means, a necessary input in framing global governance. Of course, it may be useful, up to a point, to frame the exercise of global power in legal terms. Nevertheless, an alternative regulation may be used instead. According to this view, there is nothing in law that is inherently valuable in global governance: the latter seems to conceive law as one of many means to achieve a given purpose. If international law is not appropriate for achieving that particular purpose, then it can be easily set aside (Koskenniemi 2004).

Much of contemporary international legal scholarship can be read in terms of action and reaction (Klabbers 2009). If the instrumental view of international law is the action, then it seems reasonable to look for a reaction. The reaction, in this case, is the effort to bring back the law to global governance: some of these projects adopt a top-down perspective and propose legal principles (human rights or the rule of law, for example) that contribute toward some sort of global constitutionalism. Others try to frame the matter through a bottom-up view and try to distill legal principles from the actual practice of global regulatory bodies, to form a global administrative law.

Part of the challenge these projects, and many others like them, face is that it is difficult to derive normative elements from the practice of the very community (say, international civil servants) that is being regulated. Something additional is needed. The Index, in its normative aspect, seems to have potential for both of these reconstructive projects. On the one hand, its deontological choices provide the kind of clear values that are craved by any project of global constitutionalism. These values, in turn, can be applied (with some adjustment) not only to countries, but also to international organizations, global regulatory regimes, international courts and tribunals, a UN special mandate, and so on. Could we think of, say, a Rule of Law Index score for the Security Council's Resolution 1267 antiterrorist regime? Of for foreign investment arbitration tribunals? Thus applied, the Index, and other rule of law indicators, may also provide some sort of enforcement mechanism for those same values, based on information and quantitative measurement. These are also problems of global administrative law. As the Index permeates the legal consciousness of global regulatory regimes and international bureaucracies, its normative choices become part of the discussion toward good practices of global regulatory administration.

CONCLUSION

The Rule of Law Index shows that indicators and law have many multifaceted connections. They are connected as part of the law and development agenda, but also as a problem of the expression of normative values created by law, and as part of the establishment of a community of practice that defines the very notion of the rule of law.

These connections open opportunities and challenges. Let me begin with the challenges. The first one is politics. Indicators' appeal as technologies of global governance derives from their apolitical stance. To be sure, there will always be some complaints about one indicator or the other. Indicators, though, need to be generally perceived as nonpolitical by most of those who are being measured. Otherwise, they would lose most of their appeal. However, to make sense, indicators require simplifying complex social phenomena – a process that will be necessarily influenced by some political choices. The Rule of Law Index is a case in point: clearly, defining the Rule of Law cannot be said to be a purely technical and neutral matter.

Politics comes into the equation here in a second manner. Once they are created, published, and discussed, indicators have a way of gaining a life of their own. And this life is indeed political. So, even if the expert teams that develop indicators defend their creation as a technically neutral undertaking, it is impossible to prevent their numbers from being used politically. And it would be silly to attempt to do so. The influence of an indicator derives from the fact that it is used by policymakers: otherwise, indicators would remain as a footnote in scholarly journals, with no influence in real life. However, getting involved in the messy world of politics means that indicators are also likely to become instrumentalized in political competition. Surely, Venezuela's position in the Rule of law Index will be used by the opposition in that country as an argument against Maduro and the successors of the Chavez regime.[10] And indicators may end up endorsing domestic political agendas that are different from those endorsed by the creator of the indicator.

This opens the space for a few opportunities as well. The Index, and other rule of law indicators, may be transformed into sites of contestation of the definition of what it means to adhere to the rule of law. Instead of having one obscure international civil servant decide that Fuller's or Dicey's or Raz's idea of the rule of law, or a mix of them, should be applied to evaluate domestic legal systems, the Index provides an open platform to have that discussion. The variables (the principles, factors, and subfactors) are there for everyone to agree or disagree with. Of course, WJP is unlikely to change its variables or the indicator to include, say, considerations of redistribution, or substantive equality as part of its definition of the rule of law. Their own ontological choices suggest as much. However, the very existence of the Index provides the forum to have that discussion. And this discussion is worth having. Quantitative technologies of measurement seem to be here to stay in the law and development agenda. And, as such, it seems important to engage with them, discuss them, and understand whether they reproduce, or not, prior failed efforts to bring the rule of law to the developing world.

NOTES

1　For a good example of the specific dynamic of the projects, see Merryman (2000).

2　For example, the Bank's 1949–1953 Currie Mission in Colombia (named after Canadian-born economist Lauchlin Currie) set the basis for the creation of the Departamento Nacional de Estadística (DANE) in 1953. On the Currie Mission, see generally (Alacevich 2009, 11–63). On its connection to statistics, see Adelman (2008). On its role in steering the Colombian administration towards the Bank's view of development, see Malagón Pinzón and Pardo Motta (2011).

3 On the Chile Law Project and its capture, see Dezalay and Garth (2002, 116–117). For a less critical view, see Merryman (2000, 483–490).

4 On the transformation of the Consensus from economic policy for Latin America to platform for development, see Williamson (2005).

5 For evidence of the Employing Workers Policy impact, and a summary of the main critiques, see Lee, McCann, and Torm (2008).

6 See Comments by José Manuel Salazar, Executive Director, Employment Sector, ILO at the launch of the 2009 Doing Business Report in Geneva, Monday 22 September 2008. Quoted in Bakvis (2009).

7 Since the Independent Evaluation Report, the methodology has not been revised as to suggest that the basic underlying premises of the Index (less regulation is better) have changed. Rather, marginal adjustment have been performed in the following components: (1) employing workers, in 2010 and 2011; (2) getting credit and dealing with construction permits, in 2012; and (3) paying taxes, in 2012 and 2013 (World Bank – IFC 2009, 2010, 2011, 2013).

8 Department of Peacekeeping Operations and Office of the High Commissioner for Human Rights. *United Nations Rule of Law Indicators: Implementation Guide and Project Tools* (New York and Geneva: United Nations, 2011).

9 The following use of the notion of community of practice, as well as the idea of shared understandings, is influenced by the enlightening approach proposed in Toope and Brunnée (2010, 56–87).

10 See, e.g., Chavez' critic Marta Columina's use of the Index to support voting in Venezuela's regional elections of December 2012, in Colomina (2012). Similarly, see Chavez' critic Alfredo Romero use of the Index to support criminal reform in Venezuela, in Lozano (2012).

REFERENCES

Adelman, Jeremy. 2008. "Observando a Colombia: Albert O. Hirschman Y La Economía Del Desarrollo." *Desarrollo Y Sociedad* (62): 1–40.

Agrast, Mark David, Juan Carlos Botero, and Alejandro Ponce. 2009. *World Justice Project- Rule of Law Index 2009*. Washington, DC: World Justice Project.

2010. *World Justice Project – Rule of Law Index 2010*. Washington, DC: World Justice Project.

2011. *World Justice Project- Rule of Law Index 2011*. Washington, DC: World Justice Project.

Agrast, Mark David, Juan Carlos Botero, Alejandro Ponce, Joel Martinez, and Christine Pratt. 2012. *World Justice Project- Rule of Law Index 2012–2013*. Washington, DC: World Justice Project.

Alacevich, Michele. 2009. *The Political Economy of the World Bank: The Early Years*. Stanford: Stanford University Press/World Bank.

American Bar Association. 2007. "Gates Foundation Donates $1.75 Million to Support American Bar Association's World Justice Project," March 14. http://www.abanow.org/2007/03/gates-foundation-donates-1-75-million-to-support-american-bar-associations-world-justice-project/.

Bakvis, Peter. 2009. "The World Bank's Doing Business Report: A Last Fling for the Washington Consensus?" *Transfer: European Review of Labour and Research* 15 (3–4): 419–438.

Berg, Janine, and Sandrine Cazes (2007). *The Doing Business Indicators: Measurement Issues and Political Implications*, Vol. 6. Geneva, Switzerland: International Labour Organization.

Botero, Juan Carlos, and Alejandro Ponce. 2010. *Measuring the Rule of Law*. Washington, DC: The World Justice Project – Working Paper Series / WPS 001.

Botero, Juan Carlos, Alejandro Ponce, and Christine Pratt. 2012. "The Rule of Law Measurement Revolution: Complementarity between Official Statistics, Qualitative Assessments, and Quantitative Indicators of the Rule of Law." In Juan Carlos Botero, Ronald Janse, Sam Muller, and Christine Pratt, eds., *Innovations in Rule of Law*, 8–11. The Hague/Washington DC: The Hague Institute for the Internationalisation of Law & The World Justice Project.

Colomina, Marta. 2012. "Juristas del horror: Venezuela no es Brasil." *El Universal*, December 2.

Comisión Económica para América Latina y el Caribe (CEPAL). 2009. *Informe Sobre El Desarrollo de Las Estadísticas Oficiales En América Latina Y El Caribe*. Bogotá: CEPAL.

Corte Constitucional Colombia. 2011. "Auto 226 de 2011."

Daniels, Ronald J., and M. J. Trebilcock. 2008. *Rule of Law Reform and Development: Charting the Fragile Path of Progress*. Cheltenham, UK: Edward Elgar.

Davis, Kevin E. 2004. "What Can the Rule of Law Variable Tell Us about Rule of Law Reform?" *Michigan Journal of International Law* 26: 141–161.

Davis, Kevin E., and Michael J. Trebilcock. 2008. "The Relationship between Law and Development: Optimists versus Skeptics." *American Journal of Comparative Law* 56 (4): 895–946.

De Soto, Hernando. 1989. *The Other Path: The Invisible Revolution in the Third World*. 1st ed. New York: Harper & Row.

Dezalay, Yves, and Bryant G Garth. 2002. *The Internationalization of Palace Wars: Lawyers, Economists, and the Contest to Transform Latin American States*. The Chicago Series in Law and Society. Chicago: University of Chicago Press.

Doing Business Employing Workers Consultative Group. 2011. "Final Report." www.doingbusiness.org/data/.../~/.../Final-EWICG-April-2011.doc.

Emanuel Adler. 2005. *Communitarian International Relations: The Epistemic Foundations of International Relations*. London and New York: Routledge.

Feldman, Stephen M. 2000. *American Legal Thought from Premodernism to Postmodernism: An Intellectual Voyage*. New York: Oxford University Press.

Freedom House (FH). 2005. "Nations in Transit 2005 Edition, Methodology." http://www.freedomhouse.org/report/nations-transit-2005/methodology.

2006a. "Freedom in the World: 2006 Edition, Methodology." http://www.freedomhouse.org/report/freedom-world-2006/methodology.

2006b. "Countries at the Crossroads 2006 Edition, Methodology." http://www.freedomhouse.org/report/countries-crossroads-2006/survey-methodology.

Ginsburg, Tom. 2011. "Pitfalls of Measuring the Rule of Law." *Hague Journal on the Rule of Law* 3 (2): 269–280.

Hillenbrand, Olaf. 2006. *Bertelsmann Transformation Index 2006: Toward Democracy and a Market Economy*. Gütersloh, Germany: Verlag Bertelsmann Stiftung.

Inter-American Commission of Human Rights. 2008. "Lineamientos para la elaboración de indicadores de progreso en materia de derechos económicos, sociales y culturales." Doc. 14. July 19, 2008.

International Country Risk Guide (ICRG). 2012. "ICRG Methodology." www.prsgroup .com/ICRG_Methodology.aspx.

Kennedy, David. 2005. "Challenging Expert Rule: The Politics of Global Governance." *Sydney Law Review* 27: 5–24.

2006. "The 'Rule of Law,' Political Choices, and Development Common Sense." In David M Trubek and Alvaro Santos, eds., *The New Law and Economic Development: A Critical Appraisal*, 95–173. Cambridge: Cambridge University Press.

Klabbers, Jan. 2009. "Setting the Scene." In Geir Ulfstein, Anne Peters, and Jan Klabbers, *The Constitutionalization of International Law*, 1–44. Oxford: Oxford University Press.

Knop, Karen. 1999. "Here and There: International Law in Domestic Courts." *New York University Journal of International Law and Politics* 32: 501–535.

Knop, Karen, Ralf Michaels, and Annelies Riles. 2009. "International Law in Domestic Courts: A Conflict of Laws Approach." Cornell Legal Studies Research Paper No 09016 103 (9): 1–11.

Koskenniemi, Martti. 2004. "Global Governance and Public International Law." *Kritische Justiz – Vierteljahresschrift Für Recht Und Politik* 241–254.

2012. "Hegemonic Regimes." In Margaret Young, ed., *Regime Interaction in International Law: Facing Fragmentation*, 305–323. Cambridge: Cambridge University Press.

Langbein, Laura, and Stephen Knack. 2008. "The Worldwide Governance Indicators and Tautology: Causally Related Separable Concepts, Indicators of a Common Cause, or Both?" Policy Research Working Paper Series 4669. Washington, DC: The World Bank.

Lee, Sangheon, Deirdre McCann, and Nina Torm. 2008. "The World Bank's 'Employing Workers' Index: Findings and Critiques – A Review of Recent Evidence." *International Labour Review* 147 (4): 416–432.

Llewellyn, Karl N. 1930. "Some Realism about Realism–Responding to Dean Pound." *Harvard Law Review* 44: 1222–1264.

Lozano, Diana. 2012. "Alfredo Romero: Justicia criminal está sujeta a influencia política." *El Nacional*, January 12.

Malagón Pinzón, Miguel, and Diego Pardo Motta. 2011. "Laureano Gómez, la misión currie y el proyecto de reforma constitucional de 1952." *Criterio Jurídico* 9 (2): 7–33.

Merryman, John Henry. 1977. "Comparative Law and Social Change: On the Origins, Style, Decline & Revival of the Law and Development Movement." *The American Journal of Comparative Law* 25 (3): 457–491.

2000. "Law and Development Memoirs I: The Chile Law Program." *American Journal of Comparative Law* 48: 481–499.

Miles, T. J., and Cass Sunstein. 2008. "The New Legal Realism." *University of Chicago Law Review* 75 (2): 831–851.

Nollkaemper, André. 2011. *National Courts and the International Rule of Law*. Oxford: Oxford University Press.

North, Douglass Cecil. 1990. *Institutions, Institutional Change and Economic Performance*. Cambridge: Cambridge University Press.

1991. "Institutions." *Journal of Economic Perspectives* 5 (1): 97–112.

Oman, Charles, and Christiane Arndt. 2006. *Uses and Abuses of Governance Indicators*. Paris: Development Centre of the OECD.

Parson, Jim, Monica Thornton, Hyo Eun (April) Bang, Ben Estep, Kaya Williams, and Neil Weiner. 2008. *Developing Indicators to Measure the Rule of Law: A Global Approach. A Report to the World Justice Project*. New York: Vera Institute of Justice.

Perez, Luis Eduardo. 2010. "¿Es posible medir los derechos? De la medición del acceso a bienes y servicios a la medición del disfrute de los derechos?" In Pilar Arcidiácono, Cesar Rodríguez Garavito, and Nicolás Espejo Yaksic, eds., *Derechos Sociales: Justicia, Política Y Economía En América Latina*, 463–522. Bogotá, Colombia: Universidad de Los Andes.

Pistor, Katharina. 2012. "Re-Construction of Private Indicators for Public Purposes." In Benedict Kingsbury, Kevin Davis, Sally Engle Merry, and Angelina Fisher, eds., *Governance by Indicators: Global Power through Quantification and Rankings*, 165–179. Oxford: Oxford University Press.

Podgers, James. 2007. "A Big Tent Goes Up." *ABA Magazine*, August. http://www.abajournal.com/magazine/article/a_big_tent_goes_up/.

Pound, Roscoe. 1910. "Law in Books and Law in Action." *American Law Review* 44: 12–36.

Prado, Mariana Mota, and Michael Trebilcock. 2011. *What Makes Poor Countries Poor? Institutional Determinants of Development*. Cheltenham, UK: Edward Elgar.

Sano, H. -O, and Siobhán Alice McInerney-Lankford. 2010. *Human Rights Indicators in Development: An Introduction*. Washington, DC: World Bank.

Santos, Alvaro, and David M. Trubek. 2006. "The Third Moment in Law and Development Theory and the Emergence of a New Critical Practice." In David M. Trubek and Alvaro Santos, eds., *The New Law and Economic Development: A Critical Appraisal*, 1–18. Cambridge: Cambridge University Press.

Schauer, Frederick. 2012. "Legal Realism Untamed." Virginia Public Law and Legal Theory Research Paper No. 2012–38.

Shklar, Judith. 1987. "Political Theory and the Rule of Law." In Allan Hutcheson and Patrick Monahan, eds., *The Rule of Law: Ideal or Ideology*, 1–17. Toronto: Carswell.

Skaaning, Svend-Erik. 2010. "Measuring the Rule of Law." *Political Research Quarterly* 63 (2): 449–460.

Tamanaha, Brian Z. 2004. *On the Rule of Law: History, Politics, Theory*. Cambridge: Cambridge University Press.

2007. *Law as a Means to an End: Threat to the Rule of Law*. Cambridge: Cambridge University Press.

Teubner, Gunther, and Peter Korth. 2012. "Two Kind of Legal Pluralism: Collision of Transnational in the Double Fragmentation of the World Society." In Margaret Young, ed., *Regime Interaction in International Law: Facing Fragmentation*, 23–54. Cambridge: Cambridge University Press.

Toope, Stephen J., and Jutta Brunnée. 2010. *Legitimacy and Legality in International Law: An Interactional Account*. Cambridge: Cambridge University Press.

Trubek, David M. 2006. "The 'Rule of Law' in Development Assistance: Past, Present, and Future." In David M Trubek and Alvaro Santos, eds., *The New Law and Economic Development: A Critical Appraisal*, 74–94. Cambridge: Cambridge University Press.

Trubek, David M., and Marc Galanter. 1974. "Scholars in Self-Estrangement: Some Reflections on the Crisis in Law and Development Studies in the United States." *Wisconsin Law Review* 1974: 1062.

United Nations Development Programme (UNDP). 2000. "Uso de indicadores para exigir responsabilidad en materia de derechos humanos." In *Informe Sobre Desarrollo Humano 2000*. New York: UNDP.

United Nations Secretary General. 2010. "Indicators for Monitoring the Millennium Development Goals." UN Docs E/CN.3/2011/13.

Uruena, Rene. 2012. "The Rise of the Constitutional Regulatory State in Colombia: The Case of Water Governance." *Regulation & Governance* 6 (3): 282–299.

US Department of Justice. 2009. "Assistant Attorney General Ron Weich Announces Leadership Team in the Office of Legislative Affairs," July 1. http://www.justice.gov/opa /pr/2009/July/09-ola-649.html.

Waldron, Jeremy. 2002. "Is the Rule of Law an Essentially Contested Concept (in Florida)?" *Law and Philosophy* 21 (2): 137–164.

Williamson, John. 2005. "The Washington Consensus as Policy Prescription for Development." In Tim Besley and N. Roberto Zagha, eds., *Development Challenges in the 1990s: Leading Policymakers Speak from Experience*,33–53. Washington, DC: World Bank.

World Bank – IFC. 2004. *Doing Business 2004: Understanding Regulation*. Washington, DC: World Bank and Oxford University Press.

    2009. *Doing Business 2010: Regulating Through Difficult Times*. Washington, DC: World Bank and Palgrave Macmillan.

    2010. *Doing Business 2011: Making a Difference for Entrepreneurs*. Washington, DC: World Bank and IFC.

    2011. *Doing Business 2012: Doing Business in a More Transparent World*. Washington, DC: World Bank and IFC.

    2013. *Doing Business 2013: Smarter Regulations for Small and Medium-Size Enterprises*. Washington, DC: World Bank.

World Bank Independent Evaluation Group. 2008. *Doing Business: An Independent Evaluation/Taking the Measure of the World Bank-IFC Doing Business Indicators*. Washington, DC: World Bank.

Worldwide Governance Indicators. 2014. "Worldwide Governance Indicators." Accessed January 28. http://www.govindicators.org/.

3

Measuring Corporate Accountability through Global Indicators

Galit A. Sarfaty

INTRODUCTION

During the past two decades, there has been a drive to reduce complicated concepts to simple numbers. Corruption, rule of law, human rights, and more have all been reduced to quantitative "indicators." Based on the theory that what gets measured gets done, government agencies have incorporated quantitative indicators into performance-based rules, information disclosure regimes, and self-regulation (see, e.g., Sunstein 1999; Sugarman and Sandman 2007; Carrigan and Coglianese 2011). These statistical tools have recently been used in international law to operationalize global norms and thereby improve compliance.

As a second-order abstraction of statistical information, indicators rely on numbers to represent social phenomena and evaluate performance. Backed by technical expertise and designed to produce comparability, these tools are shaping decision making by domestic and global regulatory bodies. For instance, the World Bank's Doing Business indicators produce a ranking of developing countries based on the quality of their business laws and legal institutions.[1] The Bank's classification then influences its allocation of foreign aid as well as that of the US government through the Millennium Challenge Corporation.[2] Domestic law has also incorporated indicators, as in the 2008 reauthorization of the Trafficking Victims Protection Act.[3] This law relies on performance indicators to assess foreign governments' compliance with minimum antitrafficking standards and then categorize countries into three

I am grateful to Rachel Brewster, Cary Coglianese, Kevin Davis, Oona Hathaway, Bill Laufer, Sally Engle Merry, Ariel Meyerstein, Nien-hê Hsieh, Benedict Kingsbury, Eric Orts, Adam Saunders, Amy Sepinwall, Richard Shell, David Wilkins, and David Zaring. This chapter significantly benefited from my participation as a research scholar in NYU School of Law's project on indicators and global governance and the 2012 Junior Faculty Forum at Harvard Law School.A longer version of this chapter appeared in the *Virginia Journal of International Law*, Vol. 53, 2013.

tiers.[4] Given their propensity to simplify complex concepts and translate them into quantifiable measures, indicators are often used to regulate more intangible, value-laden issues such as the rule of law (as in the Freedom House indicators), corruption (as in Transparency International's Corruption Perceptions Index), and human rights (as in the indicators developed by the Office of the UN High Commissioner for Human Rights to monitor treaty compliance).[5]

Indicators are playing an increasingly important role in regulatory governance (Davis, Kingsbury, and Engle Merry 2012). If used effectively, they can offer a number of apparent benefits: they can measure accountability to standards and norms; assess compliance with policies and specific targets; and evaluate performance with respect to stated objectives. They can also facilitate efficient processing of information and reduce the costs and resources devoted to decision making. The appeal of indicators lies in their ability to translate phenomena, such as respect for the rule of law, into numerical representations that are easy to understand and compare across actors. Moreover, their simplicity enables more effective communication with those who are governed as well as the general public, thereby promoting ideals of transparency and accountability (at least in theory). Yet legal scholarship has been largely silent about the implications of indicators for governance. Although scholars have recognized the benefits of new governance mechanisms (see, e.g., Esty 2006, 1534), they have neglected to consider the limitations when these statistical tools are applied in practice. I contend that indicators are being embraced too wholeheartedly without sufficient attention to their costs.

In this chapter, I analyze the prevalence of quantitative indicators as an emerging regulatory tool in domestic and global governance and identify the potential costs of using these tools to inform decision making. This chapter contributes to scholarly debates on the effectiveness of new governance mechanisms in regulation as well as the legitimacy of private regulatory bodies, which have become key players in international governance (see, e.g., Braithwaite and Drahos 2000; Freeman 2000; Lobel 2004; Mattli and Büthe 2005; Vandenbergh 2007).

Indicators address a visceral desire of policymakers to find mechanisms that can increase compliance with rules, a problem particularly acute in international law. Given its lack of coercive force, international law must rely on other means to affect state and nonstate behavior. Scholars have studied the roles of reputation, reciprocity, and acculturation, among other factors, in enhancing international law's ability to shape policy and decision making (see, e.g., Goodman and Jinks 2004; Berman 2006; Hathaway 2005; Guzman 2010). An emerging but as yet understudied mechanism is the power of numbers.

Private regulatory bodies have emerged as significant players in the production and enforcement of international law (see, e.g., Kingsbury et al. 2005; Meidinger 2006; Stephan 2011). However, the legitimacy of private actors is questionable given their lack of public accountability, an absence of oversight mechanisms, and possible manipulation by special interests (see, e.g., Esty 2006; Benvenisti and Downs 2011). Private regulatory bodies have recently turned to indicators to claim scientific authority, affirm legal values such as transparency and predictability, and assert their legitimacy to govern. Yet when indicators translate legal norms into quantifiable metrics, there are unintended consequences.

My analysis of indicators is based on an empirical study of the Global Reporting Initiative (GRI), a private regulatory body that has produced the leading standard for corporate sustainability reporting. The GRI guidelines include seventy-nine indicators on which corporations self-report on their social, environmental, and economic performance and are then assigned a score of A, B, or C.[6] According to a 2008 study by the accounting firm KPMG, more than three-quarters of the Global Fortune 250 companies use GRI guidelines as the basis for their reporting (KPMG International 2008). An increasing number of countries (including France, Spain, Denmark, and Sweden) have recently mandated sustainability disclosure by companies (some of which rely on GRI guidelines), while many others are actively considering such a regime and have already adopted voluntary sustainability reporting standards. In addition, mainstream institutional investors, not just socially responsible ones, are increasingly considering sustainability performance in their investment decisions and thus consulting GRI reports.

As the case of the GRI illustrates, indicators facilitate the process by which legal norms are interpreted and implemented, particularly in areas of international law where norms may be ill defined and traditional enforcement mechanisms are absent. For instance, the GRI indicators aim to make corporate sustainability reporting more mainstream as part of a larger goal of achieving corporate accountability. In this way, they are operationalizing emerging norms on corporate responsibility for human rights, among other issues. Soft law instruments such as the UN Global Compact lack independent monitoring and enforcement and have been criticized for being conceptually vague and difficult to implement.[7] While advocates have turned to US litigation under the Alien Tort Claims Act, the US Supreme Court recently limited its exterritorial application.[8] The GRI is an example of an alternative approach – information regulation through numbers – for changing corporate behavior.[9] It represents a shift in governance toward data-based tools such as quantitative indicators to enhance compliance with legal norms.

Yet my study of the GRI demonstrates that the use of quantitative indicators can be fraught with problems, which are often overlooked due to the authoritative quality of numbers. For instance, one potential cost of indicators is the promotion of box ticking and superficial compliance, as evident in the GRI's system of grading reports. Companies that issue GRI reports receive a grade of A, B, or C based on the *quantity* of indicators that they report on, rather than on the *quality* of their performance.[10] In addition, because third-party verification is optional, nongovernmental organizations (NGOs) do not trust the data behind the indicators. We therefore see that the motivation behind the GRI is not whether the reports are credible to NGOs or whether they reflect a company's good or bad performance, but that more and more companies participate, which perpetuates the existence of the GRI and raises its status as the leading standard for corporate sustainability reporting. In this way, the GRI has strayed from its original audience of consumers and NGOs, and its initial aim of corporate accountability. The use of indicators as ends, in and of themselves, has threatened the perceived legitimacy of the organization that produces and relies on them.

My analysis of the GRI applies an anthropological approach as I look inside the black box of indicators and analyze the various stages in which they are implicated in governance, including their production, implementation, and impact. Toward that end, I have conducted interviews with the producers of the indicators (members of the GRI's secretariat in Amsterdam and its New York City office), users (company officials that use GRI guidelines in their sustainability reports), consumers (investors and NGOs who read GRI reports), and US government representatives (SEC officials who are considering whether to mandate disclosure on environmental and social issues as part of securities filings). In addition, I have participated in a GRI-certified training program to look behind the numbers and understand how GRI reports are made and evaluated.

THE EMERGENCE OF THE GLOBAL REPORTING INITIATIVE AS THE LEADING STANDARD FOR CORPORATE SUSTAINABILITY REPORTING

The field of corporate social responsibility (CSR) is a fertile area for the use of indicators. Scholars have argued that companies have legal obligations under international law, particularly for violations of human rights, labor rights, and environmental protection (see, e.g., Clapham and Jerbi 2001; Ratner 2001; Kinley and Tadaki 2004; Clapham 2006; Ruggie 2007). A variety of initiatives have aimed to hold multinational companies accountable under domestic or international law but they have remained largely ineffective. The extraterritorial operations of companies are largely unregulated through domestic law, with the exception of litigation under the US Alien Tort Claims Act, whose extraterritorial application to corporations was recently curtailed by the US Supreme Court.[11] International, regional, and NGOs, such as the UN, the International Labor Organization (ILO), the Organisation for Economic Co-operation and Development (OECD), and the International Organization for Standardization (ISO), have drafted standards and principles addressed to companies (e.g., the UN Global Compact and ISO 26000) and governments (e.g., the OECD's Guidelines for Multinational Enterprises and the ILO's Tripartite Declaration of Principles Concerning Multinational Enterprises and Social Policy).[12] However, these voluntary instruments lack independent monitoring, implementation, and enforcement mechanisms; do not include performance metrics to assess compliance; and are not certifiable (Entine 2010). Self-regulatory initiatives by the private sector (e.g., codes of conduct and industry programs) may have a normative impact on corporate behavior, but are devoid of third-party accountability systems and subject to critiques of greenwashing (see Kinley and Tadaki 2004, 958–960).

As John Ruggie, the then-UN Special Representative on Business and Human Rights to the Human Rights Council, concluded:

> [T]here is no single silver bullet solution to the multi-faceted challenges of business and human rights ... [T]he tools available for dealing with business and human rights differ from those addressing State-based human rights violations, where only public international law can impose binding obligations. The business and human rights domain is considerably more complex ... Moreover, the standards that business initiatives incorporate are typically self-defined rather than tracking internationally recognized human rights. And accountability mechanisms for ensuring adherence to the standards tend to remain weak and decoupled from firms' own core oversight and control systems.[13]

This state of affairs is ripe for governance through indicators. Given that the international legal duties of corporations remain "ill-defined and ineffective," (Kinley and Tadaki 2004, 948) technologies of compliance can substitute for legal regulation (Bamberger 2010, 670–671). If incorporated into domestic law, indicators can give teeth to international legal norms by serving as a tool for evaluation and implementation.

Enter the Global Reporting Initiative. The GRI was created in 1997 as a framework for corporations to report on their environmental, social, and economic performance. Its guidelines have become the global standard for corporate sustainability reporting. They currently consist of standard disclosures (e.g., organizational profile, stakeholder engagement, and report parameters); reporting principles (e.g., materiality, stakeholder inclusiveness, and accuracy); and, most notably, a set of seventy-nine indicators (subdivided into fifty core indicators and twenty-nine additional indicators). Many indicators incorporate legal standards on such issues as corporate governance, human rights, antidiscrimination, labor, corruption, and the environment; they also reference a variety of international agreements, including ILO conventions, OECD Guidelines, and UN international human rights conventions. The indicators attempt to convert legal norms into quantifiable metrics that are easily compared across corporations and serve as a benchmark for improving performance. While the GRI framework is a voluntary self-regulatory initiative developed by a private, network-based organization, it is moving into the realm of hard law through incorporation into mandatory regulations.[14] The GRI has influenced state governments and stock exchanges to adopt binding and nonbinding corporate disclosure standards based on its guidelines. According to a recent study using data from fifty-eight countries, mandatory disclosure of sustainability information has significant consequences on socially responsible managerial practices (see Ioannou and Serafeim 2012). This research suggests that regulation based on GRI indicators has the potential to improve corporate behavior.

Overview of the GRI

"What you cannot measure, you cannot manage. What you cannot manage, you cannot change."[15] This motto has motivated the GRI since it was founded in Boston by the Coalition for Environmentally Responsible Economies (CERES).[16] Supported by the UN Environment Programme, the GRI receives funds from foundations, governments, and corporate sponsors, and also generates income by directly providing services to GRI users (e.g., training programs, executive seminars, and software tools).[17] It aims to empower civil society organizations to seek greater accountability for corporate governance (see Levy et al. 2010). Following a model of information regulation, a GRI report would presumably "mobiliz[e] its recipients to demand certain performance levels and enabl[e] activists and NGOs to reward practices considered socially responsible and exert pressure on poor performers" (95). The GRI seeks to raise sustainability reporting to the same status as financial reporting by developing metrics for companies to disclose on intangible assets such as human rights and environmental performance.[18] By presenting this information in a comparable and consistent format through quantifiable measures, the GRI attempts to signal that these intangibles have market value and can affect the financial health of a company.

The GRI bases its legitimacy on a multistakeholder consultation process among intergovernmental organizations, businesses, NGOs, and labor unions.[19] It comprises four permanent bodies: the Board of Directors, the Secretariat based in Amsterdam (employing more than fifty people), the Technical Advisory Committee, and the Stakeholder Council.[20] The Technical Advisory Committee is responsible for the development and revision of the reporting framework, while the Stakeholder Council deliberates on key strategic and policy issues, and appoints the Board of Directors. The Stakeholder Council's sixty members are geographically representative and include twenty-two seats for business, sixteen seats for NGOs, six seats for labor, and sixteen seats for so-called "mediating institutions" (which include accounting and consulting firms, foundations, and governments).[21] Most of the members of the Stakeholder Council are elected by a group of Organizational Stakeholders, which include hundreds of organizations and individuals and is dominated by large businesses and international consulting and accounting firms, with relatively few NGOs and organized labor associations (Levy et al. 2010, 88 and 96).

The GRI has formed alliances with a variety of institutional partners and promotes convergence around other corporate social responsibility guidelines and principles.[22] The most notable is between the GRI and the UN Global Compact, which was announced in October 2006.[23] As part of this alliance, the GRI's guidelines incorporate the Global Compact's requirements for signatory companies that annually report a Communication on Progress. The GRI and the Global Compact have also published a draft tool to guide companies in linking the two reporting processes. The GRI has formed linkages with other standards, including the International Finance Corporation's sustainability performance standards, the Carbon Disclosure Project (CDP), ISO 26000, and the OECD's Guidelines for Multinational Enterprises.[24] These alliances serve to deflect competition from similar initiatives such as the CDP, whose climate change reporting framework is used by more than 3,000 companies around the world.[25]

The GRI guidelines are voluntary and incremental, and include a high level of flexibility, allowing companies to decide which principles and indicators to adopt.[26] They are designed to improve over time to reflect lessons learned and the changing expectations of companies and stakeholders. The first Sustainability Reporting Guidelines were established in 2000. The GRI released its second generation of guidelines (G2) in 2002, and then its third version (G3) in late 2006 (Brown et al. 2009). The G3 guidelines were the product of a two-year development process that involved about 3,000 stakeholders worldwide and provided public comment opportunities.[27] Among the revisions from G2 to G3 are the elaboration of methods for calculating indicators, the requirement of disclosure of an organization's management approach, and broad applicability of the guidelines to private and public actors, including small and large companies, NGOs, and public agencies. The GRI has recently completed updates in the areas of human rights, gender, community impacts, and materiality, which resulted in its G3.1 guidelines (released in March 2011). Finally, in October 2010, the GRI announced that it will begin developing the fourth generation of its guidelines (G4), which are scheduled to be released in 2013.[28] The general aim behind G4 is to increase the robustness of the guidelines to further mainstream sustainability reporting and eventually combine it with financial reporting as part of one "integrated report."[29]

In accordance with the quantity (but not quality) of disclosure, companies self-declare their score as A, B, or C, which the GRI refers to as its "application level."[30] Companies at level C have reported on a minimum of ten GRI indicators, including at least one from each of the environmental, social, and economic categories. Level B means that companies have disclosed their management approach (e.g., their goals, monitoring, and relevant policies) and reported on at least twenty indicators, with at least one from each of the environmental and economic categories as well as one from each of the social subcategories of human rights, labor, society, and product responsibility. Level A means that companies have disclosed their management approach and reported on all fifty core indicators, or alternatively, explained the reason why certain indicators were omitted (such as a lack of materiality for the company). As part of this process, companies undergo a materiality test to determine which issues to report on based on such factors as what is important to stakeholders, the existence of relevant laws and regulations, and whether the issue may pose a significant risk. Level A companies must also report on indicators in its sector supplement, if one is available. Finally, companies have the option of adding a "+" to their level (e.g., an A+) if a third-party assurance provider has verified their data. Therefore, if no "+" is present, there has been no external verification of the information in a company's GRI report.

Whereas companies could choose from more than thirty different reporting frameworks in the 1990s, the GRI has now become "the de facto international reporting standard" (Maclean and Rebernak 2007, 1) According to a 2008 study by the accounting firm KPMG, more than three-quarters of the Global Fortune 250 companies and nearly 70 percent of the 100 largest companies by revenue use GRI guidelines as the basis for their reporting (KPMG International 2008). As of 2013, there were at least 5,470 organizations reporting in eighty-one countries, based on those that submitted their reports to the GRI.[31] What is the motivation for companies to use GRI?

In jurisdictions where there is no mandatory regulation to report on sustainability, there are a variety of reasons why companies nevertheless choose to do so – for example, gaining competitive advantage through "improved management of ESG [(environmental, social, and governance)] impacts and overall risk, enhancement of company reputation, and a greater ability to attract and retain both customers and talent" (Maclean and Rebernak 2007, 2–3). As part of a strategic approach, companies use the GRI guidelines to develop internal metrics that track their social and environmental performance, identify potential risks, and integrate sustainability goals with their overall business objectives. In addition, companies may feel pressure to report because their industry peers are doing so, or to deflect civil society pressure after a prominent environmental or human rights incident. In this case, reporting may be part of a public relations exercise and not reflect any real desire to enhance performance.

There have been a number of critiques of the GRI, both by NGOs and companies themselves. NGOs have criticized the GRI for its division of indicators into core indicators and additional ones that are optional and up to the discretion of companies to include, even if they may be important to certain stakeholders.

Civil society groups have also questioned the credibility of third-party verification services (usually performed by private accounting and consulting firms), given that there are no uniform guidelines to ensure their reliability (see Hess 2008, 470–471). At the same time, companies have complained that they are on a "reporting treadmill," where they spend so much time gathering data that they are left with few resources to implement changes in the organization (Leavoy 2010). Finally, there is a general concern that the GRI ranks reports based on the level of disclosure (e.g., the number of indicators that companies report on) rather than on the quality and accuracy of a firm's sustainability performance (Hess 2008, 463).

The GRI's Impact on Domestic Regulation and Financial Markets

The GRI has moved into the realm of hard law by shaping regulation by regional organizations, states, and stock exchanges. It has recently begun promoting mandatory government regulation on sustainability reporting as well as integrated reporting within the global financial framework, as evidenced by a recent session on the topic at the 2011 World Economic Forum.[32] The primary motivation behind the GRI's lobbying efforts is that the majority of companies are still not reporting on sustainability. About 4,000 companies are currently issuing CSR reports, which represents a tenfold increase since the mid-1990s.[33] Just over one-third of those reporters (about 1,400 companies) used the GRI guidelines in 2009.[34] As previously mentioned, three-quarters of the Global Fortune 250 companies use the GRI. That means that many small and medium-sized companies are still not using the GRI, or issuing sustainability reports at all. In an effort to increase participation, the GRI has recently begun encouraging regulation in the disclosure of environmental and social issues.

The GRI's promotion of regulation represents a significant shift in its role and mission, from an independent organization that encourages companies to report voluntarily on sustainability to a more advocacy-oriented organization that is partnering with governments to promote mandatory reporting. While states had historically only provided funding to the GRI and had no direct involvement in its operation, they are now actively participating in its decision-making process. In connection with this shift, the GRI established a Governmental Advisory Group in 2008 to provide advice to its Board of Directors and executive team and suggest ways of increasing GRI participation through regulatory initiatives.[35] The Governmental Advisory Group is also trying to resolve institutional and legislative fragmentation on sustainability reporting.[36] In addition, in 2009 the GRI Board signed the Amsterdam Declaration, which cites the recent global financial crisis and lack of trust in economic institutions as a justification for more transparency in economic, social, and governance (ESG) reporting.[37] The declaration calls on governments to strengthen the global sustainability reporting regime:

[T]he Board of the GRI calls on governments to take leadership by:

1. Introducing policy requiring companies to report on ESG factors or publicly explain why they have not done so.
2. Requiring ESG reporting by their public bodies – in particular: state owned companies, government pension funds, and public investment agencies.
3. Integrating sustainability reporting within the emerging global financial regulatory framework being developed by leaders of the G20.[38]

In support of the Amsterdam Declaration, the GRI is working closely with governments to pass regulations on sustainability reporting.

The current regulatory landscape reflects a movement toward more government-sponsored legislation, standards, and guidelines on sustainability reporting. According to a 2010 report, there are 142 country standards that include a sustainability-related reporting requirement or guidance. Two-thirds of those regulations are mandatory, and a number of them explicitly cite GRI guidelines (UN Environment Programme et al. 2010, 4).

European countries, in particular, are at the forefront of mandatory reporting regulations. France was one of the earliest countries to mandate ESG disclosure. Its 2001 New Economic Regulation requires all listed companies to report on forty social and environmental criteria in their annual reports.[39] The Swedish government requires state-owned enterprises to issue sustainability reports in accordance with GRI's G3 guidelines and subject to external assurance.[40] Spain similarly enacted legislation that requires state-owned companies and businesses with more than 1,000 employees to produce sustainability reports beginning in 2012.[41] As of 2009, Denmark requires disclosure of CSR activities in financial statements by both state-owned companies and companies with total assets of more than 19 million euros, revenues more than 38 million euros, and more than 250 employees – totaling about 1,100 companies.[42] In addition, Denmark's mandate extends to institutional investors, investment associations, and other listed financial businesses.[43] The guidance notes to Denmark's amended Financial Statements Act encourage the use of GRI guidelines to fulfill the reporting requirement.[44]

The other EU countries have adopted similar legislation to implement the EU Modernisation Directive on corporate disclosure of nonfinancial information. Existing EU law mandates private companies to include nonfinancial key performance indicators in their annual reports "where appropriate" and "[t]o the extent necessary for an understanding of the company's development, performance or position."[45] The European Commission is considering improvements to this policy because the requirements for disclosure (including indicators) are unclear and EU member states can choose to exempt small and medium-sized enterprises.[46] The Commission hosted a series of workshops to explore possible policy revisions in 2009 and 2010 and completed its public consultation in late January 2011.[47] Among the recommendations that are being considered is for EU policy to use the GRI guidelines as a reference point for corporate reporting.[48]

In addition to mandatory regulations, governments are issuing voluntary guidelines on sustainability reporting for companies and public agencies, many of which cite the GRI guidelines. For instance, Australia's Department of Economics and Heritage issued a guide to reporting using GRI-consistent environmental indicators, and its Minerals Council (an industry group) recommends public sustainability reporting under GRI's Mining and Metals Sector Supplement.[49] The Canadian government has also endorsed the GRI for CSR reporting by the extractive sector.[50] In 2007, Japan released its Environmental Reporting Guidelines, which cite GRI guidelines and require environmental reporting for specified corporations.[51]

Stock exchanges are another important driving force behind sustainability reporting. They are encouraging companies to be transparent as to their sustainability performance and, in some cases, mandating disclosure. Companies listed on the London Stock Exchange must disclose in their annual reports any nonfinancial information relevant to their business, although they do not have to file a full-length CSR report.[52] In Australia, companies listed on its national exchange must disclose the extent to which they have followed the Corporate Governance Principles and Recommendations, which include sustainability issues.[53] Emerging market countries are also promoting voluntary standards in CSR reporting through the involvement of local stock exchanges. All companies listed on the Johannesburg Stock Exchange are required to follow the King Report on Corporate Governance, which mandates integrated reporting that incorporates financial and nonfinancial information.[54] China's Shanghai Stock Exchange encourages companies to file annual CSR reports and develop a CSR strategy, and provides incentives for doing so, such as priority election into the prestigious Shanghai Corporate Governance Sector.[55] The Bovespa Stock Exchange in Brazil has played an influential role in raising ESG standards among companies as part of an active national movement for more sustainable investment (KPMG International 2010, 77). Many exchanges have also created socially responsible investing indices (14). The motivation for this activity includes demand from investors for sustainability-related information and the development of specialized markets for sustainable investment niches, particularly in emerging market countries. Interest in sustainability issues is not restricted to socially responsible investors. In fact, there are more than 1,100 asset owners, investment managers, and service providers with US$32 trillion in assets that are signatories to the UN's Principles for Responsible Investment, which promotes incorporation of ESG issues in investment analysis and decision making and disclosure of those issues in annual financial reports.[56]

This brings us to the United States. US-based companies have lagged in participation in the GRI, although there has been a significant increase in recent years.[57] The SEC has been at the center of regulatory efforts to mandate corporate sustainability reporting. Over the past decade, advocacy and investor groups (including some of the largest US pension funds) have successfully engaged with and formally petitioned the SEC to issue guidance on existing rules, increase shareholder rights, and develop new disclosure requirements. On October 27, 2009, the SEC reversed an existing policy (under Rule 14A-8(I)(7)) that had allowed companies to exclude shareholder resolutions requesting information on financial risks associated with environmental, social, and human rights issues.[58] In January 2010, the agency released an interpretive guidance note on the disclosure of climate change risks in financial filings.[59] The note cited the GRI as a model for sustainability reporting in its 2010 guidance note regarding disclosure related to climate change.[60] The premise behind the interpretation is that a company's 10-K annual report should include discussion of material risks, which may include climate change and other sustainability-related risks. Notably, the guidance note cited the GRI as a model framework for sustainability reporting.

There is current pressure on the SEC to require companies to assess and disclose on not only climate-related risks but also other material environmental, social, and governance risks. A petition to former SEC Chairwoman Mary Schapiro by an association of investment professionals proposed that the agency "require issuers to report annually on a comprehensive, uniform set of sustainability indicators ... and that the SEC define this as the highest level of the current version of the Global Reporting Initiative (GRI) reporting guidelines."[61]

Consistent with that request, the SEC's Investor Advisory Committee (IAC) took an initial step toward considering ESG disclosure. The IAC was created by Chairwoman Schapiro in 2009 to give greater voice to investors and was regularly attended by several commissioners as well as senior SEC officials.[62] The Committee was recently codified as a permanent institution under the Dodd–Frank Act and will soon be reconstituted with members appointed by the entire Commission.[63] Among the IAC's priorities was ESG disclosure, which was studied by the Investor as Owner Subcommittee. On May 18, 2010, the subcommittee met with a panel of experts on ESG issues, including the GRI's Director of Sustainability Reporting.[64] Before being temporarily disbanded in light of the Dodd–Frank Act, the subcommittee's final resolution reflects a recognition that ESG disclosure is a priority that should be addressed by the SEC:

The Investor as Owner Subcommittee of the Investor Advisory Committee believes that the SEC should develop dedicated internal resources to monitor and advise on developments regarding the disclosure of corporate social and environmental performance data. Activities could include

- Monitoring and evaluating the effectiveness of current US disclosure requirements and enforcement measures
- Monitoring global developments and participating in appropriate fora
- Serving as a point of contact for investors, issuers, and other stakeholders on these issues
- Making recommendations to the Commission where appropriate

The Investor as Owner Subcommittee of the Investor Advisory Committee further believes that periodic public reports on these activities be produced.[65]

The above resolution is not binding on the SEC, and it remains to be seen how much weight will be accorded to it by the yet-to-be constituted new IAC.

There are a variety of obstacles that may prevent the SEC releasing additional guidance or requirements for ESG disclosure. The agency currently does not have the requisite expertise and capacity to make meaningful decisions on the costs and benefits of mandating environmental and social reporting. SEC officials perceive that there is insufficient interest among mainstream investors, as opposed to socially responsible investors.[66] Moreover, although ESG disclosure remains on the SEC's long-term agenda, it has become less of a short-term priority given the resources needed to implement the Dodd–Frank Act.[67]

The Dodd–Frank Act includes three provisions that are particularly relevant to ESG reporting, which suggests the incremental fashion by which sustainability reporting is being mandated in the United States. Section 1502 imposes a new reporting requirement on publicly traded companies that manufacture products using certain conflict minerals.[68] For example, companies must identify whether the sourcing of the minerals originated in the Democratic Republic of Congo (DRC). If so, they must submit an independent private sector audit report on due diligence measures taken to avoid using minerals that directly or indirectly finance armed groups in the DRC.[69] Section 1503 of the Dodd–Frank Act imposes new disclosure requirements on mine safety.[70] Mining companies must disclose in their annual and quarterly reports to the SEC on the safety and health requirements that apply to mines under the Federal Mine Safety and Health Act of 1977.[71] Finally, Section 1504 requires natural resources companies to disclose certain payments made to governments for the commercial development of oil, natural gas, or minerals.[72]

Outside of the SEC, there are notable efforts by federal agencies to incorporate GRI reporting. Under an executive order signed in January 2010 entitled "Federal Leadership in Environmental, Energy, and Economic Performance," all federal agencies are required to issue a strategic sustainability performance plan.[73] In addition to developing a plan that includes quantifiable metrics and sustainability goals, agencies must also inventory their greenhouse gas emissions and set targets to reduce their emissions by 2020.[74] Each agency must also appoint a senior sustainability officer, and the Chair of the Council on Environmental Quality (CEQ) will report agency results to the president.[75] As the US Army, US Air Force, and US Postal Service already issue GRI-based reports, GRI representatives are lobbying the CEQ to recommend that all agencies issue their strategic sustainability performance plans under a GRI model.[76]

Efforts to regulate sustainability reporting in the United States are still slow compared to efforts in other countries. To raise its US profile, the GRI officially launched a focal point office in New York City on January 31, 2011.[77] The opening ceremony took place at the New York Stock Exchange (NYSE) with a panel discussion on "Why Is America Letting the World Lead in Sustainability Reporting?" This event was a clear effort to engage financial leaders and information providers who could then motivate US companies to report on sustainability using the GRI. Among the participants at the event were Bloomberg and NYSE Euronext, the leading global operators of financial markets and providers of trading technologies.[78]

An essential component of the GRI's strategy in the United States is garnering and publicizing support of the initiative among market data providers. A significant development in this direction came in late 2009 when Bloomberg began providing 120 ESG variables for public companies on its 250,000 data terminals.[79] Users now have access to these data at no additional cost and can manipulate it in the same way as traditional financial metrics. By adding ESG data, Bloomberg recognizes that mainstream institutional investors, not just socially responsible investors, will increasingly consider sustainability performance in their investment decisions. In presentations to business associations and industry groups (including the Business Roundtable, the National Association of Corporate Directors, and the National Investor Relations Institute), the GRI highlights how Bloomberg and other information providers, such as Thomson Reuters, NASDAQ, RiskMetrics, and KLD Research & Analytics, rely on GRI reports when compiling ESG data.[80] According to a Bloomberg representative, "to make our content relevant to the marketplace, we needed to display the information exactly in the format provided by GRI, as this has become the market standard."[81] For instance, when a Bloomberg user selects a company's water consumption variable, she is immediately linked to the company's GRI report. If the company has not issued a report, then the cell will remain blank. The GRI hopes that companies will therefore feel pressure from investors to disclose their social and environmental data and, over time, improve their performance.[82]

Rating agencies and sustainability indices are other potential avenues to pressure companies to report using the GRI. Many rating agencies build their methodologies around GRI indicators although they are not necessarily public about it.[83] One index that explicitly relies on GRI metrics is NASDAQ's Global Sustainability 50 Index.[84] In the fall of 2009, the index removed twenty-three firms, including Cisco, Microsoft, and Oracle, for failing to disclose on a minimum of 40 percent of core GRI indicators (Gunther 2010). Although indices and rating agencies track reporting based on the indicators, they do not track performance or improvement over time.

THE POTENTIAL COSTS OF USING INDICATORS IN GOVERNANCE

Indicators are not neutral instruments that can be applied mechanically. They are normative tools that embed certain values and shape behavior according to a standard (Koops 2008). They also carry potential costs. Whether indicators play a beneficial or harmful role in turn can influence the perceived legitimacy of the government agencies and private actors that produce and rely on them.[85] Whether civil society perceives an actor as legitimate will affect the agency's right to govern, its claim to authority, and the likelihood of compliance with its directives (see, e.g., Carron 1993, 558; Bodansky 1999, 602–603). Based on personal interviews with GRI staff in Amsterdam and New York City, and observations at a GRI-certified training session, I will identify potential costs associated with using indicators, which challenge their effectiveness in meaningfully comparing units of analysis and evaluating performance.

The Promotion of Box Ticking and Superficial Compliance

The use of indicators risks producing a box ticking approach to compliance, which entails superficial or cosmetic changes without any substantive effects on behavior. Box ticking refers to a "rigid, mechanical practice involving the use of needlessly detailed 'standardized checklists' and pursued without regard to weighing costs against benefits" (Power 2007, 153). The scientific authority of indicators and their focus on transparency can conceal behavioral changes (or the lack thereof) and lead to data gathering for its own sake, with a preference for precise but not necessarily relevant data (167). As a result, indicators run the risk of promoting business interests at the expense of public interests, thus drawing regulation away from its primary purpose and not measuring what is important.[86] Organizations that produce indicators may become more preoccupied with perpetuating their existence and raising their status, rather than using the indicators as a tool to shape behavior. In this way, the process of producing more and better indicators becomes an end in itself.

When indicators are used in regulatory governance, there can be a slippage between their initial goals and intended audience, and the goals and audience that evolve over time. For instance, the GRI training session that I attended was exclusively focused on revising indicators and disclosing more information, rather than on promoting its original aim of corporate accountability. When the GRI was founded, the intended audience for its reports consisted of communities, consumers, NGOs, and shareholders who would presumably read the reports, encourage companies to improve their performance on sustainability issues, and thereby shift the balance of power in corporate governance (Levy et al. 2010, 8). However, the focus of the GRI's activities has now become the users (the companies) – the GRI devotes significant resources to developing learning tools, training courses, and services for report preparers and users.[87] A GRI official whom I interviewed admitted that the GRI's main audience is companies and that its primary motivation is to increase company participation.[88] Here we see a gap between the GRI's stated goal of multistakeholder consensus-building and its actual operations.

The GRI is no longer aimed at empowering its original audience to hold corporations accountable. For instance, it is questionable who actually reads the reports. According to one study, "there is widespread agreement that the [GRI] reports are not studied in any detail" (Levy et al. 2010, 103). My interviews revealed that GRI officials themselves acknowledge the low readership of GRI reports.[89] Even among those actors who read the reports, many do not find them useful. A major US environmental NGO representative noted: "We don't really use GRI reports … [A] single number is not enough; we are interested in [the] strategies and plans behind the numbers" (103). Others noted that the information "does not give an adequate picture of the impacts on local communities, … [and] is too processes oriented, rather than [focused on] performance" (Brown et al. 2009, 576). NGOs also do not trust the data, which usually are not verified by a third party. They only pay attention to whether a company releases a report but not its actual content. What becomes important then is simply the procedural exercise of filling out a report or, in other words, superficial compliance.

The GRI's application levels further reinforce its focus on transparency for its own sake rather than actual improvements in behavior. Recall that the GRI attaches an application level to a report largely based on the number of indicators that a company reports on. A company receives an A if it reports on at least fifty indicators, a B for twenty, and a C for ten. That means that a company that is destroying the environment could nevertheless get an A for reporting on fifty or more indicators (as well as disclosing its management approach). Thus, the application levels are based on the level of disclosure, rather than on the quality and accuracy of a firm's actual performance. One GRI official admitted that there is a general misconception that the application levels serve as a ranking based on quality of performance, rather than an objective classification of the level of transparency:

> What we've seen is that it's … a challenge on the communication side. So often the levels have been presented as being a grade or a quality mark or a performance

related statement, which has been quite difficult for us to counteract. I mean, whenever we came across something like that we would contact the company and then ask them to change the statement, but of course, since we're an international organization you can never ensure that you find everything ... That's also inherent in the system [of] "A," "B," and "C" in a US context. It has a completely different connotation in the European context, for instance [where school grades are numeric].[90]

Another GRI official explained that it may be more worthwhile for a company to devote resources to managing change and improving performance rather than moving up levels for its own sake.[91] Moreover, external verification is only optional, and a company could add a "+" to its application level even if only a small portion of its report has been externally verified. Third-party verifiers such as accounting firms do not have to comply with a uniform assurance standard. Here we see that the motivation behind the producers of the GRI is not that the reports are actually read by NGOs or whether they reflect a company's good or bad performance, but that more and more companies participate and release reports. As the GRI enhances its profile and perpetuates its status as the market leader in sustainability reporting, it may be undermining its legitimacy and the purported goals behind its indicators.

The Dominance of Technical Experts over Decision Making

Because indicators rely on numerically rendered data, technical experts (both within government agencies and private actors) exercise considerable power over decision making and the interpretation of legal norms. Although their specialized knowledge and political neutrality can be a benefit for policymaking (see generally Landis 1938; Spence and Cross 2000), it is difficult for stakeholders to challenge the power of experts and their methodology and assumptions in producing the indicators. Because indicators carry scientific authority, they mask potential conflicts of interest among technical experts and leave little room for contestation. This is the case for the GRI, where accounting firms are heavily involved in both indicator production and data verification.

Providing assurance for sustainability reports has become a growing business, especially for accounting companies that have been seeking credibility following the Enron scandal (see Tilt 2009). As a result, "[a] large service industry comprised largely of sustainability consultancies and auditing firms has emerged around the revisions of the guidelines, preparations of reports, their verification, stakeholder outreach, and various efforts to standardize and institutionalize the above activities" (Levy et al. 2010, 97). These firms arguably derive more economic benefit from the GRI than any other stakeholder. In fact, some firms such as KPMG, PricewaterhouseCoopers, and Deloitte have recently established global sustainability practice groups that specifically focus on corporate sustainability measurement and reporting.

The role of accounting firms as independent third parties is dubious given that they are actively governing the same organization that they are presumably regulating. Representatives from large accounting firms occupy key positions in the GRI's governance structure, including the Board of Directors, from which they advise on the methodology and interpretation of indicators.[92] In an informational brochure about its sustainability practice, Deloitte advertises that it

> has been involved in every stage of the GRI's growth and development ... Deloitte member firms were involved in the 2002 revision of the GRI guidelines, as well as the 2006 revision at which the current G3 guidelines were drafted. Many Deloitte member firm professionals have played key roles in the GRI governance and stakeholder bodies ... Moreover, Deloitte member firm teams both advise clients on reporting and assurance according to GRI guidelines and collaborate ... on GRI-sponsored training. (Deloitte 2010, 2–3)

> The big four accounting firms (Deloitte, Ernst & Young, KPMG, and PricewaterhouseCoopers) have also recently sponsored the GRI's new US office for the first two years.[93] Yet these same firms also have a stake in increasing the market for their services. Given that the firms may provide other services to their clients, such as financial auditing, they have an interest in trying to package their financial and nonfinancial services together. More companies using GRI and seeking external assurance represents a significant revenue opportunity for the big accounting firms.

Given the proliferation of performance codes, standards, and other forms of voluntary self-regulation, the "third-party assurance industry" is becoming increasingly influential in the interpretation of legal norms in a variety of areas (see Blair et al. 2008). Accountants are thus exercising authority over how legal norms are valued, interpreted, measured, and verified.[94] Given their conflict of interest, sensitive issues may be left out by assurance providers for fear of upsetting their clients (O'Dwyer and Owen 2005, 227). In the case of the GRI, where the verification of data often involves law-related issues such as the application of international human rights and environmental standards, accountants arguably lack the professional competence to conduct a proper evaluation (Manetti and Becatti 2009, 291). Surprisingly, there are no legal experts on the GRI's Technical Advisory Committee, so their participation in the production of GRI guidelines and the interpretation of indicators is limited to consultations with Organizational Stakeholders.[95]

The Distortion of Public Values into Numbers

When indicators do not accurately represent the social phenomena that they are intended to evaluate, they lose their effectiveness as regulatory tools. This risk particularly applies to the use of indicators to measure public values that are noninstrumental and difficult to translate into numbers. Legal norms may then be interpreted in a managerial way that distorts their original meaning (see Edelman et al. 2001). In the case of the GRI, issues that are easy to quantify, such as greenhouse gas emissions, are prioritized. At the same time, issues such as human rights and community impact are subordinated or even diluted as they are translated into mere business risks. In this way, indicators may lead to better performance on certain issues by relying on the power of numbers, but may neglect those issues that are difficult to quantify. So instead of the maxim "what is measured gets done," in fact in reality, what is easy to measure may be the only thing that gets done.

Although quantification may be appropriate for many environmental or health and safety issues, it is difficult to capture other material information in measurable quantities. For instance, critics argue that the subjection of certain issues to cost–benefit analysis (as it is currently structured) may strip them of their intrinsic value (see Green 2001; Kysar 2010). As the GRI develops its fourth generation of guidelines, there is disagreement over the extent to which indicators can (or should) be based solely on quantitative data:

> The challenge is to what extent can we put the sustainability issues into measurable figures. Is that possible? Should we move to that completely or should we also allow for context-related information? So that's going to be a big discussion when we start up G4. But what we've seen is that the information that the investors are looking for are actually these numbers to a large extent.[96]

The debate over quantification emerged most recently over revision of the GRI's human rights indicators.

According to a report by the GRI's Human Rights Reporting Working Group, it has been challenging to develop appropriate performance indicators in this area.[97] For instance, one of the human rights indicators in the G3 guidelines is "total hours of employee training on policies and procedures concerning aspects of human rights that are relevant to operations, including the percentage of employees trained."[98] Yet the number of employee training hours does not necessarily correlate with positive human rights outcomes. Another GRI indicator is "total number of incidents of violations involving rights of indigenous people and actions taken." By exclusively relying on a quantitative measure, this indicator does not give information about the seriousness of the violations or the length of time over which they occurred. Good reporting requires more than just quantitative data:

> [I]t is necessary to disaggregate performance data ... The report should pay adequate attention to both narrative and quantitative data ... As a general point, all quantitative indicators have minimal meaning as isolated pieces of information. Numbers can indicate how often events have occurred, but will provide little or no insight into quality (e.g., 100 hours of training does not reflect whether it was effective or ineffective; 1 million Euros of revenue does not describe sources of the revenue or their relative importance to overall strategy). Therefore, all quantitative indicators must be read in the context of other information and the relative value of quantitative indicators must be judged in terms of how well it contributes to understanding in combination with the other required disclosures.[99]

In other words, public values such as human rights cannot be captured by numbers alone. Despite the working group's report, the GRI is moving in the direction of more quantification and the translation of all issues into potential financial risks.

As part of its efforts to streamline indicators and mainstream reporting, the GRI recently announced a goal that by 2020, all companies will adopt an integrated report. This means that a company would release a single annual report that includes indicators for both financial and nonfinancial information (see Eccles and Krzus 2010). The purpose of an integrated report is to raise the status of nonfinancial information and demonstrate its relationship to a company's core business strategy. Yet if integrated reporting one day became the norm and ultimately replaced sustainability reports, then the standard for including environmental and social issues would be financial materiality – that is, the same standard used for financial statements under the SEC based on what a reasonable investor would consider important in making an investment decision.[100] Therefore, issues such as human rights, which are materially important for communities and NGOs but may not necessarily be financially material, may be left out of an integrated report.[101]

The GRI's progression toward integrated reporting represents an effort to translate public values into financial terms and transform them into business risks. In the case of human rights, what is developing is a risk management approach that defines potential violations as strategic risks, which may damage a company's reputation, threaten its profits, and lead to possible litigation.[102] While risk management has become increasingly common in public and private governance (Power 2004), what are the implications for it being applied to more value-laden issues such as human rights? Translating rights into financial risks and indicators may emphasize their regulatory dimension (including their instrumental, rule-oriented, and administrative qualities) but disregard their sovereignty dimension (which invokes their universal character, symbolic valence, and emancipatory power) (see Sarfaty 2009, 2012). As a result, human rights indicators that rely exclusively on quantitative measurement may distort the legal norms on which they are based and challenge the usefulness of these tools to evaluate performance effectively.

CONCLUSION

What are the unintended consequences of using metrics in decision making? Are indicators measuring what is critical toward changing behavior? In this chapter, I have sought to answer these questions by drawing on an empirical study of the Global Reporting Initiative. I demonstrate that indicators do not just serve as instruments to regulate behavior; they themselves have normative authority and may be fraught with problems. Indicators are playing an important role in governance given their ability to simplify and translate social phenomena into a numerical representation that is easy to understand and comparable across actors. They have become particularly prevalent in international law as a mechanism to increase compliance and operationalize global norms. Yet as indicators hide behind a veil of scientific truth and neutrality, they mask potential problems: the promotion of box-ticking and superficial compliance; the dominance of technical experts over decision making; and the distortion of public values into numbers.

Like all tools, indicators can be misused and manipulated in a way that strays from their purported goals and intended audiences. Their costs threaten to outweigh their benefits if they are not designed meaningfully and if there is little confidence in the information that they provide. Therefore, regulatory bodies should not treat indicators as ends in and of themselves, but rather as a means toward evaluating performance and ultimately improving behavior.

NOTES

1 See World Bank, "Doing Business 2013: Smarter Regulations for Small and Medium-Size Enterprises" (2012).
2 Ibid. "Millennium Challenge Corporation, Guide to the MCC Indicators and the Selection Process for Fiscal Year 2013" (2012).
3 Pub. L. No. 110–457, 122 Stat. 5044 (codified as amended in scattered sections of 8, 18, 22 & 42 U.S.C.).
4 Ibid.

5 See Freedom House, "Freedom in the World" (2010), http://www.freedomhouse.org/
report/freedom-world/freedom-world-2010; Transparency Int'l, Global Corruption
Barometer (2009); Office of the U.N. High Commissioner for Human Rights, *Report on
Indicators for Promoting and Monitoring the Implementation of Human Rights*, U.N. Doc.
HRI/MC/2008/3 (June 6, 2008).

6 "Global Reporting Initiative, Sustainability Reporting Guidelines" (2011), https://www
.globalreporting.org/resourcelibrary/G3.1-Guidelines-Incl-Technical-Protocol.pdf.

7 Created in 2000, the UN Global Compact is a voluntary initiative to encourage companies
to embrace nine principles drawn from the Universal Declaration of Human Rights, the
International Labor Organization's Fundamental Principles on Rights at Work, and the
Rio Principles on Environment and Development. See *United Nations Global Compact*,
United Nations, http://www.unglobalcompact.org.

8 See Kiobel v. Royal Dutch Petroleum, 133 S.Ct. 1659 (2013). The Alien Tort Claims Act
allows US district courts to hear "any civil action by an alien for a tort only, committed in
violation of the law of nations ...." 28 U.S.C. $ 1350 (1789).

9 Information regulation has become prevalent in the field of environmental law(see,
e.g., Kleindorfer and Orts 1998; Karkkainen 2001; Esty 2004; Case 2005; Kysar and
Salzman 2008).

10 "Global Reporting Initiative, GRI Application Levels" (2011), https://www.globalreporting
.org/resourcelibrary/G3.1-Application-Levels.pdf.

11 See Kiobel v. Royal Dutch Petroleum, 133 S.Ct. 1659 (2013).

12 International Labor Organization "Tripartite Declaration of Principles Concerning
Multinational Enterprises and Social Policy" (2006), http://www.ilo.org/wcmsp5/
groups/public/--ed_emp/---emp_ent/---multi/documents/publication/wcms_094386.
pdf; "Organisation for Economic Co-operation and Development, OECD Guidelines
for Multinational Enterprises" (2000), http://www.oecd.org/dataoecd/56/36/1922428
.pdf; International Organization for Standardization, ISO 26000: Guidance on Social
Responsibility (2010); *The Ten Principles*, United Nations Global Compact, http://www
.unglobalcompact.org/AboutTheGC/TheTenPrinciples/index.html.

13 John Ruggie, Report of the Special Representative of the U.N. Secretary-General on the
Issue of Human Rights and Transnational Corporations and Other Business Enterprises,
*Draft Guiding Principles for the Implementation of the United Nations "Protect,
Respect and Remedy" Framework*, pp. 1–3 (November 1, 2010), http://www.scribd.com/
doc/44782231/Ruggie-UN-Draft-Guiding-Principles-22-Nov-2010-1.

14 In making this assertion, I disagree with a rigid hard versus soft law distinction and instead
view the division as a continuum between binding and nonbinding rules (see Abott and
Snidal 2000; Guzman and Meyer 2010; Shaffer and Pollack 2010, 712–717).

15 ISOS Group, GRI Certified Sustainability Reporting Training Program, June 2010 (on
file with author).

16 Ceres is a national network of environmental organizations, investors, and other public
interest groups with a mission of integrating sustainability into capital markets. See *Who
We Are*, Ceres, http://www.ceres.org/about-us/who-we-are.

17 Income from direct services represents about 20 percent of the GRI's budget. Interview
with representative of the Global Reporting Initiative, in Amsterdam (December 8, 2010).

18 Although its primary users are corporations, the GRI markets itself to all types of
organizations including NGOs and governmental agencies. See Global Reporting
Initiative, "GRI Sustainability Reporting: A Common Language for a Common Future"
(2012).

19 Global Reporting Initiative, supra note 6.

20 Ibid., 48.

21 Global Reporting Initiative, Rules and Procedures for the GRI Stakeholder Council (2009), https://www.globalreporting.org/SiteCollectionDocuments/SC_RulesProcedures2009.pdf.

22 See *Alliances and Synergies*, Global Reporting Initiative, https://www.globalreporting.org/information/about-gri/alliances-and-synergies/Pages/default.aspx.

23 See "Global Reporting Initiative & The Global Compact, Making the Connection: The GRI Guidelines and the UNGC Communication on Progress" (2007).

24 See Global Reporting Initiative & Int'l Finance Corp., "Getting More Value Out of Sustainability Reporting: Connecting IFC's Sustainability Performance Standards and the GRI Reporting Framework" (2010); Global Reporting Initiative & Carbon Disclosure Project, "Linking Up GRI and CDP: How Do the Global Reporting Initiative Reporting Guidelines Match with the Carbon Disclosure Project Questions?" (2010); Global Reporting Initiative, GRI & ISO 26000: "How to Use the GRI Guidelines in Conjunction with ISO 26000 (2010); Press Release, Global Reporting Initiative, New Partnership to Help Multinational Companies Operate Responsibly" (December 13, 2010), http://www.oecd.org/daf/inv/mne/oecd-gripartnershiptohelpmultinationalcompaniesoperateresponsibly.htm.

25 Carbon Disclosure Project, https://www.cdproject.net/. The GRI is distinct from the CDP because it addresses broader elements of sustainability reporting covering social and governance issues in addition to environmental issues. Yet there is considerable overlap between the GRI's environmental indicators and the CDP's questions on energy consumption and greenhouse gas emissions.

26 Indicator protocols are available to guide organizations as to how to define the relevant terms, compile data, and find potential information sources. In addition, the GRI has produced a variety of sector supplements (e.g., on financial services, electric utilities, and the mining sector) that provide additional guidance and appropriate indicators for companies in that industry.

27 The GRI follows the same multistakeholder consultative approach when developing its sector supplements.

28 See Global Reporting Initiative, "G4 Development Process Overview," https://www.globalreporting.org/resourcelibrary/G4DevelopmentProcessOverview.pdf.

29 See Press Release, IIRC, GRI and IIRC Deepen Cooperation to Shape the Future of Global Reporting (March 1, 2013), http://www.theiirc.org/2013/03/01/gri-and-iirc-deepen-cooperation-to-shape-the-future-of-corporate-reporting/. The GRI recently joined a group of professional accounting bodies, auditing firms, international organizations, companies, and NGOs to form the International Integrated Reporting Committee, whose aim is to promote the adoption of a global standard for integrated reporting among companies worldwide. For more information on integrated reporting see Eccles and Krzus (2010).

30 Global Reporting Initiative, supra note 10.

31 The GRI has been keeping an updated inventory of reports from 1999 through the present, which is available on their website. See *Reporting*, Global Reporting Initiative, https://www.globalreporting.org/reporting/Pages/default.aspx.

32 Press Release, Global Reporting Initiative, World Economic Forum Discusses Integrated Reporting (February 2, 2011), http://www.globalreporting.org/information/news-and-press-center/Pages/World-Economic-Forum-Discusses-Integrated-Reporting-.aspx.

33 CorporateRegister.com, "CR Reporting Awards '10: Global Winners and Reporting Trends 4" (2010).

34 Ibid., 6.

35 See Governmental Advisory Group, Global Reporting Initiative, https://www.globalreporting.org/network/network-structure/governmental-advisory-group/Pages/default.aspx.

36 Interview with representative of the Global Reporting Initiative, in Amsterdam (December 9, 2010).

37 Press Release, Global Reporting Initiative, The Amsterdam Declaration on Transparency and Reporting (March 10, 2009), http://www.csrwire.com/press_releases/15371-The-Amsterdam-Declaration-on-Transparency-and-Reporting.

38 Ibid.

39 See Code de Commerce [C. Com] art. L. 225-102-1 (Fr).

40 Regeringskansliet [Swedish Ministry of Enterprise, Energy, and Communications], "Guidelines for External Reporting by State-Owned Companies" (2007).

41 Ley 2/2011 de 4 de Marzo, de Economía Sostenible (B.O.E. 2011, 55) (Spain) (Spain's sustainable economy law).

42 Financial Statements Act, 2008, § 99A (Den.). The Danish law follows a principle of report or explain, which requires companies to either disclose their CSR activities or give reasons for not having any.

43 Ibid.

44 Danish Commerce & Companies Agency, "Reporting on Corporate Social Responsibility: An Introduction for Supervisory and Executive Boards" (English Version) 15 (2009).

45 See Directive 2003/51/EC, art. 1(14), of the European Parliament and of the Counsel of June 18, 2003 amending Directives 78/660/EEC, 86/635/EEC, and 91/674/EEC on the Annual and Consolidated Accounts of Certain Types of Companies, Banks, and Other Financial Institutions and Insurance Undertakings, 2003 O.J. (L 178).

46 *European Workshop on Disclosure of Environmental, Social and Governance Information*, at 16 (2010), http://ec.europa.eu/enterprise/policies/sustainable-business/corporate-social-responsibility/reporting-disclosure/swedish-presidency/files/summaries/6-final_workshop_en.pdf.

47 See *Public Consultation on Non-financial Reporting, Reporting and Disclosure*, European Commission, http://ec.europa.eu/enterprise/policies/sustainable-business/corporate-social-responsibility/reporting-disclosure/#h2-2 (last visited July 24, 2013).

48 *European Workshop on Disclosure of Environmental, Social and Governance Information*, supra note 46.

49 Australia Department of the Environment and Heritage, "Triple Bottom Line Reporting in Australia: A Guide to Reporting Against Environmental Indicators" (2003); "Minerals Council of Australia: Australian Minerals Industry Framework for Sustainable Development 'Enduring Value'" (2005).

50 The Office of the Executive Section ESR Counsellor, Building the Canadian Advantage: A Corporate Social Responsibility (CSR) Strategy for the Canadian International Extractive Sector (2009), http://web.cim.org/UserFiles/File/Building-Canadian-Advantage-CSR-Strategy-Extractive-Sector.pdf.

51 Government of Japan: "Ministry of the Environment, Environmental Reporting Guidelines: Towards a Sustainable Society" (Provisional Translation) 112 (2007); "Law

Concerning the Promotion of Business Activities with Environmental Consideration, Law No. 77 of 2004," http://www.env.go.jp/en/laws/policy/business.pdf (Japan).

52 Companies Act, 2006, c. 46, § 417 (U.K.).

53 Australian Securities Exchange, Corporate Governance Principles and Recommendations 5, 33–34 (2007). Disclosure under these recommendations is on an "if not, why" basis.

54 Institute of Directors Southern Africa, King Report on Governance for South Africa 10 (2009).

55 "Guidelines on Environmental Information Disclosure by Companies Listed on the Shanghai Stock Exchange, 2008" (China).

56 United Nations, *Principles for Responsible Investment: Annual Report 2012*, at 2 (2012), http://www.unpri.org/viewer/?file=wp-content/uploads/Annualreport20121.pdf.

57 Between 2009 and 2010, there was a 30 percent increase of GRI-based sustainability reporting in the United States although there is a still a disproportionately low percentage of assured reporting (i.e., reporting that is verified through a third-party assurance provider) (see Nazari 2011).

58 Securities & Exchange Commission Division of Corporate Finance, Staff Legal Bulletin No. 14E (CF) (October 27, 2009). Shareholder activism on environmental and social issues is becoming a significant source of pressure on companies. During the 2010 corporate proxy season, there were a record 100 shareholder-driven proposals related to climate change issues (Pizzani 2010, 35).

59 See Securities & Exchange Commission, Commission Guidance Regarding Disclosure Related to Climate Change; Final Rule, 75 Fed. Reg. 6290 (February 8, 2010).

60 Ibid., 6292.

61 Letter from Lisa Woll, CEO of Social Investment Forum, to Mary Schapiro, Chairwoman of the Securities & Exchange Commission (July 21, 2009) (on file with author).

62 See Press Release, Securities & Exchange Commission, SEC Announces Creation of Investor Advisory Committee (June 3, 2009), http://www.sec.gov/news/press/2009/2009–126 .htm.

63 See Dodd–Frank Wall Street Reform and Consumer Protection Act of 2010, Pub. L. No. 111–203, § 911, 124 Stat. 1376 (2010).

64 Memorandum from Elizabeth Murphy, Federal Advisory Committee Act Committee Management Officer, to Michael McTiernan, Division of Corporate Finance Staff Member (September 30, 2010) (on file with author).

65 Ibid.

66 Interview with SEC officials, in Washington, DC (November 2, 2010).

67 Ibid.

68 Dodd–Frank Act, supra note 63, § 1502.

69 Ibid.

70 Ibid., § 1503.

71 Federal Mine Safety and Health Act of 1977, Pub. L. No. 95–164, 91 Stat. 1290 (codified as amended in scattered sections of 30 U.S.C.).

72 Dodd–Frank Act, supra note 63, § 1504.

73 Executive Order No. 13,514, 74 Fed. Reg. 52117 (October 5, 2009).

74 Ibid., §§ 2, 8.

75 Ibid., §§ 3, 16.

76 Interview with Mike Wallace, Director of US Focal Point, Global Reporting Initiative, in New York, NY (December 2, 2010).

77 Press Release, Global Reporting Initiative, GRI Launches its Focal Point USA (January 12, 2011), https://www.globalreporting.org/information/news-and-press-center/Pages/GRI -launches-its-Focal-Point-USA-.aspx.

78 Ibid.

79 See Mindy S. Lubber, *Is ESG Data Going Mainstream?*, Harvard Business Review Blog (May 6, 2009), http://blogs.hbr.org/leadinggreen/2009/05/is-esg-data-going-mainstream .html; see also http://www.bloomberg.com/bsustainable/.

80 Mike Wallace, Director of US Focal Point, Global Reporting Initiative, GRI Reporting Trends (2010) (on file with author).

81 Ibid.

82 Client demand has spurred banks like Goldman Sachs to integrate ESG criteria into their investment research. See Goldman Sachs, "Environmental Stewardship and Sustainability Summary of 2010" (2010), http://www.goldmansachs.com/ citizenship/environmental-stewardship-and-sustainability/environmental-progress -summary/environmental-progress-summary-pdf.pdf.

83 Interview with Mike Wallace, Director of US Focal Point, Global Reporting Initiative, in New York, NY (December 2, 2010).

84 See "NASDAQ OMX, NASDAQ OMX CRD Global Sustainability Index SM Methodology" (January 2012), https://indexes.nasdaqomx.com/docs/methodology_ QCRD.pdf.

85 I am primarily interested in procedural legitimacy, which focuses on fair procedures according to principles of transparency, accountability, democratic deliberation, and participation (see Franck 1988, 1990).

86 The process by which regulated firms and special interest groups end up co-opting and manipulating the agencies that are supposed to control them is called "regulatory capture" (see Croley 2008, 17–18).

87 See *Reporting Support*, Global Reporting Initiative, https://www.globalreporting.org/ reporting/reporting-support/Pages/default.aspx (last viewed July 24, 2013).

88 Interview with representative of the Global Reporting Initiative, in Amsterdam (December 7, 2010).

89 Interviews with representatives of the Global Reporting Initiative, in Amsterdam (December 7, 8, 2010).

90 Interview with representative of the Global Reporting Initiative, in Amsterdam (December 8, 2010).

91 Interview with representative of the Global Reporting Initiative, in Amsterdam (December 7, 2010).

92 See *Board of Directors*, Global Reporting Initiative, https://www.globalreporting.org/ network/network-structure/board-of-directors/Pages/default.aspx.

93 Press Release, Global Reporting Initiative, New GRI Focal Point Helps US Companies Improve Sustainability (November 3, 2010), https://www.globalreporting.org/information/ news-and-press-center/Pages/New-GRI-Focal-Point-helps-US-companies-improve-sustain ability-reporting-.aspx.

94 A handful of law firms are beginning to catch up to accounting firms by opening corporate social responsibility practice groups, but lawyering in this area is still in its early stages. See, *e.g.*, *Corporate Social Responsibility Practice*, Foley Hoag LLP, http://www.foleyhoag .com/practices/business/corporate-social-responsibility.

95 This is particularly problematic because the GRI needs the support of lawyers before companies agree to use the guidelines. Corporate counsel must approve before a company discloses information based on corporate sustainability standards like the GRI.

96 Interview with representative of the Global Reporting Initiative, in Amsterdam (December 8, 2010).

97 Global Reporting Initiative, Report: Human Rights Reporting Working Group 7 (2009) (on file with author).

98 Global Reporting Initiative, "Sustainability Reporting Guidelines Version 3.0 33" (2000), https://www.globalreporting.org/resourcelibrary/G3-Guidelines-Incl-Technical-Protocol.pdf.

99 Ibid., 7, 8.

100 See Basic v. Levinson, 485 U.S. 224, 231–32 (1988).

101 This is the reason why some advocacy organizations do not recommend that integrated reports completely replace sustainability reports. My discussions with these organizations revealed that they believe that the audiences for the two reports are different – investors would read the integrated reports while NGOs and consumers would read sustainability reports.

102 A prominent example of this approach is the Voluntary Principles on Security and Human Rights, which promote human rights risk assessments in the extractive industries sector. *Introduction*, Voluntary Principles on Security & Human Rights, voluntaryprinciples.org/principles/introduction.

REFERENCES

Abbott, Kenneth, and Duncan Snidal. 2000. "Hard and Soft Law in International Legal Governance." *International Organization* 54: 421–456.

Bamberger, Kenneth A. 2010. "Technologies of Compliance: Risk and Regulation in a Digital Age." *Texas Law Review* 88: 669–740.

Benvenisti, Eyal, and George W. Downs. 2011. "National Courts Review of Transnational Private Regulation." *Tel Aviv University of Law Faculty Papers*, Working Papers 125. http://law.bepress.com/taulwps/art125/.

Berman, Paul Schiff. 2006. "Seeing Beyond the Limits of International Law." *Texas Law Review* 84: 1265–1316.

Blair, Margaret M., Cynthia A. Williams, and Li-Wen Lin. 2008. "The New Role for Assurance Services in Global Commerce." *Journal of Corporation Law* 33: 325–360.

Bodansky, Daniel. 1999. "The Legitimacy of International Governance: A Coming Challenge for International Environmental Law." *American Journal of Internal Law* 93: 596–624.

Braithwaite, John, and Peter Drahos. 2000. *Global Business Regulation*. Cambridge: Cambridge University Press.

Brown, Halina Szejnwald, Martin de Jong, and Teodorina Lessidrenska. 2009. "The Rise of Global Reporting Initiative (GRI) as a Case of Institutional Entrepreneurship." *Environmental Politics* 18: 182–200.

Brown, Halina Szejnwald, Martin de Jong, and David L. Levy. 2009. "Building Institutions Based on Information Disclosure: Lessons from GRI's Sustainability Reporting." *Journal of Cleaner Productions* 17: 571–580.

Caron, David D. 1993. "The Legitimacy of the Collective Authority of the Security Council." *American Journal of Internal Law* 87: 552–588.

Carrigan, Christopher, and Cary Coglianese. 2011. "The Politics of Regulation: From Institutionalism to New Governance." *Annual Review of Political Science* 14: 107–129.

Case, David W. 2005. "Corporate Environmental Reporting as Informational Regulation: A Law and Economics Perspective." *University of Colorado Law Review* 76: 379–442.

Clapham, Andrew. 2006. *Human Rights Obligations of Non-State Actors*. Oxford: Oxford University Press.

Clapham, Andrew, and Scott Jerbi. 2001. "Categories of Corporate Complicity in Human Rights Abuses." *Hastings International and Comparative Law Review* 24: 339–350.

Croley, Steven P. 2008. *Regulation and Public Interests: the Possibility of Good Regulatory Government*. Princeton, NJ: Princeton University Press.

Davis, Kevin E., Benedict Kingsbury, and Sally Engle Merry. 2012. "Indicators as a Technology of Global Governance." *Law and Society Review* 46: 71–104.

Deloitte. 2010. "Sustainability Reporting: The Emerging Challenge." http://www2.deloitte.com/content/dam/Deloitte/global/Documents/CCS/GRI_whitepaper_061710.pdf.

Eccles, Robert G., and Michael P. Krzus. 2010. *One Report: Integrated Reporting for a Sustainable Strategy*. Hoboken, NJ: John Wiley & Sons.

Edelman, Lauren B. Fuller, Sally Riggs, and Mara-Drita, Iona. 2001. "Diversity Rhetoric and the Managerialization of Law." *American Journal of Sociology* 106: 1589–1641.

Entine, Jon. 2010. "UN Global Compact: Ten Years of Greenwashing?" *Ethical Corporation*. http://www.jonentine.com/ethical_corporation/2010_11_United_Nations_Global_Compact.pdf.

Esty, Daniel C. 2004. "Environmental Protection in the Information Age." *New York Law Review* 79: 115–211.

     2006. "Good Governance at the Supranational Scale: Globalizing Administrative Law." *Yale Law Journal* 115: 1490–1562.

Franck, Thomas M. 1988. "Legitimacy in the International System." *American Journal of Internal Law* 82: 705–759.

     1990. *The Power of Legitimacy Among Nations*. Oxford: Oxford University Press.

Freeman, Jody. 2000. "The Private Role in Public Governance." *New York University Law Review* 75: 543–675.

Goodman, Ryan, and Derek Jinks. 2004. "How to Influence States: Socialization and International Human Rights Law." *Duke Law Journal* 54: 621–704.

Green, Maria. 2001. "What We Talk About When We Talk About Indicators: Current Approaches to Human Rights Measurement." *Human Rights Quarterly* 23: 1062–1097.

Gunther, Marc. 2010. "Investors Urge More Tech Firms to Follow Intel's Lead and Embrace Green." *GREENBIZ Blog*, June 1. http://www.greenbiz.com/news/2010/06/01/investors-urge-more-tech-firms-follow-intels-lead-and-embrace-green.

Guzman, Andrew T. 2010. *How International Law Works: A Rational Choice Theory*. New York: Oxford University Press.

Guzman, Andrew T., and Timothy L. Meyer. 2010. "International Soft Law." *Journal of Legal Analysis* 2: 171–225.

Hathaway, Oona A. 2005. "Between Power and Principle: An Integrated Theory of International Law." *University of Chicago Law Review* 72: 469–536.

Hess, David. 2008. "The Three Pillars of Corporate Social Reporting as New Governance Regulation: Disclosure, Dialogue, and Development." *Business Ethics Quarterly* 18: 447–482.

Ioannou, Ioannis, and George Serafeim. 2012. "The Consequences of Mandatory Corporate Sustainability Reporting." *Harvard Business School Research* Working Paper No. 11–100.

Karkkainen, Bradley C. 2001. "Information as Environmental Regulation: TRI and Performance Benchmarking, Precursor to a New Paradigm?" *Georgetown Law Journal* 89: 257–370.

Kingsbury, Benedict, Nico Krisch, and Richard B. Stewart. 2005. "The Emergence of Global Administrative Law." *Law and Contemporary Problems* 68; 15–62.

Kinley, David, and Junko Tadaki. 2004. "From Talk to Walk: The Emergence of Human Rights Responsibilities for Corporations at International Law." *Virginia Journal of International Law* 44: 931–1024.

Kleindorfer, Paul R., and Eric W. Orts. 1998. "Informational Regulation of Environmental Risks." *Risk Analysis* 18: 155–170.

Koops, Bert-Jaap. 2008. "Criteria for Normative Technology: The Acceptability of 'Code as Law' in Light of Democratic and Constitutional Values." In Roger Brownsword and Karen Yeung, eds., *Regulatory Technologies: Legal Futures, Regulatory Frames and Technological Fixes*, 157–174. Oxford: Hart Publishing.

KPMG International. 2008. "KPMG International Survey of Corporate Responsibility Reporting." http://www.kpmg.com/global/en/issuesandinsights/articlespublications/corp orate-responsibility/pages/default.aspx.

———. 2010. *Carrots and Sticks: Promoting Transparency and Sustainability.* http://www .kpmg.com/za/en/issuesandinsights/articlespublications/advisory-publications/pages/ carrots-and-sticks-2010.aspx.

Kysar, Douglas A. 2010. *Regulating from Nowhere: Environmental Law and the Search for Objectivity.* New Haven, CT: Yale University Press.

Kysar, Douglas A., and James Salzman. 2008. "Foreword: Making Sense of Information for Environmental Protection." *Texas Law Review* 86: 1347–1364.

Landis, James M. 1938. *The Administrative Process.* New Haven, CT: Yale University Press.

Leavoy, Paul. 2010. "Does CSR Reporting Help the Planet, or Just Help Reporting?" *Greenbiz Blog*, September 30. http://www.greenbiz.com/blog/2010/09/30/does-csr-reporting-h elp-planet-or-just-help-reporting?page=0%2C1.

Levy, David L., Halina Szejnwald Brown, and Martin de Jong. 2010. "The Contested Politics of Corporate Governance: The Case of the Global Reporting Initiative." *Business and Society* 49: 88–115.

Lobel, Orly. 2004. "The Renew Deal: The Fall of Regulation and the Rise of Governance in Contemporary Legal Thought." *Minnesota Law Review* 89: 342–470.

MacLean, Richard, and Kathee Rebernak. 2007. "Closing the Credibility Gap: The Challenges of Corporate Responsibility Reporting." *Environmental Quality Management* 16: 1–6.

Manetti, Giacomo, and Becatti, Lucia. 2009. "Assurance Services for Sustainability Reports: Standards and Empirical Evidence." *Journal of Business Ethics* 87: 289–298.

Mattli, Walter, and Tim Büthe. 2005. "Global Private Governance: Lessons from a National Model of Setting Standards in Accounting." *Law and Contemporary Problems* 68: 225–262.

Meidinger, Errol. 2006. "The Administrative Law of Global Private-Public Regulation: The Case of Forestry." *European Journal of International Law* 17: 47–87.

Nazari, Mehrdad. 2011. "GRI Reporting Grows by 30% in USA and 50% in Canada." *PRIZMA Blog*, March 9. http://prizmablog.com/2011/03/09/gri-reporting-grows-by-30-in-usa-and-50-in-canada/.

O'Dwyer, Brendan, and David L. Owen. 2005. "Assurance Statement Practice in Environmental, Social and Sustainability Reporting: A Critical Evaluation." *British Accounting Review* 37: 205–229.

Pizzani, Lori. 2010. "Disclosing Environmental Risks." CFA Magazine, September–October. http://www.cfainstitute.org/learning/products/publications/cfm/Pages/cfm.v21.n5.16.aspx.

Power, Michael. 2007. *Organized Uncertainty: Designing a World of Risk Management.* Oxford: Oxford University Press.

2004. *The Risk Management of Everything: Rethinking the Politics of Uncertainty.* London: Demos. http://www.demos.co.uk/files/riskmanagementofeverything.pdf.

Ratner, Steven R. 2001. "Corporations and Human Rights: A Theory of Legal Responsibility." *Yale Law Journal* 111: 443–546.

Ruggie, John Gerard. 2007. "Business and Human Rights: The Evolving International Agenda." *American Journal of International Law* 101: 819–840.

Sarfaty, Galit A. 2012. *Values in Translation: Human Rights and the Culture of the World Bank.* Stanford: Stanford University Press.

2009. "Why Culture Matters in International Institutions: the Marginality of Human Rights at the World Bank." *American Journal of International Law* 103: 647–683.

Shaffer, Gregory C., and Mark A. Pollack. 2010. "Hard vs. Soft Law: Alternatives, Complements and Antagonists in International Governance." *Minnesota Law Review* 94: 706–799.

Spence, David B., and Frank Cross. 2000. "A Public Choice Case for the Administrative State." *Georgetown Law Journal* 89: 97–142.

Stephan, Paul B. 2011. "Privatizing International Law." *Virginia Law Review* 97: 1573–1664.

Sugarman, Stephen D., and Nirit Sandman. 2007. "Fighting Childhood Obesity Through Performance-Based Regulation of the Food Industry." *Duke Law Journal* 56: 1403–1490.

Sunstein, Cass R. 1999. "Informational Regulation and Informational Standing: Akins and Beyond." *University of Pennsylvania Law Review* 147: 613–675.

Tilt, Carol A. 2009. "Corporate Responsibility, Accounting and Accountants." In Samuel O. Idowu and Walter Leal Filho, eds., *Professionals' Perspectives of Corporate Social Responsibility*, 11–32. London and Hamburg: Springer.

United Nations Environment Programme, KPMG, Global Reporting Initiative and Unit of Corporate Governance in Africa, University in Stellenbosch Business School. 2010. "Carrots and Sticks – Promoting Transparency and Sustainability: an Update on Trends in Voluntary and Mandatory Approaches to Sustainability Reporting." http://www.kpmg.com/EE/et/teenused/Noustamine/Juhtimisnoustamine/Juhtimine/Documents/Carrots-and-Sticks-2010.pdf.

Vandenbergh, Michael P. 2007. "The New Wal-Mart Effect: The Role of Private Contracting in Global Governance." *UCLA Law Review* 54: 913–970.

4

The Quest for Measuring Development

The Role of the Indicator Bank

María Angélica Prada Uribe

INTRODUCTION

Development indicators constitute a technology of global governance because of their knowledge and their governance effects. The knowledge effect is determined by the underlying development theory that is promoted by both indicator users and generators, which may be articulated through an economic, an institutional, or a rights-based frame of reference. The increased use of expert knowledge in the development field has encouraged the use of indicators as a proxy for development not only by hegemonic institutions, such as the World Bank, but also by other indicator users or generators that seek to contest the development "commonsense."[1] The World Bank remains one of the most important producers and users of indicators, and through its World Development Indicators (WDI) it has managed to promote hegemonic theories of development based on economics-based frames of reference. Although the World Bank has expanded its development discourse to include concerns of institutions and rights-based approaches, it has continuously relied on economic indicators as the main tool to measure development.

Once the knowledge that is being promoted by the development indicator is established, it becomes easier to unveil the production of standards and identities that are being shaped in the development field as a result of the use of a specific indicator. The development knowledge disseminated by the indicator in turn shapes the outcome of its governance effect. As described in the third section, indicators can have a wide range of effects on global governance; however, the most common ones for the development field are the regulatory effect and the allocation of responsibilities. The regulatory effect should be understood as a type of governance

A preliminary version of this article was published in Maria Angelica Prada Uribe (2012), "Development Through Data? A Case Study on the World Bank's Performance Indicators and Their Impact on Development in the Global South." IRPA Research Paper No. 5/2012.

at a distance, as "indicator users" can influence the performance of "indicator targets" by sending signals of the kind of society that is expected from developed societies, This effect increases when performance indicators are used to allocate aid based on the economic incentive. Furthermore, indicators have a state-centered bias; they are therefore used to allocate responsibility for failure of development and increased poverty to the receiving states, leaving the donor community unaccountable.

The use of performance indicators has increased in development assistance as a result of an ineffectiveness complex that has emerged as a result of the constant failure of development institutions to eradicate poverty and achieve development in the Global South. The oldest performance indicator is the Performance-Based Allocation System used by the International Development Association (IDA). A close look at the genealogy of this indicator shows how the changes and continuities in its content reflect the type of knowledge that is favored by IDA.

THE STRUGGLE FOR MEASURING DEVELOPMENT: THE DOMINANT POSITION OF THE WORLD BANK IN THE DEVELOPMENT FIELD

The use of indicators in development cooperation is an important part of the larger struggle for determining the development commonsense within the development field. The development field is a transnational space where national, international, and regional actors interact and struggle to determine the development commonsense that will prevail over the others. The actors who participate in such a struggle are (1) the donor institutions, whether national or multinational, (2) the receiving states, (3) the elites of the developing countries, (4) the social movements from the South, (5) nongovernmental organizations, and (6) development experts. These actors battle to determine an ideal model of delivering development to a society that is labeled as underdeveloped.

Another way to characterize these actors is by classifying them as "indicator users," "indicator generators," or "indicator targets." "Indicator users" are the actors that rely on indicators for making decisions or substantiating claims. "Indicator generators" are the entities who have the know-how to produce development indicators; this category includes not only aid agencies but also other actors such as nongovernmental organizations (NGOs) and academic or private institutions. Finally, "indicator targets" are those whose behavior the indicators are measuring (Dutta 2010, 13).

The World Bank is a predominant actor within the development field and plays a central role in the framing of development knowledge, in part through the use and generation of development indicators. Despite the fact that the International Bank for Reconstruction and Development (IBRD) had been created during the Bretton Woods Conference primarily as a tool for the reconstruction of Europe after the end of the Second World War, the Bank soon became more occupied with its secondary mandate of development. The leadership role taken by this organization was a result of three events taking place between 1949 and 1960: "the decision to attach conditions to Fund lending; the shift by the World Bank from infrastructural development plans to a broader focus on poverty; and, finally, the creation in 1960 of the International Development Association (IDA) as part of the International Bank for Reconstruction and Development (IBRD)" (Pahuja 2011, 37). Indeed, the creation of IDA was one of the most important events in the transformation of the organization into a Bank of Development and away from its original objective of reconstruction. However, it was not until 1968 with the arrival of Robert McNamara as president of the organization that the Bank explicitly and prominently became a development agency (Stern and Ferreira 1997, 534).

Despite the predominance of the Bank, its development commonsense has remained contested by different actors. The contestation of development knowledge has increased as a result of the rise new actors, especially of a non-Western origin, such as those from Japan and professionals from the Global South (Easterly 2006, 8). As the World Bank has relied on expert knowledge and quantitative methods as authorities to legitimize the production of development knowledge, contesting views of development also have to be articulated through the lens of the same expertise to gain validity. This has shifted the struggle within the field of development cooperation into one of representing realities through the dissemination of expert and quantitative knowledge. The increased demand for expert knowledge has in turn also increased the demand for indicators, as they are perceived as objective and scientific, thus legitimizing their central role in decision making. As discussed in depth in the text that follows, new "indicator generators" have sought to displace the hegemony of the World Bank through the production of indicators. For example, during the late 1980s Mahbub ul-Haq and the United Nations Development Program promoted a new debate regarding the notion of development through the publication of the Human Development Index, which aimed to challenge the hegemony of gross domestic product (GDP) as an adequate measure for development.

But the interaction between actors is not merely one of contestation. They often cooperate through networks to facilitate the production and dissemination of knowledge. Cooperation efforts among different actors may lead to the creation of epistemic communities that share discourses and promote determined worldviews and regimes of truth (Haas 1992, 2). Epistemic communities may be national, regional, or transnational. A clear example of a transnational epistemic community is the Washington Consensus, which promotes a neoliberal common knowledge established through the interaction among the World Bank, the International Monetary Fund (IMF), and the United States Treasury Department, and was later accepted by other actors.[2] The formation of an epistemic community does not necessarily involve the formal or physical meeting of its members. Collaborative work has also shaped the content of specific indicators. For example, the "specific theoretical claims embodied in the Doing Business indicators reflect ideas disseminated through networks linking elite academic economists to the World Bank" (Kevin, Kingsbury, and Merry 2012, 91). The collaboration that binds actors in different countries or institutions with common policy agendas strongly supports the existence of transnational epistemic communities within the development field (Haas 1992, 17).

The dominance of the World Bank has also been a result of its transformation into a "knowledge bank." This transformation has been most commonly related to the introduction of the Bank's knowledge-based aid agenda in the 1998–1999 World Development Report (WDR) called "Knowledge for Development" (World Bank 1999).[3] Although the policy of development knowledge within the Bank was indeed consolidated during the presidency of James Wolfensohn, the production of the World Development Reports and the World Development Indicators (WDIs) constitutes an older strategy to promote development knowledge that was initiated by Robert McNamara (Stern and Ferreira 1997, 571). Although the Bank has always been characterized by the harvest of data, with the production of the first WDR in 1978 it started using its access to data to produce "a decent statistical picture of development" (Yusuf et al. 2009, 20). At the time, this was a considerable innovation. From then on, arguments on development were expected to be backed by numbers. In this way, the WDIs, which were an annex to the earlier WDRs, helped change the nature of development discourse (Yusuf et al. 2009, 20).

The WDIs provide a window to the Bank's approach to development at a particular time, because both the use and generation of indicators in the Bank have been responsive to changes in the development agenda of the organization (Stern and Ferreira 1997, 572). As has been recognized by Terence Halliday, the use and form of indicators reflect the structure and dynamics of the ecology of the organization in which it is embedded (Davis et al. 2012, 181). Since 1996 the WDIs became a separate publication, and the traditional annex to the WDRs was replaced by a set of selected indicators that examine the progress of the world in three broad areas: people, the environment, and the economy (World Bank 1996, 180). The WDIs have become so valuable within the development field that they are issued annually in a separate volume that competes with the WDRs in size and sales (Yusuf et al. 2009, 46). The Bank has become a major data provider; as a result, every year an increasing part of the WDI is generated in-house and not just compiled from other sources by the Bank staff (Yusuf et al. 2009, 111). Therefore, through the WDIs the Bank has become the leading generator of development indicators worldwide.

As a result, the World Bank uses indicators as a tool to promote a determined knowledge of development. The development knowledge promoted by the Bank has changed over time, but has all the while been based on an economic approach to development. This common feature can be seen in the different versions of the World Bank's Performance Indicator (see the fourth section).

Identifying common frames of reference within development indicators can be very useful, as it helps to reveal the representation of the world that lies beneath the claims of expert knowledge. Among the large number of worldviews that have been promoted, three frames of reference can be identified according to the way that claims of development have been articulated: an economics-based approach, an institutions-based approach, and a rights-based approach. A frame of reference does not represent a shared set of principles or a common group of like-minded theories; it only provides a common language, set of meanings, and methodological approaches, which serve as a basis for the identification of problems and solutions. These tools, that is, the shared language, meanings, and methodology, allow each framework to harbor contesting development theories.

The economics-based approach has prevailed among most actors in the development field. This frame of reference focuses on economic relations, economic policies, and economic models for development. The institutions-based frame of reference sees development from the standpoint of political and legal theory, but more specifically from those theories that believe that the improvement of a state's institutions is either the only way to achieve development or one of its main objectives. A caveat should be made regarding the distinction between economics-based and institutions-based approaches to development. Since the late 1990s the Washington consensus has been broadened by a growing recognition that economic policies alone will not achieve economic development unless the country's institutional environment is improved (Altmann 2011, 135). Therefore, the current development commonsense, influenced by new institutional economics,[4] has bridged economics- and institutions-based-approaches to development through the belief that institutions are a key factor in the process of economic development. However, the distinction remains useful in analyzing theories of development that treat legal or institutional considerations as exogenous to economic development, such as some neoclassical theories (Douglass 1993, 5), and theories of development that regard institutions, the rule of law, or good governance as intrinsic or instrumental factors of development.[5]

The rights-based approach to development encompasses those theories that focus on social and human concerns, not just as mere means to achieve economic development but as the main objectives of the development process. It has been argued that the distinctive feature of a rights-based approach to development is that it brings an ethical and moral dimension to development cooperation, as it is based on a normative dimension of what development ought to be (Cornwall and Nyamu-Musembi 2004, 1416). Some rights-based approaches also recognized the importance of economic growth in the process of development.[6]

WHY DEVELOPMENT INDICATORS MATTER: THE KNOWLEDGE AND GOVERNANCE EFFECT

Indicators in the development field create not only realities, but also identities, as by promoting a determined development discourse they also promote the categories embedded in it. The establishment of identities, in turn, divides the development actors into a hierarchical order in which some of them are placed above the others. The place of a state in the development hierarchy depends on how far it is able to achieve the development goals and standards set by the specific indicator. During the postwar period, for example, the United States promoted the use of GDP as a proxy for development, which conveniently positioned the United States at the top of the development scale (Pahuja 2011, 64). Underneath the categorization of indicator targets lies the attribution of a moral high ground for those states that comply with the development standards, and are thus able to emulate the ideal type of a developed society. A state with good results in the economic, corruption, governance, or human rights indicators, among others, is seen as an example of development for other less successful states to follow.

The World Bank created two of the most influential indicators, based on an economic framework, which have since determined the identities not only of states but also of individuals within the development field: the division of states into Low-Income, Middle–Income, and High-Income countries depending on their income per capita[7]; and the production of a specific type of "poor" through the creation of the absolute poverty line. Regarding the division of a state into different levels of development, the World Bank realized that the division of the globe between developed and underdeveloped nations did not respond to the growing heterogeneity within the developing world. For this reason the Bank used the gross national product per person to create a new indicator that divided developing countries into Low-Income countries and Middle-Income countries. As a result, the "Third World" was broken up at the very moment in which it was expressing its collective demands. Soon, the common interest between these groups, based more on their colonial past than on a collective project of the future, disappeared, together with the possibility of collective mobilization. Furthermore, to be classified as a Low-Income or Middle-Income country had, and still has, an important governance effect because only those states categorized as Low-Income countries can receive concessional lending from the IDA, and are subject to the Debt Sustainability Framework promoted by both the World Bank and the IMF.

On the other hand, the international poverty line (IPL) created by the World Bank uses a money metric threshold of poverty. To determine an IPL the Bank compiled data on national poverty lines across thirty-three countries and proposed a poverty line for Low-Income countries of US$1 per day at purchasing power parity (PPP). The Bank established a new poverty line in 2013 of US$1.25 per day at 2005 PPP (World Bank 2013a, 375). This indicator of poverty is based on the consumption power of individuals because, according to the Bank, "consumption is thought to better capture long-run welfare levels" (World Bank 2001, 17). Through the use of an economics-based indicator of poverty the World Bank has created poor persons based on their purchasing power, without taking into account other types of noneconomic wealth that can be important for some communities. Many people around the world were transformed into poor, a new category, just for not having the power to purchase commodities. Thus, indicators are a technology of development discourse because they represent a discursive or ideological form of power that sustains a determined development agenda.

The Governance Effect

The governance effect of indicators depends highly on the type of knowledge that is being promoted through their use because indicators send a message to the receiving states regarding the development model that they should follow, and the states in turn have an incentive to accommodate such signals. Thus, indicators have a regulatory effect on the conduct of "indicator targets," which confirms the power of indicators to act as a technology of governance at a distance. The regulatory effect can be exercised by the naming and shaming of the indicators targets, primarily states, which have a poor performance in the relevant aspect of development that is being promoted by the indicator. Indicators are an important tool for this purpose, because they are used by academic researchers, economic commentators, policymakers, and policy advisers around the world. This is exemplified by the fact that the WDI database is accessed by tens of millions of subscribers around the world; of the 18.8 million registered online users 10 million are in Low- and Middle-Income countries (Yusuf et al. 2009, 111). Another form of governance at a distance is the new trend in development cooperation of using performance indicators to determine the allocation of aid. This specific use of indicators is addressed in the case study in the following section.

The promotion of development knowledge as a form of distance regulation is not the only effect of indicators. Development indicators are also a form of allocating responsibility for poverty and underdevelopment within the development field. The issue of who is responsible for poverty and the failure of development is decisive to determine what kinds of actions should be undertaken to change that situation.

Different theories have presented an answer to the question of what or who is creating poverty and "underdevelopment." Economic theories of development, such as modernization and neoliberal theories, would agree that the "developing state" is the one to be blamed for this situation because its backwardness, and they would also agree that economic growth is the ultimate means and end of development. However, they would disagree on policy changes, and on whether a regulatory state or a laissez faire economy is needed to achieve development. Institutions-based theories also locate the responsibility in the state and sometimes in a society as a whole, whether it argues that underdevelopment is caused by the states' lack of legal institutions and rule of law or continuous corruption.

In most cases those theories that promote *counter-hegemonic* or *"change of paradigm"* worldviews would have a different answer to the same question. In many cases they will use injustice (Benford, and Snow 2000, 613) and adversarial frames (Gamson 1992, 112) to articulate their claims, first by identifying the victim of a given injustice and then by determining who is to blame for the injustice. For example, dependency theories proposed a shift in the burden of development. Instead of seeing developing states as responsible for their own underdevelopment, they pointed their blaming finger to the systematic failures of the international economic arrangements. Another example is given by Thomas Pogge, who argues that the global economic order is unjust because it maintains and perpetuates global poverty. He proposes to stop thinking about world poverty in terms of helping the poor and to start thinking about institutional reforms at the global level (Pogge 2008, 30).

Development indicators play a role in maintaining developing states as the main responsible party for poverty and underdevelopment within its own borders. As has already been discussed, the use of indicators remains state-centered, because indicators implicitly send a message on the actions that are expected of the state to solve the specific problem of development that is being measured. Whether indicators are measuring GDP, corruption, or basic needs, they place the main burden of responsibility for development in the action of states (or even their inaction when the Washington Consensus is involved). The allocation of responsibility in the developing states obscures the fact that the development field is shaped by a great variety of actors, especially by the global order, and donor states and institutions. This reinforces one of the main problems in the field of development cooperation – the lack of accountability of development agencies – which has continued to flourish owing to the weak incentives that follow collective action toward broad goals (Easterly 2006, 15).

Some of the features of indicators – simplification, evaluation, standard setting (Davis, Kingsbury, and Merry 2012) – are at the same time their strength and weakness. The power of indicators as a tool for global governance is limited by its own attributes. Although possible, it would be more complex to use an indicator to represent and measure the effect that policy conditionality has had on world poverty than to establish more simple data such as the international poverty line. Indicators could not easily give an account of how the donor community is to blame for poverty and underdevelopment, because they have continuously imposed structural adjustments with an imperfect knowledge of the local environment (Nissanke 2010, 83). With a different approach, indicators could in some cases be used to shift the burden of responsibility. However, thus far, the use of indicators for this purpose has been scarce. In some cases the civil society of donor countries or the state members of aid institutions use indicators to support or contest the effectiveness of development programs, but this is done primarily to make donor institutions accountable for the expenditure of the contributors' money. For example, the World Bank has created a Corporate Score Card, which allows donor and receiving states to assess and measure the Bank's overall performance through a range of indicators (World Bank 2013b). Nevertheless, the lack of mechanisms for participation and ownership in the development field has prevented contestation by non-hegemonic development actors. The few existing mechanisms of ownership, such as the Poverty Reduction Strategy Paper (see the fourth section) in the World Bank, provide a limited space for participation, as receiving governments are expected to pick and choose development policies and goals from a set of accepted preestablished objectives that reflect the hegemonic theory promoted by the donor institution. For example, it is expected that countries negotiating a Poverty Reduction Strategy Paper include policies that would help to achieve the Millennium Development Goals (MDGs) (IDA-16 2011, 8).

THE USE OF INDICATORS IN DEVELOPMENT COOPERATION: A CASE STUDY OF THE WORLD BANK'S PERFORMANCE INDICATOR

The Expansion of Indicators in Development Cooperation

The increased demand for development indicators has also recently reached the field of development aid allocation, primarily owing to the continuous existence of poverty and underdevelopment despite the large efforts undertaken by donor institutions. Historically, the decision to allocate aid was understood to be a prerogative of each donor, who would take into consideration first and foremost its own interest and in fewer cases the recipient's needs. Many studies have identified a large number of factors that have affected the allocation of aid, such as geographical neighborhood, colonial and historical ties, linguistic and ethnic ties, political and strategic alliances, and the effect of lobbying groups in donor countries (Schabbel 2007, 91).

In the last decades a great number of scholars started to claim that the main reason why aid remained ineffective was an incorrect policy of aid allocation. The most famous and influential study was produced by Burnside and Dollar, who claim to have demonstrated, using regression analysis, that aid can be more effective in incrementing economic growth if it is allocated to those countries with the best policies (Burnside and Dollar 2000). Collier and Dollar argued that aid should be targeted to countries with good policies and severe poverty (Collier and Dollar 1999). However, other studies have challenged these results, arguing that there is no relation between good policies and aid. According to these studies, aid is more effective in the more vulnerable countries, especially when they face bad economic environments (Guillaumont and Chauvet 2001). Another persuasive critique is put forward by Easterly, Levine, and Roodman, who, by adding new data to the formula used by Burnside and Dollar, demonstrate that there is no clear relation between good policy environments and growth (Easterly, Levine, and Roodman 2004, 779).

Theoretical and empirical literature remains contested regarding the principle that aid effectiveness is enhanced when allocation is directed to countries with good policies. Regardless, many donor institutions started using selectivity as a mean for enhancing aid effectiveness. An early approach to performance indicators is the Performance-Based Allocation System used by the World Bank's IDA, which has been used since the late 1970s and has continuously evolved over time (International Development Association [IDA] 2004). In a few words, IDA allocates its resources based on each country's ranking in the IDA Country Performance Ratings (ICP), which is the result of aggregating different indicators. This model has also been followed by the African Development Bank (African Development Group 2008, 2), the Asian Development Bank (Asian Development Bank 2012), and the US Millennium Challenge Corporation (Dennis 2008, 1–6).

As with all indicators, performance-based indicators (PBIs) also have knowledge and governance effects. To determine the specific type of knowledge that a development indicator is promoting, it is necessary to analyze each one of its components, as will be done with IDA's Performance-Based Allocation System in the following section. Regarding the governance effect, the use of indicators to allocate aid could increase the incentives that receiving states have to accommodate their practices to the requirements of the indicator. For example, the US State Department's Trafficking in Persons Report claims that the PBIs used by the US Millennium Challenge Corporation have fostered national antitrafficking legislation (Johnson and Zajonc 2006, 10; Davis, Kingsbury, and Merry 2012, 84).[8]

The World Bank's Performance-Based Allocation System

Just as the rings in a tree trunk mirror past changes in the surrounding ecology, the changes in an indicator's components mirror changes in the development theory of both indicator generators and indicator users. The Performance-Based Allocation System of IDA is a good example of this, because the changes in its components from 1977 until today show how the economic frame of reference that dominated the development field has been partially riven to incorporate institutions- and rights-based approaches. Such changes in development knowledge have a direct impact on the outcome of the indicators' governance effect, as receiving states may try to accommodate the changing development commonsense to receive a higher portion of IDA's resources.

Genealogy of the Indicator

The IDA is one of the two major institutions that comprise the World Bank, and was founded as an agency in 1966 (Schabbel 2007, 15). The objective of the Bank was to help Low-Income countries repay their loans and to create an institution that would award concessional lending (Libby 1975, 1067). Only the poorest countries can access IDA's lending. Currently eighty-one countries are eligible to receive IDA's resources (World Bank 2014a). The eligibility for IDA financing depends on two factors: "(i) relative poverty defined as GNI per capita below an established threshold; and (ii) lack of creditworthiness to borrow on IBRD and market terms and therefore a need for concessional resources to finance the country's development program" (IDA 2010, 1). In 1977 IDA started using a country assessment to guide the allocation of its lending resources (IDA 2004, 1). This mechanism of assessment was originally called the Country Performance Rating (CPR); however, in 1998 it was renamed the Country Policy (Van Waeyenberge 2006, 5), and Institutional Assessment and the CPR became the aggregation index described earlier. The objective of the CPR is to measure the extent to which a country's policy and institutional framework support sustainable growth and poverty reduction; thus CPIA is used as an indicator of development effectiveness within that measurement (IDA 2010, 3).

The Performance-Based Allocation System is revised during the periodic replenishment that has been carried out every three years since the creation of IDA. Donor member countries, also known as IDA deputies, conduct the replenishment and produce a final report, on the understanding that they will provide financial support as long as their funds are being used and managed in the ways outlined in the report. The report has to be approved by IDA's executive directors and its board of governors; however, it has not been their practice to reject or amend the report. During the latest replenishments the deputies have requested several modifications of the Allocation system, which have been carried out for the most part (Faint 2003, 3–4).

During the 1980s the indicators shifted their emphasis from economic performance indicators, such as growth and saving rates, to a predominant concern with policy inputs. During the early 1980s four criteria were taken into account to allocate IDA's resources: "first, national poverty as measured through income

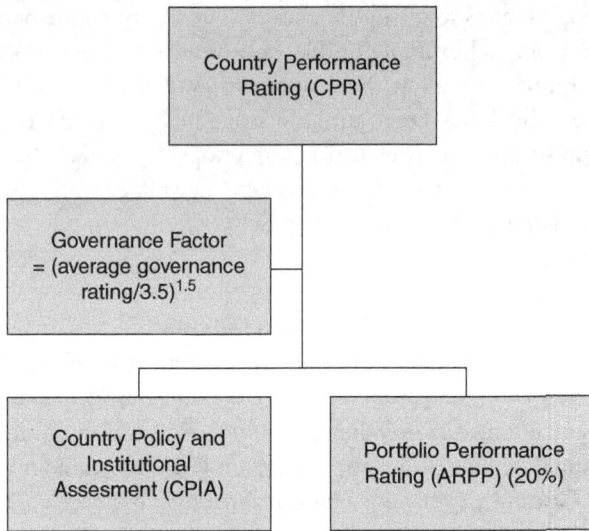

FIGURE 4.1. Country Performance Rating before 2007.
Source: IDA (2005) "Report from the Executive Directors of the International Development Association to the Board of Governors. Additions to IDA Resources: Fourteenth Replenishment."

per capita; second, creditworthiness; third, economic performance to be assessed in terms of macro indicators including growth and savings rates but also in terms of the quality of "administration and economic management" together with "the speed and direction of change"; fourth, project readiness" (Van Waeyenberge 2006, 5). These criteria clearly reflect the development commonsense promoted by the epistemic community of development professionals who advanced modernization through macroeconomic policies such as an increase in savings and, when necessary, government intervention (Kennedy 2006, 98–100).

In the 1990s the CPR included three components: "short-term economic management, long-term economic management, and poverty alleviation policies. Countries were rated in each of these three components on a scale of 1 to 5" (IDA 2007, 5). In 1993 the World Bank's Annual Report on Portfolio Performance (ARPP) was added to the CPR, and was given a weight of 20 percent (IDA 2007, 5) (see Figure 4.1). The ARPP scores are based on the percentage of IDA-funded projects in the country that are considered at risk, and these percentages are in turn translated into scores of 1 to 6 (IDA 2005, 45). The greatest change took place in 1998, when the rating was renamed the Country Policy and Institutional Assessment (CPIA) and became a determined set of twenty criteria that the Bank considered as necessary for promoting growth.

TABLE 4.1. *CPIA Criteria after 2005*

CPIA Criteria after 2005	
A. Economic Management	1. Macroeconomic Management 2. Fiscal Policy 3. Debt Policy
B. Structural Policies	4. Trade 5. Financial Sector 6. Business Regulatory Environment
C. Policies for Social Inclusion/ Equity	7. Gender Equality 8. Equity of Public Resource Use 9. Building Human Resources 10. Social Protection and Labor 11. Policies and Institutions for Environmental Sustainability
D. Public Sector Management and Institutions	12. Property Rights and Rule-based Governance 13. Quality of Budgetary and Financial Management 14. Efficiency of Revenue Mobilization 15. Quality of Public Administration 16. Transparency, Accountability, and Corruption in the Public Sector

Source: IDA (2010, 33).

Thus, the CPR was rebuilt to encompass the ARPP and the CPIA; the former continued having a weight of 20 percent and the latter was given a weight of 80 percent. In the CPIA each one of the criteria was assigned equal weight and the scale was change from 1 to 5 to 1 to 6 (IDA 2005, 5). In 2001 the CPR became more complex when the "governance factor" was added to the formula. The governance factor is calculated by dividing the governance cluster (average of the rating of the six governance criteria) of the CPIA plus the three-year moving average of the procurement flag that is an element of the portfolio rating[9] by 3.5, and then raising it to an exponent of 1.5. The result is that the rating for those governance scores above 3.5 is increased, while the rating for those below 3.5 is decreased (Nissanke 2010, 71).

From 1998 until 2005, during the IDA 14th Replenishment, the criteria that comprised part of the CPIA were modified several times, until they became the sixteen criteria that are still being used today (see Table 4.1). For example, the criterion of environmental policies was deleted in 2002 (IDA 2002) and was included again in 2005 as "policies and institutions for environmental sustainability." The "Policies for Social Inclusion/Equity" cluster was reduced from six to five criteria, its language was simplified, and the criterion of social protection and labor was newly added. The content of each one of these criteria is described in the Country Policy and Institutional Assessment Questionnaire, and the rating of each criterion is determined

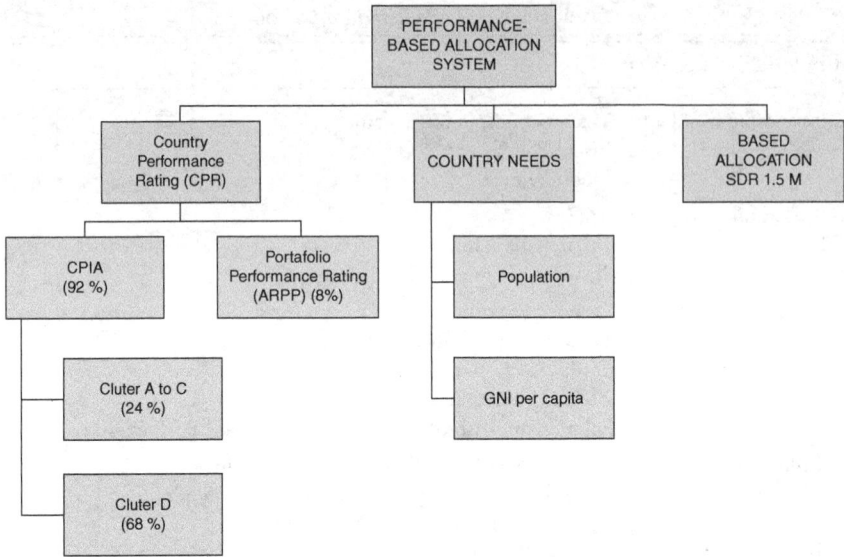

FIGURE 4.2. IDA's Performance-Based Allocation System after 2007. CPR = (0.24 × $CPIA_{A-C}$ + 0.68 × $CPIA_D$ + 0.08 × PPR). PBA = f(CPR⁵, Pop, GNIpc⁻⁰·¹²⁵) Pop is population and GNI is gross national income per capita.
Source: IDA (2010) "IDA's Performance Based Allocation System: Review of the Current System and Key Issues for IDA16."

by experts of the World Bank through the analysis of information acquired by the Bank or provided by the receiving states. These experts are also encouraged to take into account World Development indicators that measure similar phenomena when determining the score that will be given to each criterion. For example, when rating the Business regulatory environment criterion, experts are encouraged to take into account the World Bank's Doing Business Indicator (World Bank 2010, 16).

After 2005 the Performance-Based Allocation system was simplified during the IDA 15 replenishment (IDA 2010). The "Governance Factor" was eliminated; however, to maintain the predominance of good governance in the indicator the CPR was divided into different percentages (see Figure 4.2). Clusters A to C received 24 percent, while cluster D, which focuses on governance, was given 68 percent. Performance continues to be reviewed against each one of the sixteen specific criteria, and it is translated into a score from 1 (unsatisfactory) to 6 (good). Three consecutive years at 2 on a specific question automatically drops a rating to 1, while a rating at 5 over three consecutive years is automatically promoted to a 6. The final rating is the simple average score across the twenty questions. Furthermore, the Portfolio Performance Rating percentage was reduced from 20 to 8 percent. The other two elements that were added after 1998 to the Performance-Based Allocation System were variables of population and gross national income (GNI), because of the criticism that IDA did not take countries' needs into account. However, the CPIA remains the dominant factor and the countries' needs remain a moderating factor (Nissanke 2010, 72).

The Knowledge and Governance Effects

IDA has advocated the use of a Performance-Based Allocation system because it departs from arbitrary, politically driven allocation, and it provides a check on excessive aid allocation to poorly performing countries. The CPIA is seen as an accurate indicator of the quality of development policies and institutions in a country (IDA 2007, ii–3). The logic underlying the use of performance indicators to allocate development aid, as has been seen, is that they guarantee objectivity and transparency in the decision of the development donors. Furthermore, they are seen as objective because their use is supported by econometric studies, such as the one presented by Burnside and Dollar (2000), that claim to demonstrate that aid is more effective in countries with a good policy performance.

Nevertheless, the Country Performance Rating used by IDA tacitly promotes a determined development knowledge that spreads a set of standards against which a society ought to be measured. Some authors have argued that the focus on good governance promoted by IDA shows that the economic orthodoxy of the Washington Consensus is being revisited (Santiso 2001, 14). Using the notions introduced in this chapter, IDA promotes development based on an institutional frame of reference over an economics-based approach. However, "the index entirely focuses on measuring the degree of government involvement in production, distribution or consumption of goods and services, and displays a blatant anti-interventionist bias and a particular concern for the regulatory environment affecting foreign firms" (Van Waeyenberge 2006, 14). The CPIA criteria include two clusters (A and B) dedicated to measuring the economic policies of a state, emphasizing the need for adequate macroeconomic policies and institutions. Although it is true that the governance cluster has a higher percentage and, thus, a major influence in aid allocation, it is important to analyze each one of the criteria that shape this cluster.

The governance rating includes five criteria:(1) Property Rights and Rule-based Governance; (2) Quality of Budgetary and Financial Management; (3) Efficiency of Revenue Mobilization; (4) Quality of Public Administration; and (5) Transparency, Accountability, and Corruption in the Public Sector. Most of these criteria emphasize the need for improving the countries' economic institutions and environment. The property rights and rule-based governance assess, according to IDA, the extent to which private economic activity is facilitated (World Bank 2002, 21). The quality of budgetary and financial management measures whether the country has (1) a comprehensive and credible budget, linked to policy priorities; (2) an effective financial management systems to ensure that the budget is implemented as intended in a controlled and predictable way; and (3) a timely and accurate accounting and fiscal reporting. The efficiency of revenue mobilization takes into account the overall pattern of revenue mobilization (IDA 2010, 33–35). Although the first three criteria involve some sort of institutions, they are concerned primarily with economic factors of development. Therefore, only the last two criteria – quality of public administration, and transparency, accountability, and corruption in the public sector – shift from an economics-driven approach to development toward an institutions-based approach.

The macroeconomic and structural policies criteria that integrate the CPIA have been called the economic core of the indicator (Van Waeyenberge 2006, 10). However, the predominance of an economics-based approach does not outshine the fact that contesting theories of development have permeated the notion of development that is being promoted by the IDA. The Policies for Social Inclusion/Equity cluster clearly includes human and social concerns, which in other epochs remained as counter-hegemonic rights-based approaches that were merely taken into account. This confirms that the CPIA has mostly reflected the views and paradigms of hegemonic theories, and that those theories bridge with counter-hegemonic epistemic communities to expand the notion of development by incorporating new objectives. Nowadays, rights-based and institutional-based approaches have become the hegemonic theories, in part as a result of the influence exercised by the MDGs and a new "chastened neo-liberalism."

The use of CPIA suggests that in each country, regardless of its specificities, the same kind of policies (defined as good policies) promote growth and increase aid effectiveness (Schabbel 2007, 99). These policies are mostly micro- and macroeconomic, although they also value some improvements in national institutions and social and human conditions. The CPIA is an example of an eclectic mixed of ideas, given the aggregation of several indicators that promote contesting the development commonsense. Thus, the CPIA could be identified with the Post–Washington Consensus epistemic community, which is currently being promoted by several donor institutions.

The Performance-Based Allocation system used by IDA helps shape new identities within the international community. The dichotomy of "developed" and "developing" is problematized by including a division among the latter. IDA uses its own lending categories, distinguished between the

Low-Income countries, "Blend countries," and IBRD borrowers.[10] This classification divides the states in the South, creating hierarchies and stratifications among the developing states, but also in some cases the possibility to sustain affirmative actions. Low-Income Countries are IDA eligible, and therefore, they are entitled to a special treatment because of their vulnerability. However, within the

CPIA fragile states are less favored owing to their inability to achieve IDA's standards and the restricted influence of a country's needs in the indicator.

The dissemination of the Post–Washington Consensus common through the use of IDA's performance indicator sends a message to the IDA-eligible states to accommodate to the sixteen criteria to be allocated higher amounts of resources. This regulatory effect has been identified in the use of Poverty Reduction Strategic Papers (PRSPs) by the World Bank. In theory the PRSPs are a mechanism to enhance ownership of the receiving states, by encouraging them to define the policies and goals that should be promoted through development programs in their state. However, it has been proved that the CPIA serves as a guide to determine the content of PRSPs, therefore effectively regulating the receiving states' development policies (Nissanke 2010).

The underlying logic of the CPIA allocates the responsibility for development to the receiving states, premised on the belief that it is their own economic, institutional, and political performance that determines the effectiveness of aid. That is the reason why donor countries have seen the distribution of IDA's resources through the Performance-Based Allocation as a reward for the poorest states that demonstrated a commitment to good governance and the achievement of poverty reduction and economic growth (IDA 1998, 12). In other words, bad governance is punished with less aid, and it is the country's responsibility to improve its performance to avoid wasting the donor's resources. The blame for the policy failure has been placed too readily on recipient governments and institutions owing to the existence of poor policy environments. The donor community should take a fair share of the responsibility for the poor relationships that have evolved over the last decades (Nissanke 2010, 82). Abouharb and Cingranelli show how the use of structural adjustment programs by World Bank and the IMF has "lowered levels of government respect for economic and social rights, contributing to a deterioration in the situation for the mass population in these countries" (Abouharb and Cingranelli 2007, 149). Thus, the Performance-Based Allocation System can be used by the Bank to avoid its share of responsibility for the development failures that have taken place under its mandate.

Contestation and Regulation

The secretiveness that surrounded the CPIA prompted many criticisms against the World Bank, which led the Bank to start the process of disclosing all IDA information as part of its 2002 Disclosure Policy (IDA 2004, 1). CPR ratings for IDA countries were being disclosed on a quintile basis without providing the final numerical ratings or explaining the measurement process. Starting in IDA14, the numerical rating for each the CPIA and CPR criteria have been fully disclosed (IDA 2005,

44). The World Bank has expressed its intention to increase the transparency of the CPIA and to ensure ownership on the part of the receiving states. Member states of IDA have raised concerns that such transparency may cause receiving states to create pressure for changes in their ratings (IDA 2005, 7–8). Until now the receiving states have not been able to influence the elements that underlie the CPIA formula; on the contrary, IDA donors have constantly pressured for changes and adjustment to the formula and indicators (IDA 2010, 1).

Only since IDA13 replenishment in 2003 were a group of Borrower Representatives (two from Africa, two from Asia, and one each from borrowers in Europe and in Latin America) appointed with the rights to attend and speak at all deputies meetings, except those when burden sharing was being discussed (Faint 2003, 5). However, their influence remains limited compared to the leverage of the donor member States. IDA has tried to allow contestation through the use of the Result Measurement System, which is used to measure IDA's success in promoting development in the receiving states. This system is an example of indicators used to shift the burden of responsibility from the nations in the South to the donor community. However, the Result Measurement System only provides a space to discuss the results of the institutions in general, and not the use of the Performance-Based Allocation System.

Therefore, contestation and regulation of this indicator is primarily exercised by the donor member states and not by the receiving states, which could explain the lack of a broader dialogue between the mainstream development theories and contesting epistemic communities, especially those from the South promoting "change of paradigm" approaches. The absence of contestation and regulation in the production and use of the performance indicators enhances the knowledge and governance effects discussed previously. Real ownership can be achieved only through more democratic mechanisms not only in the establishment of development policies, but also in the former process of determining the development commonsense that will underlie those policies.

CONCLUSION

This chapter demonstrates that despite changes in the PBAS, IDA continues promoting a development discourse based primarily on an economics-based frame of reference. However, that commonsense does not remain merely economical, as after decades of dialogue with contesting theories of development new concerns have been added to the notion of development. This exemplifies how counter hegemonic theories of development, such as the human rights approach, have been able to permeate the hegemonic development discourse. However, the promotion of this type of knowledge by IDA sends a signal to the receiving states that economic policies and institutions remain the principal means of development. Because

IDA's indicator is used to allocate aid, eligible states interested in receiving a high amount of aid will have an incentive to accommodate to the notion of development that is being promoted by the donor agency. Furthermore, because the indicator targets of the PBAS are states, more specifically Low-Income countries, it clearly allocates responsibility for the failure or success of the development process to the performance receiving states. Leaving aside the fact that in most cases those states did not have a say in the determination of the development model that they were supposed to follow.

The predominance of economic theory also explains the hegemonic position that economic institutions, such as the World Bank and the International Monetary Fund, play in the development field. Although indicators have played a role in maintaining the struggle over the development commonsense, they have at the same time help limit the claims and discourses that can be used inside the development field. Arturo Escobar has recognized that "changing the order of discourse is a political question that entails the collective practice of social actors and the restructuring of existing political economies of truth." He argues that it would be necessary to move away from development sciences and from Western knowledge, to make room for other type of knowledge (Escobar 1995, 216). Because indicators are part of "development science," it is also necessary to move away from this technology if "change of paradigm theories" are to be included in the development discourse. The use of indicators is inherently incompatible with "change of paradigm theories," as the former advocate for context-specific notions of development while the latter, as has been shown in the chapter, seek to set universal standards against which success in development performance can be measured. Furthermore, many "change of paradigm theories" question the idea of measuring development in itself, as they argue that many of the goals pursued by a community are not quantifiable.

NOTES

1 The notion of "commonsense" should be understood as equivalent to the Gramscian notion of "hegemonic" worldview: the domination of a specific, historically determined, worldview through the insertion of its beliefs and practices as natural, universal, and rational in a community. See Gramsci (2003).

2 We use the notion of epistemic communities in a similar way as has been done by the Epistemic Communities Approach in International Relations; however, we do not subscribe to that approach primarily because of the distinction they make between knowledge and discourse. They also distinguish between decision making and epistemic communities, whereas we submit that decision makers can also be part of the epistemic community. See Haas (1992).

3 See, e.g., King and McGrath (2004).

4 See North (1990).

5 See Santos (2006).

6 For example, the Human Development Index promoted by the UNDP.

7 Today the Bank has the following four income groups, according to which economies are divided based on their 2012 GNI per capita: low income, $1,035 or less; lower middle income, $1,036–$4,085; upper middle income, $4,086–$12,615; and high income, $12,616 or more. See World Bank (2014b). "How we Classify Countries," http://data.worldbank .org/about/country-classifications.

8 An unpublished paper by Doug Johnson and Tristan Zajonc from Harvard's Kennedy School of Government shows that substantial evidence exists to conclude that the Performance Indicators used by the US Millennium Challenge Corporation influenced the conduct of several receiving states, which improved their governance environment to accommodate to the good governance standards according to which aid was allocated. See Johnson and Zajonc (2006).

9 The moving average was introduced in 2004 to reduce unwarranted volatility of the indicator. This factor was later dropped in IDA15.

10 The categories of Low-Income countries and Blend countries used by IDA, are to some extent equivalent to the income groups of low-income and lower middle income countries used by the World Bank. The difference lies in the need to distinguish between countries eligible for IDA loans and those eligible for IBRD loans. IDA loans are deeply concessional, while IBRD loans are noncessional. Blend countries are a new category created to distinguish those countries that are eligible for IDA loans because of their low per capita incomes but are also eligible for IBRD loans because they are financially creditworthy. See World Bank (2014b).

REFERENCES

Abouharb, M. Rodwan, and David Cingranelli. 2007. *Human Rights and Structural Adjustment.* Cambridge: Cambridge University Press.

African Development Bank Group. 2008. "2007 Country Performance Assessment Ratings." http://www.afdb.org/fileadmin/uploads/afdb/Documents/Project-and-Operations /30735051-EN-BANK-GROUP-CPIA-CPPR-GR-2007-DISCLOSURE.PDF.

Altmann, Matthias P. 2011. *Contextual Development Economics. A Holistic Approach to the Understanding of Economic Activity in Low-Income Countries.* New York: Springer.

Asian Development Bank. 2012. "Performance-Based Allocation Policy." http://www.adb.org/ site/adf/performance-based-allocation-policy.

Benford, Robert D., and David A. Snow. 2000. "Framing Processes and Social Movements: An Overview and Assessment." *Annual Review of Sociology* 26: 611–639.

Burnside, Craig, and David Dollar. 2000. "Aid, Policies, and Growth." *American Economic Review* 90(4): 847–868.

Collier, Paul, and David Dollar. 1999. "Aid Allocation and Poverty Reduction." *Policy Research Working Paper* No. WPS 2041:2–27. http://elibrary.worldbank.org/doi/ pdf/10.1596/1813-9450-2041.

Cornwall, Andrea, and Celestine Nyamu-Musembi. 2004. "Putting the 'Rights-Based Approach' to Development into Perspective." *Third World Quarterly* 25: 1415–1437.

Davis, Kevin E., Benedict Kingsbury, and Sally Engle Merry. 2012. "Indicators as a Technology of Global Governance." *Law and Society Review* 46: 71–104.

Dennis, Margaret. 2008. "A New Approach to Foreign Aid: A Case Study of the Millennium Challenge Account." IILJ Emerging Scholars Paper 12: 1–35. http://www.iilj.org/publications/documents/Dennis.ESP12-08.pdf.

Dutta, Nikhil K. 2010. "Accountability in the Generation of Governance Indicators." IILJ Emerging Scholars Paper 17:1–52. http://www.iilj.org/publications/EmergingScholarsPapers.asp.

Easterly, William. 2006. *The White Man's Burden*. New York: Penguin Books.

Easterly, William, Ross Levine, and David Roodman. 2004. "Aid, Policies, and Growth: Comment." *The American Economic Review* 94(3): 774–780.

Escobar, Arturo. 1995. *Encountering Development: The Making and Unmaking of the Third World*. Princeton, NJ: Princeton University Press.

Faint, Tony. 2003. "Selectivity and Accountability in IDA's Replenishments." http://siteresources.worldbank.org/IDA/Resources/selectivityreportfaint.pdf.

Gamson, William A. 1992. *Talking Politics*. Cambridge: Cambridge University Press.

Gramsci, Antonio. 2003. *Selections from the Prison Notebooks*. New York: International Publishers.

Guillaumont, Patrick, and Lisa Chauvet. 2001. "Aid and Performance: a Reassessment." *Journal of Development Studies* 37(6): 66–92.

Haas, Peter M. 1992. "Epistemic Communities and International Policy Coordination." *International Organization* 46: 1–35.

Halliday, Terrence. 2012. "Legal Yardsticks: International Financial Institutions as Diagnosticians and Designers of the Laws of Nations." In Kevin Davis, Angelina Fisher, Benedict Kingsbury and Sally Engle Merry, eds., *Governance by Indicators Global Power through Quantification and Rankings*. Oxford: Oxford University Press.

International Development Association (IDA). 1998. "Additions to IDA Resources: Twelfth Replenishment. A Partnership for Poverty Reduction." http://siteresources.worldbank.org/IDA/Resources/IDA12Report.pdf.

——— 2002. "IDA 13: Report from the Executive Directors of IDA to the Board of Governors Additions to IDA Resources: Thirteenth Replenishment." http://www.worldbank.org/ida/papers/IDA13_Replenishment/FinaltextIDA13Report.pdf.

——— 2004. "Disclosing IDA Country Performance Ratings (IDA/R2004-0210)." http://www.worldbank.org/ida/papers/IDA_Disclosing_CPR.pdf.

——— 2005. "IDA 14: Report from the Executive Directors of the International Development Association to the Board of Governors. Additions to IDA Resources: Fourteenth Replenishment." http://siteresources.worldbank.org/IDA/Resources/14th_Replenishment_Final.pdf.

——— 2007. "IDA 15: Selectivity and Performance: Ida's Country Assessment and Development Effectiveness." http://siteresources.worldbank.org/IDA/Resources/Seminar%20PDFs/73449-1172525976405/3492866-1172527584498/PBAEffectiveness.pdf.

——— 2010. "IDA 16: IDA's Performance Based Allocation System: Review of the Current System and Key Issues for IDA16." http://siteresources.worldbank.org/IDA/Resources/Seminar%20PDFs/73449-1271341193277/PBAIDA16.pdf.

——— 2011. "IDA 16: Report from the Executive Directors of the International Development Association to the Board of Governors." http://www.worldbank.org/ida/ida-16-replenishment.html.

Johnson, Doug, and Tristan Zajonc. 2006. "Can Foreign Aid Create an Incentive for Good Governance? Evidence from the Millennium Challenge Corporation." Working

Paper Series John F. Kennedy School of Government. http://www.people.fas.harvard.edu/~tzajonc/mcc_wp_apr06.pdf.

Kennedy, David. 2006. "The "Rule of Law," Political Choices and Development Common Sense." In David M. Trubek, and Alvaro Santos, eds., *The New Law and Economic Development*. Cambridge: Cambridge University Press.

Libby, Ronald T. 1975. "International Development Association: A Legal Fiction Designed to Secure the LDC Constituency." *International Organizations* 29(4): 1065–1072.

Nissanke, Machiko. 2010. "The Aid Effectiveness Debate." In George Mavrotas, ed., *Foreign Aid for Development: Issues, Challenges and the New Agenda*. New York: Oxford University Press.

North, Douglass C. 1993. "The New Institutional Economics and Development." *Economic History*, EconWPA. http://EconPapers.repec.org/RePEc:wpa:wuwpeh:9309002. http://www.deu.edu.tr/userweb/sedef.akgungor/Current%20topics%20in%20Turkish%20Economy/north.pdf.

Pahuja, Sundhya. 2011. *Decolonising International Law Development, Economic Growth and the Politics of Universality*. Cambridge: Cambridge University Press.

Pogge, Thomas. 2008. *World Poverty and Human Rights*. Malden, MA: Polity Press.

Santiso, Carlos. 2001. "Good Governance and Aid Effectiveness: The World Bank and Conditionality." *The Georgetown Public Policy Review* 7: 1–22.

Santos, Alvaro. 2006. "The World Bank's Uses of the "Rule of Law" Promise in Economic Development." In David M. Trubek, and Alvaro Santos, eds., *The New Law and Economic Development*. Cambridge: Cambridge University Press.

Schabbel, Christian. 2007. *The Value Chain of Foreign Aid. Development, Poverty Reduction, and Regional Conditions*. New York: Springer.

Stern, Nicholas, and Francisco Ferreira. 1997. "The World Bank as 'Intellectual Actor'." In Devesh Kapur, John P. Lewis, and Richard Webb, eds., *The World Bank: Its First Half Century,*. Washington, DC: The Brookings Institution.

Van Waeyenberge, Elisa. 2006. "The Missing Piece: Country Policy and Institutional Assessments at the Bank." Paper presented at the Singapore Workshop on the World Bank Papers, Singapore, September 19–21.

World Bank. 1996. *World Development Indicators 1996: From Plan to Market*. Washington, DC: World Bank.

1999. *World Development Report 1998/99: Knowledge for Development*. Washington, DC: World Bank.

2001. *World Development Report 2000/2001: Attacking Poverty*. Washington, DC: World Bank.

2002. "Country Policy and Institutional Assessment 2002. Assessment Questionnaire." http://siteresources.worldbank.org/IDA/Resources/CPIA2002.pdf.

2010. "Country Policy and Institutional Assessment. 2010 Assessment Questionnaire." http://www.worldbank.org/ida/IRAI/2010/CPIA-criteria-2010.pdf.

2013a. *World Development Report 2013: Jobs*. Washington, DC: World Bank.

2013b. "World Bank Corporate ScoreCard April 2013." http://databank.worldbank.org/data/download/World%20Bank%20Corporate%20Scorecard.pdf.

2014a. "IDA Borrowing Countries." http://web.worldbank.org/WBSITE/EXTERNAL/EXTABOUTUS/IDA/0,,contentMDK:20054572~menuPK:3414210~pagePK:51236175~piPK:437394~theSitePK:73154,00.html.

2014b. "How We Classify Countries." http://data.worldbank.org/about/country-classifications.

Yusuf, Shahid, Angus Deaton, Kemal Dervis, William Easterly, Takatoshi Ito, and Joseph E. Stiglitz. 2009. *Development Economics through the Decades A critical look at 30 years of the World Development Report.* Washington, DC: World Bank. http://www-wds .worldbank.org/external/default/WDSContentServer/IW3P/IB/2009/01/14/000334955_2 0090114045203/Rendered/PDF/471080PUB0Deve101OFFICIAL0USE0ONLY1.pdf.

5

Tradeoffs in Accountability

Conditionality Processes in the European Union and Millennium Challenge Corporation

Nikhil K. Dutta

INTRODUCTION

The American aid apparatus found itself in a quandary at the end of the last millennium. The dissolution of the Soviet Union had robbed it of one reason for being: providing material support to allies in the Cold War and bolstering friendly governments in countries in danger of succumbing to Soviet influence. Decades of anecdotal experience and recent empirical research threatened to deprive it of another, as critics suggested that US aid disbursements neither stimulated economic growth nor lessened poverty but in fact, might be correlated with worse economic outcomes in recipients. American aid budgets steadily decreased during the decade following the end of the Cold War,[1] as the commitment of other developed nations to assisting poor countries appeared to increase. By the early 2000s, with the development of the United Nations Millennium Development Goals and an apparently renewed commitment to combating worldwide poverty among countries in the Organisation for Economic Co-operation and Development, the US aid establishment appeared in need of revitalization.

The European Union (EU) faced a different challenge in the last decade of the millennium, as the anticipated accession of Austria, Finland, and Sweden in 1996 left EU expansion at a crossroads. On the one hand, the pan-European rhetoric of the post-Soviet years suggested that the countries of Central and Eastern Europe next deserved consideration for a place in the Union[2]; on the other hand, concerns about cultural, political, and economic gaps between EU members and would-be members made the former hesitant to commit to the latter's accession.[3]

The United States met the challenge to its aid institutions by creating a new organization in 2004, the Millennium Challenge Corporation (MCC), that aimed to assist only governments that had demonstrated the capacity to use this assistance to benefit their people. The EU resolved the dilemma posed by its course of expansion by committing in 1993 to the accession of its eastern neighbors provided that these countries could demonstrate that they were economically sound, respected human rights, and had the political and administrative capacity to function as members of the Union. Thus, both the United States and the European Union responded to their challenges by implementing *conditionality processes*, or *processes that conditioned the transfer of benefits to recipients on demonstration by those recipients of compliance with certain standards*.

The US and EU conditionality processes differ in important respects, but one major difference lies in the way that each assesses country compliance. The MCC uses twenty quantitative indicators[4] that purport to measure how successfully countries govern in varying respects; it compares the indicator scores of individual countries to those of other countries with similar incomes and requires passing scores on a minimum number of indicators before a country may become eligible to receive funding. The MCC thus employs what we will call a *quantitative conditionality process*, or a *conditionality process in which potential recipients of benefits are judged by reference to quantitative standards*. The EU, in contrast, does not attempt to quantify the performance of candidates for accession. Instead, it uses regular reports (based in part on third-party monitoring of candidates) and regular meetings between EU officials and officials of candidate countries to flesh out the standards applicable to candidates, judge candidates' performance, and communicate these judgments. Thus, the EU uses a *qualitative conditionality process*, or a *conditionality process in which potential recipients of benefits are judged by reference to qualitative standards*. This process is largely devoid of quantification.

As exercises of transnational power, both the EU and MCC conditionality processes raise concerns about *accountability*,[5] which we define as *giving accounts to others and permitting others to make demands as to one's conduct*.[6] These concerns are heightened by the way in which each process sets up a normative framework for how countries should be governed, and seeks to incentivize countries to adhere to this framework. The differing natures of the EU and MCC processes give us an opportunity to test some hypotheses about how the use of numbers or narratives affects accountability. In particular, we focus on three components of accountability: legibility, reason-giving, and participation.[7] Are qualitative conditionality processes more opaque? Are quantitative conditionality processes less inclined to justification and more closed to participation? This chapter explores these questions in the EU and MCC contexts.

HOW THE MCC AND EU MAKE DECISIONS

Both the MCC and the EU have sophisticated websites that make available a variety of documentation describing how their conditionality processes work (European Commission [EC] 2013g; MCC 2014i).

The MCC's Three-Step Process for Selecting Recipients

Although the MCC has tinkered with its selection approach over the years, it essentially determines who receives its assistance in three steps. It first identifies candidate countries by income level; next, it selects countries eligible for MCC assistance based on their scores on indicators developed by third parties, as well as some other considerations; and finally, it enters into compacts with countries that have developed successful project proposals and begins disbursing funds (MCC 2014k).[8] The MCC also provides smaller grants to countries that miss being selected as eligible by a narrow margin, with these grants known as "threshold programs."

As of January 2014, the MCC had approved compacts worth more than US$9 billion in twenty-five countries, and threshold programs worth more than US$500 million in twenty-two countries (MCC 2013a, 2, 2014c). The compact programs range in funding from US$65.7 million (for the Vanuatu compact signed in March 2006 and completed in April 2011) to US$698.1 million (for the Tanzania compact signed in February 2008 and completed in September 2013) (MCC 2011b, 2013h). Threshold programs are smaller than compacts, ranging from US$6.7 million (for the program agreed with Guyana in August 2008 and completed in February 2010 to US$55 million (for the program agreed with Indonesia in October 2006) (MCC 2014g, 2014h).

In its first selection step, the MCC identifies candidate countries by considering whether their per capita incomes qualify them for inclusion in either a Low-Income category or a Lower Middle-Income category.[9] This classification matters, as countries compete against their income-group peers in the second step of MCC selection.[10] The Corporation then disqualifies from consideration countries that are ineligible to receive US economic assistance because they are subject to US or international sanctions.[11]

The methodology currently used for the MCC's second selection step was introduced in fiscal year (FY) 2012 (MCC 2011c, 4); although the new methodology differs somewhat from the methodology used earlier, the principles governing this step have remained consistent throughout the MCC's existence. As currently conceived, the second step requires the MCC's Board[12] to examine the performance of candidate countries on twenty third-party indicators[13] divided into three groups: Ruling Justly, Investing in People, and Encouraging Economic Freedom. To determine whether candidate countries are eligible to enter into a compact with the MCC, the Board considers whether these countries have achieved passing scores on at least half of the indicators; for most indicators, this means that countries must have surpassed the median score of their income peer group on the indicator, though some indicators have hard thresholds that countries must exceed to pass.[14] The Board also takes into account whether candidate countries have achieved passing scores on the Control of Corruption indicator and either the Political Rights or Civil Liberties indicator in the Ruling Justly category, and considers whether candidate countries have passed at least one indicator in each category. The Board does not confine its analysis to countries' performance on the third-party indicators; it also considers supplemental information to address weaknesses in the indicators (MCC 2013c, 4–5).

Compact-eligible countries do not automatically receive MCC assistance. In the third step of MCC selection, eligible countries design compact proposals after undertaking economic analyses and consulting with their citizens and the private sector to identify ways they can use funding to stimulate economic growth and reduce poverty (MCC 2013a, 3). The MCC decides whether to approve proposals by considering if they have broad-based in-country support; are consistent with gender, environment, and procurement guidelines; and are projected to generate adequate benefit streams (as measured by economic rate of return analyses) and deliver benefits to the poor (as determined by beneficiary analyses) (MCC 2014d). Once the MCC enters into a compact with an eligible country, the compact may nonetheless be suspended or terminated if the country has "engaged in activities contrary to the national security interests of the United States," "engaged in a pattern of actions inconsistent with MCA eligibility criteria," or "failed to adhere to its responsibilities under a compact" agreement (MCC 2014j).

As noted, compacts are not the only way in which countries may receive MCC funds, though they are most important in terms of funding volume. The MCC also awards smaller grants to support threshold programs in "countries that come close to passing [the eligibility] criteria and are firmly committed to improving their policy performance" (MCC 2014a).

The EU's Three-Step Pathway to Accession

The EU also utilizes a three-step approach to determine which countries will ultimately accede to the Union, whereby applicant countries become potential candidates, candidates, and then members (EC 2013e). Countries have thus far acceded to the EU in six waves, with two such waves in the past decade bringing thirteen additional countries into the EU.[15] As of January 2014, eight countries are participating in the process of becoming EU members; five of these countries – Iceland, Montenegro, Serbia, Turkey, and the former Yugoslav Republic of Macedonia – have become official candidate countries, while three others – Albania, Bosnia and Herzegovina, and Kosovo – remain potential candidates (EC 2013c).

The textual bases for the accession process are set out in Articles 6(1)[16] and 49[17] of the Treaty on European Union. In December 1993, the EU Council (hereafter the Council) elaborated on these provisions by promulgating the "Copenhagen criteria," which require countries that wish to join the EU to have (1) stable institutions that guarantee democracy, the rule of law, human rights, and respect for and protection of minorities; (2) a functioning market economy, as well as the ability to cope with the pressure of competition and market forces at work inside the EU; and (3) the ability to take on and implement effectively the obligations of membership, including adherence to the objectives of political, economic, and monetary union (EC 2013d).

The first step countries take toward satisfying these criteria involves the grant of what is known as a membership perspective to countries seeking to join the EU, which confers the status of potential candidate on these countries and permits them to begin implementing reforms with EU support and guidance, with an eye to attaining readiness to begin the formal process of EU accession. In the Western Balkans, this first step has taken place through what is called the Stabilisation and Association Process (SAP), whereby the EU (1) offers potential candidates trade concessions and economic and financial assistance, and (2) concludes Stabilisation and Association Agreements (SAAs) with each potential candidate[18] that set out reform objectives that the country must achieve (EC 2013e; 2011, 9). The EU monitors potential candidates' progress in fulfilling the requirements of these SAAs through regular progress reports generated by the European Commission (hereafter the Commission) (EC 2013f).

The second step of the accession process begins with a decision by the Council to accept a country's application to join the EU, leading to its recognition as a candidate country. The Council makes this decision after receiving an opinion on each country's candidacy from the Commission, and must make its decision unanimously (EC 2011, 8). The Council must then unanimously agree on a framework for membership negotiations with each candidate country (EC 2013e). Once it has done so, chapter-by-chapter negotiations may commence concerning each candidate country's adoption, implementation, and enforcement of the set of EU standards and rules known as the *acquis communautaire*, or "that which has been agreed" (EC 2013d).

The *acquis* is divided into thirty-five chapters, dealing with topics ranging from "free movement of capital," to "judiciary and fundamental rights," to "foreign, security and defence policy" (EC 2013b). In a process known as screening, the Commission first examines the extent to which each candidate has adopted the *acquis* pertaining to each chapter, and then recommends that the Council either (1) set opening benchmarks that each country must meet before negotiations on a chapter may be opened, or (2) open negotiations and set closing benchmarks that must be achieved before negotiations will be closed (EC 2013e). Achieving closing benchmarks does not permanently close negotiations on a given chapter; chapters are considered to be definitively closed only at the end of the entire negotiating process (EC 2011, 11).

Candidate countries also agree to Accession Partnerships, which identify priority areas where reforms must be implemented for countries to fulfill the Copenhagen criteria and join the EU (EC 2008, 2011, 9). The Commission monitors candidate countries' progress toward adopting the *acquis* and fulfilling the Copenhagen criteria by means of publicly available regular reports, strategy papers, and clarifications on conditions for further progress, which are presented to the Council and European Parliament (hereafter the Parliament) (EC 2013d, 2013f). These reporting mechanisms are similar to those used in the SAP (EC 2008, Annex § 6). The Commission notes that these "progress reports provide valuable feedback to the countries and signal the main areas where efforts are still required" (EC 2011, 12).

Finally, once a candidate country has completed negotiations on all the chapters of the *acquis*, the terms and conditions whereby the country will accede to the Union are incorporated into a Draft Accession Treaty (EC 2011, 13). This agreement lists all transitional arrangements and deadlines, financial arrangements, and safeguard clauses that will structure and characterize the country's transition to membership (EC 2013e). After winning the support of the Council, the Commission, and the Parliament, the Treaty must be signed by the candidate country and representatives of all member countries, whereupon it is submitted to all these countries for ratification (EC 2011, 5). Once the Treaty has been ratified, accession follows on the date the Treaty enters into force (EC 2013e).

THE LEGIBILITY OF MCC AND EU DECISION MAKING

As these descriptions of the MCC and EU conditionality processes make evident, the processes differ in the way in which they make and communicate judgments about the potential recipients of their benefits. The EU depends on context-specific monitoring and reporting of countries' progress along the path to accession, though it uses benchmarks, criteria, plans, and agreements to impose some structure on this monitoring and reporting. The MCC, in contrast, uses third-party assessments of country performance that have been converted into numbers and sets up numerical thresholds for how well countries must perform on these indicators. The MCC also uses quantitative tests to evaluate the quality of country program proposals. Importantly, the MCC process also permits the Board to rely on qualitative considerations in making decisions about country eligibility and compact conclusion, so the MCC process is not purely quantitative.

We might predict that to the extent the MCC process does employ quantitative conditionality, it will be more legible than the qualitative conditionality process of EU accession, where we define *legibility* as the *ease with which an observer can identify the basis on which a decision is to be made*. Generally speaking, one of the advantages of numbers is that they appear simpler and more portable than qualitative descriptions of phenomena. As Merry (2011, 84) explains, "numbers seem open to public scrutiny and readily accessible in a way that private opinions are not," so that "[a] key dimension of the power of indicators is their capacity to convert complicated contextually variable phenomena into unambiguous, clear, and impersonal measures." Espeland and Stevens (2008, 432, 415) similarly suggest that "[t]he enduring appeal and utility of quantification is that it facilitates the production of knowledge that transcends and integrates particularities of place, language, and custom," as numbers "easily circulate and seem straightforward to interpret." Many who study indicators have noted that these appearances may be deceiving: indicators generate the appearance of simplicity by submerging complexity about the definitions of the concepts measured (Espeland and Vannebo 2007, 32; Merry 2011, 84), the comparability of dissimilar entities (Espeland and Stevens 2008, 408; Perry-Kessaris 2011, 415), the messiness of real-world measurement (Jennings 2001, 366), difficulties in interpreting data (Merry 2011, 86), and questions about whether the phenomena represented are amenable to measurement at all (Neylan 2005, 24; Perry-Kessaris 2011, 413).

If indicators secure gains in simplicity by obscuring complexity, they nonetheless enable decision-making processes that are more mechanistic and regularized than processes based on qualitative judgments. As Porter (1995, 4–5, 8) explains, quantitative methods "permit reasoning to become more uniform, and in this sense more rigorous," thus enabling what he calls "mechanical objectivity," or "following the rules." Porter cautions that quantitative decision making is no panacea; "[m]apping the mathematics onto the world is always difficult and problematic," and to the extent "[q]uantification is a way of making decisions without seeming to decide," it obscures exercises of judgment and power. Nonetheless, to the extent quantitative conditionality processes are designed to make decisions by employing easily comprehensible numbers in a mechanical fashion, we may expect them to exhibit greater legibility than qualitative conditionality processes, as they allow observers to more easily identify the mechanisms by which decisions are supposed to be made. Such legibility makes a contribution to accountability; where observers can easily discern how a decision was supposed to be made, they can more easily identify deviations in how the decision was actually made.

The Legibility of the MCC Selection Process

As we have noted, the MCC's conditionality process is not wholly determined by quantitative measures. The first one and a half steps of the process – classifying candidate countries by income level and identifying countries that have performed satisfactorily on the third-party indicators – do rely on such measures. But the second part of the second step and the third step – selecting compact-eligible countries and finalizing compacts with countries – rely not only on quantitative measures but on qualitative considerations as well. We thus might expect the first one and a half steps of the MCC process to be quite legible and the latter one and a half steps to be more opaque. This expectation is borne out in practice. However, the extent to which even the latter half of the process appears driven by quantitative decision making, though the MCC is formally permitted to exercise relatively unconstrained discretion, is surprising.

The first one and a half steps of the MCC process are, to a large extent, comprehensible even to casual observers. In the first step, the MCC borrows income data and classifications from the World Bank and International Bank for Reconstruction and Development and then subtracts from these lists those countries to whom Congress has proscribed aid under part I of the Foreign Assistance Act of 1961. In the first part of the second step, the MCC considers whether candidate countries have achieved "passing" scores on the requisite number of indicators, a task that any observer can duplicate thanks to the MCC's publication of scorecards that graphically depict each country's scores on each indicator over the past few years. These scorecards not only include lines for each indicator score chart that separate passing from non-passing performances, but they also provide color-coded squares at the top of each scorecard that show whether each candidate country has passed each of the three indicator tests (i.e., passing more than half the indicators, passing the required indicators, and passing one indicator in each indicator group) (MCC 2013a, 8–92).[19] In less than a half-hour, one can download this document from the MCC's website and determine for oneself which countries should be eligible for funding based solely on their performance on the third-party indicators.

The second part of the second step and the third step present greater obstacles to understanding how MCC decision making works. Each step involves the use of discretion based on qualitative factors, and although the MCC has enumerated the considerations that are to guide each exercise of discretion, these considerations are too vague to furnish much legibility.

MCC Selection of Compact-Eligible Countries

The MCC makes no secret of the fact that it exercises discretion in selecting eligible countries. As its FY 2014 guide to the indicators explains, "[t]he Board may also consider information to address gaps, time lags, measurement error, or other weaknesses in the indicators to assist in assessing whether MCC funds might reduce poverty and promote economic growth in a country" (MCC 2013c, 5). The MCC's report on eligible countries explains that aside from candidate countries' performance on the twenty enumerated indicators, the Board also considers

additional quantitative and qualitative information, such as evidence of a country's commitment to fighting corruption, investments in human development outcomes, or poverty rates... The Board may also take into account the margin of error around an indicator, when applicable. In keeping with legislative directives, the Board also considered the opportunity to reduce poverty and promote economic growth in a country, in light of the overall information available, as well as the availability of appropriated funds. (MCC 2006, 2013c, 4)

The need for an exercise of discretion is plain: the MCC does not claim that the indicators it has chosen exhaust the concept of "good governance," and even concedes that these indicators may not adequately measure a country's worthiness for eligibility.[20]

There can be little doubt that the MCC Board has exercised its discretion both to select as eligible countries that did not qualify based on their indicator performance and to deny eligibility to countries that did qualify based on the indicators. In FY 2011, for example, fifteen Low-Income countries satisfied the MCC's indicator criteria – Benin, Bolivia, Gambia, Ghana, Guyana, Lesotho, Malawi, Moldova, Nicaragua, Philippines, Rwanda, Senegal, Tanzania, Vietnam, and Zambia – while three Lower Middle-Income countries – Jordan, Sri Lanka, and Thailand – passed the test (MCC 2010a). Of these countries, all but seven – Bolivia, Gambia, Guyana, Rwanda, Sri Lanka, Thailand, and Vietnam – had already been selected as candidates in previous years, and had either signed or begun developing compacts with the MCC.[21] When it came time to choose FY 2011 candidates, however, the MCC's Board "selected Ghana and Georgia as eligible to develop proposals for compacts, the second for each country" (MCC 2011d). The Board thus passed over the seven countries that qualified as MCC recipients based on their indicator performance, and that had not yet signed compacts with the MCC,[22] in favor of two countries that had already been awarded compacts – including one country, Georgia, which in FY 2011 did not even satisfy the indicator criteria.[23] Nor was 2011 an outlier; in most years, the Board exercises its discretion to select as eligible some countries that do not pass the indicators test, and to deny eligibility to some countries that do pass this test.

We noted in the preceding text that when decision-making processes exhibit greater legibility, it is easier to identify when decisions are made in impermissible ways. For the MCC, which was designed in part to lessen the influence of political considerations on US aid decisions, the Board's ability to exercise largely unconstrained discretion in the second half of the second selection step would seem to make the MCC's conditionality process less legible. This in turn could fairly give rise to concerns that the MCC is selecting eligible countries based on forbidden considerations. Some commentators have indeed suggested that the Board is influenced by political considerations in selecting eligible countries. Thus, Johnson and Zajonc (2006, 6) surmise that the MCC has used its discretion "to exclude countries that, for political reasons, are deemed inappropriate recipients of US aid such as China, India, and Bhutan," and Tarnoff (2013, 8), of the Congressional Research Service, has noted that the "hold put on MCC consideration of Bolivia's compact proposal in FY2008 and its exclusion from eligibility in FY2009 appeared likely due to the political tensions existing between it and the United States rather than its performance in development related matters." However, some of these decisions are fairly explicable by reference to other, nonpolitical considerations that the Board is permitted to rely on in exercising its discretion.[24] Commentators – including some critical of the MCC – tend to agree that geopolitical considerations do not play an important role in MCC decision making (Nowels 2005, 10; Owusu 2007, 19; Collins 2009 373).

In fact, the most surprising feature of the Board's exercise of discretion in the second half of the second selection step is that although this discretion may take qualitative information into account, the Board seems to *prefer* to rely on quantitative measures; and although this discretion is formally subject to few constraints, the Board tends in practice to make its discretionary decisions by adhering to relatively simple rules that turn on indicator performance.

In FY 2013, the MCC began publishing a *Guide to the Supplemental Information Sheet* that describes the supplemental information that the Board considers when selecting countries for threshold programs and compacts (MCC 2012a, 3, 2012b, 4). Though the Board may take into account "additional quantitative *and qualitative* information" (MCC 2013e, 4), the majority of the supplemental information sources identified in this guide are quantitative – for example, the percentage of a country's economy that is in the country's informal sector, or the percentage of World Bank projects in each country that are reported "at risk" due to various implementation problems (MCC 2012a, 3–4).

And the Board's exercise of discretion often appears in practice to involve the application of simple rules involving the indicators that feature in the first half of the second selection step. Thus, Nowels (2005, 12, 8), of the Congressional Research Service, has explained that "[i]t appears ... that scoring 'substantially below' – perhaps in the lowest 25th percentile – has become a de-facto criteria for exclusion." This unspoken rule can explain why, in FY 2005, Burkina Faso, China, Djibouti, Egypt, Nepal, the Philippines, and Swaziland satisfied the indicator criteria but were not selected as eligible, and in FY 2004, the Board did not select as eligible four countries – Bhutan, Guyana, Mauritania, and Vietnam – that technically met the performance criteria. Commentators have also hypothesized, with respect to the selection methodology used before FY 2012, that the MCC refused to confer eligibility upon countries that failed all three "democracy indicators" (Political Liberties, Civil Liberties, and Voice and Democracy) in the Ruling Justly category.[25] Dunning et al. (2011, 9 n.14), of the Center for Global Development (CGD), noted in 2011 that "Bhutan and Vietnam have passed the indicators test for seven and eight years, respectively, but have never been selected as compact-eligible presumably because each country has also consistently failed all three 'democracy indicators.'" The new methodology introduced in FY 2012, which requires countries to achieve a passing score on either the Civil Liberties or Political Liberties indicators, appears to codify this previously unspoken rule (MCC 2011c, 4).

This is not to suggest that the MCC has wholly replaced its discretion in selecting eligible countries with tests driven by quantitative measures. The MCC sometimes selects countries that run afoul of the "25th-percentile rule," or that fail to pass the indicators test, so long as "recent policy changes or positive trend lines" excuse their poor performance on a single indicator – a practice that explains the selection of Bolivia, Cape Verde, Georgia, Lesotho, Mozambique, and Sri Lanka in FY 2004 (Nowels 2005, 8). Jordan's selection as eligible in FY 2006 appeared to flout the "democracy indicators" rule (Tarnoff 2007, 16). Indeed, sometimes the MCC's exercise of discretion in selecting eligible countries can seem arbitrary. To take FY 2006 as an example, Tarnoff (2007 14–15) notes that the Board's "reason for not selecting Uganda, despite having passed 12 of the 16 indicators and not falling significantly below the median on the other 4," was not clear. The Board selected two lower middle-income countries as eligible in FY 2006; however, the Board likely "could have decided to select none of the lower middle-income nations by using criteria it had applied consistently in the two previous rounds. Moreover, it was not clear why the Board chose the two that did qualify. All eight Lower Middle-Income countries that passed the performance indicator test fell significantly below the median on at least one of the indicators."

Nonetheless, the MCC appears often to replace its discretion to rely on qualitative factors in selecting eligible countries with quantitative tests based on indicator performance. To the extent the Board uses such tests, its selection becomes more regularized and comprehensible. If the second half of the second step of the MCC process is less legible than the first half of the process, then, it is nonetheless more legible than we might have expected.

Finalizing MCC Compacts with Eligible Countries

As for the third step of the selection process, the MCC (2008, 4, 2013e, 7) has made clear that "[s]ubmission of a proposal is not a guarantee that MCC will finalize a compact with an eligible country. Any MCC assistance provided under section 605 of the Act will be contingent on the successful negotiation of a mutually agreeable compact between the eligible country and MCC approval of the compact by the Board, and availability of funds." The MCC determines which projects to fund using four technical tools: constraints analyses (CA), benefit-cost analyses (BCA), economic rates of return analyses (ERR), and beneficiary analyses (Lucas 2011, 3–4; MCC 2013b, 1–2). It demands that proposed projects demonstrate a minimum

ERR[26] and makes the results of these analyses publicly available (MCC 2014d). The MCC does note, however, that "[i]n making its final investment decision, MCC considers factors other than the ERR. As a result, a project with a low ERR might be approved or a project with a high ERR might be rejected on the basis of other considerations" (Wiebe 2008, 8).

Many of the early compacts approved by the MCC shared a similar sector concentration (Tarnoff 2013, 28); to some critics, this showed that the MCC exercised its discretion in its third selection step with an unstated neoliberal bias. As Mawdsley noted in 2007, the compacts approved by the Board "are remarkably similar. It would appear that *every single country* independently identified agribusiness, rural entrepreneurial development, and transport infrastructure as their key priorities."[27] This criticism has lost some of its force in recent years, as the MCC has diversified into greater investment in governance, water supply, and sanitation and in health, education, and community services (Tarnoff 2013, 9). Moreover, despite these charges, no critic has suggested that examination of the publicly available CA, BCA, ERR, and BA analyses demonstrates that the MCC is not following these analyses in approving compacts (though the MCC does not make these analyses available for proposals that are *not* approved). We have little reason as of yet to believe that the MCC is basing its compact decisions on anything other than the results of these analyses, even though the Board is explicitly permitted to take other, qualitative considerations into account. Consequently, the third step of the MCC process appears to operate in a relatively comprehensible, regularized fashion.

Our hypothesis that the indicator-driven steps of the MCC process would be quite legible is thus confirmed in practice; these steps are more comprehensible than the parts of the process that are explicitly permitted to rely on qualitative considerations. Even in these latter parts of the process, however, the MCC often appears to *choose* to exercise its discretion in predictable, indicator-oriented ways, though it is allowed to consider qualitative factors. This suggests that constraining certain steps of a conditionality process to depend on quantitative tests may encourage reliance on quantitative considerations in other parts of the process as well. We later consider some possible explanations for this phenomenon.

The Legibility of EU Accession

In contrast, we would expect the EU's accession process, with its more indeterminate requirements and emphasis on monitoring and reporting, to be less legible. Such opacity might result from (1) challenges in understanding what subjective applications of abstract principles mean in a concrete sense; (2) difficulty in generalizing from a mass of context-driven reporting to attain a more panoptic view of how the accession process works; and (3) the likelihood that, in the absence of restrictive rubrics governing their application, qualitative requirements are not applied consistently across different countries and subject areas. In short, given the abstraction, complexity, and subjectivity of the EU accession process, we would expect observers to have difficulty understanding how it is supposed to work. This is borne out in practice.

The Indeterminacy of the EU Process

As a general rule, EU decision making is complicated; Heisenberg (2005, 65) notes that "[i]t is difficult for all but the most committed analysts of the EU to fully understand the formal process by which the EU makes decisions." The complexity of the accession process is particularly mind boggling, especially as regards adoption of the *acquis*:

> [T]he 'acquis communautaire' [has] steadily developed, and in 2001 encompassed some 90,000 pages of regulations by the Commission, as well as the precedents of the European Court of Justice over the last 50 years; all joint declarations and conclusions of the Union regarding common foreign and security politics and home and justice affairs; all international agreements of the Union with third countries; all intergovernmental agreements among single member states of the Union; and finally, all principles of *primary* EU law stemming from the Treaties of Maastricht, Amsterdam and Nice. (Behr 2007, 248)

If we set aside this complexity, however, we can discern another obstacle to understanding how the accession process is meant to work: the incomplete specification of some of its requirements.

Thus, some areas of the *acquis* present only vague standards governing the reforms acceding countries must implement. For example, as Hughes, Sasse, and Gordon (2004, 534, 547) have explained, chapter 21 of the *acquis* (dealing with regional policy and coordination of structural instruments) actually offered only "a very weak legal basis" for any particular reform requirements and no "benchmarks for compliance." This indeterminacy led EU officials to make conflicting demands on candidate countries during the fifth wave of enlargement, first demanding that countries devolve power to their regions, and then insisting that they centralize authority to simplify their dealings with Brussels.

If these problems with indeterminate requirements afflict adoption of the *acquis*, they are more relevant in regard to the other Copenhagen criteria, as "[t]he EU has no specific test to determine whether or to what extent these conditions have been met" (Grabbe 2003, 307). Not only do these vague conditions give the EU greater discretion to make policy demands on candidate countries, but they also encourage EU officials to make these demands *sub silencio*, by "minimalist directives and non-compulsory directives," leaving candidates unable to determine precisely which requirements they must meet to satisfy the criteria and qualify for accession.

Finally, even where the requisite reforms are clearly delineated, there remains uncertainty as to how to prioritize these reforms and who will judge their implementation. Grabbe (2003, 318–323) identifies "five dimensions of uncertainty built into the accession conditions": (1) the policy agenda that should be undertaken by the applicants, (2) the hierarchy of tasks, (3) timing, (4) whom to satisfy, and (5) standards and thresholds. Given the difficulty of understanding just what it is that the EU demands of accession candidates, it is not surprising that within these candidates "public opinion remained largely ignorant of what conditionality entailed, except when a few of the conditions became controversial or over-exposed" (Pridham 2006, 386).

Of course, a quantitative conditionality process like that employed by the MCC may only camouflage this problem without solving it, given the way that indicators submerge definitional issues. In terms of concrete realities, it is little clearer what it means for an MCC candidate to achieve a passing score on a Control of Corruption indicator than it is for an EU candidate to have "stability of institutions guaranteeing democracy, the rule of law, human rights, and respect for and protection of minorities." But it is nonetheless clearer what the MCC process entails *operationally* than the EU process, making the former more legible to observers.

Understanding Candidates' Progress Toward Accession

Two other factors further diminish the legibility of the EU process. To begin, though the different substantive areas in which candidates must implement reforms are all nominally of equal importance, not all of these areas are equally salient in practice. Thus, Hughes and Sasse (2003, 13) suggest that the EU's "mechanisms for enforcing and monitoring compliance on minority protection in the candidate countries are very weakly developed compared with other areas of the *acquis*." Haughton (2007, 240) agrees that due "to the poor record of some of the existing members in minority policy, provided the right language was used by the accession state, lack of policy improvement was highly unlikely to be a veto-point," which contrasted with the Justice and Home Affairs chapter of the *acquis*, a known "'potential veto-point in negotiations.'" Schimmelfennig and Sedelmeier (2004, 680–681) similarly suggest that "EU actors clearly communicated to the CEECs that the Schengen rules were a key condition for membership," while "parts of the Commission and some member states indicated that rather superficial alignment would not present an obstacle to concluding negotiations in the areas of EU social policy and to some extent … civil service reform." This uneven application of the *acquis* adoption requirements and Copenhagen criteria further inhibits the legibility of the EU process, which at the same time resembles a vague checklist and a set of hurdles with varying heights.

As for the EU's monitoring and reports, they suffer from the same defects of any evaluation that judges inherently subjective phenomena without clear benchmarks or concrete criteria: it is sometimes difficult to understand what the judgments in these reports *mean*, and it is not clear that the same standards are being applied to different candidates. Thus, Hughes and Sasse (2003, 16) contend that "there is an absence of continuity and coherence in the EU's monitoring mechanism as the Reports are characterized by ad hocism."

Reading reports supports this impression, and indeed suggests that rapporteurs may have attempted to make their judgments more legible by adopting an informal coding system. Thus, in the 2009 *Progress Report on Albania* (EC 2009, 16–32), over the course of about fifteen pages of reporting the Commission asserts that in five areas "little progress" had been made; in twelve areas, "some progress" had been noted; and in eight areas, "good progress" had been observed. Another passage of similar length reveals that in two areas "preparations" are "advancing slowly"; in nine areas, preparations are "advancing moderately" or "moderately advanced"; and in five areas, preparations are "advancing" or "advanced" (EC 2009, 27–42).[28] It seems that these quantized levels of progress and advancement must be meant to be commensurable, and to the extent this is true they help readers understand that the Commission perceives progress in some areas as more satisfactory than in others. But it is not clear why "accreditation" and "metrology," for example, deserved the assessment of "good progress" in Albania in 2009, while "conformity assessment" was judged to have displayed only "some progress." If these assessments do not simply reflect the extent to which Albania has enacted a checklist of reforms – if they attempt to measure the degree to which it has developed the capacity to integrate with the EU – it is difficult to understand how the abstract latter inquiry is carried out in practice.

What these assessments mean for Albania's chances of opening accession negotiations with the EU, and whether they are being consistently applied across countries, is even less clear. Must a country achieve a minimum number of "good progress" and "advancing moderately" assessments before it may proceed to the next stage of the accession process? Does this number vary across countries? Or does the European Commission simply rely on an impressionistic perception of whether each country has done enough to warrant advancement? In a sense, the EU reports are easily comprehensible in that they send signals to countries that they must do *more* in certain areas to achieve acceptable levels of reform. However, the reports are confusing in that they leave observers with little sense of how much progress a country has achieved, how much more the country must do before it will receive the benefit sought, and why the EU judges a country's progress in some areas to be more satisfactory than in others. Most critically, the reports do little to assist observers in determining whether an EU accession process is advancing according to a legitimate set of rules, or based on impermissible considerations.

The MCC's quantitative conditionality process hides some of these sources of confusion, converting subjective, variable judgments into seemingly objective, rigorous metrics. But although the MCC process does little to clarify – and in fact to some extent conceals – why performance in some areas or by some countries may be judged more satisfactory, it at least makes clearer what should occur operationally for a country to be deemed acceptable by the MCC. An observer studying the EU accession process will have difficulty forming an impression of how close a country is to becoming a candidate or an EU member, and whether the process is proceeding according to its design; such an observer can more easily ascertain whether an MCC candidate has fulfilled the MCC's declared requirements.

REASON-GIVING IN MCC AND EU DECISION MAKING

If quantitative conditionality processes are generally more legible than their qualitative counterparts, we might also expect such processes to display less reason-giving than qualitative conditionality processes, where we define *reason-giving* as *the extent to which decision makers offer reasoned justifications for their decisions*. Quantitative processes are likely to be perceived as more legitimate than their qualitative counterparts for two reasons: (1) the greater perceived rigor of processes based on numerical information and (2) the perception that quantitative processes are less vulnerable to deformation by impermissible considerations. As a consequence, we would expect qualitative processes to explain and justify judgments to a greater extent than quantitative processes to bolster their perceived legitimacy.

With respect to the first point, Espeland and Vannebo (2007, 31) explain that "[w]e tend to see numbers as more objective than other forms of information, perhaps because of their association with the rigors of mathematics and science," and are thus more inclined to credit judgments based on numbers. Merry (2011, 89) suggests that numbers "seem to be simple descriptions of phenomena and to resist the biases of conjecture and theory because they are subject to the invariable rules of mathematics." Because numbers seems more rigorous and credible than narrative descriptions, we would expect a decision-making process relying on the latter to be perceived as less legitimate, generating a greater need for it to justify its judgments.

As for the second point, the perceived legitimacy of quantitative processes is based not only on the credibility of numbers, but also on the way in which numbers permit processes to make decision making more regularized. This enhanced amenability to mechanical objectivity, which as described previously contributes to the legibility of quantitative conditionality processes, also bolsters their legitimacy. As Porter (1995, 8, 197–210) explains, "[a] decision made by the numbers (or by explicit rules of some other sort) has at least the appearance of being fair and impersonal," and the more mechanical the decision the greater the perception that it is free from the idiosyncrasies of personal judgment. Espeland and Vannebo (2007, 39) thus postulate that "[t]he legitimacy of quantitative authority depends on procedures, on methodology, rather than on the discretion of particular persons or the expertise of trained professionals." Qualitative decision-making processes, on the other hand, engender suspicion that personal judgments or extraneous considerations have influenced the decision. We would thus expect a quantitative process like the MCC to be able to use the appearance of regularized rigor to dispense with reason-giving, while a qualitative process like EU accession might need to explain its decisions.

Examining the MCC and EU processes reveals that these expectations are matched by reality. Although the MCC prioritizes openness and transparency, it avoids giving reasons for *not* selecting countries as eligible or *not* concluding compacts with eligible countries. The EU, on the other hand, relies on dense consultation between the EU and officials from applicant countries to elaborate on and explain accession requirements and judgments as to compliance. This reason-giving, however, takes place largely out of the public eye. We draw from these observations an additional conclusion: while the EU has an internal accountability orientation, focused on direct participants in the accession process, the MCC has an external accountability orientation focused on rendering accounts to outsiders. This external orientation explains not only the gaps in MCC reason-giving, but also its general reliance on quantitative decision-making processes.

Gaps in MCC Reason-Giving

The transparency of its processes represents an evident point of pride for the MCC. Wiebe (2008, 2), the MCC's former chief economist, has suggested that "what is truly innovative about MCC's approach is the systematic application of [its] analytical techniques to virtually every element of every program and the transparency provided by the use of these techniques and MCC's public dissemination of their output." Hewko (2010, 11), former MCC vice president, claims that the "MCC has undertaken an unprecedented level of transparency" and that it "is being praised for a level of transparency that exceeds that of other bilateral and multilateral donors." Lucas, former MCC Director of Policy and Evaluation, elaborates that

> Transparency is at the heart of accountability... For this reason, MCC makes information available along the full cycle of country engagement, from country selection through implementation to results. For all compact programs, the website

has five-year compact and project budgets, detailed project descriptions, projected outcomes, quarterly updates on financial and program progress, and results of independent impact evaluations as programs are completed. (2011, 7)[29]

It is indeed true that the MCC displays impressive transparency in some respects. Despite finding the MCC generally wanting, Chhotray and Hulme (2009, 39) note that "MCA is different from previous attempts at selectivity" in that "it proposes to use a public, transparent process to select countries to receive aid." Even Mawdsley (2007, 495), a steadfast critic of the Corporation, concedes that "[t]he calculation of the medians and how individual countries score on them is rendered relatively transparent by relying on publicly available rankings and figures derived from a number of organizations, including the World Bank and Heritage Foundation." As we noted earlier, the first, first half of the second, and third steps by which the MCC selects countries are quite legible to outside observers; though the second half of the second step involves the use of discretion in ways that are not necessarily obvious, this discretion has also sometimes been cabined by unspoken rules that rely on predictable tests based on indicators.

Given the MCC's emphasis on openness, one surprising aspect of its selection process is that when the Corporation *does* exercise discretion, it often does not trouble to explain how it has done so. Thus, the Open Society Institute (2004, 2) suggests that the MCC should "[p]rovide the public with a rigorous justification for each MCA country ultimately selected, including a detailed explanation of the factors influencing the selection process, with special onus in cases where exceptions to the basic methodology are made"; CGD agrees that this is necessary,[30] noting the "perception that use of discretion is becoming the norm more than the exception" (Herrling 2006, 1–2). Yet the MCC continues to eschew detailed reason-giving, at least with respect to some of its discretionary decisions. The MCC is required to provide three reports each year to Congress, the last of which "identifies countries determined by the Board to be eligible under section 607 of the Act ... and countries with which the MCC will seek to enter into compacts under section 609 of the Act ... as well as the justification for such decisions" (MCC 2013e, 3). In this latter report, the MCC customarily does go to some lengths to justify its selection of countries as eligible.[31] But the MCC devotes almost no effort to explaining why it has *not* selected as eligible some countries that pass the indicators test, instead presenting roughly the same generalized justifications in each year's report. In FY 2007, 2008, 2009, and 2010, these reasons consisted of the following, with minor amendments:

[A] number of countries that performed well on the quantitative elements of the selection criteria (i.e., on the policy indicators) were not chosen as eligible countries for FY07. As discussed above, the Board considered a variety of factors in addition to the country's performance on the policy indicators in determining whether they were appropriate candidates for assistance (e.g., the country's commitment to fighting corruption and promoting democratic governance; the availability of appropriated funds; and in which countries MCC would likely have the best opportunity to reduce poverty, generate economic growth and have a transformational impact). (MCC 2006, 4)[32]

More recently, the MCC has favored a somewhat different but similarly uninformative and unvarying formulation.[33] The use of such a boilerplate prevents us from considering this to be a genuine exercise in reason-giving.

This reluctance to justify the exclusion of certain formally qualified countries from MCC eligibility might suggest that the Board has no principled basis on which it distinguishes between eligible and ineligible countries. After all, the MCC is likely aware of the criticism that it provides insufficient reason-giving; Herrling, who while at CGD lodged the criticisms of the MCC's unexplained use of discretion that we described previously, is now the MCC Vice President for Policy and Evaluation (MCC 2014f). But we have noted that geopolitical considerations do not appear to play a preponderant role in the MCC selection process, and that in some respects the MCC appears to be denying eligibility to countries in unstated yet principled ways.

Much of the Board's unwillingness to furnish reasons for its exercise of discretion might be attributed to the structure of its legal obligations; as Nowels (2005, 12 n.12) explains, "[t]he MCC's authorizing legislation (section 608(d)) requires the Corporation's CEO to provide justification to Congress regarding only those countries declared as eligible for MCA assistance and for those selected for Compact negotiation. Otherwise, there is no statutory requirement for the MCC to comment on its decision-making process, including the rationale for not selecting specific countries." But it seems odd for an institution that so prizes openness to content itself with doing only the legal minimum with respect to reason-giving. This is especially so when we consider that for the MCC to motivate countries to make policy changes that render them eligible for assistance – one of its raisons d'être[34] – countries must understand on what basis the MCC makes eligibility decisions. We return to this issue later in this section, but for now note that the MCC's failure to explain its use of discretion may be partly attributable to the fact that its processes appear sufficiently transparent and rigorous that it has little need to provide more information about its selection process. The EU likely faces a different set of circumstances.

The Density of EU Communications on Accession

As we have already noted, the EU accession process is formally predicated upon monitoring and reporting, which are the key mechanisms by which the Commission,

Council, and Parliament determine whether countries have adopted the *acquis communautaire* and fulfilled the Copenhagen criteria. We have observed that this reporting by itself is likely to be difficult for observers to understand, given the vagueness of the criteria employed, the abstract judgments upon which the reporting is predicated, and the possibility that these judgments are incommensurable across issue areas and countries. Participants in the accession process – whether from candidate country governments or the Commission – appear to have dealt with these obstacles by increasing the frequency with which they consult about the process.

When the Council met in Copenhagen in 1993, it approved "a structured system of high-level political meetings" between the EU and the then-candidate countries from Central Europe[35]; since the mid-1990s, representatives of member states and candidate countries have accordingly engaged in dialogue at the ministerial level on a wide variety of subjects regarding accession (Goebel 2004, 24–25). Lower level officials in applicant countries and European countries have also had a multiplicity of contacts, including "regular visits by EU officials to countries in question, normal interchange between their governments and Brussels (which has accelerated with membership negotiations)" (Dimitrova and Pridham 2004, 102) and "[f]requent, often bi-weekly meetings ... held by working group experts from the Council, the Commission and individual applicant states, or groups of applicants" (Goebel 2004, 23).[36] Schimmelfennig (2007, 130) confirms that these contacts compensate for the opacity of EU conditionality: "although many of the democratic conditions demanded by the European Union and NATO were stated in general and vague terms, the continuous stream of communications and reports from the Western organizations during the preaccession process made sure that the candidate countries received sufficient information on their shortcomings and achievements."

If these communications between officials constitute a type of reason-giving in which representatives of the Commission and member states explain to applicant country governments how well they are advancing toward accession and what they must do to continue progressing, it is important to note that these reasons are generally *not* offered to the general public, which lessens their contribution to accountability. It is also true, however, that not all reason-giving in the EU accession process is directed only to officials from applicant countries.

Grabbe (2003) points out that "[t]he EU has also made exceptional criticisms of undemocratic practices in particular countries in '*demarches*,' i.e. public criticisms that are intended to embarrass CEE governments into making particular institutional or policy changes." Most notably, when Romania and Bulgaria displayed sluggishness in implementing reforms demanded by the EU, Enlargement Commissioner Olli Rehn sent "yellow cards" to each country in June 2005 signaling that the accession process might be delayed if certain reforms were not timely addressed (Noutcheva and Bechev 2008, 135). These cards conveyed a warning that was "straightforward and on the public record." This type of public criticism is rare, however, as is the public threat that progress might be withheld if certain conditions are not met (Grabbe 2003). The EU appears more commonly to clarify accession requirements and explain its decision making in informal contacts between officials, out of public view. This suggests that, to the extent reasons are given to bolster the perceived legitimacy of the EU decision-making process, it is perceptions among direct participants in the EU process that matter most.

The MCC's External Accountability Orientation

The EU thus seems to engage, through dense consultation with applicant countries, in nonpublic reason-giving regarding its accession decisions. In contrast, the MCC appears reluctant to justify its decisions to exclude countries from eligibility, even when its decision making is principled; moreover, it makes public technical analyses only of the programs it funds, not of those that it rejects. The MCC's emphasis on giving reasons only for its grants of eligibility to and conclusion of compacts with countries can be explained by an orientation toward external accountability: showing third parties that its decisions are defensible, and in particular that it is not wasting resources. It seems likely that this orientation encourages the MCC to focus on objectivity, technical rigor, and accessibility, thus reinforcing its nature as a quantitative process and explaining why it sometimes eschews exercising discretion based on qualitative considerations, even when reliance on such considerations is explicitly permitted.

External Pressures on the MCC

Though the MCC was originally greeted by bipartisan political and public support, it came into being, in a sense, on the defensive. American attitudes toward foreign aid have long been skeptical, which may explain why the MCC has always devoted so much effort to rigorously justifying its program selection and aid disbursement process to parties who do not directly participate in this process. The MCC's decision to focus its reason-giving on why it has chosen to make certain countries eligible and fund certain programs makes sense, moreover, in light of the difficult political environment in which it continues to find itself. The MCC's lack of natural allies, a constrained budget environment, and the mismatch between the foundational rhetoric supporting the MCC and the results it can plausibly deliver all mean that the MCC must focus on explaining why its activities are worthwhile, as opposed to defending its omissions.

As Goldsmith (2011, 159) explains, "the MCA proposal was embraced across the aisle in Congress," with the decisive vote in the House of Representatives authorizing its creation by a margin of 382 to 42. Conservative, mainstream, and liberal organizations, as well as groups within the development community, backed the MCC's creation.[37] But this support was born out of weakness, in that it was predicated on distrust in American society for the foreign aid establishment and a consequent eagerness to support a different mode of operation. Hewko (2010, 4–5) notes that US foreign aid lacks "a broad-based domestic constituency" and suggests there is a widespread belief in the US that "foreign assistance resources are often wasted and spent on corrupt regimes and white elephant projects that bring little benefit to the world's poor." Chhotray and Hulme (2009, 42) observe that "[i]n the United States, civil society is much more suspicious about the use of welfare provisions, grants, and subsidies for poverty reduction," and that "US media treat foreign aid and NGOs with much more suspicion and appear to delight in highlighting examples of development programs failing." Under these circumstances, even an initially popular aid organization would need to justify its continuing utility.

This was especially true given the MCC's status as a Bush initiative; as *The Economist* (2005) has explained, despite its initial popularity the MCC lacked "natural supporters," as supporters of foreign aid were generally suspicious of President Bush, while supporters of the President generally opposed foreign aid. Hook (2008, 161, 163) further notes that while the MCC was placed outside the flagship US aid agency United States Agency for International Development (USAID) to ensure it was "free to pursue its founding principles without parochial interference," this decision also deprived the MCC of bureaucratic allies, leaving it "exposed to congressionally imposed funding restrictions."

Of course, the MCC's first years of operations also coincided with a worsening economy, producing "[e]normous pressure on the federal budget" that led "members of Congress to ask where they will get the best value for the taxpayers' money" (Dunning et al., 2011, 2). President Bush initially planned for annual funding for the MCC to reach $5 billion by FY 2006 (Tarnoff 2007, i), but the MCC appropriation was quickly "viewed by many observers as one of the most vulnerable items in an increasingly difficult budget environment" (Nowels 2005, 20). Each year, appropriations for the MCC have fallen beneath requests, and far beneath anticipated funding levels.[38] Though President Obama appears to support the MCC,[39] funding has continued to be a problem, with Obama requesting only $1.125 billion for the MCC in his FY 2012 budget and Congress appropriating only $898.2 million (Tarnoff 2012, i); for FY 2013, the MCC's budget was then cut by $45 million (MCC 2013f).

The restricted funding for the MCC makes it difficult for the agency to fulfill one of its foundational objectives: supplying large enough grants that the prospect of qualifying for MCC compacts will motivate countries to implement needed reforms. As Collins (2009, 374) explains, "[t]he MCA was designed to have a transformative impact on recipient countries, yet this will prove difficult to accomplish when the size of the fund may not be adequate to ensure that the MCA is one of the largest aid donors for each recipient." As for the MCC's aim of inhibiting terrorism through growth, it has appeared quixotic from the beginning.[40] The MCC is thus left with little to offer to the American taxpayer by way of justification, other than the prospect that well-spent aid might improve recipient country economies and build markets for US exports.[41]

The MCC's Need to Demonstrate Results to Outsiders

Given that this is the remaining justification for the MCC's activities, and considering the difficult political environment in which it must survive, it is unsurprising that the Corporation has focused on justifying the eligibility and funding decisions it *has* made, rather than giving reasons why eligibility has been denied or compacts have not been concluded. The MCC, in short, almost certainly focuses more on external accountability toward Congress and critics of foreign aid than it does on internal accountability toward countries participating in its selection and programming process. Thus, the MCC itself declares (in the words of its former Chief Economist) that it is "accountable to country partners for providing the obligated resources and support, and also accountable to American taxpayers to deliver results" (Wiebe 2008, 12) – but does not suggest that it is accountable to candidate or eligible countries to explain how it makes its decisions, or to point the way toward how they might qualify to receive funds. Instead, the MCC emphasizes its accountability to taxpayers, promising (in the words of its CEO, Daniel W. Yohannes) that it "holds itself accountable to the American people to ensure that every taxpayer dollar generates the best possible return on investment" and "selects country partners carefully to ensure the highest returns on our investments" (MCC 2011e, 3).

Lowenheim (2008, 266) notes that "in many Western states the move towards more transparent and accountable public policy prompts governments to justify expenditures such as foreign aid according to measurable and supposedly objective benchmarks and standards." The MCC's need to justify itself to external actors has ensured that quantitative rigor remains its primary mode of accountability. Indeed, this link between external accountability and an emphasis on technical objectivity is to be expected. As internal accountability focuses on participants in a process, it should naturally focus on apprising these participants of how the process works, what is expected of them, and (if the process involves conditionality) how they will obtain benefits. External accountability, in contrast, focuses on those who observe a process from the outside, and these observers are both more likely to focus on whether the process produces the desired effects and less likely to devote significant effort to answering this question, as they are affected only indirectly by the effectiveness of the process. Quantitative rigor is thus ideally suited to external accountability: the appearance of technical objectivity is likely to impress external actors, and the use of metrics lends itself to quick appraisal by casual observers.

The MCC thus focuses on objectivity, technical rigor, and comprehensibility in discussing accountability. Wiebe (2008, 14, 7) notes that impact evaluations "are performed by independent contractors, often affiliated with universities or think tanks, whose distance from the project enables them to make objective assessments of the program's impact"; while he concedes that "[s]ubjective judgments can never be eliminated from the decision process," he stresses that benefit–cost analysis "places a premium on objective, quantitative information wherever possible and identifies those places where subjective judgment is required." Yohannes (MCC 2011e, 4) similarly highlights that "[w]hat distinguishes MCC is our commitment to technically rigorous, systematic, and transparent methods of projecting, tracking, and evaluating the impact of our programs." BenYishay and Tunstall (2011, 108), former Associate Directors of Economic Analysis & Evaluation at the MCC, emphasize that "[o]nce a compact proposal is agreed upon and implementation begins, the MCC requires strict monitoring and reporting, complemented with rigorous, independent impact evaluations"; Lucas (2011, 23), the MCC's former Director of Policy and Evaluation, notes that "2 percent of compact funds are dedicated to M&E activities during implementation." And Wiebe (2008, 3, 7) suggests that the MCC accountability "framework also enhances public engagement by providing accessible information regarding decisions, progress, and results," thus "enabl[ing] outside observers to review decisions made by country partners and by MCC and to hold both parties accountable for the use of the funds."

As Chhotray and Hulme (2009, 45, 42) explain, the MCC must be responsive to "a domestic constituency that can perhaps be persuaded that the United States is the Good Samaritan giving aid money to poor people, but wants to reiterate the neo-conservative position that aid is not for wasters." It is thus unsurprising "that MCA is premised on a tightly supervised deductive framework, where public demonstration of the proper utility of aid is as, maybe more, important as the actual reduction of poverty in the recipient countries."

MEANINGFUL PARTICIPATION IN THE EU AND MCC PROCESSES

We would have expected the MCC process to be more legible than the EU process, and it largely is. We would have expected the EU to provide more reason-giving than the MCC, and it appears to do so. We might also expect that a qualitative process like EU accession could be more readily tailored to the circumstances of candidates than a quantitative process like the MCC, which might impose a more inflexible normative framework on potential recipients. That is, we would expect qualitative processes to provide more participation than quantitative processes, where we define *participation* as *the extent to which participants in a process may influence the methods of decision making and the factors governing decisions.*

In some respects, the obstacles to comprehensibility that we have noted regarding the EU accession process are a necessary consequence of this process's qualitative nature. The more qualitative a process, and the more it eschews metrics, rankings, rubrics, and benchmarks, the greater the role that remains for discretion in (1) setting performance requirements and (2) assessing whether these requirements have been fulfilled – resulting in a less determinate process whose operation is less legible than a more mechanical process. If this is a deficit of qualitative processes, the corresponding credit is that such processes should be easier to tailor to particular circumstances given the greater residuum of discretion retained in the system.

We would expect a quantitative conditionality process to afford less scope for tailoring, and to give potential recipients fewer opportunities to participate in shaping the process, than a qualitative conditionality process. As Lowenheim (2008, 271) explains, though quantitative "examination … reduces the degree of arbitrariness of the use of power by hegemonic states and non-state actors… this also means that decision making becomes more mechanised and might disregard the unique context of each examined state." Goldsmith (2011, 161) concurs, suggesting that "hard-and-fast rules of all countries, with widely varying conditions, are bound to prove irrelevant or counterproductive in some locations. Too often, performance measures like those of the MCA make little allowance for a productive and necessary learning process."

Quantitative processes might provide less scope for participation not only because they are more constrained, but also because they are less amenable by nature to processes of compromise. Gow (2001, 60) suggests that economic forms of rationality "seek[] maximum return on investment," while "[t]he usual instruments of political action are persuasion, bargaining, and constraint"; as decision making comes to rest on optimum-seeking quantification rather than qualitative judgments, we thus might expect opportunities for participation to diminish.

This expectation, however, does not appear borne out in reality. Instead, though the EU's process is extensively consultative, with significant flows of information between the institution and countries seeking accession, this density of communication does not seem to translate into genuine opportunities for countries to participate in shaping their pathways to accession. In fact, though some have criticized the extent to which the MCC prioritizes participation, it does not necessarily appear to be *less* participatory than the EU.

Power Asymmetry and Participation in EU Accession

Since the Copenhagen criteria were promulgated in 1993, one salient feature of the EU accession process has been the asymmetry in power between the EU and applicant states. This asymmetry has a few sources, beginning with the distribution of benefits from accession. As Grabbe (2002, 13) explains, "[t]he EU has all the benefits to offer (principally accession, trade and aid), and far from all of its component member-states are sure they want all the CEE applicants to join. The CEE countries, by contrast, have little to offer the EU... This asymmetry of interdependence allows the EU to set the rules of the game in the accession conditionality."[42] Hughes, Sasse, and Gordon (2004, 524) add that "[t]he absence of alternative ideological or systemic paradigms for the Central and East European candidate (CEEC) countries, other than EU membership, has tended to reinforce the widespread perception of a power asymmetry in favour of the EU during the enlargement process." And Agh (2003, 6) notes that in the 2004 eastern enlargement, the candidates represented "the so far weakest negotiating partners," given their "low GDP in per capita terms and missing institutional capacity," as well as the "isolation effect" of "missing Western skills, networks and basic information."

As most commentators agree, the EU has taken advantage of this asymmetry to make accession a process of unconditional policy transfer. Thus, Anastasakis and Bechev (2003, 12–13) characterize "conditionality towards the post-communist countries" as "a one-way process, where conditions are defined exclusively by the EU and its Member States and must be accepted unconditionally by the eastern candidates." Haughton (2007, 235) suggests that "the term 'accession negotiations' is in many respects a misnomer, as there was very little left open to negotiation beyond the odd temporary transitional arrangement (derogation)." Raik (2004, 580) does note that the Commission "did not wish to give an impression of dictating what had to be done in the candidate countries but stressed cooperation – for example, in preparing the APs, it claimed to have 'conducted intensive discussions with each country' and 'aimed to build a broad consensus on the priorities.'" But as Anastasakis and Bechev (2003, 12–13) emphasize, the "EU assumes that its prescriptions have universal applicability and should therefore be adopted and implemented irrespective of the particularities of the different countries or regions"; as a consequence, according to Hughes, Sasse, and Gordon (2004, 537), "[t]he perception of a power asymmetry meant, as a high-ranking official at the Estonian Mission to the EU explained, that the Commission 'saw candidate countries as mice in laboratories ... anything could be asked of them.'" Schimmelfennig and Sedelmeier (2004, 683) explain that the result has been that "the scope of the outsiders to influence the content of the rules that they import is severely limited... [B]ureaucratic actors, intergovernmental or inter-bureaucratic relations, and a top-down process of rule transfer dominate the process of transferring these rules to the CEECs." Raik (2004, 588) laments that this left applicant countries with "no time to consider how best to incorporate EU norms into the existing domestic frameworks and to develop a coherent system."

The power asymmetry between the EU and applicant states, and the resulting capacity of the EU to impose conditions upon these states unilaterally, have produced some notable consequences. Arguably, the imposition without contextualization of policy changes has led to shallow reform, with formal changes unaccompanied by concrete implementation.[43] The EU's ability to dictate the terms of accession has also led over time to an increase in the volume and intrusiveness of these terms.[44] For our purposes, though, the inflexibility of EU conditionality is interesting because it demonstrates that the theoretical adaptability of a conditionality process – which we might have expected to turn on whether conditionality criteria are rigorous or amorphous, and hence whether the process is quantitative or qualitative – may matter less than the motives and opportunity of the benefit-granting institution.

Opportunities for Participation in the MCC Selection Process

Of course, the rigidity of conditionality criteria may restrain an institution to the point that it can make no allowance for participation by potential recipients; for instance, the MCC certainly has little scope to permit countries to participate in the first, most constrained step of its selection process. Though the MCC exercises discretion in the second step, and hence *could* invite participation from applicant countries, it does not do so; as we explained in the previous section, this is unsurprising in light of the MCC's external accountability orientation. It is the MCC's third step that, at least formally, provides the most room for countries to participate in setting the terms on which (1) they will be selected as compact countries, and (2) they will implement compacts. Based on the example of the EU above, however, we might expect this participation to be limited in practice; after all, the MCC would appear to enjoy a position vis-à-vis eligible countries that is just as asymmetrical as that between the EU and applicant states.

The MCC suggests that it prioritizes country participation in designing and implementing compacts, and sometimes minimizes the role that it plays in this process. Thus, Hewko (2010, 3), the MCC's former vice president, explains that after becoming eligible for funding, countries "analyze their constraints to growth; consult with their civil society and private sector to identify priority areas for MCC funding; design their MCC programs; and, where funding is provided, implement these programs." MCC documentation (2009a, 3) states that "countries have the lead in proposing how funds should be used. MCC respects the ability of the country to analyze its own impediments to growth, and expects that governments will analyze options jointly with a wide array of stakeholders." According to Hewko (2010, 11), this participatory policy "has led to a clear sense of ownership, an increase in enthusiasm and pride, and a considerable transfer of skills and know-how in economic analysis, program design, environmental and social analysis, gender sensitivity, financial accountability, procurement, and monitoring and evaluation."

There is evidence that eligible countries have genuinely participated in designing compact proposals, and that this participation has been broad-based. *The Economist* (2005) recounts that when Madagascar became eligible for MCC funding, the Corporation pushed it to "consult more widely among its own people" after initial project proposals merely included "a wish-list of all the projects that each cabinet minister wanted." In a 2008 field report, Crone, of CGD, reported that "[c]ountry ownership beyond the government in El Salvador is evident and palpable. All the Salvadoran stakeholders interviewed touted the country's ownership of the program and consider it a national priority." According to BenYishay and Tunstall (2011, 107), Armenia's "compact proposal was developed through a consultative process in which more than 1200 individuals participated and some 230 written proposals were received on particular investment projects."[45] Similarly extensive opportunities for participation in compact development have been reported in Namibia and Burkina Faso (Tarnoff 2013, 10). Collins (2009, 373) has suggested that "[r]ecipient participation, or 'ownership,' in development programs is [an MCC] feature that has received acclaim."

Some MCC documentation reinforces this depiction of its collaborative role in the program design process. We have already noted that the MCC constrains this process by requiring successful program proposals to produce acceptable results when subjected to constraints analysis (CA), benefit–cost analysis (BCA), beneficiary analysis (BA), and analysis of economic rates of return (ERR). According to the MCC (2009a, 14), "[t]he MCA-eligible country has the primary responsibility for quantifying the economic rates of return, conducting a beneficiary analysis, and incorporating expected incremental changes in beneficiary incomes as targets within an M&E plan." The MCC sometimes suggests that it plays only a friendly, avuncular role in helping countries to perform these analyses.[46]

At other times, though, the MCC appears to envision a more didactic role for itself in this process. It sometimes describes itself as an equal partner in carrying out analyses, with "MCC economists and sector specialists work[ing] closely together from the earliest phase of compact development to assess the potential costs and benefits of a project, conduct ERR and beneficiary analysis, and shape program design for maximum impact" (Lucas 2011, 20). The MCC certainly displays a lack of trust in country capacities to analyze their own proposed programs, explaining that "initial work, whether generated by country counterparts or consultants, is reviewed by MCC staff economists. These BCA models are subject to an additional peer review by economists outside the country program" (Wiebe 2008, 9). This quotation makes clear that technical analyses may be carried out by consultants as well as counterparts in eligible countries; in fact, the MCC (2010b, 2–3) sometimes suggests that it just does this analysis itself, explaining that "[a]s a first step, where appropriate, MCC will carry out diagnostics of binding policy and institutional constraints to growth." The MCC also notes its resolve to "devote increased resources and time to the preparation of threshold programs and … rely more heavily on in-house experts to develop programs."[47]

Nonetheless, even if the MCC analyzes proposed programs entirely by itself, this does not mean that it develops the proposals by itself, as well. The evidence cited in the preceding text suggests that eligible countries are empowered to some degree to generate these proposals (except for those relating to threshold programs), notwithstanding suggestions from critics that approved programs demonstrate a decided neoliberal bias. While the MCC constrains the way in which eligible countries develop proposals, it certainly seems to welcome country participation to a greater extent than the EU does in its accession process. Given the asymmetry in power between the MCC and eligible countries, and our original hypothesis that the quantitative nature of MCC conditionality would constrain participation, this result is surprising.

Nonetheless, we can hazard a couple of possible explanations for the observed levels of participation in the MCC process. As noted previously, the EU's rigid approach to conditionality has meant that formal policy reform has not always been matched by concrete implementation. The MCC may have designed its conditionality process to avoid this pitfall; the MCC may provide eligible countries with opportunities to participate in program development simply because it believes that this approach is more likely to result in effective programs. But given the magnitude of the stakes of EU accession for member states – with accession leading ultimately to the free movement of goods, services, persons, and capital, as well as substantial transfers of agricultural subsidies (Hughes 2004, 529) and structural aid aimed at bringing "applicant countries' infrastructures up to Community standards" (EC 1997a, 63) – one would imagine that the EU would have a strong interest in successful implementation of reforms in applicant countries. The EU's resistance to allowing applicant countries to shape the accession process cannot easily be explained on this basis.

An alternative explanation is more counterintuitive. The MCC's quantitative constraints upon its selection process – with countries first required to pass an "objective" indicators test, and country program proposals then subjected to "rigorous" technical analyses – may leave the MCC confident that any aid it provides will (1) go to countries with favorable policy environments and (2) be devoted to sound projects. Given this confidence, the MCC may provide eligible countries with the opportunity to design their own programs because other constraints on the selection process ensure, in its view, that these countries will make good use of this opportunity. The EU, lacking these quantitative controls, may not have had the same confidence. The inflexible, rigid nature of the eastern enlargement thus may have resulted from EU fears that applicant country participation in tailoring conditions to local circumstances might actually enable these countries to deform the process and subvert the accession requirements.

Paradoxically, then, the narrow parameters that the MCC's quantitative conditionality sets on recipients of aid and the programs they implement may liberate the MCC, allowing it to empower these recipients to participate in other aspects of the selection process.

CONCLUSION

We began this chapter by broadly classifying the MCC aid disbursement and EU accession processes as "quantitative" and "qualitative" conditionality processes, respectively, and developed some hypotheses about the modes of accountability that each process would favor based on their quantitative or qualitative character. Just as we had expected, our examination of the two processes suggested that the MCC's process was more legible than the EU's process, and that the EU did focus more assiduously on reason-giving than the MCC. In contravention of our predictions, however, we found that the EU's qualitative process did not provide more genuine opportunities for participation than the MCC's quantitative process.

It is difficult, of course, to generalize from this limited comparison. But our examination suggests that because a quantitative conditionality process's legibility may inhibit its inclination to engage in reason-giving, whether a conditionality process is quantitative or qualitative may in the end not matter decisively in determining the extent to which decision making is transparent. We posit that quantitative conditionality processes may often display a decisive orientation toward external accountability, with quantitative decision making and an external accountability orientation particularly likely to result from insecure environments in which processes' utility must be demonstrated to outsiders. Finally, regarding the provision in conditionality processes of genuine opportunities for participation, it appears that the distribution of power between decision makers and applicants may matter more than a process's quantitative or qualitative nature; indeed, quantitative processes may afford *greater* opportunities for participation because of the ways in which they otherwise constrain outcomes and thus bolster the confidence of decision makers that the desired ends will be achieved.

NOTES

1 As Hook (2008, 154) observes, "USAID suffered cutbacks during the 1990s that amounted to 25% in real terms and 50% as a share of U.S. national income."
2 Schimmelfennig (2001, 48) explains that "[s]ince the Central and Eastern European countries and their supporters in the Community did not possess sufficient material

bargaining power to attain enlargement, they based their claims on the constitutive values and norms of the EU and exposed inconsistencies between, on the one hand, the EU's standard of legitimacy, its past rhetoric, and its past treatment of applicant states and, on the other hand, its policy toward Central and Eastern Europe."

3 As Haughton (2007, 237) has noted, "[f]rom 1989 to 1993 the most striking aspect of the evolving relationship between the EC/EU and the states of CEE was the reluctance of the EC/EU to offer membership."

4 Davis, Kingsbury, and Merry (2012, 76) define an indicator as "a named collection of rank-ordered data that purports to represent the past or projected performance of different units."

5 For discussion of the "accountability deficit in the growing exercise of transnational regulatory power," see Kingsbury, Krisch, and Stewart (2005, 16).

6 Accountability may be defined in a number of ways, but there are common elements to these definitions. Dubnick (2005, 379) notes that despite the "increasingly ambiguous" nature of the concept of accountability, it retains a "core idea" that focuses on "those actions related to the social function of 'giving accounts.'" Gow (2001, 62) states that "[a]ccountability means giving account of the exercise of this responsibility and accepting the consequences." Barnetson and Cutright (2000, 288–289) define "accountability" as "providing a report of one's performance and being responsible for it." Messner (2009, 923) notes that "accountability denotes the exchange of reasons for conduct," and that "[t]o give an account means to provide reasons for one's behavior, to explain and justify what one did or did not do."

7 Kingsbury, Krisch, and Stewart (2005, 28) suggest that studies of the accountability of global administration should "focus in particular on administrative structures, on transparency, on participatory elements in the administrative procedure, on principles of reasoned decisionmaking and on mechanisms of review." We consider transparency to be related to two other administrative law concepts, legibility and reason-giving, which we examine here. We do not explore the availability of review mechanisms.

8 The MCC suggests that it utilizes a *four*-step process for selecting countries to receive aid, in which it (1) identifies candidate countries; (2) publishes selection criteria and methodology for country selection; (3) issues candidate country scorecards; and (4) selects countries eligible for program assistance (MCC 2014k). However, we find it analytically easier to conceive of this process as involving three steps because the MCC winnows the field of countries that may receive funding in three stages.

9 The former category includes those countries that are among the seventy-five lowest per capita income countries, as identified by the World Bank; the latter category includes all other countries with a per capita income that is not greater than the World Bank's Lower Middle-Income country threshold for the given fiscal year ($4,085 gross national income [GNI] per capita for FY 2014) (MCC 2013d, 4).

10 The MCC uses a slightly different methodology to identify candidate countries and to assess whether they are eligible to sign compacts, dividing Scorecard LICs from "Scorecard LMICs based on whether their per capita incomes fall below or above the World Bank's historical ceiling for International Development Association (IDA) eligibility, which was set at US$1,965 for FY 2014 (MCC 2013a, 1–2, 2013d, 4 n.1).

11 For FY 2014, this group included Burma, Cameroon, Central African Republic, Republic of the Congo, Eritrea, The Gambia, Guinea-Bissau, Madagascar, Mali, Nicaragua, North Korea, Sudan, Swaziland, Syria, and Zimbabwe. Countries are disqualified on this basis due to part I of the Foreign Assistance Act of 1961 (MCC 2013d, 6–7).

12 The Board includes "the Secretary of State, the Secretary of the Treasury, the U.S. Trade Representative, the Administrator of USAID, the CEO of the MCC and four public members appointed by the President of the United States with the advice and consent of the U.S. Senate" (MCC 2014b).

13 One indicator, Girls' Education, consists of two measures: Primary Education Completion, for Scorecard LICs and Secondary Education Enrolment for Scorecard LMICs (MCC 2013c, 4–5).

14 Candidate countries' performance is gauged against an absolute threshold for the Political Rights and Civil Liberties indicators in the Ruling Justly category, the Immunization Rates indicator in the Investing in People category, and the Inflation indicator in the Encouraging Economic Freedom category (MCC 2013c, 4).

15 The fifth wave saw the accession of Cyprus, the Czech Republic, Estonia, Latvia, Lithuania, Hungary, Malta, Poland, Slovakia, and Slovenia in 2004, and the accession of Romania and Bulgaria in 2007. Croatia then joined the EU in July 2013 (European Commission [EC] 2013a).

16 "The Union is founded on the principles of liberty, democracy, respect for human rights and fundamental freedoms, and the rule of law, principles which are common to the Member States" (EU 2006, 12).

17 "Any European State which respects the principles set out in Article 6(1) may apply to become a member of the Union. It shall address its application to the Council, which shall act unanimously after consulting the Commission and after receiving the assent of the European Parliament, which shall act by an absolute majority of its component members. The conditions of admission and the adjustments to the Treaties on which the Union is founded, which such admission entails, shall be the subject of an agreement between the Member States and the applicant State. This agreement shall be submitted for ratification by all the contracting States in accordance with their respective constitutional requirements" (EU 2006, 34–35).

18 During the prior wave of enlargement that culminated in 2004 and 2007, the role of the SAAs was played by "Europe Agreements" (Goebel 2004, 22). These agreements aimed "to provide a framework for political dialogue, promote the expansion of trade and economic relations between the parties, provide a basis for Community technical and financial assistance, and an appropriate framework to support [potential candidates'] gradual integration into the Union" (EC 1997b, 9). Even in the early stages of the Western Balkan accession process, it appears potential candidates still entered into European Partnerships (EC 2012).

19 The color-coded squares depicting which tests each country has passed are relatively new, having been unveiled in the scorecards depicting the new methodology introduced for FY 2012 (MCC 2011a, 10–191). Even before their introduction, however, one could study the scorecards and identify eligible countries in less than an hour.

20 The MCC has admitted that "[c]ountries may be generally maintaining performance [warranting selection] but not meet the criteria in a given year" because of factors such as "data improvements or revisions," "increases in peer-group medians," or "slight declines in performance" (MCC 2009b, 3). In FY 2004, the MCC explicitly noted that it would use Transparency International's Corruption Perception Index to supplement the World Bank data on which the Control of Corruption indicator is based, explaining that the World Bank data was out of date (Nowels 2005, 6).

21 At the time countries were selected as candidates for FY 2011, the following countries had signed compacts with the MCC: Armenia, Benin, Burkina Faso, Cape Verde, El Salvador,

Georgia, Ghana, Honduras, Jordan, Lesotho, Madagascar, Mali, Moldova, Mongolia, Morocco, Mozambique, Namibia, Nicaragua, the Philippines, Senegal, Tanzania, and Vanuatu. Three other countries – Indonesia, Malawi, and Zambia – were developing first compacts at the time (MCC 2010a, 1).

22 None of these seven countries were disqualified from candidacy by legal prohibitions barring the grant of US assistance to them (MCC 2010c, 4–5).

23 In FY 2011, Georgia passed only two Investing in People criteria, not the requisite three (MCC 2010a, 86).

24 As discussed further later, Bhutan's nonselection was equally well explicable by reference to its poor performance on the democracy indicators in the Ruling Justly category. Tarnoff (2007, 14–15) has suggested that "India w[as] not selected most likely because some of [its] scores were substantially below the median, which has become a marker used by the Board previously." As for China, its enormous size can by itself explain its nonselection, as the MCC explicitly states that it selects eligible countries based on "the opportunity to reduce poverty, promote economic growth and have a transformational impact in a country in light of the overall context of the information available to it as well as the availability of appropriated funds" (MCC 2007, 2). A similar rationale can support India's nonselection.

25 Before FY 2012, the Corporation used only seventeen indicators (grouped again into the same three categories) and required eligible countries to achieve passing scores within their income groups on at least three indicators in each category, as well as a passing score on the Control of Corruption indicator in the Ruling Justly category. The Ruling Justly, Investing in People, and Encouraging Economic Freedom categories contained six, six, and five indicators, respectively (MCC 2010d, 2–3).

26 "[T]he minimum acceptable ERR for both programs and individual components of MCC compacts will be the greater of: (a) two times the average real growth rate of GDP for the country for the most recent three years for which data is available; or (b) two times the average real growth rate of GDP for all of the MCC eligible countries for each country for the most recent three years for which data is available" (MCC 2009a, 9).

27 Chhotray and Hulme (2009, 44) similarly charge that "all of the 9 MCC compacts (signed until August 2006) focus on various aspects of agricultural development, private sector development, and economic growth, and it is difficult to believe that all MCC consultations came up with the same ideas."

28 Such coding is not an isolated occurrence; the European Commission's *Serbia 2013 Progress Report* (2013h), for example, features five areas in which Serbia was judged to have made "little progress," nineteen instances of "some progress," and five cases of "good progress"; in thirty-one areas, progress was "moderately advanced."

29 The MCC (2013g, 2) similarly states that it "applies principles of transparency at every stage of the MCC program life cycle; starting with the method for choosing partner countries, to the analyses that guide investment decisions after selection, to quarterly publication of expenditures and program performance, and finally the publication of data and sharing of results of independent evaluations."

30 Dunning et al. (2011, 16) recommend that "[w]hile the MCC board should continue to use a variety of supplementary information and exercise discretion in selecting countries eligible for MCC assistance, it should be explicit and transparent about the type of information it uses and when."

31   The following passage is representative: "One country was selected as eligible for the first time in FYo8: Malawi, a low income candidate, was selected under Section 606(a) of the Act... Malawi is currently participating in the Threshold Program. Malawi meets the eligibility criteria for the first time in FYo8, scoring above the median on 13 of 17 indicators, including the Corruption indicator. The Government of Malawi has demonstrated a strong commitment to fighting corruption, and is well into the implementation of a Threshold Program focused on accelerating anti-corruption reforms and improving fiscal policy. There is a significant opportunity for a Compact with Malawi to reduce poverty and promote economic growth. Roughly 7 million people (over half the population) live on less than $2 a day. Although Malawi now meets the MCA eligibility criteria for Compact assistance, successful implementation of its Threshold Program – and of the corresponding reform commitments – remains critical. Hence, the Government of Malawi will be required to demonstrate successful implementation of the Threshold Program during the Compact development process in order to reach a Compact and then to continue to receive MCA funding under a Compact" (MCC 2007, 2). The MCC has offered similar passages justifying the selection as eligible of Moldova, Ukraine, and Jordan (2006, 3); Cape Verde (2009b, 3); and Lesotho (2013e, 5).

32   In FY 2008, this justification was amended to replace "have a transformational impact" with "poverty reduction," so that it redundantly suggested that the MCC prioritized countries where it had "the best opportunity to reduce poverty, generate economic growth and poverty reduction" (MCC 2007, 3–4). In FY 2009, the superfluous "poverty reduction" introduced in FY2008 was removed, but the passage remained otherwise unaltered (MCC, 2008, 4). In FY 2010, the MCC introduced only the cosmetic substitution of "where MCC would likely have the best opportunity" for "in which countries MCC would likely have the best opportunity" (MCC 2009b, 4).

33   In FY 2013, the Board explained that: "As with previous years, a number of countries that performed well on the quantitative elements of the selection criteria (i.e., on the policy indicators) were not chosen as eligible countries for FY13. FY13 was a particularly competitive year: five countries were within the window of consideration for subsequent compacts, multiple other countries passed the scorecard (some for the first time), and funding was limited due to budget constraints. As a result, not every country that passed the scorecard was selected for MCC eligibility" (MCC 2012b, 4). The language for FY 2014 was essentially the same, with appropriate substitutions for the number of countries working to develop compacts (MCC 2013e, 5).

34   As Johnson and Zajonc (2006, 4) explain, "Bush cited two reasons for [the MCC] approach. First, because MCC funds would only go to the best governed poor countries, the funds would be better spent. Second, by basing aid on past performance, the MCC would create an incentive for good governance."

35   By 1997, the structure of this system of meetings had changed, with the European Commission (1997, 53) explaining that "[i]In light of the intensity of contacts between the Union and the applicants during the coming phase of the accession process, in the framework of the negotiations, the Europe Agreements and the Accession Partnerships, the present structured dialogue no longer appears appropriate. Most accession-related issues of principal concern to the Union and the applicants will be discussed bilaterally."

36   The European Commission (2009, 5) has thus explained, in the Albanian case, that "[t]he EU provides guidance to the Albanian authorities on reform priorities through the

European Partnership. Progress on these reform priorities is encouraged and monitored via the political and economic dialogue with Albania. This dialogue takes place through the SAA structures. The first SA Council was held in May 2009. Six sectoral working groups/sub-committees have been held since November 2008."

37 As Goldsmith (2011, 160) notes, "[t]he performance-based approach to foreign aid is endorsed by conservative think-tanks such as the American Enterprise Institute and the Heritage Foundation and also enjoys backing in the development community. Advocacy groups like Oxfam, Partners for Democratic Change, Initiative for Global Development and the Centre for Global Development approve the MCA. George Soros is very supportive, despite his otherwise disparaging assessment of Bush's foreign policy. Researchers at the mainstream Brookings Institution consider that the initiative has the potential of offering the 'biggest bang for the buck' of all US development assistance programmes and that it may turn out to be the world's leading 'venture capitalist' for promoting economic improvement in poor countries. Even international activist celebrities like Bono and Bob Geldof back the governance-oriented strategy."

38 Collins (2009, 374) observes that "[f]unding for the program has fallen far short of the initial $5 billion goal, as the MCA received funding of $1 billion in 2004, $1.5 billion in '05; $1.75 billion in '06 (at which point it should have reached $5 billion), and $1.75 billion in '07. For FY 2008, appropriations for MCA were cut to $1.54 billion."

39 Goldsmith (2011, 160) contends that "[d]espite the potential for misgivings about the previous administration's initiatives in development policy, President Obama signalled his positive view by requesting $1.4 bn to fund the MCA in 2010 – a two-thirds increase over the amount enacted in 2009."

40 As Owusu (2007, 4, 6, 11) explains, the MCC "was based on the claim that global poverty and international terrorism are linked, and therefore alleviating poverty would help combat terrorism." However, even setting aside the fact that "[t]he poverty-terrorism relationship is complex and hotly debated," the MCC's "merit-based criteria contradict the poverty-terrorism basis of the policy; that is, if we accept that terrorism thrives in nations where failed states provide safe havens for such activities, then failed states should be major recipients of MCA funding."

41 Thus, the MCC's CEO, Daniel W. Yohannes, has testified before the Senate Foreign Relations Committee that "MCC investments look to remove constraints to growth so that the private sector will invest and flourish. These investments are helping to build a foundation for U.S. exports and increased business activity, which will mean increased growth and job opportunities here at home" (MCC 2011e, 5).

42 Schimmelfennig (2001, 54) likewise attributes the weakness of the CEEC position to the fact that "[c]apital and foreign aid flow almost entirely from West to East."

43 Pridham (2006, 397–398) has argued that "[c]onditionality policy is essentially top-down in its conception but also limited in its effects, as shown by its greater impact on the institutional compared with the intermediary and societal levels; and, similarly, conditionality has been more successful in formal terms (i.e. institutional and legislative) than in concrete terms (i.e. with respect to implementation)." Noutcheva and Bechev (2008, 133) concur, stating that "the fast pace of harmonization with the *acquis* produced numerous pieces of legislation which 'courts, lawyers, regulatory bodies and others charged with implementation had difficulty understanding, applying and enforcing."

44 Pridham (2008, 373) observes that "the scope of the EU's conditionality expanded from the mid-1990s significantly beyond the (somewhat bland) formal democracy criteria utilized

in previous decades into areas of substantive democracy," elaborating that "[w]hile the Copenhagen criteria as defined in 1993 covered the stability of democratic institutions, the rule of law and human and minority rights, since then EU conditionality has also come to specify the strengthening of state capacity, the independence of judiciaries, the pursuit of anti-corruption measures and the elaboration of a series of particular human and minority rights (as well as highlighting the severe condition of the Roma); but also economic, social and cultural rights such as those relating to trafficking in women and children and gender equality. More recently, other issues have been added, notably the handing over to the Hague tribunal of war criminals from the Balkan conflicts of the earlier 1990s" (2006, 380).

45 Not all agree that the Armenian compact development process was participatory, the Social Policy and Development Center (2007, 4) has charged that "[t]hese NGOs [in the Working Group to develop Armenia's MCC proposal] were elected with no transparent criteria and procedures... [W]hen initially created by public proposal, the final paper was transformed to expert work 'independent' from the society."

46 Thus, Wiebe (2008, 5) has stated that "[a]s the first step towards submitting a proposal, MCC asks country partners to establish local teams to undertake a Constraints Analysis (CA) to identify the main bottlenecks to growth in the local economy... [T]he early CA experiences required considerable collaboration as both sides learned how to use the tool effectively."

47 Strangely enough, on the same page that it explains that it will develop threshold programs in-house, the MCC (2010b, 3) suggests that "[a] broader consultative process will also serve as an additional measure of feasibility and help ensure that the reforms sought by the Threshold Program will have the necessary degree of country ownership and political support to be truly sustainable."

REFERENCES

Agh, Attila. 2003. "Smaller and Bigger States in the EU25: The Eastern Enlargement and Decision-Making in the EU." *Perspectives* 21: 5–26.

Anastasakis, Othon, and Dimitar Bechev. 2003. "EU Conditionality in South East Europe: Bringing Commitment to the Process." Paper, S.E. Eur. Studies Programme at University of Oxford. http://www.sant.ox.ac.uk/seesox/anastasakis_publications/EUconditionality.pdf.

Barnetson, Bob, and Marc Cutright. 2000. "Performance Indicators as Conceptual Technologies." *Higher Education* 40: 277–292.

Behr, Hartmut. 2007. "The European Union in the Legacies of Imperial Rule? EU Accession Politics Viewed from a Historical Comparative Perspective." *European Journal of International Relations* 13(2): 239–262.

BenYishay, Ariel, and Rebecca Tunstall. 2011. "Impact Evaluation of Infrastructure Investments: The Experience of the Millennium Challenge Corporation." *Journal of Development Effectiveness* 3(1): 103–130.

Chhotray, Vasudha, and David Hulme. 2009. "Contrasting Visions for Aid and Governance in the 21st Century: The White House Millennium Challenge Account and DFID's Drivers of Change." *World Development* 37(1): 35–49.

Collins, Stephen D. 2009. "Can America Finance Freedom? Assessing U.S. Democracy Promotion via Economic Statecraft." *Foreign Policy Analysis* 5(4): 367–389.

Crone, Amy. 2008. "El Salvador: Field Report." Center for Global Development. http://www.cgdev.org/files/16595_file_El_Salvador_FINAL.pdf.

Davis, Kevin E., Benedict Kingsbury, and Sally Engle Merry. 2012. "Indicators as a Technology of Global Governance." *Law & Society Review* 46(1): 71–104.

Dimitrova, Antoaneta, and Geoffrey Pridham. 2004. "International Actors and Democracy Promotion in Central and Eastern Europe: The Integration Model and Its Limits." *Democratization* 11(5): 91–112.

Dubnick, Melvin. 2005. "Accountability and the Promise of Performance: In Search of the Mechanisms." *Public Performance & Management Review* 28(3): 376–417.

Dunning, Casey, Alan Gelb, Owen McCarthy, and Sarah Jane Staats. 2011. "Fine-Tuning the MCC Selection Process and Indicators." Center for Global Development. http://international.cgdev.org/sites/default/files/1425322_file_Dunning_et_al_0711_Fine_Tuning_FINAL.pdf.

Espeland, Wendy Nelson, and Mitchell L. Stevens. 2008. "A Sociology of Quantification." *European Journal of Sociology* 49(3): 401–436.

Espeland, Wendy Nelson, and Berit Irene Vannebo. 2007. "Accountability, Quantification, and Law." *Annual Review of Law and Social Science* 3: 21–43.

European Commission (EC). 1997a. "Agenda 2000: For a Stronger and Wider Union." http://ec.europa.eu/agriculture/cap-history/agenda-2000/com97-2000_en.pdf.

1997b. "Commission Opinion on Bulgaria's Application for Membership of the European Union." http://ec.europa.eu/enlargement/archives/pdf/dwn/opinions/bulgaria/bu-op_en.pdf.

2008. "2008/212/EC: Council Decision of 18 February 2008 on the principles, priorities and conditions contained in the Accession Partnership with the former Yugoslav Republic of Macedonia and repealing Decision 2006/57/EC." http://eur-lex.europa.eu/legal-content/EN/TXT/PDF/?uri=CELEX:32008D0212&from=EN.

2009. "Albania 2009 Progress Report." http://ec.europa.eu/enlargement/pdf/key_documents/2009/al_rapport_2009_en.pdf.

2011. "Understanding Enlargement: The European Union's Enlargement Policy." http://ec.europa.eu/enlargement/pdf/publication/20110725_understanding_enlargement_en.pdf.

2012. "Enlargement – Enlargement Strategy and Progress Reports 2007." Last modified August 22. http://ec.europa.eu/enlargement/key_documents/reports_nov_2007_en.htm.

2013a. "Economic and Financial Affairs – Enlargement." Last modified October 9. http://ec.europa.eu/economy_finance/international/enlargement/index_en.htm.

2013b. "Enlargement – Chapters of the acquis." Last modified June 27. http://ec.europa.eu/enlargement/policy/conditions-membership/chapters-of-the-acquis/index_en.htm.

2013c. "Enlargement – Check Current Status." Last modified December 19. http://ec.europa.eu/enlargement/countries/check-current-status/index_en.htm.

2013d. "Enlargement – Conditions for Membership." Last modified November 28. http://ec.europa.eu/enlargement/policy/conditions-membership/index_en.htm.

2013e. "Enlargement – Steps towards Joining." Last modified June 27. http://ec.europa.eu/enlargement/policy/steps-towards-joining/index_en.htm.

2013f. "Enlargement – Strategy and Progress Reports." Last modified October 23. http://ec.europa.eu/enlargement/countries/strategy-and-progress-report/index_en.htm.

2013g. "Enlargement." Last modified June 27. http://ec.europa.eu/enlargement/.

2013h. "Serbia 2013 Progress Report." http://ec.europa.eu/enlargement/pdf/key_documents/2013/package/sr_rapport_2013.pdf.

European Union (EU). 2006. "Consolidated Versions of the Treaty on European Union and of the Treaty Establishing the European Community." *Official Journal of the European Union* 321: 1–331.

Goebel, Roger J. 2004. "Joining the European Union: The Accession Procedure for the Central European and Mediterranean States." *International Law Review* 1(1): 15–54.

Goldsmith, Arthur A. 2011. "No Country Left Behind? Performance Standards and Accountability in US Foreign Assistance." *Development Policy Review* 29(S1): S157–S176.

Gow, J.I. 2001. "Accountability, Rationality, and New Structures of Governance: Making Room for Political Rationality." *The Canadian Journal of Program Evaluation* 16(2): 55–70.

Grabbe, Heather. 2003. "Europeanisation Goes East: Power and Uncertainty in the EU Accession Process." In Kevin Featherstone and Claudio M. Radaelli, eds., *The Politics of Europeanization*, 303–328, Oxford: Oxford University Press.

Haughton, Tim. 2007. "When Does the EU Make a Difference? Conditionality and the Accession Process in Central and Eastern Europe." *Political Studies Review* 5(2): 233–246.

Heisenberg, Dorothee. 2005. "The Institution of 'Consensus' in the European Union: Formal versus Informal Decision-Making in the Council." *European Journal of Political Research* 44(1): 65–90.

Herrling, Sheila. 2006. "Enhancing Transparency and Communications of MCC Operations: An Action Agenda." Center for Global Development. http://www.cgdev.org/files/14131_file_Herrling_EnhancingTransparency_Jan06.pdf.

Hewko, John. 2010. "Millennium Challenge Corporation: Can the Experiment Survive?" Carnegie Endowment for International Peace. http://carnegieendowment.org/files/millenium_challenge_corp.pdf.

Hook, Steven W. 2008. "Ideas and Change in U.S. Foreign Aid: Inventing the Millennium Challenge Corporation." *Foreign Policy Analysis* 4(2): 147–167.

Hughes, James, and Gwendolyn Sasse. 2003. "Monitoring the Monitors; EU Enlargement Conditionality and Minority Protection in the CEECs." *Journal on Ethnopolitics and Minority Issues in Europe* 2003(1): 1–36.

Hughes, James, Gwendolyn Sasse, and Claire Gordon. 2004. "Conditionality and Compliance in the EU's Eastward Enlargement: Regional Policy and the Reform of Sub-national Government." *Journal of Common Market Studies* 42(3): 523–551.

Jennings, Ann. 2001. "Social Constructions of Measurement: Three Vignettes from Recent Events and Labor Economics." *Journal of Economic Issues* 35(2): 365–372.

Johnson, Doug, and Tristan Zajonc. 2006. "Can Foreign Aid Create an Incentive for Good Governance? Evidence from the Millennium Challenge Corporation." Working Paper, Center for International Development at Harvard University. http://www.hks.harvard.edu/var/ezp_site/storage/fckeditor/file/pdfs/centers-programs/centers/cid/publications/student-fellows/wp/011.pdf.

Kingsbury, Benedict, Nico Krisch, and Richard B. Stewart. 2005. "The Emergence of Global Administrative Law." *Law and Contemporary Problems* 68(15): 15–61.

Lowenheim, Oded. 2008. "Examining the State: A Foucauldian Perspective on International 'Governance Indicators.'" *Third World Quarterly* 29(2): 255–274.

Lucas, Sarah T. 2011. "Principles into Practice: Focus on Results." Millennium Challenge Corporation. http://www.mcc.gov/documents/reports/paper-2011001052001-principles-results.pdf.

Mawdsley, Emma. 2007. "The Millennium Challenge Account: Neo-liberalism, Poverty and Security." *Review of International Political Economy* 14(3): 487–509.

Merry, Sally Engle. 2011. "Measuring the World: Indicators, Human Rights, and Global Governance." *Current Anthropology* 52(S3): S83–S95.

Messner, Martin. 2009. "The Limits of Accountability." *Accounting, Organizations and Society* 34(8): 918–938.

Millennium Challenge Corporation (MCC). 2006. "Report on the Selection of Eligible Countries for Fiscal Year 2007." http://www.gpo.gov/fdsys/pkg/FR-2006-11-17/pdf/E6-19488.pdf.

——— 2007. "Report on the Selection of Eligible Countries for Fiscal Year 2008." http://www.mcc.gov/documents/reports/cn-121307-eligiblecountries.pdf.

——— 2008. "Report on the Selection of Eligible Countries for Fiscal Year 2009." https://www.mcc.gov/documents/reports/mcc-report-fy09-countryselection.pdf.

——— 2009a. "Guidelines for Economic and Beneficiary Analysis." http://www.mcc.gov/documents/guidance/guidance-economicandbeneficiaryanalysis.pdf.

——— 2009b. "Report on the Selection of Eligible Countries for Fiscal Year 2010." http://www.mcc.gov/documents/reports/mcc-report-fy10-country-selection.pdf.

——— 2010a. "2011 Country Scorebook." http://www.mcc.gov/documents/reports/reference-2010001042001-fy11-scorebook.pdf.

——— 2010b. "MCC Threshold Program Lessons Learned." http://www.mcc.gov/documents/press/factsheet-2010002048002-threshold-program-lessons-learned1.pdf.

——— 2010c. "Report on Countries that Are Candidates for Millennium Challenge Account Eligibility for Fiscal Year 2011 and Countries that Would Be Candidates but for Legal Prohibitions." http://www.mcc.gov/documents/reports/report-2010001036301-candidate-country-report.pdf.

——— 2010d. "Report on the Criteria and Methodology for Determining the Eligibility of Candidate Countries for Millennium Challenge Account Assistance for Fiscal Year 2011." http://www.mcc.gov/documents/reports/report-2010001039502-selection-criteria-and-methodology.pdf.

——— 2011a. "2012 Country Scorebook." http://www.mcc.gov/documents/reports/reference-2011001093001-fy12-scorebook.pdf.

——— 2011b. "Final Status Report: Vanuatu Compact." https://www.mcc.gov/documents/reports/qsr-2010002032506-vanuatu.pdf.

——— 2011c. "Guide to the MCC Indicators and the Selection Process for Fiscal Year 2012." http://www.mcc.gov/documents/reports/reference-2011001066102-fy12-guide-to-the-indicators.pdf.

——— 2011d. "Press Release: MCC Board Selects Eligible Countries, Approves $350 Million Compact for Malawi." http://www.mcc.gov/pages/press/release/mcc-board-selects-eligible-countries-approves-350-million-compact-for-malaw.

——— 2011e. "Testimony of Daniel W. Yohannes Chief Executive Officer, Millennium Challenge Corporation to the Senate Foreign Relations Committee." https://www.mcc.gov/documents/press/testimony-2011001057001-2011sfrc.pdf.

——— 2012a. "Guide to the Supplemental Information Sheet." http://www.mcc.gov/documents/reports/report-2012001121001-fy13-selection-supplemental-info.pdf.

——— 2012b. "Report on the Selection of Eligible Countries for Fiscal Year 2013." http://www.mcc.gov/documents/reports/report-2012001124001-fy13-eligible-countries.pdf.

——— 2013a. "2014 Country Scorebook." https://www.mcc.gov/documents/reports/reference-2013001144301-fy14-scorebook.pdf.

——— 2013b. "Fact Sheet: MCC's Use of Evidence and Evaluation." http://www.mcc.gov/documents/press/factsheet-2013002131002-evidence.pdf.

2013c. "Guide to the MCC Indicators and the Selection Process for Fiscal Year 2014." https:// www.mcc.gov/documents/reports/reference-2013001142401-fy14-guide-to-the-indicators. pdf.

2013d. "Report on Countries that Are Candidates for Millennium Challenge Account Eligibility for Fiscal Year 2014 and Countries that Would Be Candidates but for Legal Prohibitions." http://www.mcc.gov/documents/reports/report-2013001140801-fy14-candidate-country.pdf.

2013e. "Report on the Selection of Eligible Countries for Fiscal Year 2014." http://www .mcc.gov/documents/reports/report-2013001145801-fy14-eligible-countries.pdf.

2013f. "Summary of the March 14, 2013 Meeting of the Board of Directors of the Millennium Challenge Corporation." http://www.mcc.gov/documents/reports/summary -board-031413-meeting.pdf.

2013g. "Summary of the September 12, 2013 Meeting of the Board of Directors of the Millennium Challenge Corporation." http://www.mcc.gov/documents/agreements/ summary-board-091213-meeting.pdf.

2013h. "Tanzania: Roads, Electricity and Water Supply." http://www.mcc.gov/documents/ reports/countrybrief-2013002145101-tanzania.pdf.

2014a. "About MCC." http://www.mcc.gov/pages/about.

2014b. "Board of Directors." www.mcc.gov/pages/about/boardofdirectors.

2014c. "Countries & Country Tools." http://www.mcc.gov/pages/countries.

2014d. "Economic Rates of Return, Country Spreadsheets." http://www.mcc.gov/pages/ activities/activity/economic-rates-of-return.

2014e. "Economic Rates of Return." http://www.mcc.gov/pages/activities/activity/economic -rates-of-return.

2014f. "Executive Profiles." http://www.mcc.gov/pages/about/execprofiles.

2014g. "Guyana Threshold Program." http://www.mcc.gov/pages/countries/program/ guyana-threshold-program.

2014h. "Indonesia Threshold Program." http://www.mcc.gov/pages/countries/program/ indonesia-threshold-program.

2014i. "MCC." http://www.mcc.gov.

2014j. "Policy on Suspension and Termination." http://www.mcc.gov/pages/about/policy/ policy-on-suspension-and-termination.

2014k. "Selection Criteria." http://www.mcc.gov/pages/selection.

Neylan, Julian. 2005. "Quantifying Social Entities: An Historical-Sociological Critique." *Journal of Sociology and Social Welfare* 32(4): 23–40.

Noutcheva, Gergana, and Dimitar Bechev. "The Successful Laggards: Bulgaria and Romania's Accession to the EU." *East European Politics & Societies* 22(1): 114–144.

Nowels, Larry. 2005. "Millennium Challenge Account: Implementation of a New U.S. Foreign Aid Initiative." CRS Report for Congress. http://fpc.state.gov/documents/ organization/50169.pdf.

Open Society Institute. 2004. "The Proposed Millennium Challenge Account Selection Process: A Comment by the Open Society Institute." http://opensocietypolicycenter.org/ wp-content/uploads/mca_comments.pdf.

Owusu, Francis Y. 2007. "Post-9/11 U.S. Foreign Aid, the Millennium Challenge Account, and Africa: How Many Birds Can One Stone Kill?" *Africa Today* 54(1): 3–26.

Perry-Kessaris, Amanda. 2011. "Prepare Your Indicators: Economics Imperialism on the Shores of Law and Development." *International Journal of Law in Context* 7(4): 401–421.

Porter, Theodore. 1995. *Trust in Numbers: The Pursuit of Objectivity in Science and Public Life*. Princeton, NJ: Princeton University Press.

Pridham, Geoffrey. 2006. "European Union Accession Dynamics and Democratization in Central and Eastern Europe: Past and Future Perspectives." *Government and Opposition* 41(3): 373–400.

2008. "The EU's Political Conditionality and Post-Accession Tendencies: Comparisons from Slovakia and Latvia." *Journal of Common Market Studies* 46(2): 365–387.

Raik, Kristi. 2004. "EU Accession of Central and Eastern European Countries: Democracy and Integration as Conflicting Logics." *East European Politics & Societies* 18(4): 567–594.

Schimmelfennig, Frank. 2001. "The Community Trap: Liberal Norms, Rhetorical Action, and the Eastern Enlargement of the European Union." *International Organization* 55(1): 47–80.

2007. "European Regional Organizations, Political Conditionality, and Democratic Transformation in Eastern Europe." *East European Politics & Societies* 21(1): 126–141.

Schimmelfennig, Frank, and Ulrich Sedelmeier. 2004. "Governance by Conditionality: EU Rule Transfer to the Candidate Countries of Central and Eastern Europe." *Journal of European Public Policy* 11(4): 661–679.

Social Policy and Development Center. 2007. "Participatory Processes to Millennium Challenge Account Armenia Program." http://www.cspda.org/articles/downloads/SPDC_policybrief_eng2.pdf.

Tarnoff, Curt. 2007. "CRS Report for Congress: Millennium Challenge Account." Congressional Research Service.

2012. "CRS Report for Congress: Millennium Challenge Corporation." Congressional Research Service.

2013. "Millennium Challenge Corporation." Congressional Research Service.

The Economist. 2005. "MCC hammered." June 23.

Wiebe, Franck S. 2008. "Aid Effectiveness: Putting Results at the Forefront." http://www.mcc.gov/documents/reports/mcc-112008-paper-results.pdf.

PART II

Indicators in Local Contexts

6

Rule of Law Indicators as a Technology of Power in Romania

Mihaela Serban

INTRODUCTION

On July 18, 2012, the European Commission issued its regular biannual report regarding Romania's progress on the reform of the justice system and anticorruption efforts. In light of the country's recent political turf battles between the prime minister, the president, and the judiciary,[1] the report excoriated Romania's leadership and questioned the country's "commitment to the respect of the rule of law or the understanding of the meaning of the rule of law in a pluralist democratic system" (European Commission [EC] 2012, 3). Unlike prior reports, the July report summarized five years of monitoring; also unlike prior reports, it included for the first time, albeit in footnotes, references to the country's rankings according to Transparency International (TI), Freedom House, and the World Bank's World Governance Indicators.[2]

The report illustrates well the use of rule of law indicators as a disciplinary mechanism in the Romanian context, in particular as it signals the country's ambiguous place among other EU members. This chapter examines the use of rule of law indicators as a political technology of power in Romania, to understand how indicators in general are received, contested, or resisted around the world. The theoretical framework informing the chapter is Michel Foucault's governmentality concept. Rule of law indicators are relative newcomers on the global rule of law scene, but they are increasingly popular because they promise simplification, efficiency, transparency, consistency, scientificity, objectivity, impartiality, and standard setting and evaluation, all to further better governance (Davis, Kingsbury,

For their suggestions and comments, I am grateful to the NYU Indicators Research Scholars Network, in particular Sally Merry, Benedict Kingsbury, Kevin Davis, Meg Satterthwaite, Rene Uruena, Rene Gerrets, Christopher Bradley, Jane Anderson, Terry Halliday, Tom Ginsburg, Smoki Musaraj, and Angelina Fisher; to Christine Scott-Hayward and Francesca Laguardia for their constant support; and to Lief Carter and Douglas Edlin for their insightful observations that helped me see the project in a new light.

and Merry 2011). Despite variations among them, rule of law indicators make a common set of promises: that they can encapsulate a complex reality – the rule of law – in a number or set of numbers that embodies the rule of law reformers' dreams of the past forty years.[3]

Yet not all indicators are created equal as far as the intended beneficiaries of indicators are concerned, and it is not yet clear how they are being used. In this chapter, I focus precisely on the reception of indicators in a country that is measured and governed through indicators, yet has relatively little control over these measuring techniques. The use of basic indicators, such as process and outcome indicators, is quite prevalent in Romania across the board. Composite indicators, ratio indicators, and ranking indicators are scarcer. The most frequently used ranked indicators are corruption indicators (both global and domestic) and economic indicators (not within the scope of this chapter).

The European Union's (EU's) interventions have prompted the creation and use of rule of law indicators. The EU exerts control through the Cooperation and Verification Mechanism (CVM), which defines "the rule of law" as anticorruption and judicial reform. Rule of law indicators in Romania function primarily as a political technology of control, and secondarily as a technology of reform. As a political technology of reform, rule of law indicators are unevenly mobilized by state and civil society actors. For the former, indicators belong to a discourse of modernization and governmentality, whereas for the latter, indicators are about state accountability. The appeal of indicators across the board lies in their instrumental and technocratic capacities, yet there is significant resistance to them as well. The "indicators consciousness" at the moment thus captures the backlash against indicators as a technique of control, as well as their unfulfilled promises.

The field research for this project took place primarily in the summer of 2011 and included interviews, informal conversations, collection of primary documents such as government reports, indicators databases, civil society reports and analyses, intergovernmental monitoring reports, media articles and videos, and some unpublished correspondence between the EU and Romanian state bodies. My interviewees are primarily rule of law experts and include Romanian governmental officials, civil society activists, legal academics, EU officials, funders, and foreign experts with extensive post-1989 experience in Romania and the region.

THE CVM AS A POLITICAL TECHNOLOGY OF CONTROL

The EU's Cooperation and Verification Mechanism is the main technology of power that has induced the production and use of rule of law indicators in Romania. I focus on the CVM in this section of the chapter, and on the redefinition of the rule of law as anticorruption and judicial reform that preceded and was reinforced by it. The effects of this disciplinary technique are institutional, symbolic, and discursive. A Romanian anticorruption expert captured them well in our interview: "Indicators are not a straight mirror that shows you as you are, but a distorted mirror where the Westerner wants to see himself a little thinner and if he sees a fat person does not think the mirror is problematic, but that the other person is too fat."

Post-communist chronology in Romania can be divided into three distinct periods: early 1990s, characterized by international and US-led involvement; the EU accession era (starting in 1995), when the country was heavily monitored and pressured to fulfill various rule of law related criteria; and the post-accession period, with formal, but weak, EU monitoring focused on the reform of the justice system and anticorruption mechanisms, and the corresponding ascendance of EU institutions, norms, and culture. The post-communist transition overall and accordingly the bulk of the internal focus and external funding and priorities involved democratization, market economy reforms, and achieving the rule of law. The global power map and the orientation of the country toward key international actors accordingly changed from the United States to the European Union, while the heavy hand of international organizations such as the World Bank and the International Monetary Fund held somewhat constant. Notably, the World Bank agenda, particularly in the justice area, is purposely tailored to fulfill the EU requirements for Romania. Post-accession, these requirements are embodied by the Cooperation and Verification Mechanism, a rule of law indicator tailor made for two Eastern European countries.

Romania finally became a member of the EU in 2007, together with Bulgaria and after an initial ten-member wave of Central and Eastern European countries joined in 2004. Neither Romania nor Bulgaria was unconditionally embraced, however. Although the EU does not rank its member states according to their "rule of law" proficiency, both countries are in fact monitored in this regard. Romania and Bulgaria are the only two countries in the EU to be subject to such a high level of EU scrutiny and criticism (Alegre et al. 2009, 1). For Romania, the price of admission set by the European Commission was "accompanying measures for the accession of Romania," which established a "mechanism for cooperation and verification of progress in Romania to address specific benchmarks in the areas of judicial reform and the fight against corruption."[4] The Commission Decision establishing the mechanism for cooperation and verification explicitly grounds the monitoring on the rule of law as a founding principle of the EU and an essential condition of its functioning.

The four CVM benchmarks for Romania focus on judicial reform and corruption and include (1) ensuring a more transparent and efficient judicial process by enhancing the capacity and accountability of the Superior Council of Magistracy, reporting and monitoring the impact of the new civil and penal procedures codes; (2) establishing an integrity agency with responsibilities for verifying assets, incompatibilities, and potential conflicts of interest, and for issuing mandatory decisions on the basis of which dissuasive sanctions can be taken; (3) continuing to conduct professional, nonpartisan investigations into allegations of high-level corruption; and (4) taking further measures to prevent and fight against corruption, in particular within the local government.

Every six months since the accession, the Commission has issued reports on the progress made toward the four benchmarks. The latest report, number 12, was issued in January 2013, and is only a mild improvement over the devastating prior report from July 2012. The July 2012 report was released during an ongoing political crisis and was followed by ten specific recommendations for the Romanian government. Unlike prior reports, the July report covered the entire five years since Romania joined the EU and included process, outcome, and ranking indicators. The regular reports are relatively brief yet exhaustive analyses of the areas and institutions the Commission deems crucial for progress, such as various national anticorruption agencies. The reports occasionally draw from relevant nongovernmental organization (NGO) work, such as Transparency International Romania, and refer to process and outcome indicators (particularly in the accompanying technical reports). The latest favorable report, from February 2012, comprises seven pages and focuses in some detail on recent developments in the country on the two issues of interest (judicial reform and corruption). The report discusses progress on the adoption and implementation of the new civil code and code of civil procedure, the status of high-level corruption trials, the bill on extended confiscation, the work of the National Anticorruption Directorate and the National Integrity Agency, new laws on judicial appointments and discipline, and the National Anti-Corruption Strategy. On all these items, the report makes recommendations for further necessary steps (EC, February 2012).

For the most part, the EU does not explicitly pressure states, including Romania, to make or use indicators, certainly not ranked indicators.[5] Yet achieving the CVM benchmarks implicitly requires the production and use of indicators that facilitate the EU's monitoring activities. The euphemistically named "mechanism for cooperation and verification" (as an official interviewed wryly noted, the "cooperation" part is conspicuously absent) functions as a political technology of control for Romania from at least three perspectives. First, the CVM divides EU members into countries that need to be constantly monitored – Romania and Bulgaria – and countries that do not (all of the others), thus creating a two-tier rule of law system. The very existence of the CVM suggests that Romania and Bulgaria continue to be seen as the "bottom of the heap" (Judt 2001) and the only two countries in the EU that face problems of corruption and inefficient judiciaries (a critique echoed, among others, by Gunther Verheugen, the former European Commissioner for Enlargement). The CVM is thus a symbol of Romania's inability to reach modernity and overcome its past. Rare defenders of the CVM in Romania, such as Monica Macovei, a former Minister of Justice and current center-right member of the European Parliament, argue that the CVM is a necessary sanction and that its biannual reports put the spotlight on corruption and justice issues, which in turn sparks continued public discussion.[6]

Second, the CVM circumscribes the rule of law domain for Romania to two categories, the fight against corruption and judicial reform. While the final accession report for Romania identified a number of weaknesses (including discrimination against the Roma) (Commission of the European Communities 2006, 14), the CVM focuses on only two issues – judicial reform and corruption – and within these two broad areas only on a limited number of institutional and formal mechanisms. According to an official present during the creation of the CVM, the four benchmarks were chosen in a rather arbitrary, casual manner, and the main goal was that Romania should not relax in the post-accession period.

Third, within its rather narrow reach, the CVM has ensured that virtually every step undertaken by Romania since the EU accession has aimed to conform to the CVM benchmarks. The most important ones include comprehensive national anticorruption strategies adopted by the government every three years, and the establishment of new governmental bodies specifically dedicated to the fight against corruption. Most prominently, perhaps, Romania established the National Integrity Agency (Agenția Națională de Integritate [ANI]), which began its activity in 2008 and is one of the few government bodies to gather consistently good reviews from the EU, yet also one that is rather disliked within the country.[7] The Agency's main area of activity is wealth control, specifically income declaration and incompatibilities.[8] Other key state players include a special prosecutorial body, the National Anticorruption Directorate (Direcția Națională Anticorupție [DNA]), responsible for investigating medium and big corruption, and the General Anticorruption Directorate, which is responsible for fighting corruption within the Ministry of Administration and Internal Affairs. The DNA has also received a serious boost in the pre-accession period and is similarly widely praised in the regular EU reports.[9]

Despite the CVM's existence, however, internal and external observers agree that there isn't sufficient pressure on Romania to work on its rule of law issues. The CVM is a rather toothless instrument compared to the pre-accession and accession mechanisms – it is rather unlikely the EU will expel Romania, and its deep unpopularity in the country raises questions of implementation. Possible sanctions, such as funding, are also not at issue, as Romania has in fact had trouble absorbing EU funds. Successive Romanian governments have viewed the CVM "not as a tool to help them improve the judicial system, but rather an aim in itself with their main preoccupation being the lifting of the CVM after the initial 3 years. Romanian authorities seem to have become very apt at mimicking progress in the areas they consider important for the EU with the consequence that changes are introduced not for the country's benefit in the long term but rather to please Brussels" (Alegre et al. 2009, 82). One of my interviewees noted cynically that the CVM resembles old socialist slogans – we pretend to reform, they pretend to care …

Ultimately, however, the key to understanding the CVM as a political technology of control lies at the discursive level. The CVM signifies persistent doubt about Romania's readiness to be a "civilized" member of the EU, it continues the "naming and shaming" game that was instrumental during the accession period, and it encourages competition not only with existing members of the EU (primarily Poland), but also with countries currently knocking at EU's doors. Paradoxically, the CVM's weakness and narrow focus also forestall significant rule of law reform, as well as the expansion of the discourse.

Knowledge Construction and "the Rule O'flaw"

In September 2011, the Netherlands vetoed Romania's accession to the Schengen area (removal of internal border controls for the countries part of the agreement), accusing it of lacking the rule of law. Opinions were divided among my Romanian interviewees, yet many of them agreed that there is a minimum, core rule of law in the country, best expressed by a civil society activist in the following way: "In Romania the rule of law has been internalized: for better or worse, institutions are in their place, we have moved past the post-totalitarian void and chaos, and all there is left to do now is to make sure state institutions function well, but this is not a rule of law issue" (May 2011). The rule of law, my interviewee suggests, is simply not an issue for Romania anymore. In this context, the rule of law means "institutions" and is defined in opposition to the totalitarian past. It is, moreover, a distinctly post-communist discourse.

The rule of law is not an uncontested concept, however, and its meaning has shifted in Romania over the past two decades from a broad rule of law discourse to a much narrower concept focused on corruption and institutional reform. These changes help explain the differing Dutch and Romanian views on whether Romania has the rule of law, and illuminate a less visible aspect of indicators as a political technology of control: knowledge construction. In the case of Romania, mechanisms such as the CVM build up on earlier rule of law efforts and culminate in recursive processes whereby the emphasis on rule of law issues such as corruption or judicial reform leads to the prevalence and visibility of indicators measuring corruption and institutional reform, which in turn drains the rule of law discourse of alternative meanings.

Pre-accession Romania, particularly in the early 1990s, benefitted from "unusual experimentation" from a rule of law perspective (interview data), working on everything from constitutional reform to women's rights and establishing legal advocacy NGOs, as illustrated by organizations such as Central and East European Law Initiative (CEELI, the American Bar Association's Rule of Law Initiative in the region) and the Soros foundation. The heaviest focus has been on institutions and norms, with rights and democratic participation a somewhat distant second, and building a rule of law culture (however defined) almost completely neglected. Once the country passed the initial bump of the first post-communist years and established the skeleton of a democratic, market-based, rule of law-based state, it became obsessed with the EU accession (1995–2007). Elites as well as ordinary citizens considered this the key test of the transition and a symbol of belonging to Europe and the West, and consequently all efforts were singularly directed toward acceding to EU demands. The EU singled out corruption and judicial reform as areas of insufficient progress toward EU standards. From a rule of law perspective, this meant that the earlier, relatively scattered but wide-ranging efforts to promote the rule of law and human rights essentially tapered down to these two topics.

The fight against corruption and for judicial reform is where funding, programs, attention, and indicators can be found. The EU, the World Bank, Western European countries (e.g., Matra of the Netherlands), and foundations (e.g., Konrad Adenauer Foundation, The Trust for Civil Society in Central and Eastern Europe), often in collaboration, have poured significant amounts of money in these areas. The EU has provided post-accession funding of more than €12 million for Romania, which targets, among others, the fight against corruption and judicial reform, for example, in support of the National Integrity Agency (EC July 2012, 2). Post-accession, €57 million overall have been spent on judicial reform, from both external and internal sources, and a massive €81 million has been contracted from a World Bank loan to support the reform of the judiciary.[10] The World Bank is carrying out a "Functional Review of the Romanian Judicial System" financed with EU funds and toeing the EU line.[11] Another current project, this one directly focused on indicators, seeks to "improve the capacity to gather and process judicial data and to establish optimal workload indicators across the judicial system."[12] The beneficiaries of this largesse include everyone from the Romanian government to specialized agencies such as the ANI and various NGOs.

Indicators as a technology of control have clear knowledge effects, as they redefine the very concept they purport to measure. The relationship between the concept being measured and the indicator measuring it is a constitutive one. In Romania, the EU accession led to an overemphasis on corruption and judicial reform and corresponding indicators, which in turn led to a conceptual overlap between the rule of law, anticorruption, and judicial/institutional reform. Even when noted, this effect can be difficult to resist or reverse.

This pared down version of the rule of law – "the rule o'flaw," as one of my interviewees dubbed it – has knowledge and concrete effects. First, it has a disruptive effect to the extent that it hides historical continuities, which makes Romania's rule of law efforts even more vulnerable to external definitions and pressures. A legal academic and EU expert I interviewed believed that positing the rule of law as merely a post-communist discourse misses its deeper roots in Romanian history, particularly the rule of law as a constitutive force in Romania's modernization process of the past two centuries. The CVM was thus critiqued for failing to bring together human rights, integrity and anticorruption efforts, and justice reforms in a coherent package buttressed by the rule of law. Secondarily, there is a clear disciplinary effect – once Romania won the EU-accession prize, all interest in the rule of law almost disappeared, "there is very limited understanding of the rule of law, no one asks themselves any questions, no one wonders, and you can get in trouble if you have different opinions" (interview with anticorruption activist).

The most pervasive effect, however, is the creation of gaps and silences, at discursive and institutional levels. This starts from the concept of the rule of law itself: there was hardly agreement among my interviewees on what it means, whether Romania has the rule of law, or how this could be measured since societal expectations increased, yet the range of the discourse has become narrower. Government officials and activists interviewed talked about a formal separation of powers system that is largely ignored otherwise. They pointed out problems such as the quality of governance ("we cannot create and implement public policy"); the lack of communication and collaboration between the government and Parliament; politicized public administration; predominance of executive lawmaking through the ordinance mechanism; the rise of the "unaccountable judiciary"; lack of unitary, predictable, and transparent case law; lack of transparency in the legislative process; significant expertise gaps (the flight of experts to Brussels); lack of enforcement mechanisms; and a focus on formalism rather than substance ("we have the institution, the façade, and the rest does not matter"; the example given was the People's Advocate or Ombudsman). More pessimistic experts identified the dilution of state authority and the extent to which Romania is a captive state from an economic point of view.

Rights and the relationship between the individual and the state are a more troubling gap, particularly in light of the country's recent communist past. A funder with broad experience both in the NGO sector and the European Commission noted that "we went backwards, not forward" from a rule of law perspective because "there are less organizations that work on rule of law, human rights, advocacy than there should be and used to be." Another funder noted that human rights are simply "not on the public agenda anymore, every now and then one hears something about the ECHR [the European Court of Human Rights], but it's all superficial. There is little interest in prison reform, even smaller in LGBT issues, which are marginalized because the society remains so traditional. When one uses a human rights discourse, it is taken lightly, it's seen as a soft discourse and the assumption is that it is hiding something else, a different agenda."

Both civil society activists and state officials interviewed agreed that a key problem that was ignored in the EU-accession frenzy and continues to be ignored is the relationship between the citizen and the state: "the ordinary citizen needs a peaceful relationship with the state administration, which should not be perceived as a foreign body, but as a help and support for the citizen." By contrast, "here there is a quasi-schizophrenic relationship with the state authorities. We continue to depersonalize those in power as a mechanism of distance and self-protection, for Romanian citizens the state administration is distant, depersonalized, and hostile, and the rule of law is not internalized." My interviewee, a law professor and public intellectual, used the analogy of the ant and the blinds to explain the relationship between the state and the citizen in Romania – just as an ant needs to know when the window blinds are going up and down, there is need for rules for citizens, otherwise it's anarchy, which is where Romania is now.

Similarly, an anticorruption activist talked about increasing expectations that citizens are treated with dignity and respect, are "not to be crushed by the [state] boot." This type of critique targets issues more directly connected to citizens' quality of life, from dirty streets and garbage piles to urban planning, but the ordinary person has not internalized them as citizenship privileges that belong in the rule of law sphere. The theme of responsible citizenship and rule of law internalization emerged from interviews with all types of subjects. A long-time human rights activist described the average Romanian as "legally illiterate," and the youth, in particular, as lacking minimal knowledge of their rights and responsibilities as citizens. A law professor proposed civic education classes targeted at the internalization of civic, moral, and legal standards, starting as early as elementary school. More than once during the interviews, my questions about the rule of law were met with regret combined with an acknowledgment that somehow the rule of law has fallen by the wayside post-accession: we barely passed, as a civil society funder said, with a C+, which is "mediocre," but "we're there" and this is all that matters ...

These gaps, silences, and disruptions suggest that the rule of law remains a symbolic construct and site of aspiration in the modernization process that is as yet unfulfilled. They further suggest that the rule of law and corruption are not complementary, but competitive domains. The hegemony of the corruption discourse went largely unnoticed during my field research (and is not to be confused with cynicism about anticorruption efforts, which is widespread). Only a few of my interviewees questioned it, for example, proposing that the current "fetishization" of corruption is fundamentally counterproductive to the larger rule of law project by creating a "societal psychosis," institutional multiplicity and overlap, and potentially leading to witch hunts. A rule of law funder noted that it's still "sexy" to talk about corruption, albeit the discourse is slowly losing its cache. State officials working on anticorruption efforts meanwhile see the corruption discourse as a red herring foiling both the development of clear anticorruption efforts (despite the famed national strategies) and the establishment of a "real" rule of law state.

Indicators as a Political Technology of Reform

Rule of law indicators in Romania are a political technology of control driven by EU's Cooperation and Verification Mechanism, which reinforces a rule of law discourse focused on corruption and institutional reform that is disruptive and silences alternative discourses. Yet within this narrow range, rule of law indicators also function as a political technology of reform. This section examines why and how domestic actors mobilize rule of law indicators, which in this context include primarily process, outcome, and ranking corruption and judicial reform indicators. Rule of law indicators are unevenly mobilized by state and civil society actors. State actors work within a discourse of modernization and governmentality, both predicated on a technocratic logic that is inherently opposed to politics. Civil society actors are more concerned with state accountability and are deeply politicized.

The Logic of Reform for State Actors: Modernization and Governmentality

The modernization/governmentality logic is illustrated by the creation of the Romanian government's flagship anticorruption document, the *National Anti-Corruption Strategy (2012–2015)* (the author is the Ministry of Justice). The current version includes for the first time ever five international indicators measuring corruption: the Corruption Perception Index (TI), the Global Corruption Barometer (also TI), the European Bank for Reconstruction and Development (EBRD)/World Bank Business Environment and Enterprise Performance Surveys (BEEPS) of Corruption, the Global Integrity Index, and the Nations in Transit rankings (Freedom House). The Strategy does not use these indicators simply for illustrative purposes, like the CVM reports, but rather to set targets to be attained by 2015 – for example, the Corruption Perception Index (CPI) number for Romania, currently at 3.6, by 2015 should be 6.37, which is the EU average,[13] while the number under *Nations in Transit*, currently at 4, should reach 3.27, again the EU average. This parallels global models, such as the Millennium Development Goals. Simultaneously, it reflects the technocratic logic at work for state actors involved in creating the Strategy, and the calls for state accountability by the activists that were also part of the process.

The authors of the *National Anti-Corruption Strategy* are not publicly identified, but they included both civil servants and representatives of the civil society. One of them, a long-time anticorruption activist, mentioned during our interview that it was an uphill battle to convince the group to introduce indicators in the Strategy. The resistance did not come from a specific vantage point, but rather was passive, inertia based, diffuse – "how can we do something like this, it's unheard of." Everybody in the group was familiar with indicators, and there was no disagreement that as applied to Romania, corruption indicators like the CPI are relatively accurate. Ultimately, the decision to use these five indicators in the Strategy as benchmarks for 2015 arose from the belief that they can be a useful instrument, and in particular that "when you have an indicator that is validated internationally for ten years, you don't cross it."[14]

The ANI, established under the aegis of the EU, is another example of the technocratic governmentality logic at work. The Agency focuses on wealth control and is one of the most active state bodies in terms of constructing and promoting indicators. Its leadership and staff are quite young (below 40 years) and dedicated to indicators as a technique of transparent and efficient management. Both to satisfy the European Commission and for their own purposes, the Agency has developed its own "logically integrated database" with a "clear, standardized, written, defined procedure that everyone has to follow, is efficient and transparent," and forty different reporting categories (interview). The Agency is thus able to collect data about all of its activities and to build process and outcome indicators that allow it to monitor constantly not only its own activities, but also the action (or inaction) of other state bodies. As of March 2012, the Agency had carried out nearly 4000 verifications and issued findings or referrals in more than 500 cases, but its staff keeps track of everything: number of ongoing investigations, type and outcome, number of closed investigations, number of incompatibilities, possible criminal cases, cases of administrative conflict, number and amount of fines requested, status of cases in court (when referrals were made), and so forth.[15]

For these state actors, rule of law indicators mean modernity and its accompanying rationality, and as such have been fodder for political battles. Key rule of law state bodies, such as the Ministry of Justice, the Superior Council of Magistracy, the National Integrity Agency, and the National Anticorruption Directorate are not particularly well coordinated and occasionally mutually suspicious of each other. This slows down data collection, so that multiyear efforts to construct an open format case law portal for the entire country that would include indicators measuring the performance of the justice system have been slowed down by courts not uploading their cases and other data. Indicators are not prioritized financially and strategically, and even when they are, they get bogged down in political infighting, for example, over where to house the server, who should pay for it, and who should administer it (the Ministry of Justice, or the Superior Council of the Magistracy) (interview data).

The interpretation and use of indicators, or even missing indicators, have been at the heart of larger fights over control of the justice field in Romania. In the fall of 2010, for example, the Ministry of Justice asked the Superior Council of the Magistracy to suspend the pilot program establishing optimal workloads for courts, questioning the very conception at the basis of the program and pointing out that key national indicators were missing, such as the real number of case files per court. Citing the World Bank–financed study on the rationalization of the Romanian court system by Americans Lord and Wittrup (2005), the Ministry of Justice issued a scathing critique of the Council and its analysis, based on the unquestioned legitimacy of the American study and its understanding of indicators (Ministry of Justice 2010).

Institutions such as the ANI and the DNA, meanwhile, similarly understand themselves from a modernization perspective. Because they are unpopular in the country and often attacked politically, they operate with a bunker mentality and tend to be wary even when collaborating with each other (interviews). In 2010, for example, the Constitutional Court found key provisions of the statute regulating ANI unconstitutional while ANI was investigating seven of the nine judges of the Court (Constitutional Court decision No. 415/2010; Mitan 2010). Over the past five years, judges from the Supreme Court, Constitutional Court, and members of the Superior Council of the Magistracy have also been investigated by ANI and other anticorruption agencies.[16] Occasional cooperation with civil society organizations working on corruption is also marred by a significant level of distrust (interviews). This includes indicators: while I was given access to certain proprietary statistics, I was also told that no Romanian state body has them (only the European Commission), because they "are not really interested."

Reform Discourses in Civil Society: Accountability and Politics

If state bodies mobilize rule of law indicators as a sign of modernization and transparent and efficient governance, civil society actors want to hold the state accountable. The origin of this accountability discourse, however, is at least partially determined by the EU script and is thus also connected to fighting corruption and reforming the judiciary. More surprisingly, this quest for accountability minimally mobilizes indicators and has not led to NGOs using indicators to oppose politics. On the contrary, civil society actors have themselves become embroiled in political controversies. To the extent that civil society groups mobilize indicators, they are primarily corruption indicators, both domestic and international (e.g., the National Anti-Corruption Strategy, discussed previously).

An example of domestic indicators constructed by civil society actors is the simple and user-friendly "naming and shaming" *"transparency in governance"* rankings created by the Alliance for a Clean Romania, a coalition of civil society groups that addresses issues of failed governance and institutionalized corruption, and offers a venue for ordinary citizens to participate, on a voluntary basis, in the broader fight against corruption in Romania. Member groups include NGOs such as Freedom House Romania, student groups, journalists, unions, and citizens. The Alliance's funders are The Trust for Civil Society in Central and Eastern Europe and the German Marshall Fund. The Alliance ranks both government ministries and agencies according to how transparent they are and give each between 0 and 5 stars, accordingly, with five stars indicating the utmost transparency.

The Alliance collected the following information to construct the ranking: public data from the websites of the ministries, including, among others, declarations of assets, activity reports, budgets and procurement reports; and information requested on the basis of the law of access to information of public interest, including personnel data, subcontracting data, and income. The Ministry of Justice, for example, got only four stars in this ranking system because it did not publish its annual report, budget, procurement, and some other information. The Ministry also refused to provide some information (employees who sued or were sued by the Ministry), arguing that it is not "in the public interest."

Transparency International has been active and quite visible in the country since 1999 (www.transparency.org.ro). The Romanian branch (which is financially autonomous from the headquarters) publicizes the international indicators (the CPI and the Global Corruption Barometer [GBC]) and constructs domestic indicators based on the TI methodology, primarily through the National Integrity System (NIS) Assessment (began in 2005). The latest NIS study was published in 2012 and was funded by the European Commission. The study is both a qualitative evaluation and a scoring system of thirteen "functional pillars of the integrity system" (Transparency International Romania 2012, 6). These include key government and public sector institutions, as well as nongovernmental actors (media, civil society, political parties, and the business sector). Each one of these pillars is assessed along three variables: capacity (resources and independence), internal governance (transparency, accountability, integrity), and role/efficiency from an anticorruption perspective (depending on institution). Scores are initially assigned on a 1- to 5-point scale and then transformed into a 0- to 100-point scale, in 25-point increments. Based on this methodology, the Supreme Audit Institution garnered the highest score (72), while the public sector had the lowest (24). The final report is a visually attractive and legible color-coded wheel of corruption for the country.

Civil society efforts to hold the state accountable, through indicators or otherwise, have hit two particular obstacles. First, the state attacked. Freedom House, for example, which bid and won the right to audit the anticorruption policies of Romania in 2005, was accused by the Minister of Justice (at the time) of having cheated in the process and was sued. Although this was clearly a political attack on

Freedom House and more broadly NGOs working on corruption, it nonetheless distracted, demoralized, and temporarily divided them (interviews).[17]

Second, NGOs have become part of the political machine. A recent example is the elections for the Superior Council of the Magistracy. The Superior Council of Magistracy is the constitutional guarantor of the independence of justice and sole representative of the judiciary in the Romanian system of checks and balances (arts. 1, 132 of the Romanian Constitution).[18] Originally established in 1909, it was abolished during the communist regime and re-established post 1989. Two of its nineteen members represent the civil society.[19] The Superior Council of Magistracy is a key political player whose reputation in the past decade was savaged by cases of corruption and other wrongdoing in the judiciary, which the Council did not discipline adequately. The Council was "filled with communists and the old guard," was seen as weak and timid and was in need of serious reform itself (see, e.g., reports of the Romanian Academic Society SAR [Societatea Academica Romana]; interviews). The 2010 elections promised a new Council, and the judiciary as well as the civil society threw themselves in the elections process. A number of NGOs and foundations, including the Alliance for a Clean Romania, Freedom House Romania, the Romanian Academic Society, two German political foundations, and the American Embassy created an online platform to facilitate the elections – for the candidates to present themselves, to make it easier to monitor the process, organize debates, and so forth (www.alegericsm.ro). The outcome was somewhat unexpected, as they were accused of supporting some candidates and not others, and of allowing foreign interference with the independence of the judiciary (interviews).

In addition, some of the most prominent Romanian activists working on anticorruption, judiciary reform, or human rights campaigned for the two seats reserved for the civil society.[20] This changed the dynamic of the elections, of the civil society sector, and the relationships between civil society and state bodies: from outsiders who are supposed to monitor, they became polarized insiders with a stake in the outcomes and the system. A year after the elections, during my field research, their fallout was still very much visible in public and interview setting, and contributed to the ongoing divisions among NGOs. This is a relatively small field, with perhaps ten to fifteen NGOs throughout the country truly active on matters of governance and the rule of law, so relationships matter. There are some outstanding examples of collaboration, such as the Alliance for a Clean Romania, but overall collaborations among civil society organizations are ad hoc, while with "state institutions there is no real partnership or dialogue, only on very limited topics and depending very much on context" – they are "friends with frozen smiles," as one of my interviewees vividly said.

In summary, rule of law indicators are unevenly mobilized in Romania. This uneven mobilization is primarily due to distinct reformation logics: modern governance for the state, accountability for civil society. Yet ultimately state bodies have little incentive to monitor themselves; are constantly engaged in power struggles, including over indicators; and arguably lack expertise and staff for constructing and/ or using indicators. Indicators are a long-term commitment, so politicians subject to constant reelection are more likely to focus on immediate results instead (interview with EU official). The civil society has been partially co-opted and politicized, and is internally divided.[21] Indifference or resistance to indicators does not necessarily break down along government/civil society lines, however, but along perceived technical/political lines, both within the government and civil society. This dividing line is also at the heart of the emerging indicators consciousness in the country.

INDICATORS CONSCIOUSNESS: INSTRUMENTALISM, OBJECTIVITY, OWNERSHIP

The prior two sections of this chapter examined how rule of law indicators function as political technologies of control and reform in the Romanian context. Engagement with indicators is a continuing process, and among its recursive effects is the creation of "indicators consciousness," namely the extent and manner in which producers and users of indicators accept, use, resist, or change indicators. Current indicators used in Romania, and in particular corruption indicators, created significant doubt about indicators in general and consequently produced some resistance against all indicators. Based on my interviews, attitudes toward indicators at the moment revolve around three features: their value-added, their objectivity and impartiality, and a minimal degree of ownership in the construction or use of indicators.

The appeal of indicators for my interviewees lies at the intersection of *instrumentalism* and *technocracy*. They see indicators as potential tools of governance that can promote transparency across the board, increase efficiency, help "fix governance" problems, and act as disciplinary mechanisms. The majority of my interviewees agreed, on a general level, that indicators (both ranked and unranked, although primarily unranked) could be useful instruments, and that "Romania does not have indicators, and needs them." They primarily saw indicators in a technical instrumental sense, as "measuring tools" at the center of a broader interpretive analysis, in particular when it (and the indicators) "are tailored to service specific needs." Common leitmotifs included indicators as diagnostic tools, framing tools, and standards of comparison, specifically an objective, standardized way of measuring reality horizontally and longitudinally.

As diagnostic tools, indicators "help define a problem, help diagnose problems" (anticorruption researcher), "help identify vulnerabilities in the system, the weak points," and "are useful for distilling issues, for showing us where the weak and strong points in a system are" (rule of law funder). "Numbers," in the words of a government official, "indicate where the vulnerabilities are." Anticorruption experts used an even more dramatic language: "You only see that you are corrupt if you have a mechanism of control, it's like people who are sick and know and accept they have a sickness and then get a cure, or they deny they're sick. The first step is to accept you're sick," … "is this or isn't this a disease." Indicators "help talk about a problem, frame it, understand it," and ultimately "direct the discussion," but nothing more.

From inside the government, indicators can be used for auto-evaluation – "as a mirror," while from outside the power structure they could be used for "naming and shaming." The latter, I was repeatedly reminded, helped during the accession process – the constant reinforcement of the idea that "we were always the bottom of the heap," so there is no reason it would not continue to function. Anticorruption experts in particular, whether from NGOs, think tanks or governmental agencies, wanted indicators to be used for much more than diagnostic purposes – they want to see indicators internalized as part of a process of constant, systematic evaluation and institutional development, and not just as an externally imposed mandate. They build their indicators' "wish list" on the (perceived) model of international organizations that use indicators as building blocks toward constructing concrete solutions for their problems.

Indicators, in other words, should be used for practical, policymaking purposes, not just for scientific purposes, "superficial political discussions," or no obvious purpose. A government bureaucrat talked about being "sick and tired of filling out forms and statistics only to be sent higher up," while a rule of law expert was overall skeptical about indicators because "those in power use indicators for defensive purposes only, not for real, and they have no real interest in promoting a rule of law state." People are not immune to the power of numbers, suggested a rule of law funder, so they have "educational power" that could be harnessed to change mentalities, for example, in the area of corruption. Ultimately, of course, "any type of indicator is in theory helpful if those in power take them into account."

The lack of value added is a key reason for resistance against indicators, as well. Corruption and rule of law indicators aim to measure complex phenomena, and my interviewees questioned the value added of a measuring process that means simplification, reductionism, decontextualization, and a "one size fits all" approach that draws from outdated data (indicators as inherently backward looking). From a user perspective, if rule of law indicators are seen as not adding any new information, they are likely to be ignored. As many of my interviewees noted, "we know where we are, and anyway no one wants to find out they're last." There is no added value, as well, to the extent that indicators conform to expectations, which is particularly true for countries such as Romania that tend to score in the middle ranges on most rule of law indicators.

The value-added of indicators can also be fatally damaged by their lack of *credibility*, either because the producers lack credibility, or because of doubts about how indicators are used. The producers may lack legitimacy either because they are a virtual monopoly for a particular indicator ("it's like state capture," argued an interviewee), or if they are embroiled in political controversies. Transparency International Romania, for example, has been a contentious organization in recent years: it is perceived by other civil society members to be in "continuous crisis," "very political and controversial," and affiliated with political agents. Its leader, moreover, a young lawyer wearing many hats – public servant, NGO leader, attorney, aspiring government member – has been embroiled in a number of public scandals and lawsuits with the National Integrity Agency, which had found him incompatible with membership in the Superior Council of the Magistracy, the top administrative body within the judiciary (*MediaFax* May 2, 2012; Transparency International News Flash May 18, 2012). The fact that two key anticorruption actors have been publicly sparring for the past three years has damaged the credibility of both, as well as their work. In its National Integrity System Assessment, for example, Transparency International Romania evaluates poorly the National Integrity Agency, yet this evaluation, in light of their public battle, is not seen as credible, which in turn raises questions about the entire assessment (see, e.g., Transparency International Romania 2012; interviews). In this battle, indicators end up as collateral damage.

The lack of credibility and thus value-added can also arise from the perception that indicators are easy to manipulate and use for political or cosmetic purposes only, that they are merely the latest gimmick and that "it's all a game." As an example, when a Romanian NGO interested in indicators did its own preliminary research on indicators, they talked to foreign organizations that routinely use indicators. One of them candidly admitted that the reason their country scored well is because there was a "cozy relationship" between them and their government, and they calculate the final score "until it comes out right." This was enough to deter the Romanian NGO from seriously considering indicators.

My interviewees were also concerned value-added suffers if indicators are hard to interpret, for example, in the case of corruption, both domestic and international corruption indicators found an apparent increase in corruption from 2010 to 2011, yet its meaning is unclear because it can indicate either an increase in corruption, or a better anticorruption effort (National Anti-Corruption Agency 2010). Indicators also pose risks to those using them, in terms of finding out unwanted information, and are easy to fetishize (in particular the implicit and unquestioned faith in numbers). Turning off key audiences, such as magistrates vis-à-vis corruption indicators (because they think "they miss most of the picture, don't capture what's really going on"), leads to more resistance to indicators overall.

The instrumental value of indicators is directly connected to their *objectivity* and *impartiality*. Cautious supporters of rule of law indicators embrace them only to the extent that they can be "objective," used to reform the system, and build up from process indicators – for example, measuring the evolution of cases in the judicial system, measuring the extent to which laws are equally implemented, how often they change and how transparent is the process, what happens to corruption cases once they get to court. Interestingly, EU experts see rule of law indicators as potentially helpful for defining the rule of law itself across Europe, as a "neutral," technical concept-building mechanism. Yet their origin – domestic or international – was not seen as particularly relevant, as opposed to their technical, objective, impartial ability to "measure reality," itself based on faith in numbers and their capacity to stymie politics and ideology.

The vast majority of my interviewees rejected current indicators because they measure perception, not reality, and thus cannot establish an objective, standard way of measuring reality that would allow Romania to measure itself both against comparable countries, and against itself over time. As a former accession official remarked, "we get to know each other better through comparison, and indicators would thus allow comparisons among states." Critiques of the Corruption Perception Index (CPI), in particular, which is seen as inherently subjective and flawed, are a key reason for the desire to have "reality" indicators that rely upon "hard data" and a standardized system that could be used universally. Objective, impartial indicators are attractive because they can be used to measure the impact of policies, the extent to which specific policies work, and the impact on the average person. The objectivity trope also surfaced in the context of constructing indicators, specifically the need to separate the collection of data from data analysis so that any possibility of bias and subjectivity is avoided.

Finally, attitudes toward indicators and in particular resistance to indicators emerged from lack of *ownership* and control in the process of constructing indicators and end use. My interviewees pointed out that Romania lacks expertise and money to build its own indicators, especially those that require a complex methodology, and therefore has to rely on external ones. External indicators are problematic because data flows up. Under the CVM, Romania is required to provide very detailed statistics in a number of areas, but not specific indicators (interview corruption official). There is some pressure to develop outcome indicators for the judiciary in last year's CVM report,[22] and Romania also participates in a number of other European initiatives. Process and outcome indicators measuring the judiciary are created by the European Commission for the Efficiency of Justice (CEPEJ) (belonging to the Council of Europe system), a meticulous and extensive evaluation of all participating European justice systems. Its reports (the latest one was issued in 2010, with data from 2008) cover all areas of the judiciary systems, from public expenditures to courts, alternative dispute resolution, court activity, execution of judgments, lawyers, and so forth.[23]

From a Romanian perspective, however, it does not matter whether indicators are the result of the CVM or part of the Council of Europe reports, because the process and results are the same: Romanian bodies provide the raw data according to a set questionnaire and predetermined methodology (see, e.g., CEPEJ 2009 Romanian answers), which is then processed, analyzed, and interpreted "out there," in Brussels or Strasbourg. There is similarly little national control over the end result, which further weakens any interest that might exist in indicators.

CONCLUSION

This chapter examined rule of law indicators in Romania as political technologies of control and reform. The EU's Cooperation and Verification Mechanism is the key site of control that is important from symbolic, institutional, and discursive perspectives. Its existence signifies the continuous second-rate status of Romania in Europe and its inability to reach modernity, while its focus on anticorruption and judicial reform privileges these institutions and discourses while obscuring or silencing alternatives. Rule of law indicators are less prominent from a reform perspective and are unevenly mobilized by domestic state and civil society actors. Their main appeal for state actors lies in their embodiment of modern, efficient governance. NGOs are driven primarily by their desire for state accountability, yet they have only minimally deployed indicators for this purpose or concrete reforms. Across the board, indicators are appropriated to the extent that they can prove their added value, neutrality, objectivity, and credibility, and rejected if they are seen as subjective or superfluous and if there is no domestic ownership in either their construction or use.

What are the implications of this case study for rule of law indicators (and perhaps other indicators)? First, the acceptance of indicators cannot be taken for granted. Different constituencies mobilize them for distinct purposes that are highly context dependent, and the meaning of indicators and of the concepts they purport to measure will morph accordingly. This jeopardizes indicators' very raison d'être: clarification, simplification, universality. A second implication is that the indicators main strength is also their weakness, in particular the extent to which they embody neutrality and objectivity that both insulates them from politics but also leaves them vulnerable to political battles. The third implication is that no indicator is an island – the prominence of narrower rule of law indicators in Romania (corruption and judicial reform) and their performance impact the entire indicators field and the reception of new indicators.

NOTES

1 For summaries, see, e.g., Kim Lane Scheppele's guest editorial in *The New York Times* on July 5, 2012, http://krugman.blogs.nytimes.com/2012/07/05/guest-post-romania-unravels-the-rule-of-law/.

2 The accompanying technical report further included a plethora of data on the country's judiciary, such as numbers of cases processed at every level of the judicial system, outcomes, staffing changes, magistrates' workloads, budgets, and changes over time.

3 Four major efforts to construct or refine global rule of law indicators currently include the World Bank's Governance Indicators, the World Justice Project Rule of Law Index, the Vera–Altus Indicators, and the United Nations Rule of Law Indicators.

4 For Bulgaria, the accompanying measures also include the fight against organized crime.

5 Officially, the EU does not use ranking indicators, as it would antagonize its member states too much and would be against a widely perceived EU ethos (politically, naming and shaming and reputation are quite valuable controlling mechanisms) (interview data).

6 Macovei has been working to establish a pan-European anticorruption policy, including indicators to measure corruption in the EU. The indicator would be focused on public procurement, and would compare countries in the EU with each other. www .monica-macovei.ro; www.monicamavei.eu.

7 See www.integritate.eu. Tellingly, even the Agency's website has an EU domain name.

8 Under Romanian law (Law no. 176/2010), public officials have the obligation to declare all their income and wealth, part of broader measures of preserving integrity and transparency in governance and fighting systemic corruption. The Agency's responsibility is to collect, publicize, evaluate, and investigate the income statements, and to the extent it finds cause, alert other state bodies for further investigation and potentially prosecution. The Agency maintains a large public database of wealth statements on its website, which includes approximately 3 million statements and can be searched using eleven different search criteria.

9 The July 2012 report notes approvingly that the number of indictments has risen from 167 cases against 415 defendants in 2007 to 233 cases against 1,091 defendants in 2011. Since 2007, DNA has indicted, among other, a former prime minister, a former deputy prime minister, former ministers and members of Parliament, prefects, mayors, county councilors, and heads of state-owned enterprises (EC July 2012, 12).

10 A significant portion so far has been spent on building and renovating courts; another portion is for an integrated IT system for resource management (EC July 2012 Technical Report, 9).

11 The review was contracted in February 2012 and should be complete in nine to twelve months. The review is assessing the resourcing, organization, functioning, and performance of the judicial system. It should provide short-, medium-, and long-term recommendations to guide the direction of judicial reform, as well as a vehicle for reinvigorating structural and capacity reforms (EC July 2012 Technical Report, 12).

12 This is currently being undertaken by consultants financed from a World Bank loan (EC July 2012, 6 fn 13).

13 The CPI runs from 0 – most corrupt, to 10 – least corrupt.

14 Aiming for a 6 in two years, in this interviewee's opinion, is a realistic goal that, even if not achieved, would still allow us to measure progress.

15 Every one of these categories is further broken down, e.g., by prosecutorial and court outcomes, reasons for each (lack of criminal intention, deed does not exist, etc.), duration of investigations and court cases, final outcome (e.g., as of July 2011, out of 1,438 complaints against administrative fines applied by the Agency, courts found in favor of the Agency in an overwhelming 84 percent of cases) (interview with agency official), and many other types of statistical breakdown. For the most part, these are relatively simple statistics, with some ratios and no rankings, and also with relatively little analysis. They do allow for rough temporal comparisons, however.

16 For example, the Jipa affair, described by the Alliance for a Clean Romania (http://www.romaniacurata.ro/cristian-jipa-magistrat-la-inalta-curte-de-justitie-chemat-la-dna-in-d-838.htm). The Alliance (www.romaniacurata.ro) has a public database keeping track of these cases.

17 This video shows the Minister of Justice launching a diatribe against key anticorruption activists: http://www.realitatea.net/video_186612_t-chiuariu–lupta-anti-coruptie-este-baz ata-pe-licitatii-trucate_91741.html video. The entire controversy was extensively covered by the press at the time, e.g., the newspaper *Cotidianul* in an article entitled "Ministerul de Justitie da in judecata pentru o greseala de tipar" [The Ministry of Justice Sues for a Typo" (September 25, 2007)], and *Romania Libera*, "Freedom House Demonteaza Acuzatiile Ministrului Chiuariu" ["Freedom House Demolishes the Accusations of Minister Chiuariu"] http://www.romanialibera.ro/actualitate/eveniment/freedom-ho use-demonteaza-acuzatiile-ministrului-chiuariu-106953.html, and "Chiuariu devine un pericol pentru Romania" ["Chiuariu Becomes a Danger for Romania"] http://www.romanialibera.ro/actualitate/eveniment/freedom-house-chiuariu-devine-u n-pericol-pentru-romania-108168.html.

18 Similar bodies throughout the world include France, Italy, Côte d'Ivoire, Rwanda.

19 Fourteen members are elected by judges and prosecutors from among themselves, two represent the civil society and are elected by the Romanian Senate, and ex officio the Minister of Justice, the President of the Supreme Court and the Prosecutor General. Members of the Council serve for nonrenewable six-year terms. The Council's powers are expansive and include the recruitment, promotion, disciplining, suspension, and proposals for termination of judges and prosecutors (including submitting proposals for appointment for the highest judicial functions in the country), as well as overseeing the organization and well functioning of all courts and prosecutors' offices in the country.

20 For example, Cristina Ana from Romanian Academic Society, the main Romanian think tank; Simina Tanasescu, the Vice Dean of the Bucharest Law School; Victor Alistar, the head of Transparency International Romania.

21 The business sector is narrowly and relatively happily focused on its interests, having evolved from the early 1990s as vocal promoters of the rule of law, in particular vis-à-vis property and contracts, to a relatively self-absorbed sector once those demands were fulfilled. However, the recent push toward judicial accountability is justified, at least in part, with an effort to create honesty and quality in the judiciary, an issue of great interest to businesses, as well (World Bank 2005 proposal).

22 "The judicial system does not possess and has not developed effective performance indicators to inform total resource needs and resource allocations within the judicial system. Romania has recently recognized these weaknesses and they will now be addressed by a project funded by the World Bank which will prepare and pilot revised case and workload indicators by early 2013" (EC July 2012, 9).

23 The report includes a lengthy warning that it only "aims to give an overview of the situation of the European judicial systems, not to rank the best judicial systems in Europe, which would be scientifically inaccurate and would not be a useful tool for the public policies of justice." It further emphasizes that "comparing is not ranking" (pp. 8–9 of the 2010 Report, which has 390 pages and can be found at http://www.coe.int/T/dghl/ cooperation/cepej/default_en.asp 9). Yet countries are commonly ranked in color-coded categories, e.g., by level of expenditure for legal aid. As another example, countries are ranked according to the level of computerization in their judicial system.

REFERENCES

Alegre, Susie, Ivanka Ivanova, and Dana Denis-Smith. 2009. "Safeguarding the Rule of Law in an Enlarged EU: The Cases of Bulgaria and Romania." The Centre for European Policy Studies. http://www.ceps.eu/book/safeguarding-rule-law-enlarged-eu-cases-bulgaria-and-romania.

American Bar Association. 2007. "Rule of Law Initiative. Romania (past program)." http:// apps.americanbar.org/rol/europe_and_eurasia/romania.html.

American Bar Association, Central and East European Law Initiative (CEELI). 1993. "Country Strategies for the Rule of Law Program for Albania, Bulgaria, Croatia, Czech Republic, Estonia, Hungary, Latvia, Lithuania, Macedonia, Poland, Romania, and Slovakia." Submitted to the U.S. Agency for International Development, August 23, 1993.

Bazon, Irina. 2010. "Gunter Verheugen: The Mechanism for Cooperation and Verification Is Not Right, Although It Was Necessary." *CorectPolitics*, December 5.

Commission of the European Communities. 2006. "Commission Staff Working Document, Romania, May 2006 Monitoring Report." http://ec.europa.eu/enlargement/pdf /key_documents/2006/monitoring_report_ro_en.pdf.

Davis, Kevin, Benedict Kingsbury, and Sally Engle Merry. 2011. "Indicators as a Technology of Global Governance." Institute for International Law and Justice, Working Paper 2. http://www.iilj.org/publications/documents/2011.8.IndicatorsasaTechnologyofGlobal Governance.pdf.

European Commission (EC). 2007–2012. "Mechanism for Cooperation and Verification for Romania and Bulgaria. Progress Reports." http://ec.europa.eu/cvm/ progress_reports_en.htm.

European Commission for the Efficiency of Justice (CEPEJ). 2008. "European Judicial Systems. Efficiency and Quality of Justice." www.coe.int/cepej.

Freedom House. 2005. "The Anti-Corruption Policies of the Romanian Government. An Evaluation Report." http://www.just.ro/Portals/0/Lupta%20impotriva%20coruptiei /Documente/Audit%20SNA/FH_audit_RO_16_031.pdf.

Harvard University, John F. Kennedy School of Government. 2008. "Indicators of Safety and Justice: Their Design, Implementation and Use in Developing Countries." Workshop Held at Harvard University, March 13–15.

Judt, Tony. 2001. "Romania: Bottom of the Heap." *The New York Review of Books*, November 1. http://www.nybooks.com/articles/archives/2001/nov/01/romania-bottom-of-the-heap/.

Kaufmann, Daniel, Aart Kraay, and Massimo Mastruzzi. 2009. "Governance Matters VIII: Aggregate and Individual Governance Indicators 1996–2008." The World Bank

Development Research Group. https://openknowledge.worldbank.org/bitstream/ handle/10986/4170/WPS4978.pdf?sequence=1.

Lord, Terry, and Jesper Wittrup. 2005. "Study on Romanian Court Rationalization." www .just.ro.

Ministry of Justice, Romania. 2010. "The Institutional Position of the Ministry of Justice Regarding the Evaluation of the Results of the Pilot Program Establishing the Optimal Workload for Courts and Tribunals." www.just.ro.

2012. "National Anti-Corruption Strategy for 2012–2015." http://www.just.ro/LinkClick.aspx ?fileticket=T3mlRnW1IsY%3d&tabid=2102.

Mitan, Madalina. 2010. "National Integrity Agency: The Decision of the Constitutional Court Endangers the Report on the Justice System." *Ziare.com*, April 16. http://www .ziare.com/ccr/decizii/ani-decizia-ccr-pune-in-pericol-raportul-pe-justitie-1009719.

National Anti-Corruption Agency. 2010. "Activity Report." http://www.pna.ro/faces/obiect2 .jsp?id=144.

Permanent Representation of Romania to the European Union. 2007. "Romania-EU Accession Assistance." http://ue.mae.ro/en/node/456.

Rule of Law Symposium. 2009. "The History of CEELI, the ABA's Rule of Law Initiative, and the Rule of Law Movement Going Forward." *Minnesota Journal of International Law* 18: 304–342.

Skaaning, Svend-Erik. 2010. "Measuring the Rule of Law." *Political Research Quarterly* 63: 449–460.

Tamanaha, Brian. 2004. *On the Rule of Law: History, Politics, Theory.* Cambridge: Cambridge University Press.

Transparency International (TI) Romania. 2012. "National Integrity System." http://media .transparency.org/nis/cogs/index.html?Country=ro.

2012. "Press Release." http://www.transparency.org.ro/stiri/comunicate_de_presa/2012 /18mai/index.html.

United Nations. 2011. "Rule of Law Indicators. Implementation Guide and Project Tools." http://www.un.org/en/events/peacekeepersday/2011/publications/un_rule_of_law_ indicators.pdf.

United Nations Office of the High Commissioner for Human Rights. 2006. "Report on Rule of Law Tools for Post-Conflict States. Monitoring Legal Systems." http://www.ohchr.org /Documents/Publications/RuleoflawMonitoringen.pdf.

United Nations Security Council. 2011. "The Rule of Law and Transitional Justice in Conflict and Post-Conflict Societies." http://www.unrol.org/files/S_2011_634EN.pdf.

"Victor Alistar Prohibited from Occupying Public Office until August 7, 2012." 2005. "Project Appraisal Document on a Proposed Loan in the Amount of €110Million ($130 million) to Romania for a Judicial Reform Project." www.worldbank.org.

World Bank. 2012. "Victor Alistar Prohibited from Occupying Public Office until August 7, 2012." *MediaFax*, May 2, 2012. http://www.mediafax.ro/politic/ani-victor-alistar-are-interdictie -de-a-ocupa-functii-publice-pana-in-7-august-2012-9586028.

7

Indicators, Global Expertise, and a Local Political Drama

Producing and Deploying Corruption Perception Data in Post-Socialist Albania

Smoki Musaraj

INTRODUCTION

This chapter explores the production and circulation of a corruption perception survey in Albania. The indicator in question acts as a semiprivate quasi-indicator: "semiprivate" insofar as its design and production involve both private institutions (transnational consultancy firms, local market research centers) and public institutions (governmental funding agencies); and a "quasi-indicator" insofar as, like the indicators described by Davis, Kingsbury, and Merry (2012a, 2012b), it compares institutions to one another and over time, yet, unlike those of other indicators, its rankings are not compared or translatable to other countries or other rankings. The chapter examines the ways in which this survey acts as a "form of knowledge" and a "technology of governance" (Davis, Kingsbury, and Merry 2012b). The first part of the chapter draws attention to the heterogeneous "ecology" (Halliday 2012) of indicators, through a discussion of the institutions and sources of expertise involved in the making of its questionnaires. The second part traces the intended and unintended uses of indicators in the local political context. I trace the impact of the 2008 and 2009 survey data on a local political drama that enfolded around the allegations of *afera korruptive* (corruption affairs) involving the highest levels of government. In the public debate of this event, the United States Agency for International Development (USAID)/Institute for Development Research and Alternatives (IDRA) survey became an important actor in the public debacle between the US Ambassador John Withers, Public Prosecutor Ina Rama, and Prime Minister Sali Berisha.

The focus of this story is the "Corruption in Albania: Perceptions and Experience" survey conducted by the local market research institute, the Institute for Development Research and Alternatives (IDRA) with funding from the USAID Rule of Law funding from 2005 to 2010. The survey was known locally as "the USAID corruption perception survey," despite the fact that it is IDRA that conducts the whole process of data collection, SPSS (Statistical Package for the Social Sciences) aggregation, and the distillation of the data into the final report. In January of 2008, I started an internship with IDRA while conducting research on the multiple notions of corruption in Albania. IDRA's director, Auron Pasha, kindly allowed me to be a part of IDRA's 2008 corruption perception survey data collection. During my three months at IDRA, I witnessed the various parts of the data collection process – from the in-office training workshops of interviewers to be dispatched across the country, to following up on the completed questionnaires, to finally waiting for the results from the aggregated data to identify patterns of perceptions of corruption in Albania. Throughout my time at IDRA I also enjoyed the friendship and company of many of the staff. They patiently discussed with me their experiences and impressions of corruption in Albania and the evolution of the survey. Needless to say, the opinions expressed in this chapter do not reflect those of USAID or IDRA.

AN ACT OF TRANSLATION

Unlike prior events of the kind, the launch of the 2008 USAID/IDRA survey "Corruption in Albania: Perceptions and Experience" took on a special political significance. Taking place at the University of Tirana's facilities, the press conference included an unprecedented speech from then-US Ambassador to Albania, John Withers. As IDRA's staff noted, previous press conferences of this kind usually involved lower level officers of the US Embassy or the USAID. Ambassador Withers' presence and pronouncements at the press conference grabbed the main headlines of next day's news with dramatic titles such as "Corruption: USA Slaps the Government."

In his opening remarks, Withers cited a number of survey findings with an alarming tone: "92% of Albanians say that corruption is widespread among public officials," "about 70% of interviewed said they had paid a bribe to receive a medical service," and "60% of the interviewed have little trust in the justice system" (Shekulli 2008, 4). Further, Withers moved on to provide stories of petty corruption told to him by local people. Next, Withers appealed to local cultural traditions and virtues – "honesty, integrity" and the honor code (*besa*) – to make a case that corruption was not a "symptom of the local culture." Instead, Withers targeted the political elite as the main culprit in the widespread corruption. Finally, Withers outlined actions that institutions can take to combat corruption. Specifically, he provided one policy prescription regarding the proposed law on lifting the immunity of high-level officials – a law that was under discussion at the Albanian parliament at the time.

The launch of the 2008 survey findings thus provided a platform that granted legitimacy to the ambassador's allegations of corruption toward high-level officials in the Albanian government. In particular, the launch presented an opportunity for the ambassador to articulate his disapproval of Prime Minister Sali Berisha, and his support for the prosecutor general, Ina Rama. At the same time, the form and scale of the event in turn strengthened the survey's status as an objective and authoritative source of expertise on corruption and governance. Other local actors – including members of the opposition party and the prosecutor general – drew on the survey as a mean of strengthening their own opposition to an increasingly authoritarian political leadership.

Linking the indicator data to the specific local events and debates and further into a concrete form of action, I argue in this chapter, entailed several acts of translation. I use the term translation pace actor-network theory to describe a displacement of concerns and questions from one realm to another (Callon and Latour 1986, 34).[1] Here the survey data constituted a source of expertise to be trusted and used as basis for political assessment and decision making. This act of translation entailed several types of displacements. One such displacement involved moving the indicator data from the realm of apolitical opinion polling expertise to that of political negotiation and decision making. How did this particular corruption indicator come to count as a source of expertise and as a tool for political action? The first part of this chapter addresses this question by looking into the ecology of institutions involved in the production of the survey questionnaire. Mapping out this ecology provides insight into how private quasi-indicators such as USAID/IDRA's Survey are entangled with heterogeneous actors – global/local, public/private – and thus partake in a transnational form of expertise.

Recent work on indicators has brought attention to them as a form of knowledge and as a technology of governance (Merry 2011; Davis, Kingsbury, and Merry 2012a, 2012b). Sally Merry (2011), for instance, notes that, increasingly, global indicators have been taking after corporate forms of audit cultures (Power 1999; Strathern 2000). Merry warns about the political implications of this expansion of audit cultures in the sphere of human rights, health, and governance: "Indicators typically conceal their political and theoretical origins and underlying theories of social change and activism" (2011, S84). By looking at the various acts of displacement and translation – of forms of knowledge and political action – I seek to make visible the complicated origins and movements of expertise involved in the creation of the USAID/IDRA corruption perception survey. I argue that the content of this survey's questionnaire came into existence through dispersed acts of sharing, negotiating, and transferring of knowledge across various nodes of knowledge production – the local research center in Albania, global private consultancies, American higher education institutions' opinion-polling centers, and USAID-sponsored polls in Latin America.

THE POLITICAL ECOLOGY OF A CORRUPTION INDICATOR

Although not part of a broader cross-country index (such as, e.g., the rival index, the Corruption Perceptions Index [CPI] by Transparency International [TI]), similar to other indicators discussed in this volume, USAID/IDRA's survey draws on a global type of expertise, both in its methodology (measuring perception as a means of measuring the phenomenon; using statistical knowledge and survey methods to assess complex social and political configurations) as well as in its content – the keywords and forms of questions used in the questionnaire draw on a global register of the "anticorruption world" (Sampson 2005).

For instance, the key data that Ambassador Withers headlined in his speech – that 92 percent of Albanians say that corruption is widespread among public officials – corresponded to the question: "How much, in your opinion, is corruption spread among government officials?" The answer choices were: widespread, somewhat widespread, not widespread. Other typical perception questions include: "How much do you trust in the Parliament?" (the answer choices being: very transparent, somewhat transparent, not transparent, I don't know/do not want to answer) (IDRA 2008, SYS.8) and "[On a scale of 1 to 10, where 1 is very honest and 10 is very corrupt] according to you, how corrupt or honest are the representatives of the following institutions?" (USAID/IDRA 2008, PC1–PC19). This set of questions is modeled after other corruption perception indicators (such as TI's CPI, for instance, Kaufmann et al. 2006). The questionnaire also includes experiential questions (such as "Over the past year has any policeman asked you to give a bribe? [IDRA 2008, Q EXC2]) – also mirroring similar questions in corruption perception surveys and bribe indices (e.g., the TI's Bribe Payers' Index). Finally, the USAID/IDRA survey contains a set of questions that attains little media spotlight but that, unlike other corruption perception surveys, gauges local notions of legitimacy or illegitimacy of given transactions (such as, "If a minister accepts a bribe of ten thousand dollars from a private enterprise, do you think the minister is (1) corrupt and should be punished, (2) corrupt but justified, (3) not corrupt, (0) don't know?" [IDRA 2008, Q AOC1]).

Further, other international reports on governance and corruption make reference to the USAID/IDARA survey as a source of data about corruption in Albania that is comparable in its legitimacy and credibility to other major governance indicators. A 2011 World Bank report on "Governance in Albania: A Way Forward for Competitive Growth, and European Integration," for instance, referenced many of IDRA's surveys alongside other indicators (such as TI's CPI, Doing Business, Freedom House' Freedom in the World Index, etc.) (World Bank 2011, 21, 27–28, 43). As the title of this report suggests, this assemblage of indicators, including the USAID/IDRA's data on corruption, provide a source of expertise that enables World

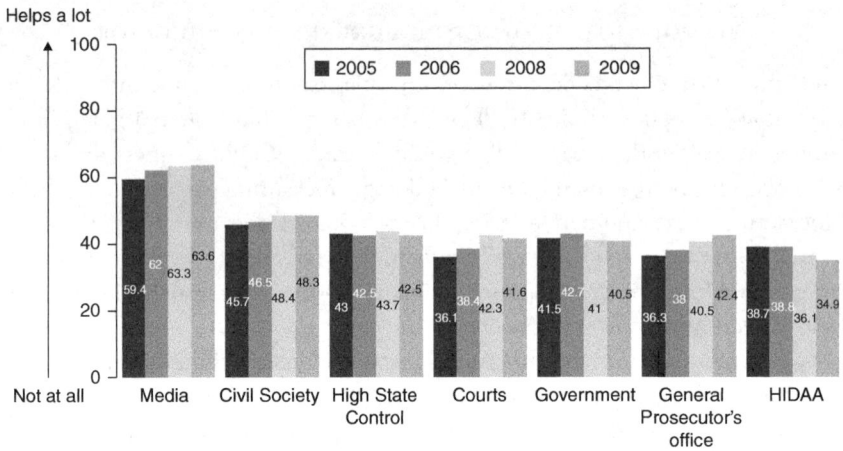

Helps a lot

100

■ 2005 ■ 2006 ■ 2008 ■ 2009

80

60

40

20

0

Not at all

Media: 59.4, 62, 63.3, 63.6
Civil Society: 45.7, 46.5, 48.4, 48.3
High State Control: 43, 42.5, 43.7, 42.5
Courts: 36.1, 38.4, 42.3, 41.6
Government: 41.5, 42.7, 41, 40.5
General Prosecutor's office: 36.3, 38, 40.5, 42.4
HIDAA: 38.7, 38.8, 36.1, 34.9

FIGURE 7.1. Extent to which institutions help to fight corruption – General Public samples.
Source: IDRA, Corruption in Albania, Survey. "The General Prosecutor's office has shown the biggest improvement from 2005 with a 6.1 point increase [from 36.3 to 42.4 points]." IDRA 2009:13.

Bank experts to make assessments and recommendations that target economic and political matters (namely, competitive growth and European integration).

Much like the indicators described by Davis, Kingsbury, and Merry (2012a, 6), the USAID/IDRA survey compares ranking of institutions to one another and over time. Thus the 2010 survey provided an overview of the rankings of institutions between 2005 and 2009 (Figure 7.1).

As *a form of knowledge*, the USAID Corruption survey needs to be situated within the broader context of an anticorruption assemblage emerging in the mid-1990s, a network of "global integrity warriors" (Sampson 2005), an "industry" (Sampson 2010) consisting of "hundreds of specialists, embedded in a myriad of programmes, initiatives and institutions, using hundreds of millions of dollars to combat corruption" (Sampson 2010, 267). This assemblage was set in motion by a movement within the World Bank declaring war on "the corruption eruption" (Naím 1995) and the emergence of TI, a global anticorruption organization that can be credited with popularizing the use of indicators as tools to measure and compare corruption cross-culturally.[2]

Over the last two decades, writes Sampson (2010), this anticorruption assemblage has evolved from "a movement" to an "industry" that favors "comparable statistical measures and rankings that can be easily 'crunched'" over "qualitative, intensive studies keyed to specific situations or countries" (Sampson 2010, 269). The USAID/IDRA survey is one such tool, though unlike its sister indicators – most notably,

TI's CPI – it does focus on one country, Albania, all the while using a similar form of knowledge – measuring perceptions of corruption as a means of gauging levels of corruption, using SPSS data aggregation and comparative ranking of local institutions over time.

As *a technology of governance*, the USAID/IDRA survey takes different forms. The UDAID/IDRAs survey emerged at the peak of a local grassroots movement with a strong antigovernment energy exploding especially since 1997, the year of the pyramid scheme collapse.[3] This local political energy expressed a growing popular frustration with the political leadership (of both the Democratic Party and the Socialist Party). This general antigovernment energy was, in turn, was channeled toward the anticorruption movement. Various institutions promoted and supported this movement, including international organizations such as the World Bank, country-specific Development Agencies (e.g., the USAID), and European Union (EU) and Council of Europe institutions such as GRECO (The Group of States Against Corruption, a Council of Europe body) (see also Kajsiu 2013).

The context within which the USAID/IDRA's survey emerged highlights the intersection between local and international political institutions and histories. The USAID/IDRA survey was one of the many USAID Rule of Law sponsored local initiatives to raise "awareness" and "educate" locals about corruption. The USAID hired the Washington-based consultancy firm Management System International (MSI), which in 2001 organized and set up the Albanian Coalition Against Corruption (ACAC). Funded alongside other local civil society organizations, the USAID/IDRA survey was initially tasked to also serve as a means of self-audit – previous questionnaires, for instance, asked respondents about their awareness of the USAID-funded civil society institutions, such ACAC and the Citizens Advocacy Office (CAO) (Seligson and Baviskar 2006). This in itself reflects an increasing shift toward indicators (rather than, say, activist groups) in the broader world of anticorruption funding.

Despite setting out as a politically neutral civil society movement, the anticorruption movement had a significant political impact in early 2000s Albania. Although the coalition was a nonpartisan network of civil society actors, its activities contributed to the electoral victory of the then-opposition party, Partia Demokratike (PD, the Democratic Party), which campaigned against the incumbent Partia Socialiste (PS, Socialist Party) under the banner of "the war on corruption" (*lufta ndaj korrupsionit*). Alas, the subsequent two-term rule of PD did by no means end or lower corruption in the country. On the contrary, during the time of my research (2008–2009) corruption was once again a dominant keyword in local news headlines as well as remaining a key policy concern for international bodies evaluating the country's eligibility for grants and aid. Most importantly, corruption continues to be a key marker of ineligibility of the country to EU membership.

However, since the first anticorruption protests and campaigns, the *type* of corruption that most concerned local and international actors has changed – while in the late 1990s the anticorruption movement targeted petty corruption (bribes and favors to low-level public sectors workers), by 2008, the public debate on corruption honed in on *afera korruptive* (corrupt affairs) or instances of appropriation of big money through legal processes of public procurement. These changes in local discourse around corruption (see also Kajsiu 2013) reflect a shift of focus within the global anticorruption industry toward the types of corrupt transactions defined as "state capture" or "legal corruption" (see, e.g., Hellman and Kaufmann 2001; Kaufmann and Vicente 2005).

Three important points emerge from this brief history of USAID/IDRA's survey. The first is the embedded assumption that people on the ground needed to be educated about corruption – this speaks to a general understanding of post-socialist Albania as well as other countries in the developing world as lacking in knowledge about rule of law and good governance. The second point – and this pertains to the a rise of "audit cultures" (Strathern 2000) across the board – is the important role of private sector intermediaries such as MSI in conducting work traditionally associated with the public administration. The third point speaks to the intended and unintended political "translations" of such indicators on the ground.

TRANSLATING GLOBAL EXPERTISE

The USAID/IDRA survey was a product of a heterogeneous ecology of actors and forms of expertise. The questionnaire used for the USAID/IDRA survey was designed with the help of two consulting firms that mediated the work between the USAID and IDRA, namely Casals and Associates and DPK Consulting. These two are also acknowledged in some of the surveys. During my time with IDRA, I never met anyone from DPK Consulting – which was the consultancy USAID had partnered with for the 2008 survey – nor was their input visible to me through the course of my internship. My understanding is that the consulting firms participate as bookends to the process of producing the survey; they approve the design of the questionnaires and revise the final report of the summary of findings. They interact only with the head of the center and have no direct involvement in the most labor-intensive aspect of the project. Here we see the mirroring of the global pattern of the division of labor – designers and consultants in the North, the physical labor in the South – and a separation and distancing between these nodes of knowledge production.

A key consequence of this particular distribution of labor is the broader pattern of the privatization of means of governance – a phenomenon that characterizes a global shift from liberal to neoliberal forms of governance (Barry, Osborne, and

Rose 1996; Miller and Rose 2008). In other words, the division of labor within the corruption industry reflects a much broader business model of "the contract state" (see Cordella and Willcocks 2010) whereby work traditionally performed by public officials and administrators is increasingly outsourced to private sector companies competing for public contracts. Thus, one of the two consultancy firms subcontracted by the USAID to mediate the contract with IDRA represents itself as a private institution with expertise on "operat[ing] in fragile, conflict or post-conflict settings, providing quick action to support fledgling democratic institutions until political transitions are solidly entrenched" (Casals and Associates website http://www.casals.com/capabilities/). As such, this and other similar global consultancies, have taken on tasks that have traditionally been the domain of public institutions.

Another intermediary institution played a role in the very design of the IDRA questionnaire and in its methodology. The opinion poll center Latin American Public Opinion Project (LAPOP), based in Vanderbilt University and conducting opinion-polling survey throughout Latin America, also contributed this process. A LAPOP representative had visited Albania and helped design the initial surveys in 2004–2005[4]; by the time of my research, neither LAPOP nor Casals and Associates were interacting with IDRA. Yet, the initial collaboration in 2004–2005 has left its imprint on the present form, content, and methodology of the survey. Comparing the questionnaires, one can easily notice that the sections and questions in the questionnaire for the general public were very much the same as the LAPOP's model questionnaire. In addition, as I was to learn from sitting in the training sessions, the methodology of recruiting respondents was also introduced by LAPOP based on their experience in South America. IDRA staff referred to this methodology as "the random route method" and, as my supervisor at the time noted, this was a method designed for places "like Albania" where there is a lack of a systematic way of locating people, a lack of reliable government census data.

This brief genealogy of the making of IDRA's questionnaire calls for an approach to the politics of indicators that attends to the circulation of indicator expertise across various sites of knowledge production, validation, interpretation, and deployment. These circulations are fraught with friction and complicated ecology and political institutions and other semiprivate actors.

The question at stake here is not simply the status of statistical knowledge as a form of objective truth (after all, statistics as such is not a new science in Albania – let's not forget that socialist states were also deploying similar technologies of biopower in registering and controlling population through statistical forms of knowledge; see, for instance, Kipnis 2008; Cohen 2011). What happens when this form of knowledge becomes commoditized (see also Poovey 1998), what happens when measuring corruption and the rule of law becomes subject to the competition for a public contract or grant, and what happens when the process of production and validation of surveys such as IDRA's goes through several nodes of intermediaries? These questions speak to broader concerns about the "outsourcing" of public competences to the private domain.[5]

One key consequence of such transfers of knowledge is also a tendency toward homogenization of governance and rule of law assessments; such homogenization tends to efface differences across distinct cultural contexts (see also Merry 2011) as well as erase the political histories behind culturally and historically specific concepts of just rule. Thus, the transfers/transplantation of particular research frames from one place to another – in this case, from South America to Albania – ignore differences in the very meaning and definition of terms such as "corruption" and "transparency." Such transfers conceal the historical origins of these concepts while generating new forms of political action.[6] Given these pathways of knowledge transfers, it is important to see how contexts of "political transition" and "instability" become sites of experimentation (Bockmann and Eyal 2002; Dezalay and Garth 2010) and how indicators as forms of knowledge and as technologies of governance play a role in these processes of experimentation.[7]

One of the ways to challenge such homogenizing efforts is to attend to the ways in which governance indicators are used on the ground – the unexpected political action that they might set into motion – the actors or networks that they might mobilize, strengthen, or weaken. The second part of this chapter traces the political effects of two editions of the USAID/IDRA survey – the 2008 and 2009 editions – exploring their imbrications with a local political drama involving Ambassador Withers, Public Prosecutor Ina Rama, and Prime Minister Sali Berisha.

THE GËRDEC AFFAIR

Withers' passionate and political speech at IDRA/USAID launch mentioned earlier came at the peak of heated local spectacle around the *afera korruptive* (corrupt affairs) that allegedly surrounded the explosions of a munitions depot in the village of Gërdec, outside the capital, Tirana. On March 15, 2008, a chain of explosions erupted in the depot of Gërdec, killing 22 people and injuring 300 others (see also Chivers 2008). The explosion sent shocks throughout the major metropolitan area of Tirana-Durrës – I heard its deafening sound and felt the reverberations while in Durrës, fifteen miles away from the site of the explosion. As images of destruction, the dead and the wounded dominated the airtime of major television networks through the weeks that followed, a number of questions emerged in public debate: To what extent were safety measures breached in locating the depot near inhabited areas? What was the nature of the public procurement process for the warehouse and the contracts that allowed for the disassembly and sale of outdated ammunition stored at the Gërdec depot?

In the months that followed, local opposition leaders as well as international actors such as key officials of the American Embassy pressed on Prosecutor General Ina Rama to investigate the possible high-level corruption that may have contributed to the irresponsible procurement and unsafe conditions of the Gërdec depot. Mention of the Gërdec explosion by a *New York Times* article investigating an American military private contracting company fueled this local media spectacle.[8] The *New York Times* article targeted a private defense company AEY Inc., led by the twenty-two-year-old Efraim Diveroli and registered in Miami, Florida; AEY, wrote the *Times*, "was one of the many previously unknown defense companies to have thrived since 2003, when the Pentagon began dispersing billions of dollars to train and equip indigenous forces in Afghanistan and Iraq" (Chivers et al. 2008). In 2004, AEY won a lucrative contract with Pentagon for selling ammunition to the Special Forces.

Among others, the *New York Times* article revealed a chain of companies that facilitated the transfer of more than forty-year-old Chinese ammunition from the Gërdec depot in Albania to the US-supported Afghani troops. Thus, AEY operated on the ground through the Albanian private subcontracting company Albademil. The ammunition was not bought directly from the state company MEICO but via yet another intermediary, Evdin Ltd., an obscure company registered in Cyprus. The article related, among other findings, evidence from a conversation between Efraim Diveroli and the middleman Kosta Trebicka, an Albanian citizen briefly involved with the repackaging of the ammunitions in Albania. Trebicka claimed that the Evdin purchases were a "flip": "Albania sold ammunition to Evdin for $22 per 1,000 rounds, and Evdin sold it to AEY for much more. The difference, I suspected, was shared with Albanian officials" (Chivers et al. 2008). Among others, the officials suspected to be involved included MEICO director Ylli Pinari and former Minister of Defense Fatmir Mediu (Chivers et al. 2008).

American representatives in Albania took special interest in what came to be known as "the Gërdec case" (*dosja e Gërdecit*) given the implication of the weapons contractor AEY Inc., and the possible breach of US and NATO military rules and regulations on ammunition standards.[9] AEY sold parts of the disassembled ammunition from the Gërdec depot to Afghan troops, despite their substandard condition. In the meantime, under NATO instructions, MEICO was supposed to oversee the dismantling and destruction of 2,000 tons of ammunition deemed to be in poor condition. AEY had misled the US army to think that the ammunition sold to the Afghan forces was from Hungary rather than Albania. Overall this circuit of sales contradicted the United States' $2 million investment in Albania to destroy obsolete weapons such as those repackaged and sold through AEY.[10]

From the time of the Gërdec explosion (March 15, 2008) to the time of the USAID/IDRA's survey launch (May 7, 2008), the Gërdec investigations were cast in local public debate as yet another *afera korruptive* (corrupt affairs). *Afera korruptive* is a common local idiom describing transactions that in the anticorruption industry fall under the definitions "legal corruption" or "state capture" (Hellman and Kaufmann 2001). *Afera korruptive* refers to transactions that unlike petty corruption – for instance, bribing low-level public servants – involve more sophisticated and ambivalent practices of appropriation of public goods for private gain or abuse of entrusted power for public gain. The predominance of talk of *afera korruptive* in local debate speaks to historically specific changes in the discourse of corruption on the ground; this shift in discourse reflects broader changes in local political culture and of citizens' relations to the state (Gupta 2005). While targeting primarily petty corruption in the late 1990s, over the last decade, local publics have become increasingly concerned with the high-level (or state) corruption, captured in the notions of *afera korruptive*. These instances of corruption are harder to trace and prove through the public record and hence difficult to investigate and prosecute. This shift in the Albanian public discourse parallels a similar development among the global anticorruption policymakers who, increasingly, make a distinction between petty corruption (bribery and favors among low-level officials) and state capture, noting the graver consequences on the latter on national political and economic prospects.

Given the implication of the American military private contractors in this web of transactions around the Gërdec affair, Ambassador Withers pressed harder on local authorities to come to the bottom of the case. Prosecuting the Gërdec affair thus became a test of the integrity and transparency of the judiciary – one of the branches of government with some of the poorest records of transparency and trust in institutions in previous USAID/IDRA surveys. Following the *New York Times* article, Ambassador Withers repeatedly appealed to local institutions for a fair investigation into the public procurement of the contracts and money flows between MEICO, Evdin Ltd., Albademil, and AEY Inc. These appeals became a public expression of support for the Prosecutor General Ina Rama and a challenge to the executive and the legislative bodies, pressing the latter to refrain from influencing the investigations. In the investigations, all eyes were on Fatmir Mediu, then-minister of defense, and Ylli Pinari, director of MEICO. Mediu resigned from the post of minister immediately after the explosion but remained a member of parliament – which also granted him immunity from prosecution – and continued to hold his post as leader of the Republican Party – a strong ally of the majority party, PD.[11] Through the course of the investigations into the Gërdec affair, Ambassador Withers therefore increased his public support for new legislation on lifting the immunity of high-level officials and thus enable the Rama to fully investigate MP Fatmir Mediu.

Precisely because of this fortuitous timing – a month and a half after the Gërdec explosion – the launch of the 2008 IDRA/USAID corruption survey results read as an official verdict over the Gërdec affair. Over the course of the Gërdec investigations, American Ambassador John Withers cited data from the survey as (1) evidence of state capture and (2) the basis for a direct policy recommendation regarding the proposed law on lifting the immunity of high-ranking officials (including members of parliament) (*Shekulli* 2008). The law had become particularly contentious at a time when Prosecutor General Ina Rama requested lifting the immunity of MP Fatmir Mediu for the purpose of pursuing her investigations into the Gërdec affair. By connecting the survey data to the Gërdec affair, Ambassador Withers performed an act of translation: he applied data that measured perceptions of (mostly petty) corruption to a case of alleged grand corruption (or state-capture). This move reflected a gap that existed at the time (and, to my knowledge, continues to be the case to this day) between the type of corruption that perception surveys such as USAID/IDRA's (but also, TI's CPI) – petty corruption – and the type of corruption that major international bodies are turning their attention to – state capture/grand corruption in public procurement contracts (see also Malito 2013, 25). Thus, the survey played an important role in the local debates over legal and political action. These gaps draw attention to the various forms of displacements through which the survey becomes an (often unpredictable) actor in local political debacle.

First, a temporal translation: The interviews for the 2008 IDRA survey were conducted through January and February, and thus before the Gërdec explosion, which took place on March 15 of that year. Meanwhile, the results were aggregated and made public after the explosion – on May 7. In other words, as the final summary report noted, the opinions of the survey did not reflect people's perception of corruption in the aftermath of the Gërdec explosion.[12] In conversations with IDRA staff, some argued that were they to conduct the survey after the explosion, the results would have been much worse.

Second, a translation of terms: A second displacement implicit in the ambassador's speech pointed to the various definition of "corruption" at play. Although there is by now a broad consensus that corruption is "bad" for democracy and economic development (Kaufmann 1997; Rose-Ackerman 2002; Tanzi and Davoodi 2002), defining and measuring corruption remains a point of contention (Thompson and Shah 2005; Sampson 2010). The USAID/IDRA survey questions measured people's perception of "corruption in government," "transparency of institutions," and "trust in institutions." But these questions are vague in terms of *what* counts as corruption, transparency, or trust for people on the ground and *how* these are measurable.[13] Other questions in the survey questionnaire ask about bribes given/requested by public officials. While tackling more experiential (and countable) means of measuring corruption, these questions are inevitably limited to measuring petty corruption rather than state capture. In other words, linking the data that corresponds to the question, "How widespread is corruption among public officials?" to specific *afera korruptive* inevitably entails a potential mistranslation.

These two sets of displacements further enabled the ambassador to make a specific translation of the survey data into political and legislative action. Having set out the general scene of deteriorating perceptions of corruption in the government, Withers then moved on to introduce a specific policy recommendation:

> The political elite of Albania should lead by example. One important straightforward step that can be done is *to change the immunity law*, which protects senior officials in courts, in Parliament and in other offices from prosecution. They should be as liable to prosecution as any Albanian citizen. Put another way, none should be immune from prosecution or illegal acts. And the political leadership of Albania should empower the institutions that seek justice; *empower the prosecutors* who go after the criminals; and, should make clear that whoever the suspect is, regardless of wealth, regardless of family ties, regardless of political connections, is subject to prosecution. (Withers 2008a, emphasis added)

Through this specific call for concrete action, Withers was addressing the Albanian parliament in reference to the proposed law on lifting the immunity of high-ranking officials (including members of parliament). The law had become particularly contentious at a time when Prosecutor General Ina Rama requested lifting the immunity of MP Fatmir Mediu for the purpose of pursuing her investigations into the Gërdec affair.

This translation of survey data into legislative action speaks more generally to the ways in which corruption indicators have become important actors in political decision making (see also Davis, Kingsbury, and Merry 2012a, 15–16) by way of their status as an objective "form of knowledge." At the same time, the forms that such action may take are not always anticipated. Thus, as I explain in the next section, in addition to providing a new form of expertise in an established political practice (namely, the interventions in local legal/political decision making by American representatives), the survey also played a new role for local actors seeking legitimacy and political strength. Indirectly, the survey strengthened the position of Public Prosecutor Ina Rama in her efforts at asserting the independence of the judiciary vis-à-vis the executive branch. I turn to the role that the survey played in the enfolding of a political drama between the heads of two branches of government – Prime Minister Sali Berisha and Prosecutor General Ina Rama – and on international player – American Ambassador John Withers.

INA RAMA: THE ALBANIAN SILVIA KONTI

PG Ina Rama became a focal point for the enfolding of a rift within the Democratic Party from 2008 to 2009. Rama's rise to power within the judiciary has been cast as the story of the triumph of the underdog. Rama was appointed as Prosecutor General by President Bamir Topi (a former member of DP) in late 2007. She received broad bipartisan support in her confirmation by parliament. Ina Rama's two predecessors had been accused of taking bribes. Her appointment was intended as a radical change in an institution plagued by accusations of corruption. Rama's profile also broke away from tradition. She was the first young woman to take on the position of prosecutor general in a country where the highest levels of hierarchy within the judiciary were traditionally occupied by men educated under the communist legal regime. Appointing a female prosecutor of the post-1990s generation of law school graduates also signaled a departure from the communist legacy in judicial structures.

Rama was initially seen by leaders of the opposition party (the Socialist Party) as a blind soldier of DP who appointed her. Yet, with the Gërdec case, Rama demonstrated a degree (albeit slight) of independence. For this reason, through the course of the Gërdec investigations, she received Ambassador Withers' full-fledged support. In a speech given at the workshop on the Coordination of Institutions Against Money Laundering, Ambassador Withers made the following remarks regarding Rama:

> I would like to begin by expressing my congratulations and admiration for Prosecutor General Ina Rama. In the past, Ms. Rama has been compared to the fictional character Silvia Conti. As you know, Ms. Conti was dedicated and determined to fight crime no matter what was thrown against her, no matter the difficulty of the circumstances, or the opposition against her. That comparison is apt but it does not go far enough. That is because the character of Silvia Conti was fictional and the tasks that Ms. Rama has taken on are very real. (Withers 2008b)

It was PM Berisha who had first drawn the analogy between Ina Rama and Silvia Conti, the uncompromising prosecutor in the Italian television miniseries *La Piovra* (The Octopus, from the Italian metaphor for the Mafia) (Likmeta 2012). By recalling this earlier analogy, Ambassador Withers appealed to a recent local history of allegories that portrayed an image of integrity of the young female prosecutor – an image Rama enjoyed before her falling out of favor with Berisha. The specific analogy to characters of the television series *La Piovra* bring to life once again local sensibilities of, to use Raymond William's term, "structures of feeling" (Williams 1978) lived through the nostalgic viewing of the Italian television show at a time when most Italian television programming was viewed surreptitiously or barely made it past the censorship of late socialist cultural watchdogs (see also Mai 2004; Musaraj 2012).

La Piovra, produced in Italy between 1984 and 1999, was broadcast in the highly censored Albanian (only) television station between 1987 and 1988. The TV series was extremely popular in late socialist Albania as well as in the former USSR and Bulgaria. The series passed the test of censorship because it was cast as evidence of the culture of corruption and injustice that permeated the neighboring western nation of Italy. The series painted a grim picture of the Italian Mafia and its multiple tentacles into the highest levels of government – hence the metaphor of the octopus. The plot is told from the perspective of one uncompromising police detective (Comissario Cattani) who eventually loses his closest family members to the fight against the Mafia networks. In contrast with the utter corruption of politicians and public officials, Silvia Conti, the deputy prosecutor, is one of the few characters who defies any external influence and threats.

The comparison of Ina Rama to Silvia Konti evokes the image of integrity of lone actors surrounded by a culture of corruption that cuts across state and private entities (see also Coronil 1997). The analogy also draws on similarities in gender and age and the general sense of vulnerability and innocence attached to those two demographics. Withers' resurrection of this analogy underscored his support for Prosecutor Rama's pursuit of leads to the Gërdec affair. At the time of Withers' pronouncement, the Gërdec investigations had begun to stall. On one hand, the key witness to the case, Kosta Trebicka, was found dead in a rural road near his car. The police declared the death an accident. On the other hand, the speaker of the parliament, Jozefina Topalli, a fervent Berisha supporter, was pushing for a new law that would enable the parliament to question and/or investigate the prosecutor general – a law that, according to Withers, violated the principle of the separation of powers (*Tema* 2009).

Despite Berisha's initial endorsement of Rama as the Albania Silvia Konti, soon after taking office in October 2007, Rama quickly found herself in the middle of a battle zone. Expected to conform to the party that elected her, in other words, expected to obey Berisha's authoritarian rule, Rama also faced increasing pressure from international bodies demanding transparency in the justice system, namely the courts and the office of the general prosecutor, which overall persistently scored as some of the least trusted and least transparent public institutions in the USAID/ IDRA's surveys (Figures 7.2 and 7.3).[14] The Gërdec affair presented an opportunity for Rama to live up to her popular image as the Albanian Silvia Konti.

Reforming the justice system and raising the number of prosecutions of high-level public officials has been at the forefront of the USAID Rule of Law programme in Albania. For the US Embassy as well as other international representatives in Albania, the appointment of Ina Rama thus presented an opportunity for change. Rama's courageous request to the parliament for the lifting of the immunity of MP Fatmir Mediu (and her subsequent investigations into Lulëzim Basha) marked an

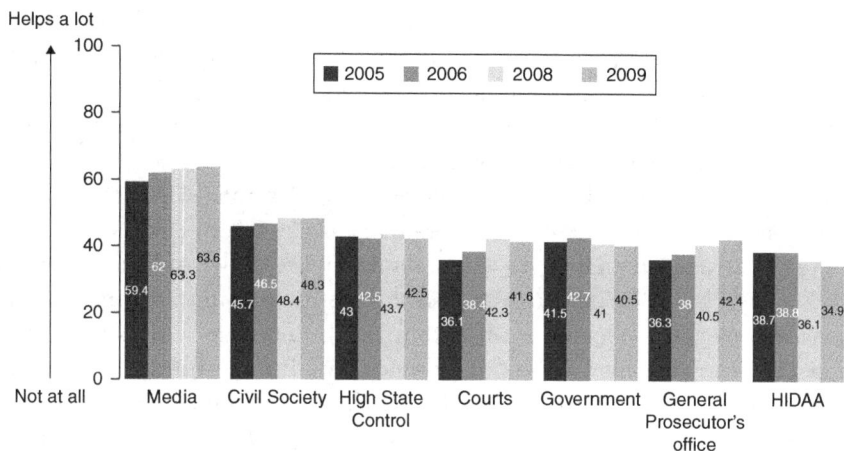

FIGURE 7.2. Trust in institutions – General Public samples.
Source: USAID/IDRA 2010.

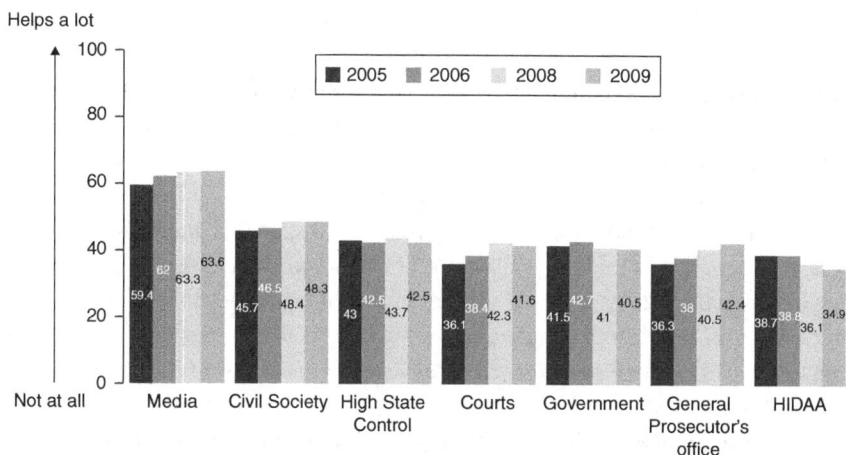

FIGURE 7.3. Institutional transparency (selected institutions) – General Public samples.
Source: "Perceptions of Transparency of Institutions over Time [2005–2009]. USAID/IDRA 2009.

unprecedented maneuver by the prosecutor's offices, which traditionally remained loyal, if not subordinated, to the incumbent party.

Likewise, Rama found an important ally in the ambassador at a time when her former supporters within the DP turned against her. For her investigations into high-profile PD public officials, through her tenure, from 2007–2012, Rama was viciously attacked by many of her former supports as "a witch" and "a street prostitute." As Rama investigated two of Berisha's most trusted ministers – Minister of Defense Fatmir Mediu and Minister of Transportation Lulëzim Basha – Berisha's supporters in the parliament proposed a law that would require the prosecutor general to respond directly to the parliament.[15]

The 2008 USAID/IDRA survey findings came at a time when the DP was undergoing an internal fracture – a fracture that became visible in the very room where the survey launch took place: Ina Rama sat next to the ambassador during the launch while PM Berisha was absent. The open confrontations between Rama and Berisha reflected a rift within the Democratic Party with Rama's supporter, President Bamir Topi, on one side, and Prime Minister Berisha and his supporters on the other.[16] Internal cables from the ambassador released in 2013 by WikiLeaks brought new evidence to the ongoing efforts of Ambassador Withers in support of the Topi-Rama camp within the Democratic Party (see, e.g., Withers 2008c).

In an impassioned cable titled "Ripples from a Boulder" Withers reflects on the conflicting response to the 2008 USAID/IDRA survey from various officials who were also members of PD. Following the event, reports Withers, President Topi echoed the ambassador's concerns about the rise of corruption within the political elite. Meanwhile, Berisha remained silent on the subject for two days following the launch and, when he finally referred to the ambassador's allegation of corruption, he belittled it as "a leaf in a tree" by comparison to the broader successful efforts of his government against corruption (Withers 2008d). The cables reveal how the launch of the 2008 USAID/IDRA survey provided a space for the articulation and display of these rifts in the local political scene. They also underscore the important ways in which the survey provided another source of legitimacy for the ambassador's intervention in this scene. In addition, however, this event provided legitimacy to actors such as PG Ina Rama in their local struggle for asserting the independence of institutions.

Thus, throughout 2008, the prosecutor general turned to the American ambassador and to other US authorities as a source of protection and legitimacy. Local media outlets repeatedly featured photos of the two sitting together or exchanging friendly gestures in public events. In the Gërdec investigations, Rama made several requests for expertise from the FBI and other US military experts. In an interview given at the end of her tenure (on January 2012) for the pro-government television program *Opinion*, Rama explained that the recurring call for help from the United States was meant to ensure better expertise *and* increase credibility of the prosecutor's office (*Opinion* 2012). This tactic reflects a broader pattern in local political culture whereby outside actors – especially US and EU authorities – are often called on to act as arbiter for local disagreements.

With this context in mind, ambassador Withers' public statements and impassioned speeches take on additional significance. Withers' specific reference to the law of immunity in his speech at the USAID/IDRA launch in May 2008 was one of his many direct statements in support of Rama's struggle to establish an independent judiciary. In a similar vein, in May 2009, as Rama faced fervent opposition by the majority in the parliament, the ambassador once again came to her defense by highlighting the expertise of the following USAID/IDRA survey, the 2009 findings.

Citing IDRA's 2009 data on the comparative perceptions of corruption of different political institutions (Figure 7.1), Withers noted:

> Albania must dedicate itself to the defense of the prosecutors to ensure its democratic progress. Any threat to their independence is a clear step backwards ... The USAID survey shows that the Albanian public still has a negative perception of its own public institutions, but especially of their ability to fight corruption. *However, the good news is that the public perception of the public prosecutor has improved more than any other institution.* (Withers, cited in *Tema* 2009, 7, emphasis added)

The first set of comments – the case for defending the independence of institutions – made explicit reference to the law proposed by the majority in parliament that would require the Prosecutor General to account to the parliament. The ambassador thus expressed his lack of support for such measure. The second set of comments – the evidence of increase of public trust in the prosecutor – referred to the specific data from the USAID/IDRA survey.

As noted in the summary of findings of the 2009 USAID/IDRA survey, by contrast to other institutions "The Prosecutor General's office show[ed] the biggest improvement from 2005 with a 6.1 point increase (from 36.3 to 42.4 points)" (IDRA 2009, 13). Further, according to another comparison in the same survey, trust in the prosecutor general increased by 10 points from 2005 to 2009 – the most of all measured institutions (see also Figure 7.3).

Note that by comparison to other institutions, the prosecutor's office remained one of the least trusted – it was at par with the Supreme Court (47 percent), better than the central government (42 percent), and significantly worse than the military (60 percent). Nevertheless, it was the comparative ranking of perceptions over time that, for the ambassador, constituted a key indicator of improvement in the assessment of the prosecutor general. In a sense, through the course of 2008–2009, one notices how different actors – local and international, human and nonhuman – come into various associations thus increasing each other's strengths (see also Latour 1993, 2005). Thus, Rama's own credibility increased by her association with the ambassador, the latter continuously relied on the USAID/

IDRA survey as an independent source of legitimacy for his political intervention; finally, the survey itself became an important actor by the various citations in the public debates.

CONCLUSION: GLOBAL EXPERTISE AND LOCAL POLITICAL ACTION

Ambassador Withers explicit political stance throughout 2008–2009 is not surprising in and of itself. However, the repeated appeals to the USAID/IDRA survey as a source of legitimacy and expertise reflect a shift also prevalent in global forms of governance; namely, the increasing use of indicators as a source of expertise in political decision making (Sampson 2010; Bhuta 2012; Davis, Kingsbury, and Merry 2012b). By following the production and circulation of this particular survey, this chapter has sought to explore how a wide array of actors – global/local, private/public – come to play a part in the consolidation of indicators as a form of knowledge and as a technology of governance (Davis, Kingsbury, and Merry 2012a).

One key concern that emerges from this study pertains to the forms of knowledge implicit in indicators and used as a means of governing. The very genealogy of the survey in question, for instance, raises questions about the "corporate form" (Merry 2011) embedded in the questionnaires used on the ground by virtue of the history of their funding and design. Increasingly, country or cross-country indicators are produced through various intermediaries that cut across boundaries between private and public institutions. Thus, the making of IDRA's questionnaire involved expertise from an American research and polling center housed at Vanderbilt University, research based on opinion polling in Latin America, global private consulting companies subcontracted by the US government, and a local research center with experience in market research and corruption perception research. For one thing, this assemblage of actors speaks to the distributed agency behind the making of governance indicators. Such distribution is not entirely even – rather, it often replicates a hierarchical North/South division of labor – the North tasked with designing the survey, the South tasked with conducting the survey.

Further, this particular configuration reflects broader changes in the modes of governance across the globe – a shift from liberal toward neoliberal forms of governance – whereby public service is increasingly delegated to the private sector. When applied to the political realm, decisions are made based on the availability of funding, or funding categories rather than, for instance, the needs of the public. Assuming that the USAID/IDRA survey had an important role as a diagnostic of progress or deterioration of corruption in Albania, its abrupt interruption in 2010 – due to the end of the respective funding stream – raises questions about the continuity of such indicators – an aspect so crucial to the comparative nature of the evidence that they provide. As such, the USAID/IDRA survey serves as a limit case that points to a tension between the business models that enable the production of governance indicators and specific features – continuity, consistency in methods and samplings, repetition – of the type of data they produce over the course of time.[17]

A second concern addressed in this chapter relates to the effects of governance indicators on the ground. In addition to echoing other accounts of indicators as the making of global expertise, the chapter sought to open up new ways of researching how such indicators influence local decision making, how they impact local politics. Here I traced various "translations" of two editions of USAID/IDRA survey data –2008 and 2009 – in relation to a local political drama enfolding between Prime Minister Sali Berisha, Prosecutor General Ina Rama, and American Ambassador John Withers.

One specific aspect of the survey that came to play a key role in this drama was the comparative data on the change of perceptions of corruption *over time*. This comparative aspect is arguably the survey's most important component as it provides a measure of change in institutions or lack thereof. Locally, these comparative data took on crucial significance as they translate into an indirect "grade" toward institutions and/or specific officials.[18] In other words, the USAID/IDRA survey came to constitute an important actor in the enfolding of a local political confrontation between various institutions and political forces.

As the Gërdec case enfolded, the survey data – which, as per its form, aims at depoliticization by way of its status as scientific expertise – was in turn repoliticized as it travelled on the ground through various actors that endorsed it and/or disputed it. But, as discussed previously, one cannot understand the strength of the data in this particular survey – and by extension of other types of governance and corruption indicators – without taking into account the various acts of translation, the political networks and associations between various actors, and the specific local political culture.

The survey's strength drew on its status as global expertise – the transfers of knowledge through various nodes of calculation – but also, locally, it gained "strength by association" (Latour 1993) with specific actors. The survey and Ambassador Withers increased each other's strength – Withers repeatedly cited the survey as a source of independent expertise, while the public image of the survey itself became more visible and legitimate through these citations. In addition, Withers appealed to local cultural imaginaries – such as the analogy between Ina Rama and Silvia Konti – to increase the truth value, the strength of the survey data.

This hybrid repertoire of actors, actions, and associations speaks to the increasing role of indicators in various scales of decision making; it also speaks to their limitations. Thus, this particular survey gained more strength as a result of the various performative acts by various actors and the displacements and translations of its data to specific local events. These gaps constitute productive sites that enable creative spaces for a more differentiated approach to the rise of "audit cultures" (Strathern 2000) in various areas of governance – an approach that looks into how such forms of knowledge and techniques of governance get appropriated and deployed on the ground, and how they are in turn translated into unintended actions.

Of all actors involved in the Gërdec case, the Prosecutor General Ina Rama came to gain perhaps the most strength from the USAID/IDRA's circulations on the ground. She was able to do so not just because of the survey's own status as independent arbiter of perceptions of corruption but also as a result of a specific association between various human and nonhuman actors as well as a local political culture that consistently turns to external actors as a source of local political strength. Yet, ultimately, these associations were not enough to push her investigations forward, leaving the actual record on prosecutions of high-level corruption in Albania remarkably low. Strengthening such actors remains an issue of high priority for people on the ground.

NOTES

1 I use the term "translations" after actor-network theory, which defines it as "all the negotiations, intrigues, calculations, acts of persuasion and violence, thanks to which an actor or force takes, or causes to be conferred on itself, the authority to speak or act on behalf of another actor or force" (Callon and Latour 1986, 279).

2 In particular, see speech by former World Bank President, James Wolfensohn in 1996, which set out an agenda around anticorruption as an antidote to lack of economic development.

3 The collapse of the pyramid schemes in Albania in 1997 set out widespread antigovernment protests. The then-president Sali Berisha responded to the protests with the use of force which backfired as military leadership did not follow orders and led to a vacuum in political leadership across the south of Albania. The ensuing anarchy that swept the country and the increased international pressure on Berisha led to his resignation and the humanitarian intervention, Operation Alba, led by the Italian troops (see Musaraj 2011).

4 The first survey was not conducted by IDRA. The second, in 2005, was the first conducted by IDRA. For an explanation of differences as well as comparisons between these two years, see Seligson and Baviskar (2006).

5 This subject has received attention from anthropologists of the state (Coronil 1997), political scientists concerned with the privatization of the state in Africa (Hibou 2004; Bayart 2009), and legal scholars concerned with "the contract state" in liberal Ango-American states (Cordella and Willcocks 2010).

6 One example that speaks to the particular history of concepts such as "international human rights" in Latin America in the context of the Cold War is the historical and comparative work of Dezalay and Garth (2010).

7   Not coincidentally, the transfer of the survey methodology from South America to Eastern Europe follows a path similar to that of the Washington consensus tenets (also known as the shock therapy reforms) – also compiled on the basis of the experience in South America and "transplanted" to Eastern Europe in the first years of post-socialist transformations (see also Bockmann and Eyal 2002). Tracing the intersections between these parallel flows of expertise would be a fascinating project.

8   Chivers, C. J. et al. (2008). "Supplier Under Scrutiny on Arms for Afghans," *The New York Times*, March 27. http://www.nytimes.com/2008/03/27/world/asia/27ammo .html?ref=albania.

9   Following the investigations, all federal contracts to AEY were suspended.

10 Chivers (2008). See also http://graphics8.nytimes.com/images/2008/03/27/world/2008 ammomap.jpg.

11 Although the Republican Party is not a contender for the majority in parliament or the government, it is one of the main allies of the Democratic Party. It traditionally forms a coalition with DP in exchange for one or two seats in the ministries. Fatmir Mediu's appointment as Minister of Defense was a result of this coalition.

12 In the opening remarks of the survey's Summary of Findings, the authors inserted the following note: "This survey was carried out prior to the March 15, 2008 explosion in Gërdec. Whatever impact the ensuing political debate or media coverage of that event may have had on public opinion, it is not reflected in this survey's findings" (IDRA and DPK Consulting 2008, 3).

13 On the shortcomings of using quantitative measures to assess noncountable things such as governance, state failures, and corruption, see also Bhuta (2012).

14 It is worth noting that the survey asks several questions gauging the transparency/ corruption of institutions. In the 2008 survey, these questions included: SYS11 &16. [Trust in institutions]: [On a scale of 1 to 7, where 1 is very little, and 7 is a lot] How much do you trust the Prosecutor General/the High Court? COR8. [On a scale of 1 to 7, where 1 is very little, and 7 is a lot] How much do you think that the courts help in the war against corruption? TRAN9 & 10. How transparent is the General Prosecutor's Office/the Courts? (very transparent/somewhat transparent/not transparent/don't know) EXP8 & 9. Have you in the past year given a bribe to the prosecutor's office/the courts? PC8 & 12. [On a scale of 1 to 10, where 1 is very honest and 10 very corrupt] how honest/corrupt are judges/prosecutors?

15 Former Minister of Transportation Lulezim Basha was investigated for his role in signing a public procurement contract with the company Bechtel-Enka for building one of the largest highways in Albania. The case was closed on the basis of procedural errors.

16 The Albanian political system in parliamentary representative democratic system, with a multiparty system. The prime minister is the head of the government and usually represents the majority in parliament. The president is also appointed by the parliament yet plays a more limited role in government. Both Berisha and Topi were members of the Democratic Party. As per the constitutions, Topi resigned his party membership when he became president in Juy 2007. After the end of his tenure as president, he formed a new party, the Democratic Spirit Party.

17 Similar questions of continuity in the production of the data emerge also from internal debates about the best methodological tools used. This is, for instance, an issue that applies also to the recent changes in TI's CPI which changed it methodology, thus making it impossible to compare data from the 2011 CPI to the 2012 CPI (TI 2012).

18 Pasha, Auron, interview with author, Tirana, Albania, February 2008.

REFERENCES

Barry, Andrew, Thomas Osborne, and Nicholas Rose, eds. 1996. *Foucault and Political Reason: Liberalism, Neo-liberalism and Rationalities of Government.* Chicago: University of Chicago Press.

Bayart, Jean-François. 2009. *The State in Africa: The Politics of the Belly.* 2nd ed. Malden, MA: Polity Press.

Bhuta, Nehal. 2012. "Governmentalizing Sovereignty: Indexes of State Fragility and the Calculability of Political Order." In Kevin Davis, Angelina Fisher, Benedict Kingsbury, and Sally Engle Merry, eds., *Governance by Indicators: Global Power through Quantification and Rankings,* 132–164. Oxford: Oxford University Press.

Bockmann, Johanna, and Gil Eyal. 2002. Eastern Europe as a Laboratory of Economic Knowledge: The Transnational Roots of Neoliberalism. *American Journal of Sociology* 108(2): 310–352.

Callon, Michel, and Bruno Latour. 1986. "Unscrewing the Big Leviathan; or How Actors Macrostructure Reality, and How Sociologists Help Them to Do So?" In John Law, ed., *Power, Action, Belief: A New Sociology of Knowledge?,* 196–229. Keele, U.K.: Metheun.

Chivers, C. J., Eric Schmitt, and Nicholas Wood. 2008. "Supplier under Scrutiny on Arms for Afghans." *New York Times,* March 27, 2008. http://www.nytimes.com/2008/03/27/world/asia/27ammo.html?ref=albania.

Cohen, Susanne. 2011. "Transparency between East and West" SOYUZ Annual Symposium: New Postsocialist Ontologies and Politics. University of Illinois at Urbana-Champaign, March.

Cordella, Antonio, and Leslie Willcocks. 2010. "Outsourcing, Bureaucracy and Public Value: Reapraising the Notion of the 'Contract State'." *Government Information Quarterly* 27(1): 82–88.

Coronil, Fernando. 1997. *The Magical State: Nature, Money and Modernity in Venezuela.* Chicago: University of Chicago Press.

Davis, Kevin, Benedict Kingsbury, and Sally Engle Merry. 2012a. "Introduction: Global Governance by Indicators." In Kevin Davis, Angelina Fisher, Benedict Kingsbury, and Sally Engle Merry, eds., *Governance by Indicators: Global Power Through Quantification and Rankings,* 3–28. Oxford: Oxford University Press.

——— 2012b. "Indicators as a Technology of Global Governance." *Law and Society Review* 46(1): 71–104.

Dezalay, Yves, and Briant Garth. 2010. *The Internationalization of the Palace Wars: Lawyers, Economists and the Contest to Transform Latin American States.* Chicago: University of Chicago Press.

Foucault, Michel. 1991. "Governmentality." In Graham Burchell, Colin Gordon, and Peter Miller, eds., *The Foucault Effect: Studies in Governmentality,* 87–104. Chicago: University of Chicago Press.

Gupta, Akhil. 1995. "Blurred Boundaries: The Discourse of Corruption, The Culture of Politics and the Imagined State." *American Ethnologist* 22(2): 375–402.

——— 2005. "Narratives of Corruption: Anthropological and Fictional Accounts of the Indian State." *Ethnography* 6(1): 5–34.

Halliday, Terence. 2012. "Legal Yardsticks: International Financial Institutions as Diagnosticians and Designers of the Laws of the Nations." In Kevin Davis, Angelina Fisher, Benedict

Kingsbury, and Sally Engle Merry, eds., *Governance by Indicators: Global Power Through Quantification and Rankings*, 180–216. Oxford: Oxford University Press.

Hellman, Joel, and Daniel Kaufmann. 2001. "Confronting the Challenge of State Capture in Transition Economies." *Finance and Development* 38(3). http://www.imf.org/external/pubs/ft/fandd/2001/09/hellman.htm

Hibou, Beatrice. 2004. *Privatizing the State*. New York: Columbia University Press.

Institute for Development Research and Alternatives (IDRA). 2009. *Corruption in Albania: Summary of Findings. Survey 2009*. Tirana, Albania: IDRA and USAID.

———. 2010. *Corruption in Albania: Summary of Findings. Survey 2010*. Tirana, Albania: IDRA and USAID.

IDRA and DPK Consulting. 2008. *Corruption in Albania: Summary of Findings. Survey 2008*. Tirana, Albania: IDRA and USAID.

Kajsiu, Blendi. 2013. "The Birth of Corruption and the Politics of Anti-Corruption in Albania, 1991–2005." *Nationalities Papers: The Journal of Nationalism and Ethnicity* 41(3): 1–18.

Kaufmann, Daniel. 1997. "Why is Ukraine's Economy – and Russia's – Not Growing?" *Transition* 5–8. Washington, DC: World Bank.

Kaufmann, Daniel, and Pedro C. Vicente. 2005. "Legal Corruption." Working Papers and Articles. World Bank Institute: Governance and Anti-corruption. World Bank, 2005. http://siteresources.worldbank.org/INTWBIGOVANTCOR/Resources/Legal_Corruption.pdf

Kipnis, Andrew B. 2008. "Audit Cultures: Neoliberal Governmentality, Socialist Legacy, or Technologies of Governing?" *American Ethnologist* 35(2): 275–289.

Latour, Bruno. 1988. *Science in Action: How to Follow Scientists and Engineers through Society*. Cambridge, MA: Harvard University Press.

———. 1993. *The Pasteurization of France*. Translated by Alan Sheridan and John Law. Cambridge, MA: Harvard University Press.

———. 2005. *Reassembling the Social*. Oxford: Oxford University Press.

Likmeta, Besar. 2012. "Saying Farewell to an Albanian Hero in the Fight against Corruption." *Foreign Policy*, November 16.http://transitions.foreignpolicy.com/posts/2012/11/16/saying_farewell_to_an_albanian_hero_in_the_fight_against_corruption

Maho, Armand. 2008. "Withers: Nismat e qeverise kunder prokurorise jolegjitime." (Withers: The Government's Initiatives against the Prosecutor's Office Are Illegitimate). *Tema*, October 17.

Mai, Nicola. 2001. "Italy Is Beautiful: The Role of Italian Television in the Albanian Migratory Flow to Italy." In Russell King and Nancy Wood, eds., *Media and Migration: Constructions of Mobility and Difference*, 95–109. London: Routledge.

Malito, Debora Valentina. 2013. "Measuring Corruption Indicators and Indices." Framing Paper. Global Governance by Indicators: Measuring Corruption and Corruption Indices Workshop. Florence, Italy: European University Institute.

Merry, Sally Engle. 2011. "Measuring the World: Indicators, Human Rights, and Global Governance." *Current Anthropology* 52(S3): S83–96.

Miller, Peter, and Nikolas Rose. 2008. *Governing the Present: Administering Economic, Social and Personal Life*. Cambridge, UK: Polity Press.

Musaraj, Smoki. 2011. "Tales from Albarado: The Materiality of Pyramid Schemes in Postsocialist Albania." *Cultural Anthropology* 26(1): 84–110.

———. 2012. "Alternative Publics, Alternative Temporalities: Reflections on Marginal Collective Practices in Communist Albania." In Andrea Hemming, Gentiana Kera, Enriketa Papa, eds., *Albania: Family, Society and Culture in the 20th Century*, 175–186. Berlin: LIT Verlag Münste.

Naím, Moisés. 1995. "The Corruption Eruption" *Brown Journal of World Affairs* 2 (2): 245–261.

Opinion. 2012. "Interview with Ina Rama," by Blendi Fevziu. TV Klan. January 26.

Poovey, Mary. 1998. *A History of the Modern Fact: Problems of Knowledge in the Sciences of Wealth and Society*. Chicago: University of Chicago Press.

Power, Michael. 1999. *The Audit Society: Rituals of Verification*. Oxford: Oxford University Press.

Rose-Ackerman, Susan. 2002. "Political Corruption and Democratic Structures" In Arvind K. Jain, ed., *The Political Economy of Corruption*, 35–62. London: Routledge.

Sampson, Steven. 2005. "Integrity Warriors: Global Morality and the Anticorruption Movement in the Balkans." In Dieter Haller and Chris Shore, eds., *Corruption: Anthropological Perspectives*, 103–130. London: Pluto Press.

——— 2010. "The Anti-corruption Industry: From Movement to Institution." *Global Crime* 11(2): 261–278.

Seligson, Mitchell, and Sidharta Baviskar. 2006. "Corruption in Albania: Comparisons between 2004 and 2005 Surveys." Arlington, VA: Casals and Associates. http://www.vanderbilt.edu/lapop/albania/GoodGovernanceinAlbaniav82r.pdf

Shekulli. 2008. "Withers: Fatkeqesisht 92% e qytetareve pranojne korrupsionin." (Unfortunately 92% of Albanians Agree that There Is Corruption), May 8.

Strathern, Marilyn, ed. 2000. *Audit Cultures: Anthropological Studies in Accountability, Ethics and the Academy*. 1st ed. New York: Routledge.

Tanzi, Vito, and Hamdi Davoodi. 2002. "Corruption, Growth, and Public Finances." In Arvind K. Jain, ed., *The Political Economy of Corruption*,89–110. London: Routledge.

Tema. 2009. "Withers: Politika nuk duhet te ushtroje presion ndaj qeverise." (Politics Should Not Exert Pressure on the Government), May 7.

Thompson, Theresa, and Anwar Shah. 2005. "Transparency International's Corruption Perceptions Index: Whose Perceptions Are They Anyway?" Working Papers and Articles. World Bank Institute: Governance and Anti-Corruption. Washington, DC: World Bank. http://siteresources.worldbank.org/INTWBIGOVANTCOR/Resources/Transparency InternationalCorruptionIndex.pdf

Transparency International. 2012. *Corruption Perceptions Index 2012: Technical Methodology Note.*" http://ti-ukraine.org/sites/default/files/u/124/docs/g._technical_methodology_note_-_corruption_perceptions_index_2012_0.pdf.

USAID Albania: Rule of Law Program. 2010. http://albania.usaid.gov/print.php?aid=220&gj=gj2.

Williams, Raymond. 1978. *Marxism and Literature*. New York: Oxford University Press.

Withers, John. 2008a. "Remarks by U.S. Ambassador John L. Withers II at the Launch of the 2008 Corruption Perception and Experience Survey Conducted by IDRA and Funded by USAID." http://tirana.usembassy.gov/08pr_0507.html.

——— 2008b. "Remarks by U.S. Ambassador John L. Withers at the Workshop on the Coordination of Institutions against Money Laundering Tirana Prosecutor's Office. Cable #08_1016. October 16. http://tirana.usembassy.gov/08pr_1016.html.

——— 2008c. "This Week in Albania, May 31 – June 6, 2008." Embassy Tirana (Albania). Cable #08Tirana426. http://wikileaks.org/cable/2008/06/08TIRANA426.html.

2008d. "Ripples From a Boulder: Ambassador's Remarks Renew Debate on Corruption, Immunity." Embassy Tirana (Albanian). Cable #08TIRANA398.http://wikileaks.org/cable/2008/05/08TIRANA398.html.

Wolfensohn, James. 1996. "People and Development." Address to the Board of Governors at the Annual Meetings of the World Bank and the International Monetary Fund. Reprinted in *Voice for the World's Poor: Selected Speeches and Writings of World Bank President James D. Wolfensohn, 1995–2005*. Washington, DC: World Bank.

World Bank. 2011. "Governance in Albania: A Way Forward for Competitiveness, Growth, and European Integration." Poverty Reduction and Economic Management Unit Europe and Central Asia Region. A World Bank Brief. Report No. 62518-AL. http://siteresources.worldbank.org/INTALBANIA/Resources/Governance_profile_English.pdf.

8

Evaluating the Impact of Corruption Indicators on Governance Discourses in Kenya

Migai Akech

INTRODUCTION

International organizations, civil society, and governments of developed and developing countries alike have all declared war on corruption. In developing countries, corruption is seen as a major contributory factor to their failure to attain economic development. Indicators that measure corruption, or public perceptions thereof, have become a significant tool in this war. The indicators adopt various methodologies and are used for different purposes, including raising public awareness, advocating for institutional reforms, and assessing the extent to which such reforms are being implemented.

In Kenya, the government and Transparency International (TI)-Kenya now measure corruption annually, for different purposes. TI-Kenya produces an annual Bribery Index, which forms part of its efforts "to inform the fight against corruption with rigorous and objective research and analysis" (TI-Kenya 2006, 3). It has been producing the index since 2002. It has also been producing regional bribery indices since 2009. TI-Kenya sees the bribery index as a survey that "captures corruption as experienced by ordinary citizens in their interaction with officials of both public and private organizations" (TI-Kenya 2006, 3). It is compiled from information provided by respondents "on the organizations where they have encountered bribery during the year, where they paid bribes, how much and for what" (TI-Kenya 2006, 3). Respondents are also asked to assess the changes they have observed in these organizations. According to TI-Kenya, both the country and regional bribery indices are tools for measuring "petty bribery," which it sees as "a general indicator for other forms of corruption in a particular country" (TI-Kenya 2010, 1). The Bribery Index has a value range from 0 to 100, where the higher the value, the worse the performance. The Bribery Index seeks to influence or shape discourses on governance, given that TI sees corruption as a manifestation of bad governance. The Index should be seen in the context of TI's mission to encourage "governments to establish and implement effective laws, policies and anticorruption programs" (Wang and Rosenau 2001, 31).

For its part, the Government of Kenya has been measuring corruption since fiscal year 2007/2008, in the context of ongoing performance contracting reforms. It has developed "corruption eradication" performance indicators and tasked the Ethics and Anti-Corruption Commission (EACC) to monitor and evaluate their implementation. The EACC was established by Article 79 of the Constitution of 2010, and replaces the Kenya Anti-Corruption Commission (KACC). To enable it to perform this function, the EACC measures corruption through methods such as public perception surveys.

This chapter seeks to evaluate the impact of these two approaches to measuring corruption in Kenya. How are these indicators produced? How is corruption conceptualized, and what kinds of questions are asked in the surveys that inform these indicators? To what extent do these indicators reflect the "true picture" of corruption? Do these indicators contribute to decision making on corruption in Kenya? How do these indicators affect or influence the work of policymakers, civil society, institutions, and government? What impact have these indicators had on the fight against corruption?

The chapter examines the production and use of the corruption indicators by TI-Kenya and the government in the context of the fight against corruption and institutional reform in Kenya over the last decade. It is based on a review of the literature on the subject; public deliberations of the indicators in advocacy, policy, and legal discourses; interviews with key informants; and analysis of the coverage of the indicators in the media. The chapter makes two arguments. First, although TI-Kenya's approach to measuring corruption is useful, it is not only incomplete because it is largely concerned with bribery but has also had little impact on governmental decision making on corruption. Although the Bribery Index rankings name and shame "corrupt" institutions, they neither explain the causes of corruption nor give such institutions incentives to do better, apart from removal from the Index. Second, the government's approach to measuring corruption promises to reduce public sector corruption as it is an essential component of performance contracting, which requires public institutions, and gives them much needed incentives, to undertake institutional reforms. Nevertheless, the TI-Kenya Bribery Index remains a useful tool for monitoring the effectiveness of governmental efforts to eradicate public sector corruption.

The second part consists of a conceptual framework. It explains why corruption is difficult to define, observe, and measure. It also outlines existing approaches to measuring corruption. It contends that any efforts to measure corruption should be informed by contextual and institutional factors, if they are to guide policymakers and activists in designing suitable anticorruption initiatives. The third part then examines the contextual and institutional factors that explain the prevalence of corruption in Kenya, and that ought to inform the measurement and eradication of corruption in Kenya. The fourth part provides a brief background of TI-Kenya and examines the production and limitations of its Bribery Index. The fifth part evaluates the impact of the Bribery Index, and compares it to the Government of Kenya's approach of using performance contracting to measure and eradicate corruption. The sixth part concludes the chapter.

MEASURING CORRUPTION: PURPOSES, CHALLENGES OF DEFINITION, AND DIFFERENCES OF PERCEPTION

International development organizations such as the World Bank see corruption as a great obstacle to development (Andersson and Heywood 2009, 747). They consider combating corruption as necessary for the realization of development. In particular, they see the establishment of good governance as an important tool for combating corruption (Andersson and Heywood 2009, 747). On the one hand, they view governance as "the traditions and institutions by which authority in a country is exercised for the common good" (Kaufmann 2005, 82). On the other hand, they define corruption as "the abuse of public office for private gain" (Kaufmann 2005, 82). Essentially, therefore, they see corruption as a product or consequence of the abuse of governmental power. In this context, a need arises to diagnose the causes and magnitude of corruption to facilitate the targeting of good governance reforms. The idea is that if the causes and magnitude of corruption can be measured with some accuracy, then it can be combated effectively.

However, corruption is an elusive concept and therefore difficult to measure. Transparency International (TI) itself defines corruption as the misuse of entrusted power for private gain (TI 2006). Further, it distinguishes between "according to rule corruption" and "against the rule" corruption, and therefore applies the term to both legal and illegal activities (TI 2006). The former category consists of facilitation payments, where a bribe is paid to receive preferential treatment for something that the bribe receiver is required to do by law (TI 2006). Conversely, the latter category consists of bribes paid to obtain services the bribe receiver is prohibited from providing (TI 2006). This definition has been faulted for "explicitly refer[ring] to the payment of bribes, whereas many forms of corruption may not involve any form of financial transaction" (Andersson and Heywood 2009, 748). For example, it is argued that private actors who peddle influence with the aim of distorting public policy decisions are also engaging in corruption (Andersson and Heywood 2009, 749). From this perspective, corruption should be defined more broadly as "the misuse of power in the interests of illicit gain" to embrace the idea that those who do not enjoy "entrusted" power, including private actors, are also often involved in corrupt activities (Andersson and Heywood 2009, 748). Accordingly, to be "meaningfully applicable," a definition should embrace the "many different types of corruption, which vary according to the sector in which they occur (public or private; political or administrative), the actors involved (for instance, state officials, politicians, entrepreneurs and so forth), the impact they have (localized or extensive) and the degree to which they are formalized (embedded and systemic or occasional and sporadic)" (Andersson and Heywood 2009, 749). Arguably, the United Nations Development Programme (UNDP)'s definition of corruption meets this test of meaningful applicability. The UNDP defines corruption as "the misuse of public power, office or authority for private benefit – through bribery, extortion, influence peddling, nepotism, fraud, speed money or embezzlement" (UNDP 1998, 6).

Defining corruption is also difficult because it is perceived differently in different political and cultural settings (Andersson and Heywood 2009, 749). There is no international consensus on the meaning of corruption (Soreide 2006, 4), and people do not agree on what is the uncorrupt state of affairs (Andersson and Heywood 2009, 750). Further, people's personal experiences and the media considerably influence their perceptions of corruption (Rahim and Zaman 2008, 11). In this respect, TI's perspective on corruption has been criticized for being "blind to the ground realities of a developing society, especially one in the process of rapid transition from tradition to modernity" (Chadda 2004, 122). It could therefore be argued that international discourses on corruption are shaped by the views of the dominant Western liberal democracies, but that may not be very helpful in diagnosing and combating corruption in non-Western societies. As a result, the institutional reforms recommended by international agencies for combating corruption in these societies may not be suitable. For example, it has been argued that there are fewer corrupt transactions in rich countries because bureaucrats receive adequate salaries (Rahim and Zaman 2008, 16). In contrast, their counterparts in poor countries are underpaid, a fact that leads to "substantially greater exposure of [the] general public to corrupt transactions" (Rahim and Zaman 2008, 16).

Corruption is also difficult to observe because it is usually hidden (Kalnins 2005, 4). Hence the observation that "We know corruption exists, but direct witnesses are few; often, those with direct knowledge have an interest in keeping it secret" (Johnston 2000, 4). And because corruption is a clandestine phenomenon, it has been argued that it is virtually impossible to measure it with precision (Gephart 2009, 18). It follows from this premise that empirical attempts to measure corruption "can never be better than approximations" (Johnston 2000, 5). And to ensure that these approximations are as close to reality as possible, the three predominant approaches to measuring corruption are often used in combination.

The first approach measures the perception of target groups concerning corruption, and is based on the assumption that there is an association between the perception and actual corruption (Kalnins 2005, 7). The usefulness of this approach is doubtful for two reasons. First, "factors such as media coverage of specific corruption scandals may excessively amplify popular perceptions about the overall level of corruption" (Kalnins 2005, 7). Second, "the highly secretive nature of corrupt transactions… may contribute to the underestimation of corruption in people's perception" (Kalnins 2005, 7).

The second approach asks people about their actual experiences or incidences of corruption. Under this approach, for example, researchers seek to determine whether and how often individuals solicited, offered, paid, or were compelled to pay, bribes over a given period, say one year. Again, this approach has drawbacks. For example, because corruption is usually illegal and morally objectionable, there is a possibility of deflation (Kalnins 2005, 8). That is, respondents may report less corruption than they experienced. Further, it is unlikely that those who view corruption experiences as mutually profitable transactions will reveal them (Kalnins 2005, 9). The final approach consists of the evaluation of corruption by elites, such as businessmen (both local and international) and nongovernmental organization (NGO) actors. This approach has equally been faulted. For example, it is argued that the evaluations of businessmen are biased because they often offer bribes (Hungarian Gallup Institute 1999, 6). Second, it is said that international businessmen are often not accustomed to local customs and language, and as a result tend to use bribes to obtain quick solutions to their problems. Third, it is claimed that elite knowledge is often narrow, as it is "limited to a particular government ministry or economic sector and difficult to generalize since elites do not constitute a national probability sample" (Mishler 2008, 7).

Alina Mungiu-Pippidi has also offered a useful perspective on the diagnosis and treatment of corruption that should influence how it is measured (Mungiu-Pippidi 2006, 86). She laments that although global expenditures in anticorruption have grown to approximately US$100 million per year, few successes have resulted from this investment. She contends that "many anticorruption initiatives fail because they are nonpolitical in nature, while most of the corruption in developing and postcommunist countries is inherently political" (Mungiu-Pippidi 2006, 86). She takes the view that whereas corruption in developed countries usually consists of individual cases of infringement of the norms of integrity, in developing countries it typically takes the form of "particularism," which she defines as "a mode of social organization characterized by the regular distribution of public goods on a non-universalistic basis that mirrors the vicious distribution of power within such societies" (Mungiu-Pippidi 2006, 86–87). She contrasts "particularism" with "universalism," which she defines as the norm and practice of individualistic societies, where equal treatment applies to everyone regardless of the group to which one belongs (Mungiu-Pippidi 2006, 88). In this type of society, individuals expect equal treatment from the state. In the former, however, their treatment depends on their status or position in society, and people do not even expect to be treated fairly by the state. She then suggests that anticorruption strategies in developing countries fail for two reasons. First, anticorruption strategies do not attack the roots of corruption in such societies, which are to be found in the distribution of power. Second, these strategies are "adopted and implemented in cooperation with the very predators who control the government and, in some cases, the anticorruption instruments themselves" (Mungiu-Pippidi 2006, 87).

Mungiu-Pippidi's analysis is useful in understanding the practical choices that many powerless citizens of such societies face on a daily basis. For example, such citizens often offer or pay bribes to circumvent inequality, as "bribing an official may be the only way to secure equal treatment" (Mungiu-Pippidi 2006, 88). In such contexts, a preoccupation with measuring petty bribery may not be a particularly useful strategy for combating corruption. Her analysis is also useful in understanding the fact that institutions such as the police and the judiciary – which in countries such as Kenya are sites where citizens report that they often encounter bribery – are directed by the guardians of a corrupt, and largely particularistic, system (Mungiu-Pippidi 2006, 93–94). From this analysis, she suggests that a proper diagnosis of corruption in any given society requires a qualitative strategy that is informed by the distribution of power. She writes:

> For each society, we must ask: Are we dealing with modern corruption, where corruption is the exception to the norm of universalism? Or are we dealing with particularism and a culture of privilege, where corruption itself is the norm? Or, as is frequently the case in the postcolonial world where the modern state was defectively implanted on a traditional society, are we dealing with a combination of the two? If so, to what extent is the government guided by universalist norms and to what extent is its main task to promote patronage and cater to specific interest groups? (Mungiu-Pippidi 2006, 91–92)

In terms of diagnosing corruption in particularistic societies, she recommends the use of "indirect" indicators, including persistence of widespread popular perceptions of government corruption despite changes in government; influential jobs being held by the same individuals or groups regardless of the outcome of elections; high political migration from opposition parties to the party in government; a widespread perception that politicians are above the law; a situation in which access to resources is intermediated by oligarchic networks; and failure to take legal action against even the most notoriously corrupt members of high-status groups (Mungiu-Pippidi 2006, 92). Such indicators should help us to understand the causes of corrupt behavior, with a view to building accountable and fair governments, and constructing societies that "embrace universalism as the supreme principle governing relations between the people and government, and among the people themselves" (Mungiu-Pippidi 2006, 96). This entails designing institutions that ensure that no official has monopoly control over resources, linking the power of officials to mechanisms of accountability and minimizing room for discretionary judgment (Warren 2004, 330).

Proponents of diagnostic data and analysis on corruption and governance contend that this type of research serves useful purposes, such as awareness-raising, advocacy, and policymaking (Hakobyan and Wolkers 2004, 2). In particular, they favor local or national instruments, which they claim "often provide more in-depth analysis of the phenomenon from different angles" (Hakobyan and Wolkers 2004, 2). Such instruments diagnose the extent and level of corruption across different segments of the population, institutions, and sectors, with a view to identifying the causes and consequences of corruption, and tolerance toward corrupt practices, among others (Hakobyan and Wolkers 2004, 2). Such tools also enhance the visibility and profile of the civil society organizations that produce them, such as TI. It is also claimed that they are useful resources for governmental authorities to draw on in order to better target their policy and reform efforts (Hakobyan and Wolkers 2004, 2). As we will see in Kenya's case, however, the extent to which some of these tools influence the behavior of governmental institutions or citizens remains speculative. For example, to what extent does raising the awareness of citizens and police officers (through the publication of TI-Kenya's Bribery Index) contribute to combating corruption in the absence of reforms that can alter the fundamental rules of an essentially particularistic system? What choices do citizens really have when they are confronted with demands for bribes in such situations? And what choices do junior police officers really have when their seniors, who wield immense discretionary powers, prevail upon them to solicit bribes?

The foregoing challenges of defining and measuring corruption notwithstanding, the existing approaches are nevertheless useful in guiding policymakers and activists in designing anticorruption initiatives.

INSTITUTIONAL FACTORS AND THE DIAGNOSIS
AND TREATMENT OF CORRUPTION IN KENYA

I have argued elsewhere that corruption in Kenya should be attributed to institutional failure (Akech 2011, 1). That is, dysfunctional or failed institutions often facilitate the abuse of governmental power, thereby creating opportunities for corruption. I have therefore attributed the prevalence of corruption to the predominance of arbitrary power, especially in the statutory (as opposed to constitutional) order. Typically, the Kenyan statutory order grants executive, legislative, and judicial actors broad powers without establishing effective procedural mechanisms to circumscribe their exercise. For example, the Immigration Act[1] conferred on the minister and immigration officers wide discretionary powers to consider applications for citizenship, and they were not required to give any reasons for the grant or refusal of applications. In the absence of effective regulation, law often aids the abuse of power and corruption. In other words, "in the absence of fear of penalty or sanctions, there is nothing to deter [those who wield power from] fraudulently enriching themselves" and violating the law (Egbue 2006, 84). In this scenario, government actors often disregard the prescriptions of law, especially where they view legal requirements as hindering the attainment of short-term political objectives or other ends. Because law is dispensed with whenever it is convenient, a culture of impunity emerges where law ceases to be authoritative.

Furthermore, the president, government ministers, and senior public servants often use the law to intimidate their juniors into silence or into obeying illegal commands, largely because of the absence of accountability mechanisms. Indeed, junior public servants are often unwilling accomplices to abuses of power or corruption. Moreover, until the promulgation of a new constitution in August 2010, the law did not restrict the president's ability to make decisions without consulting the cabinet or undermining the independence of the judiciary, nor did it restrict the chief justice's ability to compromise the decisional independence of judges, or the ability of legislators to become hired mercenaries for the highest bidder. In the case of the legislature, the failure to institutionalize codes of conduct functions as a license for legislators to breach conflict of interest rules with impunity. In addition, state secrecy laws such as the Official Secrets Act[2] have ensured that the citizenry have little or no information about the activities of government. Invariably, the citizenry learn of abuses of power and corruption only long after they have occurred, by which time the damage caused is nearly irreparable. Even new laws enacted to aid the fight against corruption, such as the Public Officer Ethics Act,[3] may actually be used to strengthen the hand of power wielders, who often interpret such laws in a manner that enhances their ability to intimidate public servants. In these circumstances, I have contended that constitutional reform must be accompanied by comprehensive democratization of the legal order.

More particularly, I have suggested that institutional mechanisms that increase political accountability – for example, by encouraging punishment of corrupt individuals or reducing the informational problems related to government activities – may reduce the incidence of corruption (see also Lederman et al. 2001, 3–4).

Indeed, and as we shall see, abuse of power is prevalent in the organizations that typically feature in the Bribery Index. Take the police for example. The exercise of the powers of the police is characterized by wide discretionary powers, which are prone to abuse because they are largely unregulated. In addition, internal regulations of the police force give senior officers the power to dismiss their juniors using summary procedures that have no due process mechanisms. In such circumstances, it is understandable why junior police officers often carry out the orders of their seniors, including soliciting bribes. Until the promulgation of the Constitution of 2010, there was also no objectivity and accountability in investigations and prosecutions. As a result, the power to prosecute was often abused and exercised selectively.

In the case of the public service, Kenya is hopefully now emerging from a past in which public officers served at the pleasure of the president. Thus the president could – and often did – terminate their services at will. In this environment, public officers did what they were told by the president or government ministers, even when the instructions were illegal. As a result, they were often accomplices in corrupt activities. The courts even sanctioned the transfer of public officers from one position to another without due process.[4] In addition, public officers seeking to safeguard the public interest were easily intimidated into implementing illegal instructions, which were invariably verbal.

And in the case of the legislature, the absence of proper regulation has meant that legislators can serve on committees even though their membership would entail a conflict of interest – either because they face allegations of corruption, are allegedly allied to corruption cartels, or have commercial interests that are overseen by these committees (World Bank 2008, 24). There are also allegations that legislators have taken bribes from fellow legislators and other wealthy politicians to influence the deliberations of the legislature (Rugene 2009). Such corruption facilitates impunity and hinders efforts to hold the corrupt to account.

The absence of effective accountability mechanisms has meant that government actors either fail to follow the prescriptions of law or manipulate them. For example, the executive has selectively applied the law, with the result that the idea of "equality before the law" is greatly undermined. This failure to apply the law consistently has been pronounced in grand corruption investigations, where conspiracies among executive agencies has encouraged inaction as the responsible agencies of government engage in turf wars that only result in the law not being applied. Such conspiracies by the executive agencies to undermine the rule of law do not engender public confidence in the fairness of the law as petty corruption investigations, which are invariably taken to their logical conclusion, are seen to be treated differently. A further indication that the citizenry are losing faith in the law is to be found in the increasingly common practice of deploying clientelism that is based on personal relationships with judicial officers to access the courts, instead of trusting in the capacity of the judiciary to give blind justice. Because the citizenry do not have faith in judicial procedures and processes to produce just outcomes, they are inclined to "work the system" by seeking the intervention of judicial officers so that they are given favorable treatment.

Fortunately, Kenya's Constitution of 2010 seeks to address some of the foregoing institutional factors that contribute to corruption. In particular, it establishes principles and mechanisms that can circumscribe the exercise of power. For example, it establishes "guiding principles of leadership and integrity" that include (1) selection of public officers on the basis of personal integrity, competence, and suitability; (2) objectivity and impartiality in decision making, and in ensuring that decisions are not influenced by nepotism, favoritism, other proper motives or corrupt practices; (3) selfless service as demonstrated by honesty and the declaration of any personal interest that may conflict with public duties; and (4) accountability to the public for decisions and actions.[5] Further, it imposes a duty on state officers to "behave, whether in public and official life, in private life, or in association with other persons, in a manner that avoids any conflict between personal interests and public or official duties."[6] However, these provisions of the constitution will make a difference only if they are translated into policies and procedures that govern the day-to-day conduct of public officers.

Apart from the predominance of arbitrary power, the prevalence of corruption in Kenya can be attributed to the fact that systems and processes of public administration are often manual and inefficient, with the result that citizens often experience long delays before they receive the services they seek. In some cases, these services are denied altogether. This induces the largely helpless and desperate citizens to bribe public officers if they are to receive services in a timely manner. But it also induces public officers to not only deny citizens timely services unless they are bribed, but also to resist computerization and other initiatives that seek to speed up their administrative processes and minimize room for discretionary judgment. Further, efforts to computerize systems and processes have been resisted in some cases.

The Pensions Department of the Ministry of Finance provides an excellent illustration of this reality. It is responsible for administering the pension schemes of public officers. There have been allegations that the Pensions Department takes too long to process claims even after it has received all the necessary documents from retirees or their dependants (KACC 2008b, 5). Further, it has been alleged that claims take long to process because of deliberate loss of documents and files, and that some files cannot be traced in the Department especially when certain officers have an interest in them (KACC 2008b, 5). These officers, often in collaboration with middlemen (or "brokers"), have also been accused of exploiting retirees and their dependents by promising to fast track the processing of their benefits if they pay bribes. The KACC confirmed these allegations in an examination of systems and processes that it undertook in 2008. It established that these systems and processes contribute to corruption in various ways. First, the department's operations are centralized at the Head Office in Nairobi, meaning that the majority of the pensioners and their dependents who reside upcountry have to travel to Nairobi for any service. Many of them are desperate because they often lack accommodation in Nairobi, but also do not understand the processes of the Department. They are therefore easy prey to corrupt department officers and middlemen. Second, it took the Department more than six months to process a claim on average, even when it possessed all the required documents. However, the officers had discretion to fast track claims. This created an incentive for the officers to delay processing claims unless they were bribed to fast track them. Third, the officers assessed the pension awards due without the aid of appropriate operational manuals. This unregulated exercise of discretion often led to the miscalculation of dues. In addition, the Department had no system for recording complaints reported to it and therefore could not track the action taken on specific complaints.

This experience is replicated in other institutions. For example, in the public health care system, there have been prolonged delays spanning four to ten years in the determination of disciplinary cases involving health professionals (EACC 2011, 16). Among other things, such delays create room for the affected professionals to pay bribes so that their cases can be considered favorably. The Ministry of Medical Systems has also issued regulations for the management of waivers and exemptions from paying fees. These guidelines require each hospital to form a committee to handle waivers and exemptions. However, the EACC has established that some hospitals have not established these committees, and that where they have been established, they rarely meet (EACC 2011, 33). As a result, unauthorized officers have been approving waivers and exemptions. This has presented an opportunity for corruption: those who pay bribes are granted waivers and exemptions, while deserving cases are denied such services (EACC 2011, 33, 35).

Let us now see whether, and the extent to which, the existing approaches to measuring corruption in Kenya have taken the foregoing factors into account.

TI'S BRIBERY INDEX

TI's Approach to Measuring Corruption

Transparency International is a transnational network devoted to fighting corruption. It was founded in Berlin in 1993 by Peter Egen, a former World Bank executive, together with a group of like-minded individuals, including Joe Githongo, then head of a Kenyan accountancy firm, whose son John was later to head TI-Kenya (Norwegian Agency for Development Cooperation 2011, 7). TI's mission is to increase government accountability and curb both international and national corruption. It seeks to realize this mission by promoting and strengthening international and national integrity systems. At the national level, it targets reforms that minimize the discretionary power of public officials, strengthen autonomous oversight mechanisms, reduce conflicts of interest, and increase public supervision of the government (Wang and Rosenau 2001, 31). In terms of approach, TI "has eschewed investigation into particular cases, and has tended to stop short of overt confrontation with centres of power, whether in government or business" (Norwegian Agency for Development Cooperation 2011, 7). Instead, it has preferred "to work with organizations from the inside, with a strong focus on technical solutions to corruption problems" (Norwegian Agency for Development Cooperation 2011, 7).

TI carries out its work through national chapters, which are supported by a secretariat based in Berlin. The secretariat also coordinates the work of these chapters, gives them advice, leads the organization's international agenda, and serves as a knowledge management centre (Norwegian Agency for Development Cooperation 2011, 7). According to TI, the movement, through the national chapters, "brings together people of integrity in civil society, business and government to work as coalitions for systemic reforms."[7] TI now has some ninety accredited national chapters, which are supposed to be financially and institutionally independent, but are required to observe the movement's guiding principles of noninvestigative work and independence from government, commercial, and partisan political interests.

As far as governance is concerned, TI's ultimate decision-making body is the Annual Membership Meeting (AMM), which convenes once a year. It consists of official chapter representatives and individual members, the latter being "experienced anti-corruption practitioners who are judged to make a significant personal contribution to the movement at global level" (Norwegian Agency for Development Cooperation 2011, 12). The next important body is the International Board of Directors, whose members are elected by the AMM. In turn, this Board appoints the managing director of the secretariat. Another important body is the Advisory Council consisting of "some 30 highly experienced individuals" (Norwegian Agency for Development Cooperation 2011, 12). This council is appointed by the Board and advises it.

TI's best-known product is the Corruption Perception Index (CPI), which it has issued annually since 1995. The CPI ranks countries in terms of their degree of corruption, based on the perceptions and opinions of people working with multinational corporations and international institutions (Wang and Rosenau 2001, 32). It uses country scores, which range from one to ten (with ten representing the lowest levels of corruption). Because it is based on perception, the CPI is therefore not an objective measurement of corruption. In fact, TI acknowledges the limitations of the CPI's methodology, which has been widely challenged (Norwegian Agency for Development Cooperation 2011, 31). However, the annual publication of the CPI attracts wide publicity all over the world. For example, it "generates a great deal of media coverage, which brings public attention to the issue of corruption, as well as to TI itself" (Wang and Rosenau 2001, 35). Further, governments around the world are sensitive to their standing on the CPI (Wang and Rosenau 2001, 35). Academic researchers also use the CPI as a basis for comparative studies (Norwegian Agency for Development Cooperation 2011, 31). It therefore has tremendous value as an advocacy tool.

Perhaps because of the limitations of the CPI, and the controversy it generates, TI has sought to supplement it with other indices and assessments, some of which are the initiatives of the national chapters.

TI-Kenya's bribery index should be seen against this background. Like other national chapters, TI-Kenya – which was established in 1999 – has tried to steer clear of exposing specific cases of corruption and confronting government. In one interesting episode in 2005, it prevailed upon its then executive director to resign on the basis that "she had behaved rudely to government officials and had made unsubstantiated allegations about official sleaze" (Maclean 2005). However, sections of the media thought that the real reason she was fired was because some elements of the TI-Kenya Board were "too close to the ruling regime," and were therefore uncomfortable with the vocal manner in which she had articulated corruption issues (Okwatch 2005). For example, this executive director had alleged that a government minister had stolen KES 750 million and stashed it in overseas banks. At the time, the chairman of the TI-Kenya Board was "a close friend and confidante" of the president, who had even appointed him as the chancellor of one of the public universities. Indeed, this particular individual remains a member of TI's Advisory Council. Her successor was also fired in controversial circumstances, and was reportedly sacked for "being vocal on corruption involving some board members" (*East African Standard* 2006). Further, the current TI-Kenya Board include a former head of the public service, a member of the Monetary Committee of the Central Bank of Kenya, and a former permanent secretary in the Office of the Vice President and Minister for Home Affairs. These circumstances perhaps explain why media and civil society skeptics claim that "true anti-corruption crusaders" have been removed from TI-Kenya (Oloo 2005). And although it is said that TI has resolved the governance issues that have dogged the TI-Kenya Board (Norwegian Agency for Development Cooperation 2011, 20), the latter remains open to criticism on the ground that it is rather closely associated with powerful elements in government.

Nevertheless, TI-Kenya produces the Bribery Index, a survey that captures corruption as experienced by ordinary citizens in their interactions with officials of public institutions, although a few private organizations are also included. The survey is conducted at the household level, and sampled households and respondents are picked through random sampling (TI-Kenya 2010, 3). It uses a sampling frame based on a census of the target population, which makes it possible to make inferences about the population as a whole, taking into account margins of error (TI-Kenya 2010). Further, the survey is structured around four key experiential questions: (1) which institutions the respondents interacted with in the last twelve months while seeking services; (2) whether a bribe was expected or demanded during the interaction; (3) whether the respondents paid a bribe and how much was paid; and (4) whether the respondents received the services sought after paying the bribe (TI-Kenya 2010). In addition, the survey now asks respondents about the frequency of demands for and payment of bribes.[8] By asking these questions, TI-Kenya hopes to capture the situation on the ground concerning corruption in particular institutions.[9] The services sought are categorized into law enforcement (i.e., avoiding the consequences of wrong-doing and/or harassment by the relevant authority); access to services such as medical treatment, water, and electricity; business, such as obtaining contracts and expediting payments; and employment matters, such as securing jobs, promotions, transfers, and training (TI-Kenya 2008, 3).

In addition to the foregoing experiential questions, the survey includes the following questions of perception: (1) why the respondents think they did not get service even after paying a bribe; (2) whether they were satisfied with the services they received after paying a bribe; (3) whether they complained or reported the bribery incidences to any authority or person; (4) why they did not report or complain about the bribery incidences; (5) how satisfied they were with the action taken after they reported the incidences; (6) how they would describe the current state of corruption in Kenya; (7) whether the state of corruption has increased, remained the same, or decreased during the preceding year; (8) whether the state of corruption will increase, remain the same, or decrease in the next year; and (9) whether the government is doing enough to fight corruption.

The collected data are analyzed using six indicators, namely (TI-Kenya 2008, 3–4).

1. **Incidence**, defined as the proportion of survey respondents who have interacted with an institution and have reported encountering bribery situations in their official dealings with it. This indicator measures "the opportunity for and propensity of officials in an organization to ask for or to accept bribes."

2. **Prevalence**, defined as the proportion of survey respondents who are victims of bribery in an institution. These are the respondents who reported paying a bribe or were badly treated or not served for failing to do so. This indicator measures "the impact of bribery in an organization on the population is serves."

3. **Severity**, defined as the frequency of denial of service if bribes are not paid. This indicator measures "the deleterious impact of this form of corruption on the public's ability to access that to which it is entitled."

4. **Frequency**, defined as the average number of bribes paid per client. This indicator measures "the scale of the bribery activity in an organization among those who interact with it."

5. **Cost**, defined as the average expenditure on bribery per person. This indicator measures "the extra 'tax burden' that results from such practices."
6. **Size**, defined as the average size of bribes paid. This indicator measures "the premium that citizens put on a particular service or cost/penalty avoided or, conversely, the value that those demanding/receiving such bribes believe their 'services'… are worth."

In constructing the Bribery Index, TI-Kenya gives each indicator equal weight. The result is an aggregate index based on these indicators and "has a value range from 0 to 100, where the higher the value, the worse the performance" (TI-Kenya 2008, 4). Whereas the first three indicators are entered into the aggregate index as raw percentages, the other three are actual values and "are scaled by the lowest to the highest value to obtain a normalized score range of 0–100" (TI-Kenya 2008, 3). Only organizations mentioned by at least fifty respondents are ranked (TI-Kenya 2008, 8). As Table 8.1 indicates, the Kenya Police has consistently obtained the highest aggregate score. The Judiciary, the Ministry of Lands, and Nairobi City Council have also featured several times in the top ten. All of these institutions are characterized by wide discretionary powers and citizens interact with them frequently owing to the nature of their services. Although the Ministry of Education has been in the news in the recent past following a major corruption scandal, it has not featured in the top ten of the TI-Kenya rankings. Another significant institution that various commentators and the media allege is a den of corruption is Parliament (the legislature), although it has featured only once in the rankings.

TI-Kenya has drawn a number of inferences from these indices over the years. First, bribes are on average demanded (or offered) in two out of three encounters with public officials. Second, law enforcement matters have emerged as the most corrupt, followed by regulatory functions. Third, poor people (with low income and low education) are the most vulnerable to bribery. Fourth, most bribes involve relatively small sums paid frequently. Fifth, the majority of respondents do not report bribery incidences to the relevant authorities; they prefer to pay the bribes and keep quiet. For example, the East African Bribery Index for 2010 states that about 89 percent of the respondents did not report cases of bribery to any person in authority (TI – Kenya 2010, 18). TI-Kenya attributes this behavior to factors such as the fear of legal culpability, avoidance of the inconveniences that involvement in court proceedings are likely to cause, and lack of faith in the anticorruption systems (TI-Kenya 2006, 8; 2011, 8). Many of them believe that no action would be taken against corrupt officials following their reports or are afraid that the authorities will intimidate them (TI-Kenya 2009b, 17). However, many of them are increasingly reporting incidents of corruption to the media, which TI-Kenya attributes to increased access to and ease of communication by cellular phones (TI-Kenya 2006, 8).

TABLE 8.1. *Rankings of Select Organizations 2002–2010*

Organization	Aggregate Score and (Rank) in KBI (2002)	Aggregate Score and (Rank) in KBI (2003)	Aggregate Score and (Rank) in KBI (2004)	Aggregate Score and (Rank) in KBI (2005)	Aggregate Score and (Rank) in KBI (2006)	Aggregate Score and (Rank) in KBI (2007)	Aggregate Score and (Rank) in KBI (2008)	Aggregate Score and (Rank) in EABI (2009)	Aggregate Score and (Rank) in EABI (2010)
Kenya Police	69.4 (1)	57.3 (1)	72.4 (1)	60.3 (1)	46.6 (1)	Not available	57 (1)	66.5 (1)	76.9 (2)
Judiciary	32.4 (11)	24 (12)	23.7 (4)	27.8 (6)	21.3 (12)	Not available	Not ranked (under 50 interactions)	54.4 (3)	70.1 (5)
Ministry of Lands	30.3 (13)	24.5 (10)	23.6 (5)	25.5 (8)	19.7 (17)	Not available	37 (3)	45.6 (5)	69.1 (6)
Nairobi City Council	33.8 (9)	26.2 (7)	27.4 (7)	21.3 (13)	Not ranked	Not available	31 (7)	42.9 (6)	84.5 (1)
Ministry of Education	25.8 (26)	14.3 (22)	12.7 (18)	14.7 (21)	20.4 (15)	Not available	25 (12)	26.4 (17)	45.9 (19)
Parliament	Not ranked	Not ranked	Not ranked	Not ranked	21.1 (13)	Not available	Not ranked	Not ranked	Not ranked

KBI, Kenya Bribery Index; EABI, East African Bribery Index; (Rank), position of organization in Bribery Index.
Source: Transparency International, Kenya Bribery Indices 2002–2010.

TABLE 8.2. *Bribery Prevalence in East Africa 2010–2011*

Country Rank	Country	Bribery Prevalence 2011 (%)	Rank in 2010	Bribery Prevalence 2010 (%)
1	Burundi	37.9	1	36.7
2	Uganda	33.9	2	33.0
3	Tanzania	31.6	4	28.6
4	Kenya	28.8	3	31.9
5	Rwanda	5.1	5	6.6

Source: Transparency International, East African Bribery Index 2011.

Sixth, new policies, laws, and regulations impact on opportunities for bribery. For example, in 2005 TI-Kenya noted a sharp escalation of the size of bribes paid to the police in rural areas following the introduction of new public service vehicle rules (TI-Kenya 2005, 5). Conversely, in 2007 TI-Kenya contended that the government's Rapid Results Initiative, and the elimination of road licences contributed to the decline of law enforcement and service-related bribes (TI-Kenya 2007, 8). Seventh, the majority of respondents do not think that corruption is decreasing. In the East African Bribery Index for 2010, for example, TI-Kenya reports that about 90 percent of Kenyan respondents perceive the country as being between corrupt and extremely corrupt. Many of them believe that the government is not taking sufficient action to combat corruption (TI-Kenya 2010, 29).

Since 2009, TI-Kenya has been producing an East African Bribery Index (EABI), which compares the levels of corruption in the East African countries of Burundi, Kenya, Rwanda, Tanzania, and Uganda. The EABI adopts the same methodology as the Kenya Bribery Index, and has two objectives. First, it ranks all institutions where citizens experienced bribery in the five countries. It then uses this ranking to compare the performance of similar institutions, such as policing agencies and public utility companies. Second, it uses the data to compile a country ranking of corruption prevalence. That is, it aggregates the indices of the ranked organizations for each country, a figure that is then divided by the number of ranked organizations to produce a "corruption prevalence" figure for each country. It then lists and compares the corruption prevalence figures of the five countries. It should be noted that in the 2011 report, TI-Kenya uses the term "bribery prevalence" and not corruption prevalence (TI-Kenya 2011, 1). Table 8.2 shows the bribery prevalence figures for 2010 and 2011. TI-Kenya uses these figures to target institutional reform at the level of the East African Community. For example, the 2009 EABI report notes that corruption in the affected sectors contributes to deepening poverty and increasing the cost of doing business in East Africa, and calls on the Community "to create the right environment if the member countries are to attract and retain foreign domestic investments" (TI-Kenya 2010, 6).

It is worth noting that TI-Kenya appreciates the limitations of its methodology. For example, it notes that survey responses are subject to unavoidable respondent bias since corruption is a form of stigmatizing behavior. Depending on their attitudes to particular issues, respondents may therefore understate or overstate the level of activity. This may explain why certain institutions feature prominently in the Index only in particular years. For example, the Department of Defence has tended to feature prominently during years in which there have been widespread media allegations of bribery in the recruitment of servicemen (TI-Kenya 2009b, 18). The same can be said of the legislature. Second, TI-Kenya is aware of self-selection bias, in the sense that people who have something to hide are likely to decline to respond. Third, the survey is not designed to capture high-level corruption, such as bribery in big public procurement projects (TI-Kenya 2004, 7). Fourth, TI-Kenya appreciates the fact that computing aggregate indices invariably entails making subjective judgments about what to include and what not to include, what measures to use, whether or not to attach weights to individual components, and if so what weights to attach. In this respect, it admits that the decision to give each of the six indicators an equal weight is a value judgment because some of the indicators are arguably more critical than others. Fifth, it acknowledges that a representative sample of the population does "not adequately capture the bribery in an organization that affects a very specific, small segment of the population, even though this may be systemic and severe" (TI-Kenya 2004, 7). Finally, the Index only encompasses institutions where citizens have experienced bribery. But critics of the Index assert that public institutions that citizens do not ordinarily interact with are probably more corrupt than the included ones.[10]

Evaluating the Impact of the Bribery Index

To what extent has the Bribery Index influenced or shaped local discourses on corruption and governance? According to TI-Kenya, the Index is a useful tool insofar as it demonstrates the severity and impact of corruption.[11] In addition, it provides an indicator that can be tracked and evaluated over time, thereby enabling various actors to gauge corruption trends in organizations, especially public ones.[12] The Index measures bribery which, unlike other forms of corruption, is measurable, or so TI-Kenya argues. And because bribery can be measured, TI-Kenya takes the view that the Index is a useful tool for coalescing public attention on corruption. In other words, TI-Kenya sees, and uses, the Index primarily as a policy advocacy tool. This explains why whenever TI-Kenya launches the Index, it invites government actors, the media, civil society groups, and members of the public to a meeting at which it gives a speech about the status of corruption in the country. In 2010, for example, it noted that corruption had remained a part of public practice as many of the institutions established after 2002 to promote good governance had failed to tackle it (TI-Kenya 2010, 5). Further, TI-Kenya aims to provide "a snap-shot view of bribery and corruption levels inherent in critical public institutions so that further in-depth studies of these institutions may be undertaken and requisite reforms implemented" (TI-Kenya 2009b, 6). In this respect, TI-Kenya sees the Index as an indication of weak governance structures in the ranked organizations.[13] The Index may therefore be a useful tool for governmental agencies such as KACC.

According to TI-Kenya, government officials, who now refer to it quite often, have accepted the Index.[14] The government and the donor community use it for their programming. Foreign investors seeking to set up shop in Kenya also use it as part of their due diligence.[15] So do academic researchers (see African Capacity Building Foundation 2007, 39; Ngunjiri 2010, 100–104) and business information websites.[16] Further, it assists TI-Kenya to prioritize its interventions.[17] For example, the Kenya Police has consistently been ranked first in the Index for the last decade. TI-Kenya has now working with the Kenya Police with a view to strengthening its governance systems.[18]

As a reaction to their poor ranking in the Index, organizations such as the Teachers Service Commission (TSC), the Kenya Ports Authority, the Kenya Power & Lighting Company (KPLC), the Kenya Wildlife Service, and the Kenya Commercial Bank have all approached TI-Kenya to carry out integrity assessments of their governance systems.[19] The cases of the TSC and KPLC are instructive (TI-Kenya 2009b, 15–17). Following the ranking of TSC as the second most corrupt institution in Kenya in the 2005 Kenya Bribery Index (KBI), the management of TSC approached TI-Kenya to investigate and recommend institutional reforms with a view to reducing corruption in the Commission. The investigation found that the most corrupt unit in the Commission was the Staffing Department followed by the Administration, Finance & Accounting and Internal Audit departments. The study also found that several officials were engaging in corrupt practices. The investigation further indicated that the corruption in the exercise of recruiting teachers was particularly to blame for TSC's adverse mention in the KBI. Although TSC devolved the recruitment of teachers to the district and divisional levels, it failed to establish transparency and accountability systems, thereby creating opportunities for corruption. The study also established that the TSC's integrity division, which was launched in early 2006, was encountering obstacles such as lack of financial autonomy, lack of resources, discrimination, and favoritism in employment; threats of dismissal to potential whistle blowers; lack of goodwill and support from other units in the TSC; and lack of proper structures for its operations. Following the investigations, TI-Kenya made a number of recommendations, including the need to (1) strengthen the Integrity Division by hiring personnel whose moral standing was beyond doubt and reproach; (2) educate members of staff on corruption; (3) ensure that guilty individuals are prosecuted; (4) establish effective monitoring and evaluation mechanisms; and (5) computerize systems.

TI-Kenya reports that by June 2008, the Integrity Division had implemented a number of these recommendations. This led to achievements among them administration of wealth declarations for income, assets, and liabilities; formation of a corruption prevention committee and corruption prevention subcommittees in all service areas; and networking and linkages with watchdog agencies, namely the KACC, the National Anti-Corruption Campaign Steering Committee, and TI-Kenya. Further, the division (1) initiated systems processes and procedures for audit by KACC; (2) instituted reporting mechanisms, including installing corruption reporting boxes at the TSC headquarters in Nairobi; (3) undertook corruption risk assessments; and (4) formulated a corruption prevention plan. It also punished culprits through existing administrative procedures.

In the case of KPLC, TI-Kenya carried out an integrity assessment of governance systems in 2009 (TI-Kenya 2009c). It made a number of useful findings. First, members of the Board of Directors meddled in procurement processes and participated in decision making where they had conflicts of interest. The institution did not even have rules on conflict of interest. Second, although KPLC established an Ethics & Integrity Office in 2006, integrity issues remained peripheral. This office also lacked independence because it was headed by an officer who reported to the company secretary instead of reporting directly to the chief executive officer. Third, KPLC had not established a system for the protection of whistle blowers. To deal with these deficiencies, TI-Kenya recommended that KPLC should conduct periodic risk assessments in all its divisions, recruit the head of the Integrity Office competitively and enhance its independence, and reassign or redeploy key personnel to arrest corrupt tendencies resulting from staying too long in a certain position or division.

For organizations that are sufficiently embarrassed by appearing in the Bribery Index, this tool may therefore precipitate internal institutional reforms. In this respect, TI-Kenya makes the assumption that organizations are capable of reforming themselves. And it asserts that its interventions have helped institutions such as the Kenya Commercial Bank to strengthen their governance systems. It therefore takes credit for the fact that this bank no longer appears in the index.[20] Beyond this micro-level, however, it is arguable that the Index offers a limited tool for diagnosing and combating system-wide public sector corruption.

The Index and National Discourses on Corruption

It is difficult to say whether TI-Kenya's bribery indices influence national discourses on corruption given that the existing evidence is anecdotal. Some civil society organizations make reference to these indices in their literature and advocacy campaigns (see Africa Centre for Open Governance 2009a, 3). The Department of Governance and Ethics in the Office of the President, which has since been abolished, also took notice of the Bribery Index. It perceived the Index as "a clear demonstration of the ways in which civil society can complement and contribute to government efforts to address corruption."[21] In 2004, for example, it saw that year's Index as a vindication of the government's campaign against corruption.[22] It also commended the organizations that registered improvements in their rankings in the Bribery Index.[23] As we shall see, the Kenya Anti-Corruption Commission (KACC; now the Ethics and Anti-Corruption Commission [EACC]) also begun carrying out corruption perception surveys, and it is plausible that it was partly influenced by TI-Kenya's approach to measuring corruption. In addition, the EACC carries out corruption risk assessments of public institutions. The indices have featured prominently in the media since their inception, and have arguably enhanced and sustained public awareness of corruption. For the most part, media reports consist of verbatim accounts of the Bribery Index as contained in press briefings issued by TI-Kenya. To determine the impact of these media reports on public perceptions of corruption, an opinion survey would be useful.

Despite the annual production and dissemination of corruption indices, however, public sector corruption (both grand and petty) seems to be on the increase. Powerful political and economic elites have hatched various schemes to embezzle public funds or otherwise defraud the public. Goldenberg, Anglo-Leasing, and the Maize scandal provide good examples of such scams. The Goldenberg scandal revolved around a deal between government officials and a businessman, in which the businessman agreed to remit US$50 million annually to the Central Bank of Kenya on condition that the government would give him a monopoly on gold and diamond exports from Kenya and a compensation of 35 percent on his exports. No such exports took place, however. Instead, the businessman exported "fictional commodities to fictional companies that paid for them in fictitional foreign exchange" (Lawson 2009, 80). For its part, the Anglo Leasing scandal involved government contracts for goods and services that were paid for but never received from companies that did not exist. These contracts resulted in the loss of millions of dollars. And the more recent maize scandal revolved around the sale of imported maize (see Africa Centre for Open Governance 2009b). Here, briefcase millers (individuals and companies with no milling premises or capacity) were awarded large quantities of maize by the Strategic Grain Reserve at a time when the country was facing a serious shortage of maize in the market. These briefcase millers subsequently sold the maize to genuine millers, making exorbitant profits in the process. This meant that the government's goal of providing the ordinary citizen with affordable maize flour was defeated.

There is also pervasive corruption involving the irregular or illegal allocation of public land, including important natural resources such as the Mau Forest, which is an important water tower (see Republic of Kenya 2004). And more recently, a corruption scandal involving the National Hospital Insurance Fund came to light (see Lakin 2012). Such corruption has an adverse impact on the livelihoods of many citizens, and undermines environmental conservation efforts. Similarly, political and economic elites have stolen from health funds, such as those meant for the management of the HIV/AIDS pandemic (see Mutiga 2005). These elites then use their ill-gotten wealth to distort the political and judicial processes, thereby ensuring that they remain in power and that they are never punished for their crimes. The troubling culture of impunity that has taken root in the country can be attributed to this distorting effect of corruption (Akech 2009, 81).

Further, corruption is no longer solely attributable to the executive. There are widespread and credible allegations that the legislature and the judiciary are also abusing their powers and engaging in, or facilitating, corruption (see *Daily Nation* 2005; Republic of Kenya 2010). These allegations have led to questions about the ability and legitimacy of these branches to hold the executive to account. For example, there is a perception that legislators are no less corrupt than the executive actors they purport to hold accountable (see Rugene 2009). Further, the legislature's ability to function as a watchdog is compromised because some of its key committees are headed by legislators who have been implicated in corruption scandals. There are also concerns that legislators are influenced by special interests and may not be credible guardians of the public interest. The judiciary is equally culpable. As a result of allegations of abuse of power and corruption, significant segments of the citizenry perceive the judiciary as having lost its legitimacy as a dispute resolution forum. But in the case of the Judiciary, the adoption of competitive recruitment and governance reforms promise to enhance the decisional independence of judicial officers, with the likelihood that they will be less prone to capture by corrupt elements.

At the same time, ordinary citizens are typically compelled to bribe government officials – such as police officers, local authority councilors, clerks in government ministries, and school functionaries – to obtain services that they are entitled to at little or no cost. Accordingly, life becomes quite precarious for many of those who are unable to bribe these government officials. For example, the liberties of these citizens are often under threat from police officers, who often detain them or continue to detain them as a result of their inability to pay bribes. Further, these citizens are often unable to access healthcare services because they have no money to pay the bribes demanded by health officials. In addition, they do not have security of tenure in many cases because their land is often grabbed by powerful political and economic elites in collusion with bureaucrats at the Ministry of Lands.

In official policy, successive governments have acknowledged the magnitude of the problem of corruption and have established various mechanisms to fight it, including the enactment of anticorruption laws, one of which established the KACC.[24] In practice, however, government has been accused of not doing enough to fight corruption. Those accused of corruption, especially the powerful elites, are never held to account, and continue to hold public office. The implementation of the new laws has been dismal at best. Further, the KACC, which was supposed to be the premier anticorruption agency, failed to carry out its mandate effectively. Instead, it was embroiled in a blame game with the Attorney-General's Office as to which of the two agencies was frustrating the fight against corruption. As a result of persistent prevarication by government, many citizens have had little or no confidence in the government's commitment to fight corruption (Africa Centre for Open Governance 2008, 3).

PERFORMANCE CONTRACTING AND THE DIAGNOSIS AND ERADICATION OF CORRUPTION

A question therefore arises as to how public sector corruption can be diagnosed properly and treated. Arguably, measures of corruption would be more useful if they were part of a governmental system that rewards good performers and punishes poor ones. In such a system, corruption rankings would create "integrity competition" among organizations, thereby giving them an incentive to fight corruption. This perhaps explains why the government is now making the measurement of corruption an integral part of performance contracting reforms, which are already enhancing the effectiveness and responsiveness of public institutions, according to some accounts. For this approach to work, however, the measurement of corruption needs to be informed by an understanding of the contextual and institutional factors that explain the persistence of corruption.[25] For example, indicators need to target the incentives of the responsible governmental actors if they are to contribute to the diagnosis and treatment of corruption. In this regard, Alina Mungiu-Pippidi's qualitative strategy of attacking the roots of corruption in societies characterized by particularism by developing indirect indicators for measuring corruption constitutes an instructive approach for countries such as Kenya. Unless we tackle the roots of corruption, for example, organizations such as the Kenya Police, which TI-Kenya considers to be impervious to change, will continue to take their pride of place in the Index.

The diagnosis of corruption in Kenya should therefore be based on qualitative indicators that take contextual and institutional factors into account. In this respect, the KACC developed a fairly comprehensive guide, which public institutions implementing performance contracts have been required to use to determine the levels of corruption since fiscal year 2007/2008. This guide was motivated by the inclusion of a "corruption eradication" indicator in the annual performance contracts that public institutions have been signing with the government since 2004 (KACC 2008a, 2). The idea was to mainstream anticorruption prevention and detection strategies in the management systems of public institutions; the guide was supposed to help them to attain this objective (KACC 2008a, 2). The corruption eradication indicator required the realization of the following measures: (1) formulation of an institutional anti-corruption policy; (2) operationalizing corruption prevention and integrity committees; (3) developing corruption prevention plans; (4) developing a code of conduct; (5) integrity training; and (6) conducting surveys on corruption perception (KAAC 2008a, 2).

The survey was supposed to monitor corruption levels in institutions over time and evaluate the impact of their corruption prevention programs. The KACC survey instrument was designed to measure levels of corruption, the magnitude of corruption, and service delivery ratings within an institution. It sought to generate information about corrupt practices, including a clear understanding of the activities and actors involved in "creating a situation of corrupt practices" and actual acts of corrupt behavior. Like the Bribery Index, it sought to measure the degree to which customers of an institution were subjected to direct or indirect pressure to participate in corrupt practices, for example, instances in which a customer was asked for money, gifts, or favors to have a service provided or problem solved. Third, it sought to measure the magnitude of corruption, as reflected in customers' assessment of the spread of corruption in the institution. Finally, it sought to measure customers' expectations about the future of corruption, as reflected in their expectations about the *capacity* of the institution to curb corruption. Each public institution was required to send an analytical report of its annual survey findings to the Public Sector Reforms and Performance Contracting Department and the KACC.

The EACC has embraced this approach to fighting corruption. Further, the Corruption Eradication indicator has been upgraded to a performance criterion. The Performance targets under the 2010/2011 Corruption Eradication Criterion focus on the implementation of corruption prevention plans and strategies therein to fight corruption. Further, it requires the implementation of the following activities geared toward the realization of Chapter 6 of the Constitution, which establishes guiding principles of leadership and integrity: (1) integrity vetting for public officers; (2) capacity building on corruption risk assessment and management for Corruption Prevention Committee members, Heads of Departments and Integrity/Ethics officers; (3) developing or reviewing Codes of Conduct in line with Chapter 6 of the Constitution and the Public Officer Ethics Act; (4) ensuring that any public officer suspected of corrupt practices is suspended to allow room for investigation; (5) ensuring that any professional suspended by the respective professional body is suspended from public service until investigations are complete; and (6) submitting quarterly reports to the EACC. Institutions are also required to establish mechanisms and measures to address corruption related audit queries, and undertake integrity testing in collaboration with the EACC. The expectation is that the implementation of the Corruption Eradication performance indicators will enhance internal controls, based on the corruption risk assessment surveys and implementation of the corruption prevention plans (Log Associates 2010, 39).

The survey instrument contains much-needed qualitative indicators. On the magnitude of corruption, it asks respondents to indicate how widespread corruption is among state officials and employees – that is, whether all officials and employees, or most, or only a few are involved in corruption. Second, it asks respondents to indicate what forms or practices of corruption they encountered in the course of seeking services, and lists the practices of abuse of office, bribery, extortion, favoritism, tribalism/nepotism, misuse, and misappropriation of government resources, un-procedural tendering, and others. Third, it seeks to determine the motive of bribe givers, and asks whether they gave bribes voluntarily as a token, to obtain a service, because of too much delay in service delivery, or because it was demanded. Fourth, the survey instrument seeks to determine the reasons for customer assessments of corruption levels, by asking whether they base their assessments on personal experience; discussions with relatives and friends; or information from the institution, the media, the EACC, politicians, a place of worship, or other sources of information. Fifth, it asks them to indicate whether the level of corruption has changed in the institution over the last year, and what they would attribute their answers to. Finally, the instrument seeks to determine what customers would do if they experience delays while waiting for a service, and asks whether they would, for example, offer bribes or gifts to officials, use influential people to help them, lodge a complaint with the top management, report to the EACC, or do nothing and give up.

The measurement of corruption in the context of performance contracting therefore promises to reduce this vice. A performance contract is a written agreement between the government and the head of a state agency (such us a government ministry, state corporation, or local authority) that delivers services to the public in which quantifiable targets are specified for a period of one financial year (July to June) and performance measured against agreed targets (Obong'o 2009, 73). In this contract, the government agrees to give the state agency certain units of capacity in exchange for which the agency undertakes to provide the performance due for each unit of capacity (Obong'o 2009, 73). The idea behind performance contracting is that "the institution of performance measurements, clarification of corporate objectives, customer orientation and an increased focus towards incremental productivity and cost reduction can lead to improvements in service delivery" (Government of Kenya 2003). It entails four activities: (1) establishing performance targets for ministries/ departments, groups, or individuals in carrying out specific work assignments; (2) performance planning, which is a process of establishing a shared understanding of what is to be achieved, how it is to be achieved, and managing resources to ensure successful implementation; (3) performance monitoring and reporting; and (4) performance appraisal (Obong'o 2009, 72).

The performance contracting and evaluation process works as follows (Government of Kenya 2012). First, an institution is required to prepare a strategic plan, which forms the basis of its performance contract with the government. Where it does not have a strategic plan, developing one constitutes one of the commitments and responsibilities of its permanent secretary or other accounting officer. The idea is to obtain "specific, easily understood, attainable, measurable and time bound" strategic objectives that can form terms of the performance contract. Each contract contains a matrix that specifies the weights attached to the performance criteria. At present, there are six criteria: Finance & Stewardship (20 percent), Service Delivery (20 percent), Non-Financial (15 percent), Operations (25 percent), Dynamic/ Qualitative (15 percent), and Corruption Eradication (5 percent). The process of identifying performance targets occurs after the government has completed its annual budget process and institutions have been informed about the financial resources allocated to them. The idea is to ensure that any targets established in the performance contract will be realistic and achievable within the available resources.

The second step consists of pre-negotiation consultations. At this stage, the parties perform a SWOT (strengths, weaknesses, opportunities, and threats) analysis to determine the institution's performance capacity. The aim is to ensure that the targets being established are realistic, achievable, measurable, growth oriented, and benchmarked to the performance of similar institutions. Negotiations then follow. At this stage, all the issues agreed on are included in the performance contract. It is interesting to note that the contract now include a commitment by the government that it will ensure that public officers suspected of corrupt practices step down to allow room for investigations. Next, the draft contract is submitted to the Performance Contracting Secretariat for vetting, a process whose objective is to ensure that the contract complies with established guidelines and are linked to the institution's strategic objectives. The parties then sign the contract.

To facilitate continuous monitoring and reporting on performance, the institutions are required to submit quarterly and annual performance reports in prescribed formats to the secretariat. Each institution is then evaluated on the basis of the contract and the annual performance report. Performance evaluation involves rating the actual achievements against the targets established at the beginning of

TABLE 8.3. *Performance Contract Ranking Criteria*

Attribute	Criteria
Excellent	Achievement of 30% to 100% above target
Very Good	Achievement of set target up to 129% of set target
Good	Achievement of between 70% and 99.99% of set target
Fair	Achievement of between 50% and 69.99% of set target
Poor	Achievement of between 0% and 49.99% of set target

the financial year. The resultant differences are resolved into raw scores, weighted scores, and ultimately denominated into composite scores. Evaluation occurs in two stages. First, each agency evaluates itself using an automated system. Next, the results of each agency are moderated by an ad hoc Evaluation Task Force, which consists of experts drawn from professional associations, the academy, the business community, and retired public officers. The performance of institutions is rated based on the attributes and criteria outlines in Table 8.3.

The institutions are then ranked according to performance, and the good performers are rewarded at an annual public ceremony officiated by the president and/or the prime minister. It should be noted that the performance contracting system does not measure performance in terms of who are the best and worst performers. It is merely an indicator of improvement in the performance of the ranked institutions (Log Associates 2010, 36–37).

Performance contracting "has compelled government agencies to restructure extensively," and there is "significant improvement in delivery of services" (Obong'o 2009, 79). According to the government, performance contracting has enhanced efficiency, accountability, and service delivery in public institutions (Government of Kenya 2012, 14). However, the performance contracting program has been criticized on various grounds. First, it is argued that it applies a standardized instrument that attaches rigid weight to evaluation criteria to a range of public institutions involved in very different operations (Institute of Public Administration of Canada & Africa Development Professional Group 2009, 13). Second, the capacity of moderators and evaluators to negotiate appropriately ambitious and result-oriented targets has been doubted (Institute of Public Administration of Canada & Africa Development Professional Group 2009, 13). So has the capacity of the Secretariat to verify performance reports (Institute of Public Administration of Canada & Africa Development Professional Group 2009, 13). Critics also maintain that there is a need for clear rewards and sanctions for performance outcomes apart from publicizing the rankings (Institute of Public Administration of Canada & Africa Development Professional Group 2009, 13). Because of these shortcomings, it is then asserted that the rankings may not reflect the situation on the ground. For example, it has been noted that although the Ministry of Internal Security was ranked as the best performing ministry in 2007/2008, the police force (which falls under this ministry) was recorded by the Office of the Ombudsman as the institution against which they received the most service delivery complaints (Institute of Public Administration of Canada & Africa Development Professional Group 2009, 13). Indeed, government ministries consist of many departments, and the performance contracting methodology may not be particularly effective in distinguishing their performance.

Nevertheless, performance contracting can be a useful tool for ensuring transparency and accountability in the management of public institutions (Obong'o 2009, 74). In particular, the performance contract strategy includes citizens' service delivery charters and customer satisfaction surveys, which "may lead to reduced incidences of corruption" (Obong'o 2009, 75). As we have noted, it also includes a corruption eradication criterion that is supposed to help public institutions to prevent and detect corruption. According to Sylvester Odhiambo Obong'o, who works on public sector reforms in Kenya, performance contracting can help the fight against corruption in several ways.[26] First, it encourages a collegial approach to management, which means that an entire organization is involved. This helps to fight corruption, which thrives where a clique runs the show and information is controlled, as happens in a traditional bureaucracy. Second, because it is based on the development of strategic plans, which requires the participation of all actors in an institution, it enhances transparency and forestalls situations in which resource allocation and utilization is controlled by a small clique. Finally, its performance-based reward system encourages competitive merit based recruitment and promotion, for the simple reason that no institution would want to hire incompetent managers who would affect its performance adversely. To that extent, performance contracting can close the door to purely patronage based appointments, which in his view constitute the highest avenue to corruption in the public sector.

All public institutions are required to submit their quarterly performance reports to the Specialized Agencies, in addition to the Performance Contracting Secretariat. As far as the eradication of corruption is concerned, the EACC has been designated a Specialized Agency. This means that it is tasked with overseeing and evaluating the extent to which corruption is being eradicated in all public institutions (Government of Kenya 2010, 13). Further, it is required to submit quarterly reports of its analysis of the extent to which these institutions are making progress in eradicating corruption (Log Associates 2010, 39).

Has the performance contracting approach to fighting corruption made any difference? The personnel of the Performance Contracting Secretariat and the

EACC think it has. According to a senior officer of the secretariat, this approach is contributing positively to the fight against corruption as it is based on establishing systems that will prevent corruption.[27] The idea is to ensure that each organization develops a corruption management plan. The EACC then works with the organization to ensure that it has the systems and the capacity to implement this plan. In addition, whenever the EACC receives the quarterly reports on corruption eradication, it visits the institutions and tests their integrity systems with a view to establishing strengths and weaknesses. In the opinion of this officer, this approach is better than TI-Kenya's because it also targets institutions which do not have interface with the public. In addition, the systems approach is helping them to not only detect corruption, but also reduce incidences of corruption. Unlike before where incidences of corruption came to light long after they had transpired, this officer thinks that it is now becoming possible to learn about them early enough to prevent substantial damage from occurring. Performance contracting may therefore make it possible to prevent the kinds of high-value scandals we have witnessed in the past. Further, automation of services is a key indicator in performance measurement and evaluation. According to this officer, automation has already contributed to the reduction of corruption in institutions such as the Immigrations Department. Another useful indicator that can reduce corruption is service delivery innovation. For example, those who want express services in public institutions should be required pay higher fees. An instance would be where one requires a passport urgently. The success of this approach is also reflected in the nation-wide customer satisfaction surveys that the Secretariat undertakes annually. For example, the 2009 survey indicated customer satisfaction levels of about 63 percent. Performance contracting has also enhanced agency compliance with statutory obligations, for example, those relating to public procurement. This also reduces corruption. And in terms of dealing with petty corruption, the newly established Commission on the Administration of Justice (CAJ) has also been designated a Specialized Agency. In this capacity, it is responsible for certifying that all public institutions have resolved the maladministration complaints made against them. Further, the CAJ is required to submit quarterly reports of its analysis of the extent to which these institutions are making progress in resolving maladministration complaints.

For the EACC, the performance contracting approach has been attractive because it permeates all public institutions.[28] When it began measuring corruption in the context of performance contracting, the KACC (predecessor to the EACC) thought that it would be ideal if all the public institutions involved in performance contracting – which now number 471 – carried out baseline surveys on corruption. The surveys ranked institutional corruption on a scale of 1 to 10, one being on the lower side and ten on the higher side. But many of these institutions did not have the capacity to carry out these surveys, and invariably outsourced this task. However, most of them hired consultants who would tell them what they wanted to hear. Thus most surveys indicated that institutional corruption oscillated between 0 and 1. The KACC was not therefore getting a true picture of the situation on the ground, and often asked the institutions to redo the surveys, a process that consumed precious time. In any case, the KACC itself had been carrying out a national corruption perception survey, an enterprise corruption survey, and a public officer corruption survey. These surveys produced results that did not tally with the institution surveys. In addition, the Commission was receiving complaints from the public about corruption in many of these institutions.

This institutional survey approach was therefore abandoned in the last annual review of performance contracting, which took place in April 2012. Instead, it is proposed that the EACC should now be tasked with carrying out the surveys of corruption in public institutions. But the EACC faces a huge capacity challenge in this regard: how can it carry out baseline surveys for 471 institutions? An option would be for the EACC to subcontract this work but establish mechanisms for managing the process. Either option would require massive resources in terms of funding and personnel.

In terms of monitoring how institutions are implementing the Corruption Eradication performance indicators, the EACC has adopted a phased approach. In phase one, it requires the institutions to establish anticorruption structural frameworks, policies, code of conduct, and baselines. In phase two, it requires institutions to begin implementing their corruption prevention plans. In phase three, it requires them to establish mechanisms to address corruption-related queries raised by external auditors. Such audit queries usually arise because of internal weaknesses in organizational systems. In phase four, it requires them to build capacity by training corruption prevention committees.

Various agencies have also faulted the method of evaluating the implementation of the Corruption Eradication performance indicators. At present, the ad hoc Task Force is responsible for evaluating performance, including performance of cross-cutting issues such as corruption, automation, gender mainstreaming, and public complaints. However, the Task Force does not have expertise on anticorruption, for example. Accordingly, there is a feeling that the EACC itself should evaluate the implementation of the Corruption Eradication performance indicators. But again, the EACC faces a hurdle as it does not have the capacity to evaluate the performance of 471 institutions. One option would be to develop an interactive Web-based portal with online feedback capability, and that would allow the EACC to track implementation.

All in all, the EACC is optimistic about the potential of the performance contracting approach to fighting corruption. However, this approach can work only if the EACC is able to closely track implementation of the indicators on a regular, say quarterly, basis. In this respect, it would be helpful if the institutions submitted electronic, and not manual, quarterly reports. Further, the capacity and resources of the EACC's Prevention Department need to be enhanced extensively. Despite the huge potential of the prevention approach to fighting corruption, the EACC devotes only about 25 percent of its employees to preventive work; the other 75 percent work in the Investigations and Legal Department.

In my estimation, although corruption eradication only accounts for 5 percent of the performance criteria, performance contracting needs to be evaluated as a holistic process that seeks to enhance the efficiency and accountability of government institutions. To the extent that it improves financial management and service delivery, for example, performance contracting can contribute to eradicating corruption. As we have seen, for example, corruption in Kenya can partly be attributed to the prevalence of manual and inefficient systems and process in government institutions. Again, the bribery that often occurs in these institutions is an indicator of weak governance structures, as the Bribery Index attests.

Despite the promise that performance contracting holds, however, it is arguable that it will be derailed by the institutional and contextual factors that explain the prevalence of high-value corruption in Kenya. This is largely because significant actors who benefit from corruption, such as members of parliament, continue to wield broad unregulated powers. For example, it is doubtful whether the legislature will give the EACC the resources it desperately needs to implement its hugely promising prevention approach to fighting corruption. However, there is increasing evidence that an assertive judiciary might contribute to creating the environment required for performance contracting to succeed. For example, the High Court is now outlawing patronage based appointments, which as we have seen arguably constitute the highest avenue to corruption in government institutions. In *Trusted Society of Human Rights Alliance v Attorney General & 2 others*,[29] for example, the court held that an individual who had been appointed by the president to the position of chairperson of the EACC had not passed the constitutional test of integrity and suitability, and could not therefore assume office. It based its decision on the finding that the individual in question had unresolved allegations that linked him to financial impropriety that he allegedly committed while he was the legal officer of a government corporation. In making this decision, the court agreed with the petitioners that given the very serious and plausible allegations raised against him, the executive and parliament both had a constitutional duty to investigate and resolve the allegations one way or the other before either nominating or approving his appointment. According to the court, therefore, the constitution does not merely require the legislature to go through the motions in vetting candidates for public office; it must conduct a proper inquiry into the pertinent issues raised against such candidates. This approach is now possible because of the principles and values of Kenya's revolutionary new constitution that, if implemented, will no doubt facilitate the democratization of the legal order and circumscription of the exercise of power, the punishment of corrupt individuals, and elimination of the informational problems that have all too often hindered citizen access to information on the activities of government institutions.

CONCLUSION

Indicators of corruption can be useful tools for its eradication. However, much depends on what phenomena are being measured and how the measures are used. As we have seen, measures are likely to be useful if they define corruption broadly and take into account contextual and institutional factors that explain the distribution and exercise of power, and the character of bureaucratic systems. In this respect, the approach of the Government of Kenya is arguably more useful and sustainable than that of TI-Kenya. Further, unlike TI-Kenya which only undertakes integrity assessments depending on the goodwill of the leadership of institutions listed in the Bribery Index, the government has the capacity to compel these institutions to implement the Corruption Eradication performance indicators. The performance contracting approach also promises to reduce corruption in public procurement by including and evaluating compliance with statutory obligations such as the Public Procurement and Disposal Act and its regulations. Another useful performance indicator that can reduce corruption is service delivery innovation, which is already making a difference in institutions such as the Immigrations Department. Chapter 6 of the Constitution of 2010 has also introduced innovations that can enhance the effectiveness of performance contracting. As we have seen, the government is now committing in the performance contracts to ensure that any public officer suspected of corrupt practices is suspended to allow room for investigation. Thus the government, in seeking to fulfill its part of the performance contract, is beginning to take a broad approach to the question of giving its institutions the capacity they need to deliver services to the public.

Nevertheless, the TI-Kenya Bribery Index remains a useful accountability and public information tool, and can be used to monitor the extent to which the government is eradicating corruption as part of implementing the performance contracting program. In addition, the Bribery Index and performance contracting are similar to the extent that both seek to underscore how weak governance structures might contribute to corruption. TI-Kenya could also augment the capacity that the EACC needs to evaluate the implementation of the Corruption Eradication performance indicators. Ultimately, however, the usefulness of indicators of corruption should be assessed against the background of the contextual and institutional factors that explain the nature and characteristics of corruption in different polities. While such country-specific factors should influence the design of corruption indicators, they also show policymakers where they need to invest resources if they want to eradicate corruption. Where such a broad approach is taken, corruption indicators are likely to be a valuable tool for monitoring progress toward eradicating corruption.

NOTES

1 Immigration Act, Chapter 170, Laws of Kenya (repealed by the Kenya Citizenship and Immigration Act No. 12 of 2011).
2 Official Secrets Act (1968), Cap. 187, Laws of Kenya.
3 Public Officer Ethics Act (2009), Cap. 183, Laws of Kenya.
4 See Republic v. The Permanent Secretary/Secretary to the Cabinet and Head of Public Service Office of the President and the Permanent Secretary, Ministry of Gender, Culture and Social Services ex parte Stanley Kamanga and the Kenya National Library Services Board, Nairobi High Court, Misc. Civ. Appl. 612 of 2004, [2006] eKLR.
5 Constitution of Kenya 2010, Article 73(2).
6 Ibid., Article 75(1).
7 http://tikenya.org.
8 Interview with Executive Director, TI-Kenya, May 23, 2012.
9 Ibid.
10 Interview with Senior Officer Prevention, Ethics and Anti-Corruption Commission, May 18, 2012.
11 Interview with Officer, TI-Kenya, April 21, 2011.
12 Ibid.
13 Ibid.
14 Interview with Executive Director, TI-Kenya, May 23, 2012.
15 Ibid.
16 See, e.g., business-anti-corruption.com.
17 Interview with Executive Director, TI-Kenya, May 23, 2012.
18 Ibid.
19 Ibid.
20 Interview with Executive Director, TI-Kenya, May 23, 2012.
21 Statement of the Permanent Secretary, Department of Governance and Ethics, Office of the President, February 24, 2004 at 2.
22 Ibid., 1.
23 Ibid.
24 On the legislative front, the government has enacted a number of laws on corruption in the last decade, namely the Anti-Corruption and Economic Crimes Act, the Public Officers Ethics Act, the Public Procurement and Disposal of Assets Act, the Government Financial Management Act, the Privatization Act, and the Political Parties Act. The government has also ratified both the United Nations Convention against Corruption and the African Union Convention on Preventing and Combating Corruption.
25 See "Institutional Factors and the Diagnosis and Treatment of Corruption in Kenya."

26 Interview with Sylvester Odhiambo Obong'o, Rapid Results Approach Coordinator, Public Service Transformation Department, Office of the Prime Minister, Government of Kenya, May 12, 2011.
27 Interview with senior Performance Contracting Officer, Office of the Prime Minister, May 16, 2012.
28 Interview with Senior Officer Prevention, Ethics and Anti-Corruption Commission, May 18, 2012.
29 Trusted Society of Human Rights Alliance v Attorney General & 2 others [2012] eKLR.

REFERENCES

African Capacity Building Foundation. 2007. "Institutional Frameworks for Addressing Public Sector Corruption in Africa." Harare, Zimbabwe: Author.
Africa Centre for Open Governance (AfriCOG). 2008. "An Audit of the Kibaki Government's Anti-Corruption Drive 2003–2007: Shattered Dreams," 3. Nairobi, Kenya: Author.
  2009a. "Five Years On: How Effective Is the KACC in Kenya's Fight against Corruption?" Nairobi, Kenya: Author.
  2009b. "The Maize Scandal." Nairobi, Kenya: Author.
Akech, Migai. 2009. "Ethics of the Rule of Law: Impunity, Public Perceptions of Justice and Governance in Kenya." In Elizabeth W. Gachenga et al., eds., *Governance Institutions and the Human Condition* LawAfrica 81.
  2011. "Abuse of Power and Corruption in Kenya: Will the New Constitution Enhance Government Accountability?" *Indiana Journal of Global Legal Studies* 18: 1.
Andersson, Staffan, and Paul M. Heywood. 2009. "The Politics of Perception: Use and Abuse of Transparency International's Approach to Measuring Corruption." *Political Studies* 57: 746.
Chadda, Maya. 2004. "India: Between Majesty and Modernity." In Johnson, Roberta Ann, ed., *The Struggle against Corruption: A Comparative Analysis*, 109–144. London: Palgrave Macmillan.
Egbue, N. G. 2006. "Africa: Cultural Dimensions of Corruption and Possibilities for Change" *Journal of Social Science* 12: 83.
Ethics and Anti-Corruption Commission, 2011. *Report of the Examination into the Service Delivery Systems, Policies, Procedures and Practices of Provincial and District Hospitals in Kenya.*
Gephart, Malte. 2009. "Contextualizing Conceptions of Corruption: Challenges for the International Anti-corruption Campaign." Working Paper No. 115. Hamburg, Germany: German Institute of Global Area Studies.
Government of Kenya. 2003. "Economic Recovery Strategy for Wealth and Employment Creation."
  2004. *Report of the Commission of Inquiry into Illegal/Irregular Allocation of Land.*
  2010. *Final Report of the Task Force on Judicial Reforms.*
Government of Kenya, Office of the Prime Minister, Performance Contracting Department. 2010. *Performance Contracting Guidelines*, 7th ed.
  2012. *Report on the Evaluation of the Performance of Public Agencies for the Financial Year 2010/2011.*

Hakobyan, Anna, and Marie Wolkers,. 2004. *Local Corruption Diagnostics and Measurement Tools in Africa.* Bergen, Norway: Ulstein Anti-Corruption Resource Centre, Chr. Michelsen Institute.

Hungarian Gallup Institute. 1999. *Basic Methodological Aspects of Corruption Measurement: Lessons Learned from the Literature and the Pilot Study.* Budapest, Hungary: Author.

Institute of Public Administration of Canada & Africa Development Professional Group, 2009. Evaluation of the Results for Kenyans Programme.

Johnston, Michael. 2000. "The New Corruption Rankings: Implications for Analysis and Reform." Paper prepared for Research Committee 24, International Political Science Association World Congress, Quebec City, Canada, August 2.

Kalnins, Valts. 2005. "Assessing Trends in Corruption and Impact of Anti-Corruption Measures." Discussion Paper, Anti-Corruption Network for Transition Economies 6th General Meeting, May 30–31, Istanbul, Turkey.

Kaufmann, Daniel. 2005. "Myths and Realities of Governance and Corruption." Munich Personal RePEc Archive (MPRA) Paper No. 8089.

Kenya Anti-Corruption Commission (KACC). 2008a. "'Corruption Eradication' Indicator for Performance Contracts in Public Service: A Guide for Corruption Base Line Survey."

    2008b. *Report of the Examination into the Systems, Policies, Procedures and Practices of the Pensions Department, Ministry of Finance* 5.

Lakin, Jason. 2012. "Civil Servants Health Insurance Scandal: What Happened on the Way to Mumias?" *East African,* August 4.

Lawson, Letitia. 2009. "The Politics of Anti-Corruption Reform in Africa." *Journal of Modern African Studies* 47(1): 73.

Lederman, Daniel, Norman V. Loayza, and Rodrigo R. Soares. 2001. "Accountability and Corruption: Political Institutions Matter." World Bank Policy Research, Working Paper No. 2708, 3–4. Washington, DC: World Bank.

Log Associates. 2010. "Evaluation of Performance Contracting." Nairobi, Kenya: Author.

"MPs in 'Most Corrupt' League." 2005. *Daily Nation* (Nairobi), December 10.

Maclean, William. 2005. "Leader of Kenya's Anti-Corruption Watchdog Resigns." African Platform – the Opinion Centre. https://beta.groups.yahoo.com/neo/groups/africa-oped/conversations/messages/13535.

Mishler, William. 2008. "Seeing Is Not Always Believing: Measuring Corruption Perceptions and Experiences." Paper prepared for the Elections, Public Opinion and Parties 2008 Annual Conference, September 12–14, University of Manchester, United Kingdom.

Mungiu-Pippidi, Alina. 2006. "Corruption: Diagnosis and Treatment." *Journal of Democracy* 17: 86.

Mutiga, Murithi. 2005. "Kenya: Sh300m Aids Scandal at Health Ministry." *East African Standard,* June 5.

Ngunjiri, Irene. 2010. "Corruption and Entrepreneurship in Kenya." *Journal of Language Technology & Entrepreneurship in Africa* 2: 93.

Norwegian Agency for Development Cooperation, 2011. "Evaluation of Transparency International." Oslo, Norway: Author.

Obong'o, Sylvester Odhiambo. 2009. "Implementation of Performance Contracting in Kenya." *International Public Management Review* 10(2): 66.

Okwatch, Douglas. 2005. "TI Director Forced Out of Office." *East African Standard,* April 16.

Oloo, Onyango. 2005. "How Transparent Is Transparency International?" http://demokrasia-kenya.blogspot.com/2005/04/how-transparent-is-transparency.html.

Rahim, Faiz and Asad Zaman. 2008. "Corruption: Measuring the Unmeasurable." International Institute of Islamic Economics. http://ssrn.com/abstract=1309131.

Rugene, Njeri. 2009. "Bribery Rampant in Kenya's Parliament." *Sunday Nation*, May 17.

"Sacking Linked to Anglo-Leasing Remarks, Says Ex-TI Boss." 2006. *East African Standard*, June 26.

Soreide, Tina. 2006. "Is It Wrong to Rank? A Critical Assessment of Corruption Indices." Working Paper 2006:1. Bergen, Norway: Chr. Michelsen Institute (CMI).

Transparency International. 2006. "Frequently Asked Questions about Transparency International."

Transparency International (TI)-Kenya. 2002. Kenya Bribery Index.

    2004. Kenya Bribery Index.

    2005. Kenya Bribery Index.

    2006. Kenya Bribery Index.

    2007. Kenya Bribery Index.

    2008. Kenya Bribery Index.

    2009a. East African Bribery Index.

    2009b. "Corruption Trends Analysis: Tracing Corruption Trends in Kenya's Public Sector."

    2009c. KPLC Integrity Baseline Survey Report.

    2010. East African Bribery Index.

    2011. East African Bribery Index.

United Nations Development Programme (UNDP). 1998. "Fighting Corruption to Improve Governance." New York: United Nations.

Wang, Hongying, and James N. Rosenau. 2001. "Transparency International and Corruption as an Issue of Global Governance." 7 *Global Governance* 7: 25.

Warren, Mark E. 2004. "What Does Corruption Mean in a Democracy?" *America Journal of Political Science* 48(2): 328.

World Bank. "Understanding the Evolving Role of the Kenya National Assembly in Economic Governance in Kenya: An Assessment of Opportunities for Building Capacity of the Tenth Parliament and Beyond." Report No. 45924-KE, May 2008. Washington, DC: World Bank.

9

Measuring Labor Market Efficiency

Indicators that Fuel an Ideological War and Undermine Social Concern and Trust in the South African Regulatory Process

Debbie Collier and Paul Benjamin

[L]aws created to protect workers often hurt them.... More flexible labor regulations boost job creation.

World Bank (2007, 19)

The effects of labour law may be more indeterminate than previously thought....... [T]here is evidence to suggest that the economic effects of labour laws are not just highly varied and complex ... but also that they may be efficiency- enhancing in certain contexts ...

Deakin and Sarkar (2008, 481)

INTRODUCTION

The laws that regulate the labor market – that intangible domain where transactions for labor take place – have not escaped the gaze of indicators.[1] Since the turn of the century a multitude of labor market indicators have been produced within a strained ecology of international organizations concerned with the performance of labor markets. In some cases these organizations are concerned only with one dimension (the "efficiency") of labor market regulation, notwithstanding the complex multidimensional[2] character of labor law,[3] its origins in social policy,[4] its indeterminate economic effect (Deakin and Sarkar 2008), and indeed notwithstanding its original purpose of injecting equity into an otherwise unequal relationship.[5]

Plotted on a continuum, the international organizations involved in the transnational shaping of the legal norms and institutions that regulate the labor

The authors are grateful for the helpful comments and suggestions of Sally E. Merry, Terence C. Halliday, and René Urueña and scholars participating in the Indicators and Global Governance project of the NYU Institute for International Law and Justice (IILJ) at the International Conference on Law and Society, Honolulu, Hawai'i, June 5–8, 2012, where the ideas expressed in this chapter were first presented, and for the financial support of the IILJ.

market are poles apart in their mandates and worldviews. These organizations range from a powerful private international organization, funded almost entirely by private enterprise, with an agenda that pushes for labor markets governed primarily by private ordering and market principles to a public international law organization that promotes a coordinated regulatory framework enabling equitable participation in the labor market. This divergence of views among international organizations undermines the development and coherence of legal norms and standards for worker security and creates a fractious transnational legal order that has implications for the domestic debate on labor market regulation.

The aim of this chapter is to critically examine this ecology of organizations and the growth and dynamics of their indicators. The chapter considers specifically the powers of governance (Davis et al. 2012) of the influential "neoliberal" indicators underpinned by orthodox economic theory in which labor laws are viewed as inefficient "external interferences with market relations" (Deakin and Sarkar 2008, 455).[6] These indicators promote a particular brand of law reform advocating free markets and a limited role for the state in organizing the economic and social affairs of society (Krever 2013, 131–150). The South African labor market, a regulated market located in a complex social, economic, and political reality, will provide a focal point for the analysis and the chapter considers four organizations and their indicators. These are, ranging in orientation from neoliberal to coordinated market, the World Economic Forum's Labour Market Efficiency (LME) Pillar of Competitiveness, the World Bank's (controversial and short lived) Employing Workers Indicator (the EWI),[7] the Organisation for Economic Co-operation and Development (OECD)'s Indicators of Employment Protection (IEP), and the International Labor Organization (ILO)'s as yet incomplete Decent Work Indicators (DWI), although in terms of the Davis, Kingsbury, and Merry (2012, 73–74) working definition of an indicator, the ILO's approach produces something other than an indicator.[8] In contrast to the ordinal structure and the element of ranking typical of global indicators, the ILO, a UN specialized agency and the international law organization responsible for setting labor standards,[9] has not succumbed to reductionism. The ILO instead provides a narrative – a *Decent Work Country Profile*[10] – for each country under review rather than the aggregations or "mash-up" compilations (Ravallion 2010, 74) typical of global indicators.

This chapter consists of five parts. The first part briefly sketches the social, political, and economic dynamics of the South African labor market to provide a context for the discussion on labor market indicators. The second part plots the evolution of, and explores the difference, and duplication, in the labor market indicators under review in this chapter. The third and fourth parts focus more closely on the governance powers of the "neoliberal" labor market indicators produced by the World Economic Forum and the World Bank. The final part of the chapter predicts future developments and explores the potential for dialogue and equilibrium to be restored to both the transnational and domestic legal processes governing the production of legal norms and institutions for regulating the labor market.

SOUTH AFRICA'S LABOR LAWS AND LABOR MARKET FAILURE IN CONTEXT

South Africa transitioned from apartheid to democracy in April 1994. The struggle to end apartheid saw the emergence of a strong trade union movement, enabled by amendments to the 1956 Industrial Conciliation Act.[11] The labor movement fought not only for workers' rights but also for political equality, and remains relevant and politically active as a party in the tripartite alliance in power in South Africa.[12]

Although a founder member of the ILO, South Africa was forced to withdraw from the ILO in 1964 on account of its apartheid policy. In 1994 South Africa rejoined the organization, and today plays a key role in the organization (Van Niekerk 2012, 20).

In 2010 the ILO and the social partners (through the National Economic Development and Labour Council) signed the Decent Work Country Programme for South Africa. South Africa has ratified the core ILO conventions and has enacted a suite of laws to give effect to these. Labor rights in South Africa are embedded in the Constitution of the Republic of South Africa, 1996 and explicitly strive to advance social justice[13] as well as economic development. The Constitution, in Section 23, explicitly provides for the right to fair labor practices and the right to engage in collective bargaining. The regulatory framework for sustaining employment rights, which was agreed to at the time through robust engagement between the stakeholders,[14] consists of the Labour Relations Act of 1995 (LRA), the Basic Conditions of Employment Act of 1997 (BCEA), and the Employment Equity Act of 1998 (EEA), which provide workers with a comprehensive floor of rights in the employment relationship and, primarily through measures in the EEA, also a framework for achieving substantive equality. In addition, the Skills Development Act of 1998 (SDA) provides a framework for work-related training. The LRA provides protection against unfair dismissals and unfair labor practices and regulates collective bargaining while the BCEA provides a floor of minimum statutory rights in regard to, for example, overtime, hours of work, and leave, and although no national minimum wage is established, provision is made for sectoral determinations by the Minister of Labour to determine conditions of service in vulnerable sectors where collective bargaining structures are weak. The EEA prohibits unfair discrimination in the workplace and provides a framework for affirmative action and the SDA provides a framework to develop strategies to improve the skills of the South African workforce.

Although the voice of labor is vibrant, and South Africa's labor laws progressive, the legacy of apartheid South Africa's discriminatory laws and practices are experienced as strongly as ever. Today high levels of poverty, unemployment,[15] and income inequality[16] continue to afflict the lives of millions of South Africans, with a disproportionate impact on black people[17] and the youth. The problem is exacerbated by high rates of unemployment of low-skilled workers and a skills shortage at the top end of the labor market (Altman 2006, 24).[18] The resulting extreme disparities, largely along racial lines, undermine social cohesion and prospects for economic growth,[19] and a range of legal and policy interventions attempt to address the imbalance.[20] Labor market regulation must be crafted and tailored, and assessed and measured, within this complex multidimensional context. Putting in place effective policies to respond to market failure will require open social dialogue, a commitment to social justice, and trust between the social partners.

Although labor markets are a dynamic space and its rules constantly subject to reflection and revision, this process is increasingly tense as we experience not only the global struggle for labor laws' new identity,[21] but also the waning of consensus that existed when our new laws were promulgated on what the core goals and substance of our labor laws should be. A protagonist gaining traction in South Africa is the Free Market Foundation,[22] an organization that is currently challenging, through highly publicized litigation, the constitutionality of certain provisions of the LRA. The Free Market Foundation has strengthened its arguments for deregulation on the back of neoliberal labor market indications. In a online publication, the Foundation links South Africa's poor economic outcome to labor laws, making the claim that

> The World Economic Forum ranks South Africa as the 7th worst country out of 139 in the world in terms of its labour laws and regulations. This has created two significant problems for the country: the highest unemployment rate in the world (because labour laws and regulations do not promote job creation) and low rates of economic growth (because South Africa's labour force is unproductive in comparison with its peers, the rest of the developing world).
>
> Two sets of laws are particularly problematic. Firstly, collective bargaining ... has caused wage escalations to exceed labour productivity growth over the past 15 years. Secondly, dismissal protections (i.e. legal protections afforded to employees that protect them from dismissal despite performing poorly on the job) have caused labour productivity, on average, to be very low. (Sharp n.d.)

At the same time, union membership is in decline and industrial action is increasingly prevalent and violent. Government struggles with capacity constraints and, as Godfrey argues "[t]he overall picture presents a rather pessimistic prognosis for the industrial relations system and the employment standards of workers" (Van Niekerk 2012, 15).

The competing legal norms, articulated in the globally produced labor market indicators, have steered the labor market debate into dangerous territory and arguably have altered the trajectory of the social justice project in South Africa. The sections that follow analyze, in more detail, four of these indicators and consider critical comment on the ideology, methodology, and accuracy of the indicators.

EVOLUTION, DIFFERENCE, AND DUPLICATION: THE FOUR LABOR MARKET INDICATORS IN CONTEXT

Of the four organizations under review, the ILO comes closest to replicating the domestic social systems in which labor laws typically evolve, with its member delegations comprising representatives from government, business, and labor. The ILO was constituted in 1919 with the explicit mandate of promoting social justice and, through extensive negotiation, has developed a comprehensive body of labor standards (Van Niekerk 2012, 20). Today the ILO seeks to actualize standards through the realization of worker security[23] within its contemporary decent work agenda.[24] As the global system of economic governance evolves, however, the ILO increasingly faces challenges of marginalization and must reinvent the ways in which labor standards are most effectively promoted (Royle 2010, 249–271).

Having recognized and debated at length the need to monitor and assess progress toward decent work, the ILO, finally in 2008, convened an international meeting of experts on the Measurement of Decent Work, and later that year presented a framework of Decent Work Indicators to the International Conference of Labour Statisticians (ILO 2012). The ILO recognizes ten thematic areas of decent work,[25] which it measures through Statistical Decent Work Indicators (DWI), largely comprising National Labour Force Survey results and Legal Framework Indicators, and that are communicated through the *Decent Work Country Profiles* recently piloted in several countries including South Africa. Although styled as "Indicators," the DWIs, unlike the indicators of the World Bank, the World Economic Forum, and the OECD, are not constituted by a "collection of rank-ordered data" (Davis, Kingsbury, and Merry 2012, 73) and take the form rather of a narrative of progress toward decent work in the thematic areas. Countries are not ranked alongside each other; rather, a detailed Country Profile, a living document, is produced for each country containing "all available data on decent work, statistical and legal indicators, as well as analysis of gaps and trends on decent work …[to]… facilitate the evaluation of progress made towards decent work and inform national planning and policymaking" (ILO 2011, 18). The ILO's approach is context specific and normative and involves engagement with all of the social partners that is facilitated, in South Africa, by the National Economic Development and Labour Council (NEDLAC). In the *Decent Work Country Profile* (2011, 18) for South Africa the ILO presents statistics that reveal that on average the female employee continues to earn less than the average male employee, and that an earnings gap between employees of different races persists, hence suggesting the continued need for employment equity legislation. The ILO country profile reveals gaps in South Africa's ratification of ILO Conventions,[26] and in its concluding chapter on proposal for monitoring indicators, suggests that these conventions be ratified and evidence of compliance be provided. In addition, a comprehensive range of recommendations are included in the profile. In particular, it is recommended that steps be taken to ensure that labor administrators provide effective services; that persons with disabilities have greater access to productive and decent employment through inclusive job-rich growth; that sustainable and competitive enterprises (including cooperatives) create productive and decent jobs, in particular among women, youth, and persons with disabilities; that skills development include employability of workers and inclusiveness of growth; that more people have access to better managed and more gender equitable social security and health benefits; that workers and enterprises benefit from improved health and safety conditions at work; that the world of work respond effectively to the HIV and AIDS epidemic; and that strengthened labor market institutions contribute to effective social dialogue and sound industrial relations (ILO 2011, 55–57).

The ILO's approach to the labour market necessarily envisages a negotiated and coordinated regulatory framework at least compliant with its labor standards. The OECD[27] too envisages a high level of protection although it measures flexibility in its Indicators of Employment Protection, it does not promote a free market approach to flexibility.[28] A very different perspective is reflected in the World Economic Forum (WEF) and the World Bank indicators, which is evident from the brand of law reform (expressed in ideas such as "heavier regulation brings bad outcomes" and "one size can fit all") (World Bank 2004) being promoted by these organizations. The approach of these organizations, a private international organization representing the interests of business,[29] and an international financial institution that makes loans to developing countries,[30] adhere largely to a free market economic growth model of development in which equity is viewed largely as a function of efficiency and in which efficiency is advocated through reforming and reducing laws that bind the hands of business. The idea is that markets, including labor markets, should be liberalized to encourage economic growth and state intervention in the market should be discouraged (Fischl 2011, 947–958).[31] From this perspective, laws are viewed with particular suspicion. The argument is that labor market flexibility – the ability of firms to "hire and fire" with ease (including through the use of temporary and fixed-term contracts); to move employees from one task to another; and to pay wages in response to labor market conditions (Michie and Sheehan-Quinn 2001, 287–306; Michie and Sheehan 2005, 445–464) – is a key factor in promoting the competitiveness of firms and the economic health of nation-states that leads to social and economic benefits for the individual.

The notion of competitiveness, a contested[32] notion, underpins the WEF's indicators and it is this organization's Labour Market Efficiency indicator in particular that fuels the current debate on labor market regulation in the South African context. The WEF relies extensively on an annual Executive Opinion Survey in which business executives are asked for their subjective views on aspects of flexibility and efficiency within their country's regulatory landscape. For example employers are asked to indicate, on a scale of 1 ("impeded by regulations") to 7 ("flexibly determined by employers"), "How would you characterize the hiring and firing of workers in your country?" Implicit in the question is the assumption that regulated protections limit efficiency and competitiveness, and a respondent in South Africa who subscribes to a free market approach to the labor market is likely to react to the question very differently from a respondent whose benchmark is the ILO standards on dismissals.

Local business and employers perceive the current regulatory framework as particularly rigid,[33] and South Africa's poor performance[34] in the WEF's largely perception-based Labour Market Efficiency indicator reflects this. Yet when more objective methods to obtain data are used in similarly constructed indicators also concerned primarily with the rigidity of hiring and firing practices (but with some variation on their choice of proxy for rigidity), such as the World Bank and the OECD labor market indicators, South Africa's laws are portrayed more favorably, as Table 9.1 demonstrates. In terms of method, the World Bank explicitly recognizes the lack of objectivity in the perception-based approach and adopts "a new approach to measurement" that involves a more objective consideration of the textual provisions in laws and regulations (World Bank 2004, viii–x). The OECD evolves this method further by adopting a more rigorous, nuanced approach and unlike the binary Yes/ No options provided by the World Bank, the OECD provides respondents with a scale of possible answers. The OECD explicitly argues that its approach is more comprehensive than the World Bank labor market indicators, but acknowledges that there is some consistency among the results of the two (Venn 2009).[35] In the case of South Africa, many of the countries that are ranked as less flexible than South Africa in the OECD study are ranked as more flexible in the World Bank and World Economic Forum as Table 9.1 illustrates. Table 9.1 compares the rankings of fifteen countries across the three flexibility indicators and ranks, from 1 (most flexible) to 15 (most rigid), the countries within each dataset.

Although there are some consistent results among these three indicators, in particular the United States (1, 1, 1)[36] and the Netherlands (10, 10, 10), there are also some inconsistencies, such as China (15, 8, 11) and Denmark (8, 3, 2). However, the most inconsistent of the results is probably South Africa (5, 9, 14), which tends to suggest that business's perception of the rigidity of South African employment law, as recorded by the WEF, is overly critical in comparison with the perception

TABLE 9.1. *A Comparison of Labor Market Indicators and Their Ranking of Fifteen Selected Countries*

	OECD 2008 Employment Protection Index		World Bank 2008 Employing Workers Rank		World Economic Forum 2008 Labor Market Efficiency Rank	
	Scale of 0–6	Ranking 1–15	Ranking 1–178	Ranking 1/15	Ranking 1–134	Ranking 1/15
Australia	1.38	6	8	2	9	5
Belgium	2.61	13	36	7	79	13
Brazil	2.27	11	119	13	91	15
Canada	1.02	2	19	5	7	3
China	2.80	15	86	8	51	11
Denmark	1.91	8	10	3	5	2
Estonia	2.39	12	156	15	29	9
Germany	2.63	14	137	14	58	12
Netherlands	2.23	10	92	10	30	10
New Zealand	1.16	4	13	4	10	6
Russian Federation	1.84	7	101	11	27	8
South Africa	1.35	5	91	9	88	14
Sweden	2.06	9	107	12	26	7
United Kingdom	1.09	3	21	6	8	4
United States	0.85	1	1	1	1	1

of businesses abroad. Further, if South Africa's World Bank score and rank are adjusted to correct for the calculation errors identified by Benjamin and Theron (2009, 204–234) (these errors are discussed in "Public Power Reined In: The Rise and Fall of the World Bank's EWI") then the perceptions for South Africa recorded by the WEF are even more starkly out of kilter with the OECD and World Bank findings. Although there is variation in the choice of proxy for flexibility among the three indicators, flexibility in hiring and firing practices remain central enquiries in all three indicators.

The 2008 country survey of South Africa by the OECD was the first time South African labor law was analyzed in terms of the OECD's index. The OECD concluded that of the OECD's twenty-nine members only the United States has less restrictive laws than South Africa on hiring and hours of work. South Africa's dismissal laws are given a less flexible rating, but were nevertheless found to be more flexible than the average for OECD countries. The OECD study shows that South Africa's employment protection legislation is more flexible than that of countries such as Brazil, Chile, China, and India despite public perceptions that South Africa's laws are more rigid. The OECD study makes the point that despite the significant level of labor market flexibility in South Africa, there is a widespread perception that our labor market is highly regulated.

The OECD results reflecting South Africa as "flexible" have been dismissed by South Africa's free market zealots as being the product of government officials and bureaucrats from thirty-four countries, whereas the WEF, which crystallizes perceptions into problems, is "[t]he world's most august and powerful body of businesses" (Adcorp Employment Index 2011), whose analysis on South Africa validates employer claims that South Africa has the "fifth-worst labour laws in the world" (Sharp 2011). Research by Bhorat and Cheadle (2009) to the contrary is dismissed as being the dubious product of "two Professors at the University of Cape Town" that are "apparent experts in labour law and regulation" (Adcorp Employment Index 2011), who are funded by the Department of Labour "which lends the possibility of bias and consequently a lack of credibility to the results" (Adcorp Employment Index 2011).

In South Africa business and employers rely on the WEF's annual perception surveys to push their free market agenda, and after publication of the *Global Competitiveness Report*, employer organizations, which typically use any opportunity to extol the virtues of a free labor market,[37] bask in the luster and fuss accompanying the launch of the glossy report[38] and use the opportunity to generate, from the survey results in which South Africa invariably scores poorly, alluring sound bites – such as "Labour market takes the shine off SA's competitiveness" (Khuzwayo 2012) – to advance their arguments for business-friendly labor reforms. These sound bites reverberate through the media, capture the public imagination, and provide authority for the demand for less regulation in the labor market. Critical trade union or academic responses commenting on these influential indicators, or the free market approach more generally are treated with disdain, with the author usually being labeled partisan and an enemy of the unemployed. A dangerous ideological war rages, further polarizing stakeholders in the labor market and undermining possibilities for cohesion, cooperation, and consensus on the future shape and design of labor standards. In the process, national stability and individual well-being are affected and effective labor rights often remain elusive.

The problem with the influential neoliberal indicators, which capture business and the media's attention, is their ideological bias toward a free market approach to flexibility (Michie and Sheehan 2005, 445–464; Deakin and Sarkar 2008). This promotes an inferior approach to equity and growth (Ostry and Berg 2011), and obscures the fact that flexibility, if it is desirable in a particular market, can be achieved in more than one way. In a laissez-faire or free market capitalist economic system government intervention will be kept to a minimum and the conditions and price of labor left to the forces of supply and demand. On the other hand, in a social welfare or welfare state system the approach is likely to integrate both labor market flexibility and worker security, such as the European model of "flexicurity,"[39] which resonates with the South African Constitutional commitment to social justice and is, politically, more feasible, yet, blinkered by free market rhetoric, this is not the brand of flexibility that South African employers are likely to promote or agree to, for the tradeoff for this flexibility is likely to be higher taxes.

In the next two parts of this chapter, the ideology, methodology, and accuracy, and the governance powers, of the influential neoliberal indicators of the WEF and the World Bank are analyzed in more detail.

UNFETTERED PRIVATE POWER: THE WEF'S LABOR MARKET EFFICIENCY INDICATOR

The World Economic Forum (so named in 1987) has a membership limited to "the 1,000 leading companies of the world" and now also 200 smaller companies,[40] and started life in 1971 as the European Management Forum, a private nonprofit organization, established, as mentioned in note 29, by German Economist Klause Schwab, at the time motivated by a "stakeholder theory" of management as a tool for corporate success. The focus of the organization shifted swiftly to global economic, social, and political issues, most evident in its annual meeting where it engages world leaders on pressing concerns in Davos, Switzerland. As a private organization, the activities of the WEF are largely funded by its members.

In 1979 the WEF published its first index of competitiveness: the *Report on the Competitiveness of European Industry* which, at the time, surveyed just sixteen European countries. This has evolved into the current annual glossy *Global Competitiveness Report* (GCR), which measures, compares, and ranks "12 pillars of competitiveness"[41] (each pillar is reduced to a numerical score between 1 and 7), including the *Labour market efficiency* pillar of competitiveness, in more than 140 countries, with the explicit aim of governing by "provid[ing] benchmarking tools for business leaders and policymakers to identify obstacles to improved competitiveness, stimulating discussion on strategies to overcome them" (Schwab 2008, 3).

The WEF fixates on the notion of competitiveness, which it defines as "*the set of institutions, policies, and factors that determine the level of productivity of a country*" (Schwab 2008, 3). In the WEF model both "the value of a nations' products and services, measured by the prices they can command in open markets, and the efficiency with which these products can be produced" are important for determining productivity (Schwab 2008, 44). The model supports an economic growth theory of development, the idea being that "[p]roductivity supports high wages, a strong currency, and attractive returns to capital – and with them a high standard of living" (Schwab 2008, 44).

Lall (2001), in a critique of the GCR, points out the lack of an accepted definition and measure of competitiveness, and suggests that although the notion of competitiveness may suffice at company level in terms of relative market share or profitability analysis, its applicability to national economies is questionable. Although Krugman (1994, 44) goes so far as to argue that "competitiveness is a meaningless word when applied to national economies," Lall (2001, 1505) suggests that there may be value in competitiveness analysis if it helps developing countries to "overcome market deficiencies that impede the realization of dynamic comparative advantage," but, more generally, that it is important that the underlying assumptions about government capabilities and the nature of the market failures that affect dynamic comparative advantage are valid. Here, Lall criticizes the WEF's implicit assumption that markets are efficient and the high values placed on, for example, freer trade and intellectual property protection that "ignores valid arguments for intervention" (Lall 2001, 1506–1507) in the case of infant industries and non-innovating countries. Similarly, Bergsteiner and Avery (2012, 406) observe that "the WEF's bias is all in one direction, namely towards Anglo/US capitalism. It represents the polar opposite of another business model called the Rhineland model, also known as social market economics, stakeholder-centered capitalism, or simply as the Continental model." This explains why the WEF assigns a more negative (less efficient) score to a regulated labor market than to a labour market largely left to private ordering, notwithstanding the complex relationship between labor law and economics and cogent arguments that the economic effect of labor law may, in certain contexts, be a positive one (Deakin and Sarkar 2008). Evidence of this bias is reflected in the questions (and scoring method) in the Executive Opinion Survey, a controversial method used by the WEF to gather data. For example, business executives in the 2012–2013 survey were asked the questions in Table 9.2.

The lower the score, the more "inefficient" the labor market: a less regulated labor market is therefore the benchmark, or standard, set by the WEF. Underlying this approach is the orthodox economic assumption that less employment protection, no centralized bargaining, and lower wages ("a race to the bottom") will create more jobs and enhance company (and national) performance. For Bergsteiner and Avery (2012, 391) this approach is "ethically reprehensible because research shows that these practices and behaviours, when compared with other approaches, are sub-optimal in the results they produce for individuals, corporations and nations."[42] Lall too questions the validity of the proposition that the ability of firms to hire and fire workers freely is universally good for competitiveness and points out a number of other "spurious causal connections" (Lall 2001, 1515) such as the impact of regulatory

TABLE 9.2. *Sample Questions from the GCR*

How would you characterize the hiring and firing of workers in your country?		
Impeded by regulations	1 2 3 4 5 6 7	Flexibly determined by employers

How are wages generally set in your country?		
By a centralized bargaining process	1 2 3 4 5 6 7	Up to each individual company

standards and environmental regulations on income, that reveal the organizations' "commitment to free markets." In the 2008–2009 GCR, hidden on page 53 of a 513-page report, the WEF itself concedes that "two areas of policy – taxation and labor market regulations – deserve special discussion because they have no simple linear relationship to prosperity" (Schwab 2008, 53). The report concedes that labor markets tend to be more regulated in countries with highly developed institutions, yet the WEF, somewhat deceptively given its concessions, persists with its flawed, and socially dangerous, approach to labor market regulation.

The perception-based Executive Opinion Survey is the primary method for gathering data about labor law and the labor market being measured in the indices. In South Africa the sample size is relatively small: between 2008 and 2011 the number of respondents has varied between thirty-nine and fifty-seven business executives. The survey is conducted through partner institutions in each country (in South Africa these are Business Unity South Africa and Business Leadership South Africa who also act as ambassadors of the report at the time of its launch and bring the report to the media's attention). The opinion survey data is, in some cases, complemented by "hard data derived from various international sources" (Schwab 2008, 67), as the left-hand column in Table 9.3 reflects. Lall and others[43] criticize the extensive use of qualitative responses. Lall (2001, 1518) points out that "answers may be misleading not just because the questions are ambiguous but also because respondents use different (implicit) benchmarks. Most respondents are local businesses, with different access to information, experience of technology, and perspectives on international standards. Even if they are answering very clear and straightforward questions their responses can reflect such contextual difference." Lall (2001, 1519) argues that there are many repetitive and redundant questions, and finds it disturbing that such subjective data are at the core of the Forum's report which "[d]espite all these methodological problems ... give an impression of precision and authority."

Steeped in neoliberal ideology, the Executive Opinion Survey suggests to respondents that social policy interventions are problematic, in the same way that

TABLE 9.3. *South Africa's Overall Ranking and Disaggregated Performance in Pillar 7: Labor Market Efficiency 2008–2013*

Sub-indexes in Labor Market Efficiency (Seventh Pillar of Competitiveness)	Year of Report (SA overall ranking/number of countries ranked)				
	2012–2013 (52/144)	2011–2012 (50/142)	2010–2011 (54/139)	2009–2010 (45 / 133)	2008–2009 (45 / 134)
1. Cooperation in labor-employer relations (Source: Executive Opinion Survey)	144	138	132	121	119
2. Flexibility of wage determination (Source: Executive Opinion Survey)	140	138	131	123	123
3. Non-wage labor costs (Source: Social security payments and taxes)	N/A	N/A	N/A	N/A	14
4. Rigidity of employment index (Source: World Bank variable from the *Doing Business* Report)	N/A	90	86	84	81
5. Hiring and firing practices (Source: Executive Opinion Survey)	143	139	135	125	129
6. Firing costs / Redundancy costs (Source: World Bank variable from the *Doing Business* Report)	33	46	44	40	39
7. Pay and productivity (Source: Executive Opinion Survey)	134	130	112	105	81

Sub-indexes in Labor Market Efficiency (Seventh Pillar of Competitiveness)	Year of Report (SA overall ranking/number of countries ranked)				
	2012–2013 (52/144)	2011–2012 (50/142)	2010–2011 (54/139)	2009–2010 (45 / 133)	2008–2009 (45 / 134)
8. Reliance on professional management (Source: Executive Opinion Survey)	13	18	19	21	16
9. Brain drain (Source: Executive Opinion Survey)	47	48	62	79	72
10. Female participation in labor force (Source: National data collected by the ILO)	85	76	64	61	103

Variables 1 to 6 are categorized as "efficiency" and together constitute 50 percent of the score in the 7th pillar of competitiveness, while variables 7 to 10 are categorized as "efficient use of talent," which constitutes the remaining 50 percent.

crime and corruption are problematic. In the opinion survey, respondents are asked to select the most "problematic" factors in their country – from a list of fifteen factors, in which "Tax rates" and "Restrictive labour regulations" are listed alongside factors such as "Corruption," and "Crime and theft" – and to rank them between 1 (most problematic) and 5.

In its analysis the WEF model recognizes three stages of development – factor-driven, efficiency-driven, and innovation-driven – and allocates its pillars of competitiveness, and adjusts its weighting, among these stages. South Africa, although rated as efficiency driven, ranks poorly in the basic requirement indices for factor-driven economies yet performs relatively well in the innovation and sophistication indices. This likely reflects South Africa's complex colonial history, in which the platform of a first-world economy was built in an environment where the basic requirements were denied to a disadvantaged majority of the population.

The labor market analysis in the GCR, the LME indicator, when disaggregated consists of the sub-indexes (the number changes periodically) listed in Table 9.3, in which a score of between 1 and 7 is awarded per sub-index. South Africa's ranking in each of these sub-indices between 2008 and 2013 are plotted in Table 9.3.

Table 9.3 unequivocally reflects that South Africa's performance or ranking in the seventh pillar of competitiveness (labor market efficiency) falls way below South Africa's overall competitiveness ranking, and the WEF specifies South Africa's "restrictive labor regulations" as one of the most problematic factors for doing business (Schwab 2008, 302). In South Africa, business and employers use this rhetoric to treat labor market regulation as an aberration, yet South Africa's performance in labor market efficiency in fact aligns well with comparator countries in the efficiency-driven stage of development as Figure 9.1 illustrates. The real aberration is health and primary education.

The GCR and its twelve pillars of competitiveness provide well-presented, tantalizingly simple rankings – catchy slogans – that play a role in fuelling the debate in South Africa on labor market flexibility and result in common assaults on labour market regulation such as "South Africa ranks 143 out of 144 in 'hiring and firing practices'" (Schwab 2012, 325). This hardens the resolve, and strengthens the hand, of business. The fact that South Africa is one of the world's most unequal societies, with a structural unemployment problem that will not be resolved simply by relaxing employment protections, is filtered from the debate by the powerful assumptions, the "neoliberal common sense" (Krever, 2013), underpinning certain legal indicators, including the GCR.

South Africa's labor market regulatory regime needs revising, but the WEF's standards and rankings are unhelpful and they establish an unrealistic expectation around the possibilities for deregulation. Political infeasibility aside, a free market approach to labor market regulation in South Africa would establish an inferior brand of efficiency and equity. In its current iteration, the WEF's norms do not resonate with existing domestic laws and are a catalyst for an increasingly polarized debate on labor market regulation in South Africa.

The World Bank, which has also produced a "neoliberal" labor market indicator, has had to reassess its own legal norms, and has entered into a phase of revision through a dynamic, recursive[44] process.

PUBLIC POWER REINED IN: THE RISE AND FALL OF THE WORLD BANK'S EWI

The EWI forms part of the annual *Doing Business* report, first published in 2004, produced by the International Finance Corporation (IFC), a member of the World Bank Group. The *Doing Business* (2004) report advances the World Bank's private sector development agenda and explicitly seeks, through country benchmarking, to identify regulations that enhance business activity (specifically of local firms) and

Stage of development

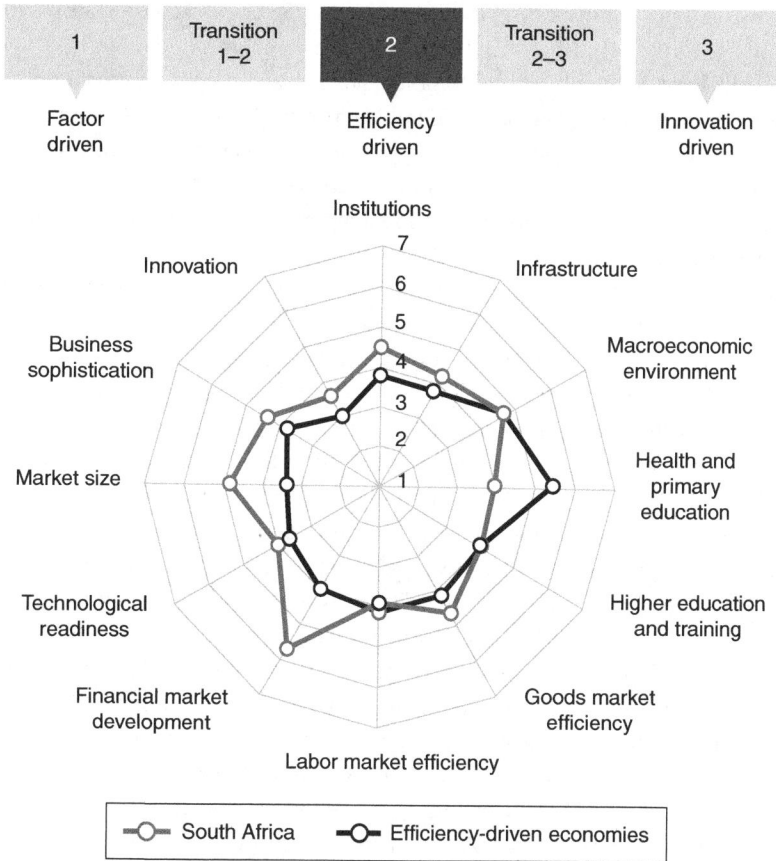

FIGURE 9.1. A comparison of South African and other efficiency-driven economies. *Source*: Schwab 2012, 324.

regulations that constrain it in an effort to motivate for, and inform the design of, reform.

The annual *Doing Business* report provides a ranking of the business regulations of more than 150 countries in several indicators, which, in 2004, included Starting a Business, Hiring and Firing Workers, Getting Credit, Enforcing a Contract, and Closing a Business and has been expanded over the years to include Dealing with Licenses, Registering Property, Protecting Investors, Paying Taxes, and Trading across Borders. In each of these, the report assesses and ranks countries on an "ease of doing business" scale from 0 to 100: the higher the score the greater the burden on business. In terms of method, the World Bank improves on, and distinguishes itself from, perception-based approaches such as that of the WEF by explicitly recognizing that "many existing indicators rely on perceptions, notoriously difficult to compare across countries or translate into policy recommendations" and instead the World Bank sets out "a new approach to measurement," relying on "factual information concerning laws and regulation in force" (*Doing Business* 2004), and therefore which can be replicated.[45] Improvements, however, seem to end there and numerous concerns,[46] some of which are discussed in the text that follows, about method, methodology, the underlying ideology, and the accuracy of the indicators have been raised.

The 2004 report identifies four bodies of labor law: employment regulation, social security laws, industrial relations, and workplace safety and indicates that the 2004 report will investigate employment regulation only, but points out that subsequent reports will analyze the remaining areas of labor law (*Doing Business* 2004, 30). However, only the employment regulation indicator has been pursued in subsequent reports, which in 2004 consisted of a composite of three indices: (1) the flexibility of hiring index, (2) the conditions of employment index, and (3) the flexibility of firing index. In each of these three a value between 0 and 100 is given, and the employment regulation index is an average of the three. The following were assumed about the worker and the company: "[t]he worker is a nonexecutive, full-time employee who has worked in the same company for 20 years, has a nonworking wife and two children, and is not a member of a labor union (unless membership is mandatory). The business, a limited-liability manufacturing company that operates in the country's most populous city, is 100 percent domestically owned and has 201 employees." (*Doing Business* 2004, 5–6). However, as Benjamin and Theron (2009, 210) point out, a worker with twenty years' service is an unusual scenario and a business employing more than 200 workers is large in the South African context and "not the kind of business that has been the focus of the debate about labour market regulation" (Benjamin and Theron 2009, 214). These assumptions have subsequently been amended.

The World Bank (2006, 81) advises that the EWI methodology was adopted from a study by Botero et al. (2004). Although legal provisions rather than perceptions are relied on, the manner of assessment used is fairly crude: for example binary Yes/No questions are asked, whereas exemptions and exceptions are often available in domestic law that cannot be fully articulated in this approach. In addition, collective bargaining (private) arrangements are often more protective than the provisions of law, yet the model used does not assess contractual "rigidity." Davidov summarizes criticism of the Botero et al. index, pointing out arguments that it focuses on "law on the books" and ignores "law in action" by failing to consider "the extent to which laws are actually being enforced; the size and characteristics of the informal economy (i.e., the scope of labor law's actual application); and the impact of extra-legal norms that dictate employment standards, possibly making some legislative interventions unnecessary" (Davidov 2008, 285). This, for example, would give inaccurate and misleading results on employment standards in Sweden and Germany where standards are often established by collective agreement (Davidov 2008, 285). In addition, Davidov (2008, 285) points out, "Botero et al pretty much ignored the existence of judge-made law." This goes to the heart of criticism articulated against Botero et al.'s premise that legal origin determines country's regulatory approach to markets.

At an ideological level, concerns are summed up by Faundez (2009, 16), who laments that the "Bank's decision to reaffirm the Washington Consensus and to quietly discard the alternative vision of development ... is regrettable. ... [hence] law continues to be seen as a negative device that protects citizens against power-hungry governments and provides a neutral mechanism for the development of market transactions. This view about the role of the law is far too narrow as it neglects to take into account that law does not merely have an economic dimension, but is deeply embedded in all aspects of social life, including the important political process of democratization."

Of the various indicators in the *Doing Business* report the EWI has proven the most controversial: countries that have little or no protection for labor rights are likely to score more favorably than those who provide a responsible level of protection to workers. For example, a small island nation, the Marshall Islands, which is not a member of the ILO and has no legislation concerning maximum hours of work, occupational safety and health, child labor, or forced labor, was repeatedly ranked in the top spots on employing workers and has been promoted in *Doing Business* as a good practice economy for Employing Workers.[47] This is testimony to the deregulatory thrust of the *Doing Business* ratings and demonstrates the total lack of concern for the social rationale of employment law. South Africa, a democratic country with a labor regime reflective of the ILO standards, receives a less favorable ranking than Swaziland, an absolute monarchy where trade unions are repressed. The World Bank's own Independent Evaluation Group (IEG) admits that the EWI analysis cannot distinguish between "well regulated" and "unregulated" economies (Independent Evaluation Group 2008, 32). Improving economic performance is a more complex task than simply reforming law and policy to improve an economy's *Doing Business* rankings, as Georgia has experienced.[48]

South Africa's performance in the *Doing Business* report, and specifically in the EWI, is plotted in Table 9.4.

Benjamin and Theron (2009, 204–234) took up the challenge of "replicating" the EWI method of assessment in the case of South Africa's laws and found the reliability of the results wanting. On the "flexibility-of-hiring" index, South Africa is incorrectly indicated as a country that permits fixed term contracts only for

TABLE 9.4. *South Africa's Performance in Doing Business
Report and EWI (2006–2012)*

Year	Ease of Business Rank	EWI Rank
2006	28 / 155	Not available
2007	29 / 175	87 / 175
2008	35 / 178	91 / 178
2009	32 / 181	102 / 181
2010	34 / 183	102 / 183
2011	34 / 183	Rankings not available
2012	35 / 183	Rankings not available

temporary work (Benjamin and Theron 2009, 219),[49] a result that negatively impacts
on South Africa's score on flexibility, when in fact employers have considerable
flexibility to employ staff on fixed-term contracts. On the question of the ratio of the
mandated minimum wage for a trainee or first-time employee to the average value
added per worker, the researchers explore the very limited instances (where the
employer is covered by a bargaining council agreement) where a learner might be
covered by a minimum wage, and argue that the putative employer "is not covered
by a bargaining council agreement, and that there is, therefore no 'mandated
minimum wage'" (Benjamin and Theron 2009, 222). However, in terms of the
EWI, South Africa's ratio was 0.46 in 2006 and 0.67 in 2007, yet "[t]he basis for
this calculation is not apparent from either the research or the website and there is
no published or accessible information indicating what assumptions were made or
why there is such a large increase between the two years" (Benjamin and Theron
2009, 222). On the second index, "rigidity of hours," Benjamin and Theron (2009)
point out the following error: South Africa is incorrectly, negatively, rated on the
question of whether night work is unrestricted. The basic employment conditions
legislation in South Africa does not impose limitations, or premium pay, on night
work but provides that employees who work at night may be compensated through
an allowance or a reduction of working hours,[50] and hence this rating is inaccurate.
Insofar as the third index, the "flexibility-of-firing" index, which focuses primarily
on redundancy, is concerned, Benjamin and Theron point out the following
errors. On the question whether the employer needs to notify a third party (such
as a government agency) to terminate one redundant worker, South Africa is
incorrectly rated as if such notice needs to be given when in fact no such notice
is required. The only notice that needs to be given in South Africa is when an
employee is a union member, in which case notice to that trade union needs to
be given; however, the *Doing Business* assumption is that the employee is not a

trade union member (Benjamin and Theron 2009, 225). Likewise, on the question of whether the employer needs to notify a third party to terminate a group of more than twenty redundant workers, South Africa again receives an incorrect negative rating, for the same reason that notice need only be given to a trade union in the event that employees are members. A third error on this index is made in relation to the question of whether the law requires the employer to reassign or retrain a worker before making the worker redundant.[51] South Africa received a negative rating, yet there is no substantive obligation to reassign or retrain. The employer is obliged only to disclose alternatives that the employer considered before proposing retrenchments. Benjamin and Theron (2009, 227) conclude that

> it appears that two out of the three ratings for the 'difficulty of hiring' index are incorrect, one out of five of the rigidity of hours is incorrect and two out of eight of the ratings in the 'difficulty of firing' index are incorrect. This is a significant level of error (5 out of 16) which could alter South Africa's overall standing in the 'rigidity of employment' index. Only one of these errors was corrected in 2007, and there were no further adjustments in the 2008 and 2009 surveys. (Original footnote omitted)

The researchers adjust for these errors and recalculate South Africa's score in the "employing workers" indicator using the World Bank methodology and the result is a much more flexible labor market: the authors conclude that "if South Africa's rating in respect of three of the five questions which we suggest are wrong were corrected, it would receive a slightly better ranking than Namibia which is rated the 34th most flexible labour market .... Correcting all five errors would place South Africa among the twenty most flexible labour markets in the world" (Benjamin and Theron 2009, 227).

South Africa's uncorrected score and poor rankings were internalized into domestic policy by the Department of Trade and Industry in a 2007 assessment of investment climate (Clarke et al. 2007). The assessment relied heavily on South Africa's performance in the EWI to conclude that "South Africa performs worse on most measures than the comparator countries and performs considerably worse on the two [Difficulty of Hiring and Difficulty of Firing Indices] indices than OECD and several of the comparator countries.... this assessment is quite sobering" (Clarke et al. 2007, 68–69).

Certain changes to the *Doing Business* methodology have been implemented from time to time: for example, in 2008 "improvements were made to align the *Doing Business* methodology with ... (ILO) Conventions.... First, the calculation of firing costs was modified.... Second, restrictions on night work ... are no longer coded as rigidities" (World Bank 2007, 68). Amendments were also later introduced with respect to the methods of calculating minimum wages and calculating redundancy costs so that certain employee protections in this regard were no longer regarded as rigidities, and in addition changes in approach to "paid annual leave and a ceiling for working days allowed per week [were introduced] to ensure that no economy benefits in the scoring from excessive flexibility in these areas" (World Bank 2010, 111). Notwithstanding these changes, fundamental flaws remain in the *Doing Business* approach and the World Bank continues to report on engagement with stakeholders to review its methodology in light of ILO core labor standards (*Doing Business* 2012, 58).

The Writing on the Wall for the EWI

The ILO's critical reaction[52] to the EWI was taken on board by the Independent Evaluation Group (IEG), an independent unit within the World Bank Group in its 2008 evaluation of the *Doing Business* survey (Independent Evaluation Group 2008). In its evaluation, the IEG (2008, xvi) notes that "[t]he controversial *employing workers* indicator is consistent with the letter of relevant International Labor Organization (ILO) conventions, but not always their spirit, insofar as it gives lower scores to countries that have chosen policies for greater job protection."[53]

Shortly thereafter, in April 2009, the World Bank announced revisions to the EWI and that it would adjust the scores in *Doing Business* 2010 "to accord favorable scores to worker protection policies that comply with the letter and spirit of the relevant ILO Conventions, recognizing that well-designed worker protections are of benefit to the society as a whole" (World Bank, 2009b). In addition the announcement noted that the EWI would no longer serve as a guidepost in the Country Policy and Institutional Assessments (CPIA), and further that a guidance note would be issued clarifying that the EWI "does not represent World Bank policy and should not be used as a basis for policy advice or in any country program documents that outline or evaluate the development strategy or assistance program for a recipient country" (World Bank, 2009). The note emphasizes the importance of regulatory approaches that facilitate the creation of more formal sector jobs but with adequate safeguards for workers' rights and that guard against the shifting of risk from firms to workers and low-income families and undertook to convene a working group that would include "representatives from the ILO, as the international standard setting body, trade unions, businesses, academics and legal experts ... [to] serve as an important source of advice on revising the EWI and on the establishment of a new worker protection indicator, as well as offering broader ideas on labor market and employment protection issues – with a view to creating regulations that help build robust jobs with adequate protection in the formal sector that can withstand future crises" (World Bank, 2009b).

Doing Business 2010 contained the EWI rankings for a final time and, in an annex on worker protection (World Bank 2009, 70), the report indicates that *Doing*

Business "plans to develop a new worker protection indicator ... [and] ... [t]he ILO, which has leadership on the core labour standards, will serve as an essential source of guidance in this process" (World Bank 2009, 70). A further update is reported in *Doing Business* 2013 which indicates that "[b]etween 2009 and 2011 the World Bank Group worked with a consultative group – including labor lawyers, employer and employee representatives, and experts for the ILO, the OECD, civil society and the private sector – to review the employing workers methodology and explore future areas of research" (World Bank 2013, 127). Further, the 2013 report notes that, in the previous year, additional data on worker protection regulations has been collected that will be used to develop "a joint analysis of worker protection by the World Bank Group and the ILO and for developing new areas of research in the area of worker protection measures" (World Bank 2013, 131).

This interaction and cooperation between the World Bank and the ILO bodes well for future developments.

FROM DIVERGENCE TO CONVERGENCE: RESTORING EQUILIBRIUM AND OPENING SPACE FOR DIALOGUE

The role that labor law should play in regulating the labor market and the evolving world of work is a contentious social, economic, and political issue, the detail of which is usually negotiated by stakeholders in the domestic setting. While in the past these negotiations may have been mediated by the labor standards of the ILO, increasing global economic interconnectedness has thrown the field wide open and, over the past decade, a steady flow of transnationally constructed and discordant legal norms, conveyed by indicators and actors from different international organizations with different agendas, has intensified the debate (Shaffer 2010, 4).

The push of diverging perspectives on labor law and labor market regulation: the free market model on the one hand, and the coordinated market model on the other, has resulted in a fragmented, fractured, and dysfunctional transnational legal order concerned with labor market regulation. Although the ILO has a long and established history in producing transnational legal norms for worker security,[54] its role and influence over development policy became more limited in the 1980s and 90s as a result of the powerful ideology underlying neoliberal thinking and the structural adjustment programs promoted by the dominant economic powers (Rodgers 2009).

A similar divergence of views is evident in South Africa, not only between stakeholders but even within stakeholders. Within the ranks of government, on the one hand, the Department of Trade and Industry (DTI) demonstrates an affinity for the norms articulated by the World Bank evidenced by its alignment with an Assessment of the Investment Climate in South Africa (Clarke et al. 2007) that is based on the World Bank indices, while, on the other hand, the Department of Labour, which works closely with the ILO, initiated a process of interrogating the World Bank indicators. The Treasury takes a similar position to the DTI and has at times made public calls for business-friendly labor law reform. This in fact led to Cabinet intervening, stating that "the Department of Labour is the lead department on all labour matters and ... [that] ... the only labour law amendments being considered at present are those being processed by the Minister of Labour through the NEDLAC processes."[55] The statement was seen as a closing of "the space for ministers such as Finance Minister ... and National Planning Minister ... to express their views on SA's labour dispensation in public" (Ensor and Mkokeli 2011). Preparatory documents published as part of the process of developing South Africa's National Development Plan reflect an acceptance that the OECD indicators provide the most useful comparative assessment of South Africa's labor laws. Despite this, the OECD studies receive little public attention when compared to the subjective rankings promoted by the WEF.

Although a convergence of norms and the opening of space to navigate the labor market regulatory terrain currently seems unlikely in South Africa, a positive move toward convergence, and therefore the development of more coherent and widely accepted norms, may have occurred at the international level, where the ILO, irked by the World Bank's controversial EWI, has focused its attention and forced engagement on concerns about the erosion of worker protection. ILO intervention in the process ultimately led to changes in World Bank methodology and, more recently, the exclusion of the employing workers data from the *Doing Business* rankings while a representative working group refines the methodology, with the ILO playing a core role in this regard.[56] The norms and proposed institutional forms[57] that emerge from this recursive, and discursive, process largely *between* international organizations should, after some lag, narrow domestic divergence and increase domestic space for negotiating the regulatory landscape for the labor market. A stumbling block in South Africa's case is the World Economic Forum's subjective analysis of labor markets and its proclamations on South Africa's "rigid" laws which, ironically, have received greater attention after the WB admitted to the shortcomings of its labor market index.[58] But perhaps emerging legal norms from the ILO/World Bank interaction may result in changes in the Forum's approach:[59] with an engaged global citizenship its future may just depend on it.

CONCLUSION

South Africa's labor market is in particularly poor shape. Bulging at the seams with unskilled labor while experiencing a shortage of skilled labor, you might compare it to an obese but malnourished person whose dietary intake contains too many empty calories and not enough nutrition. How to treat the resulting lethargic, inefficient, and unhealthy system will depend on a proper diagnosis and a detailed assessment of the particulars of the unhealthy system, much like the approach in the ILO's decent work agenda. There is no "silver bullet," no "one-size-fits-all" solution to remedy a seriously dysfunctional system and fixating on a free market model of "labour market flexibility" as being the answer is a flawed, mono-dimensional, and biased approach to a multifaceted problem. Yet, buoyed by the results and rhetoric of the labor market indicators embedded in neoliberal economic theory, this is precisely what many prominent businesses and employers would have us believe is the answer.

The messages being conveyed in the neoliberal labor market indicators are influential and have captured the minds of many in South Africa and have fuelled the rhetoric of the "strictness" of South Africa's laws. Yet even its champions admit that "some of the changes we propose are more politically feasible than others" (Sharp and Black 2010, 117). Business, labor, and government need to find the space where the discussion is not about free markets and "rigid" laws but rather about the dual goals of equity and efficiency and the design of governance and regulatory mechanisms to pursue these goals. Perhaps the closing of the gap between the ILO and the World Bank's norms and institutions for labor market regulation will provide this space.

NOTES

1 See Davis, Kingsbury, and Merry (2012, 73–74) and infra note 8. More generally on the proliferation of indicators and the use of rule of law indicators as a tool of governance see Davis et al. (2012).

2 Labor laws are a socially negotiated and evolving institution that manages the expectations (of both equity and efficiency) of social parties, and will necessarily have redistributive effect (see infra note 5) and therefore will be a matter of dispute (Deakin and Sarkar 2008).

3 While the term "labor law" has no universally agreed definition it is conventionally understood to mean the regulatory framework governing workplace relationships, including the regulatory structure for workers' rights to organize in trade unions and to bargain collectively; workers' rights to a fair dismissal; workers' rights to minimum standards of employment, including minimum wages; and workers' rights to be treated equally. See, e.g., Blackburn (2006, 143–144).

4 Although labor law is embedded in social policy, modern conceptions of labor law do factor in broader concerns in economic policy; hence Klare in Collins, Davies, and Rideout (2000, 68) suggests the following objectives of modern labor law: promoting allocative and productive efficiency and economic growth; macroeconomic management (by achieving wage stabilization, high employment levels, and international competitiveness); establishing and protecting fundamental rights; and redistributing wealth and power in the employment context.

5 Sir Otto Kahn Freund (cited by Benjamin in Le Roux and Rycroft (2012, 21)), widely recognized as the "founding father of British academic labor law," articulates the

dynamics of the employment relationship and the purpose of labor law as follows: "[T]he relation between an employer and an isolated employee or worker is typically a relation between a bearer of power and one who is not a bearer of power. In its inception it is an act of submission, in its operation it is a condition of subordination, however much the submission and subordination may be concealed by that indispensable figment of the legal mind known as the 'contract of employment'. The main object of labour law has always been and we venture to say will always be, to be a countervailing force to counteract the inequality of bargaining power which is inherent and must be inherent in the employment relationship." This "famous dictum" of Kahn Freund was cited with approval in the Constitutional Court in South Africa in Sidumo & Another v Rustenburg Platinum Mines Ltd & Others 2007 (28) ILJ 2405 (CC) at para [72].

6 Deakin and Sarkar (2008, 455) articulate an alternative approach that argues that labor law rules and regulations are "endogenously generated by a combination of economic and political forces operating at the level of nation states" and should be understood "as devices for coordinating the expectations of actors."

7 The EWI proved to be so controversial that within several years of first being published the indicator was withdrawn following an assessment by the World Bank's Independent Evaluation Group (IEG), which concluded that the EWI is not always compliant with the spirit of the ILO conventions (Independent Evaluation Group 2008, xvi). See the discussion in "Public Power Reined In: The Rise and Fall of the World Bank's EWI."

8 Davis, Kingsbury, and Merry provide the following working definition of an indicator: "An indicator is a named collection of rank-ordered data that purports to represent the past or projected performance for different units. The data are generated through a process that simplifies raw data about a complex social phenomenon. The data, in this simplified and processed form, are capable of being used to compare particular units of analysis (such as countries, institutions, or corporations), synchronically or over time, and to evaluate their performance by reference to one or more standards."

9 ILO standards come in the form of conventions, recommendations, and declarations. The ILO's Governing Body has identified the following eight conventions as core standards: Freedom of Association and the Right to Organise Convention, 1948 (No. 87); Right to Organise and Collective Bargaining Convention, 1949 (No. 98); Forced Labour Convention, 1930 (No. 29); Abolition of Forced Labour Convention, 1957 (No. 105); Minimum Age Convention, 1973 (No. 138); Worst Forms of Child Labour Convention, 1999 (No. 184); Equal Remuneration Convention, 1951 (No. 100); and Discrimination (Employment and Occupation) Convention, 1958 (No. 111). These core rights are further expressed in the ILO's Declaration on Fundamental Principles and Rights at Work, adopted in 1998.

10 Each Country Profile contains a number of so-called Statistical Decent Work Indicators, primarily consisting of the empirical results of national Labour Force Surveys. In addition the Country Profiles contain a number of Legal Framework Indicators that consist of a narrative of the country's regulatory framework assessed against relevant ILO conventions.

11 On recommendation of the Wiehahn Commission, the 1956 Act was amended in 1979 to extend trade union rights to black employees. On the development of South Africa's labor laws see generally Van Niekerk (2012) and the sources cited therein.

12 The governing party, the African National Congress (ANC) has an (increasingly troubled) alliance with the South African Communist Party (SACP) and the Congress of South

African Trade Unions (COSATU). This alliance contests elections as a unitary party, and COSATU and SACP members hold senior positions in the ANC-led government.

13   The Constitution, in its preamble, explicitly adopts the text of the Constitution as the law of South Africa to "heal the divisions of the past and establish a society based on democratic values, social justice and fundamental human rights." This commitment to social justice is reinforced in the context of the labor market in the Labour Relations Act, Section 1, which iterates that the purpose of the Act is "to advance economic development, social justice, labour peace and the democratisation of the workplace."

14   Proposed labor laws, and amendments to existing laws, are negotiated and agreed upon by government, labor, and business at the National Economic Development and Labour Council (NEDLAC) before being enacted by Parliament.

15   Unemployment in South Africa, in the second quarter of 2012, excluding discouraged job seekers, measured at 24.9 percent. Unemployment disproportionately affects the young as well as members of the workforce with low levels of education and skills – whereas there is a shortage of highly skilled labor, there is an oversupply of unskilled or low skilled workers. The unemployment rate by population group for the second quarter of 2012 is as follows: Black/African (28.7 percent); Coloured (24 percent); Indian/Asian (9.5 percent); White (5.7 percent). Quarterly Labour Force Survey (Statistics South Africa, July 2012). When an expanded definition of unemployment is used, that is, when the unemployment rate is adjusted to include discouraged persons who, although able to work, do not actively seek work, the overall unemployment rate in 2010 was 35.8 percent – the rate for men was 31.5 percent and for women, 40.7 percent. ILO *Decent work country profile: South Africa* (2011, v).

16   South Africa remains one of the most unequal societies in the world (for a comparative perspective of Gini index scores see http://data.worldbank.org/indicator/SI.POV.GINI). High unemployment exacerbates poverty and inequality, which not only has profoundly negative health and welfare consequences for individuals, but also undermines the economic, social, and political stability of the country as a whole.

17   The term "black people" is defined in Section 1 of the Employment Equity Act of 1998 as "a generic term which means Africans, Coloureds and Indians."

18   While the formal sector cannot absorb more unskilled (primarily African) labor, and remunerates unskilled labor poorly, "scarce skills" at the top end of the labor market are often excessively remunerated by contrast. Even the informal economy is unable to provide many unemployed an opportunity to etch out a livelihood. The unemployed are sometimes labeled "unemployable" (see McCord 2002, 20), and see also Caspi et al. (1998, 63) for a discussion of the negative impact that a lack of high school qualifications, poor reading skills, low IQ scores, and limited parental resources has on the employment prospects of young adults. Many of these attributes can be ascribed to apartheid and apartheid education policy.

19   The idea that paying attention to inequality may have benefits for economic growth is gaining ground. See, e.g., Berg and Ostry (2011). On inequality, law, and policy in the South African context see generally Collier, Idensohn, and Adkins (2010) and Massie, Collier, and Crotty (2014).

20   Policies to address labor market failures include the New Growth Path, the Industrial Policy Action Plan, the Expanded Public Works Programme, and the National Development Plan.

21 In the global context see generally Barnard, Deakin, and Morris (2004) and in the South African context Le Roux and Rycroft (2012).

22 See, e.g., *Jobs Jobs Jobs* (2011), a publication compiled by Nolutshungu, a director of the Free Market Foundation. The South African–based Free Market Foundation boasts an extensive members list comprising organizations such as the Chambers of Commerce, and corporate and individual members.

23 The ILO Programme on Socio-Economic Security, *Economic Security for a Better World* (2004), articulates seven components of work-related security, namely income security, labor market security, employment security, work security, skill reproduction security, job security, and voice representation security.

24 With gender equality as a cross-cutting objective, the four pillars of the ILO's approach are (1) creating jobs; (2) guaranteeing rights at work; (3) extending social protection; and (4) promoting social dialogue.

25 These are (1) Employment opportunities; (2) Adequate earnings and productive work; (3) Decent hours; (4) Combining work, family, and personal life; (5) Work that should be abolished; (6) Stability and security of work; (7) equal opportunity and treatment in employment; (8) Safe work environment; (9) Social security; and (10) Social dialogue, workers' and employers' representation.

26 The ILO *Decent Work Country Profile* identifies the following conventions as not have been ratified: the Labour Administration Convention, 1978 (No. 150); the Employment Convention, 1964 (No. 122); the Social Security (Minimum Standards) Convention, 1952 (No. 102), Part IV; the Employment Promotion and Protection against Unemployment Convention, 1988 (No. 168); the Minimum Wage Fixing Convention, 1970 (No. 131); the Minimum Wage-Fixing Machinery (Agriculture) Convention, 1951 (No. 99); the Hours of Work (Industry) Convention, 1919 (No. 1); the Hours of Work (Commerce and Offices) Convention, 1930 (No. 30); the Holidays with Pay Convention (Revised), 1970 (No. 132), the Holidays with Pay Convention, 1936 (No. 52) the Holidays with Pay (Agriculture) Convention, 1952 (No. 101); the Maternity Protection Convention, 1919 (No. 3); the Maternity Protection (revised), 1952 (No. 103); the Maternity Protection Convention, 2000 (No. 183) nor the Social Security (Minimum Standards) Convention, 1952 (No. 102).; the Workers with Family Responsibilities Convention, 1981 (No. 156); the Termination of Employment Convention, 1982 (No. 158); the Employment Injury Benefits Convention, 1964 (No. 121); the Labour Inspection Convention, 1947 (No. 81), its 1995 Protocol; the Labour Inspection (Agriculture) Convention, 1969 (No. 129) the Promotional Framework for Occupational Safety and Health Convention, 2006 (No. 187); the Invalidity Old-Age and Survivors' Benefits Convention, 1967 (No. 128); and the Medical Care and Sickness Benefits Convention, 1969 (No. 130).

27 The OECD is an international organization, whose members are primarily governments from European and other developed countries, created in 1960 to promote policies that enhance social and economic well-being and therefore contemplates state intervention in the market.

28 Although the OECD acknowledges the important social benefits that flow from employment protection, it is conscious of a potential impact on firms, productivity, and growth if employment protection is over-strict and therefore periodically publishes estimates of the strictness of employment protection, focusing only on aspects of dismissals and temporary contracts for OECD countries and, in 2008, measured also ten emerging economies, including South Africa.

29 The WEF, which is the brainchild of a German economist, dates back to 1971.

30 The WB Group, a Bretton Woods institution, was created in 1944.

31 For a lucid account of why labor, because of its social nature, is not a market like any other, see Fischl (2011). According to Fischl (2011, 957–958), a more socially engaged approach would pursue "governance reform in the name of social values such as democratic and humane ordering."

32 The late Sanjaya Lall, a leading development economist, critically analyzes the economic foundations of the Forum's "competitiveness" approach, and its methodology, and finds that the "underlying model tends to lack rigor and clarity, with a propensity to use a large number of variables without theoretically justifying their causal relations to the dependent (and often without measuring them correctly)" (Lall 2001, 1508). For a more recent critique of the *Global Competitiveness Report* see Bergsteiner and Avery (2012).

33 Employer levels of frustration with South Africa's labor laws are evident in Duncan (2011).

34 In the 2012/13 Report South Africa was ranked 113 out of 144 in the labor market efficiency pillar of competitiveness, which, when disaggregated, saw South Africa ranked as 143rd in hiring and firing practices and 144th in cooperation in labor–employer relations.

35 Venn (2009, 15) points out that "[v]ariations between the two are likely to reflect the inclusion in the Doing Business index of regulations on working hours and minimum wages, along with more comprehensive information on employment protection included in the OECD indicators, including remedies in cases of unfair dismissal, regulation of temporary work agency contracts and collective bargaining provisions for a number of countries."

36 The United States ranks first in all three of the indicators, suggesting that a neoliberal economic theory of development underlies the methodology of each. See generally Bergsteiner and Avery (2012) and Krever (2013).

37 See, e.g., the contributions in *Jobs Jobs Jobs* (2011) compiled by Temba A Nolutshungu and published by the Free Market Foundation and the many online publications of Loan Sharpe, a South African labor economist with Adcorp Holdings Limited.

38 As Lall (2001, 1519) perceptively puts it, the WEF's presentation of the indicators gives "a misleading impression of precision, robustness and sophistication," concealing the many "analytical, methodological and quantitative weaknesses."

39 See the Common Principles of Flexicurity agreed by the Working Party on Social Questions of the Council of The European Union (15497/07 SOC 476 ECOFIN 483). The term was first used to describe Denmark's regulatory framework, which accommodates flexibility in the labor market by providing for worker protection through social security and active labor market policies.

40 This is perhaps as a sop to allegations that the organization is an exclusive "rich man's club" (this term is used in a question on http://www.weforum.org/faq).

41 These are (1) *institutions*, which measures the national legal and administrative framework; (2) *infrastructure*, which measures the provision of electricity, transport, and communications services; (3) *macroeconomic environment*, which considers government's budget balance and debt, gross national savings, inflation, and country credit rating; (4) *health and primary education*; (5) *higher education and training*; (6) *goods market efficiency*, which measures factors such as intensity of competition and extent of market dominance, the effectiveness of anti-monopoly policy, the extent and effect of taxation, the number of days and processes to start a business, and the prevalence of trade barriers and the level of buyer sophistication; (7) *labor market efficiency* (see Table 9.3); (8) *financial*

market development such as the availability and affordability of financial services, venture capital availability, the regulation of securities exchanges, and the soundness of banks; (9) *technological readiness* measuring the availability of latest technologies and the absorption of technology at the firm level, FDI and technology transfer, number of Internet users and broadband subscriptions and Internet bandwidth; (10) *market size*, both domestic and foreign; (11) *business sophistication*, being a consideration of factors such as local supplier quantity and quality, the value chain breadth, the extent of marketing, willingness to delegate authority, and the production process sophistication; and (12) *innovation* measured through factors such as research and development expenditure and activities, the availability of scientists and engineers, and the number of utility patents granted.

42 See also Michie and Sheehan-Quinn (2001) and Michie and Sheehan (2005) and the studies referenced therein.

43 The WEF has been widely criticized, including by the World Bank, for its use of perception in the construction of its indices. See, e.g., Bergsteiner and Avery (2012) and Krever (2013).

44 Halliday and Carruthers' concept of *recursivity* in the context of transnational legal processes is explored in Shaffer (2010).

45 An exercise that Benjamin and Theron (2009) undertake.

46 See generally Perry-Kessaris (2002); Berg and Cazes (2008); Lee, McCann, and Torm (2008); Faundez (2009); AJ Kerhuel and Fauvarque-Cosson (2010); and Pistor in Davis et al. (2012). More specifically, on the employing workers indicator in South Africa see Bhorat and Cheadle (2007); Bhorat and van der Westhuizen (2008); Benjamin and Theron (2009); and Benjamin, Bhorat, and Cheadle (2010).

47 The World Bank (2008, 17) indicates that "*The following economies are also good practice economies for Employing Workers: Marshall Islands, Singapore*".

48 Georgia is often cited as a country that deliberately set out to improve its rankings, and was able to improve its overall ranking by 100 places. Among the reforms that it implemented was to abolish the Labour Inspectorate, hence undermining monitoring and enforcement of labor standards; allow employers to bypass trade unions and negotiate with individual employees; stop employer contributions to the social security fund; and not adjust the minimum wage in line with inflation (ITUC 2009). The impact on economic performance has been questionable, demonstrating the dangers of blindly seeking to enhance ratings. In this regard see generally Gylfason and Hochreiter (2009).

49 The error appears to result from an incorrect reading of the provisions of the South African Labour Relations Act 66 of 1995 (LRA) in terms of which the failure to renew a fixed term contract, where the employee has an expectation of renewal, amounts to a dismissal. The LRA, however, does not otherwise restrict the use of fixed-term contracts, although proposed amendments to the LRA may, in future, impose certain restrictions on the use of fixed-term contracts.

50 Section 17 of the BCEA.

51 Prior to 2009, the question was whether the law required an employer to *consider* reassignment or retaining options before redundancy termination. See Benjamin and Theron (2009, 226).

52 See in particular Berg and Cazes (2008) and Lee, McCann, and Torm (2008).

53 More specifically, the IEG (2008, 33) found that four of the measures on the costs and difficulty of firing workers did not reflect the spirit of the ILO provisions on redundancy.

54 By October 1919, the ILO had already adopted six International Conventions dealing with hours of work, unemployment, maternity protection, night work for women, minimum age, and night work for young persons in industry. The ILO was awarded the Nobel Peace Prize on its 50th anniversary in 1969. For information on the ILOs origins and history see http://www.ilo.org/global/about-the-ilo/history/lang--en/index.htm.

55 Statement on Cabinet Meeting, August 24, 2011, http://www.gcis.gov.za/newsroom/releases/cabstate/2011/110825.html.

56 The ILO has galvanized its efforts and has established the Regulating for Decent Work (RDW) Research Network Project that will focus on effective labor market regulatory design for both social and economic progress. See http://www.ilo.org/travail/whatwedo/projects/WCMS_122341/lang--en/index.htm.

57 This term is borrowed from Shaffer (2010).

58 For recent developments in this regard see the *Independent Panel Review of the Doing Business Report* (June 2013), http://www.dbrpanel.org/sites/dbrpanel/files/doing-business-review-panel-report.pdf.

59 The WEF, in its most recent report, outlines its evolving approach to measuring sustainable competitiveness that involves both social sustainability and environmental sustainability. Perhaps these will influence the direction of the WEF's future labor market analysis (Schwab 2012, 49–68).

REFERENCES

Adcorp Employment Index. 2011. "SA Labour Laws 7th Most Restrictive in World." *PoliticsWeb*.

Altman, Miriam. 2007. "Low Wage Work in South Africa." Pretoria: Human Sciences Research Council (HSRC).

Barnard, Catherine, Simon Deakin, and Gillian S. Morris. 2004. *The Future of Labour Law Liber Amicorum: Sir Bob Hepple QC*. Oxford: Hart Publishing.

Benjamin, Paul. 2012. "Labour Law Beyond Employment." In R. Le Roux and A. Rycroft, eds., *Reinventing Labour Law: Reflecting on the First 15 Years of the Labour Relations Act and Future Challenges*. Cape Town: Juta.

Benjamin, Paul, Haroon Bhorat, and Halton Cheadle. 2010. "The Cost of "Doing Business" and Labour Regulation: The Case of South Africa." *International Labour Review* 149(1): 73–91.

Benjamin, Paul, and Jan Theron. 2009. "Costing, Comparing and Competing: The World Bank's Doing Business Survey and the Bench-Marking of Labour Regulation." *Acta Juridica* 204–234.

Berg, Janine, and Sandrine Cazes. 2008. "Policymaking Gone Awry: The Labour Market Regulations of the Doing Business Indicators." *Comparative Labor Law & Policy Journal* 29: 349–381. Also published as "The Doing Business Indicators: Measurement Issues and Political Implications:" Economic and Labour Market Paper 2007/6 (2007) Geneva: International Labour Office.

Berg, Andrew G., and Jonathan D. Ostry. 2011. "Inequality and Unsustainable Growth: Two Sides of the Same Coin?" IMF Staff Discussion Note, April 8, 2011 SDN/11/08.

Bergsteiner, Harald, and Avery, Gayle C. 2012. "When Ethics Are Compromised by Ideology: The Global Competitiveness Report." *Journal of Business Ethics* 109: 391–410.

Bhorat, Haroon, and Halton Cheadle. 2009. "Labour Reform in South Africa: Measuring Regulation and a Synthesis of Policy Suggestions." DPRU Working Paper 09/139.

Bhorat, Haroon, and Carlene van der Westhuizen. 2008. "A Synthesis of Current Issues in the Labour Regulatory Environment." Development Policy Research Unit (DPRU), School of Economics: University of Cape Town.

Blackburn, D. 2006. "The Role, Impact and Future of Labour Law." Labour Law: Its Role, Trends and Potential. International Labour Organization: Labour Education 2–3 No. 143–144.

Botero, Juan C., Simeon Djankov, Rafael la Porta, Florencio Lopez-de-Silanes, and Andrei Shleifer. 2004. "The Regulation of Labor." Quarterly Journal of Economics 119 (4): 1339–1382.

Caspi, Avshalom, Bradley R. Entner Wright, Terrie E. Moffitt, and Phil A. Silva. 1989. "Early Failure in the Labor Market: Childhood and Adolescent Predictors of Unemployment in the Transition to Adulthood." American Sociological Review 63: 424–451.

Clarke, George R. G., James Habyarimana, Michael Ingram, David Kaplan, and Vijaya Ramachandran. 2007. An Assessment of the Investment Climate in South Africa. Washington, DC: World Bank.

Collier, Debbie, Kathy Idensohn, and Jill Adkins. 2010. "Income Inequality and Executive Remuneration: Assessing the Role of Law and Policy in the Pursuit of Equality." South African Journal of Labour Relations 34(2): 84–109.

Collins, H., P. L. Davies, and R. Rideout. 2000. Legal Regulation of the Employment Relation. London: Kluwer Law International.

Council of the European Union, Working Party on Social Questions. 2007. "Common Principles of Flexicurity." 15497/07 SOC 476 ECOFIN 483. Brussels: Council of the European Union.

Davidov, Guy. 2008. "Unbound: Some Comments on Israel's Judicially-Developed Labour Law." Comparative Labor Law & Policy Journal 30: 283–311.

Davis, Kevin, Angelina Fisher, Benedict Kingsbury, and Sally Engle Merry, eds. 2012. Governance by Indicators: Global Power through Quantification and Rankings. Oxford: Oxford University Press.

Davis, Kevin E., Benedict Kingsbury, and Sally Engle Merry. 2012. "Indicators as a Technology of Global Governance." Law and Society Review 36(1): 73.

Deakin, Simon, and Prabirjit Sarkar. 2008. "Assessing the Long-Run Economic Impact of Labour Law Systems: A Theoretical Reappraisal and Analysis of New Time Series Data." Industrial Relations Journal 39(6): 453–487.

Department of Communications, Republic of South Africa. 2011. Statement on Cabinet Meeting 24 August 2011.

Doing Business Employing Workers Consultative Group. 2011. Final Report. April, 25, 2011.

Duncan, Felicity. 2011. "South Africa's Labour Annus Horribilis? Will 2011 Be the Year that Labour Laws Finally Throttle Us?" Discovery Invest/Moneyweb.

Ensor, Linda, and Sam Mkokeli. 2011. "Cabinet Slap for Manuel, Gordhan on Labour Laws." BusinessDay.

Faundez, Julio. 2009. "Rule of Law or Washington Consensus: The Evolution of The World Bank's Approach to Legal and Judicial Reform." Warwick SSRN Working Paper.

Fauvarque-Cosson, Bénédicte, and Anne-Julie Kerhuel. 2010. "Is Law an Economic Contest? French Reactions to the Doing Business World Bank Reports and Economic Analysis of the Law." The American Journal of Comparative Law 57: 811–830.

Fischl, Richard M. 2011. "Labor Law, the Left, and the Lure of the Market." Marquette Law Review 94: 947–958.

Gylfason, Thorvaldur, and Eduard Hochreiter. 2009. "Growing Apart? A Tale of Two Republics: Estonia and Georgia." *European Journal of Political Economy* 25(3): 355–370.

Halliday, Terence, and Bruce Carruthers. 2010. "Transnational Legal Process and State Change: Opportunities and Constraints." International Law and Justice Working Papers, IILJ Working Paper 4.

International Labour Organization (ILO). 2004. *Economic Security for a Better World.* Geneva: ILO.

    2011. *Decent Work Country Profile: South Africa.* Geneva: International Labour Organization.

International Trade Union Confederation (ITUC). 2009. Internationally Recognised Core Labour Standards in Georgia: Report for the WTO General Council Review of the Trade Policies of Georgia. Geneva: ITUC.

Khuzwayo, Wiseman. 2012. *BusinessReport.* http://www.iol.co.za/business/business-news/labour-market-takes-the-shine-off-sa-s-competitiveness-1.1376811

Krever, Tor. 2013. "Quantifying Law: Legal Indicator Projects and the Reproduction of Neoliberal Common Sense." *Third World Quarterly* 34: 131–150.

Krugman, Paul. 1994. "Competitiveness: A Dangerous Obsession." *Foreign Affairs* 73(2): 44.

Lall, Sanjaya. 2001. "Competitiveness Indices and Developing Countries: An Economic Evaluation of the Global Competitiveness Report." *World Development* 29: 1501, 1508.

Lee, Sangheon, McCann Deirdre, and Nina Torm. 2008. "The World Bank's "Employing Workers" Index: Findings and Critiques – A Review of Recent Evidence." *International Labour Review* 147(4): 416–432.

Massie, Kaylan, Debbie Collier, and Ann Crotty. 2014. *Executive Salaries in South Africa: Who Should Have a Say on Pay?* Auckland Park, South Africa: Jacana Media.

McCord, Anna. 2002. "Public Works as a Response to Labour Market Failure in South Africa." CSSR Working Paper No. 19. Cape Town: University of Cape Town, Center of Social Science Research.

Michie, Jonathan, and Maura Sheehan. 2005. "Business Strategy, Human Resources, Labour Market Flexibility and Competitive Advantage." *The International Journal of Human Resource Management* 16(3): 445–464.

Michie, Jonathan, and Maura Sheehan-Quinn. 2001. "Labour Market Flexibility, Human Resource Management and Corporate Performance." *British Journal of Management* 12: 287–306.

Nolutshungu, Temba A., ed. 2011. *Jobs Jobs Jobs.* South Africa: Free Market Foundation.

Organisation for Economic Co-operation and Development (OECD). 2008. "Employment Protection in OECD and Selected Non-OECD Countries." OECD Indicators on Employment Protection. Paris: OECD.

Perry-Kessaris, Amanda. 2002. "The Relationship between Legal Systems and Economic Development: Integrating Economic and Cultural Approaches." *Journal of Law and Society* 29(2): 282–307.

Pike, Richard, Loane Sharp, and Ted Black. 2010. *The New Divide: Will High Wages and a Lack of Leadership Create an Unemployed Majority?* Johannesburg: Terranova.

Pistor, Katharina. 2012. "Re-Construction of Private Indicators for Public Purposes." In Kevin Davis, Angelina Fisher, Benedict Kingsbury, and Sally Engle Merry, eds., *Governance by Indicators: Global Power through Quantification and Rankings* Oxford: Oxford University Press.

Ravallion, Martin. 2010. "Mashup Indices of Development." Policy Research Paper No. 5432 Washington, DC: The World Bank.

Rodgers, Gerry, Eddy Lee, Lee Swepston, and Jasmien Van Daele. 2009. *The International Labour Organization and the Quest for Social Justice, 1919–2009*. Geneva: International Labour Organization.

Royle, Tony. 2010. "The ILO's Shift to Promotional Principles and the 'Privatization' of Labour Rights: An Analysis of Labour Standards, Voluntary Self-regulation and Social Clauses." *The International Journal of Comparative Labour Law and Industrial Relations* 26(3): 249–271.

Schwab, Klaus. 2008. *The Global Competitiveness Report 2008–2009*. Geneva: World Economic Forum.

2009. *The Global Competitiveness Report 2009–2010*. Geneva: World Economic Forum.

2010. *The Global Competitiveness Report 2010–2011*. Geneva: World Economic Forum.

2011. *The Global Competitiveness Report 2011–2012*. Geneva: World Economic Forum.

2012. *The Global Competitiveness Report 2012–2013* Geneva: World Economic Forum.

Shaffer, Gregory. 2010. "Transnational Legal Process and State Change: Opportunities and Constraints." International Law and Justice Working Papers, IILJ Working Paper 4.

Sharp, Loane. 2011. "Role of Business Is Vital." *BusinessDay*.

2012. "South Africa's Labour Laws in Context." South Africa: Free Market Foundation.

Sidumo & Another v Rustenburg Platinum Mines Ltd & Others 2007 (28) ILJ 2405 (CC).

Statistics South Africa. 2012. "Quarterly Labour Force Survey." Pretoria: StatsSA.

Van Niekerk A. 2012. *Law@work*. South Africa: LexisNexis.

Venn, Danielle. 2009. "Legislation, Collective Bargaining and Enforcement: Updating the OECD Employment Protection Indicators." OECD Social, Employment and Migration Working Papers, No. 89. Paris: OECD Publishing.

World Bank. 2004. *Doing Business in 2004: Understanding Regulation*. Oxford: Oxford University Press.

2006. *Doing Business in 2006: Creating Jobs*. Washington, DC: The International Bank for Reconstruction and Development/The World Bank.

2007. *Doing Business 2008*. Washington, DC: The International Bank for Reconstruction and Development/The World Bank.

2008. *Doing Business 2009: Country Profile for South Africa*. Washington, DC: The International Bank for Reconstruction and Development/The World Bank.

2009. *Doing Business 2010: Reforming through Difficult Times*. Washington, DC: The International Bank for Reconstruction and Development/The World Bank.

2009b. "Revisions to the EWI Indicator." http://www.doingbusiness.org/methodology/~/media/FPDKM/Doing%20Business/Documents/Methodology/EWI/EWI-revisions.pdf

2010. *Doing Business 2011: Making a Difference for Entrepreneurs* Washington, DC: The International Bank for Reconstruction and Development/The World Bank.

2012. *Doing Business 2012: Doing Business in a More Transparent World*. Washington, DC: The International Bank for Reconstruction and Development/The World Bank.

2013. *Doing Business 2013: Smarter Regulations for Small and Medium-Size Enterprises* Washington, DC: The International Bank for Reconstruction and Development/The World Bank.

World Bank Independent Evaluation Group (IEG). 2008. *Doing Business: An Independent Evaluation Taking the Measure of the World Bank – IFC Doing Business Indicators*. Washington, DC: The World Bank.

10

Conclusion

Contesting Global Indicators

David Nelken

We will have a kind of symbolic and secularized society based on the premise that people voluntarily conform to the decisions of authorized expert knowledge. But while order is being established, responsibility may be vanishing.

Bengt Jacobsson (2000, 40)

(T)he inequality between one who gives orders and one who must obey is not as radical as that between one who has a right to demand an answer and one who has the duty to answer.

Milan Kundera (1991, 110)

The studies in this collection, building on previous important contributions to the discussion (see especially Davis, Kingsbury, and Merry 2012a, 2012b), offer a set of rich and insightful discussions of social indicators that have potentially global implications.[1] The focus here is on the wider relevance of those indicators that seek to compare levels of political freedom, the rule of law, corruption, good governance, and corporate responsibility.[2] In their introduction, the editors explain what is distinctive about their approach. They tell us that most of the literature on indicators focuses on how to develop effective, reliable, and valid measures. It looks at how to conceptualize what is to be measured, how to operationalize broad and vague concepts, what data sets are available that can be used, how to label indicators so that they will be easy to understand, and how to persuade governments, donors, and other potential users of the indicator to pay for and use them. In contrast, this collection asks what difference indicators make to governance and law. It examines how indicators work in practice, why some become successful.

My task in this afterword is to reflect on what the chapters in this book tell us by way of answers to these questions.[3] In particular I shall point to some of the difficulties of actually separating the question of explaining the causes of what they call an indicator's "success" from the search for developing more effective indicators. The editors themselves tell us of their concern about the way indicators present themselves as more effective and reliable and valid than is truly warranted. For them, indicators strive to appear objective and neutral and they need to maintain that appearance to be credible. But they are in essence political creatures. Social and political processes determine their creation, use, and effects on policies and publics.

Can (and should) anything be done to overcome the attempt to use indicators to "de-politicize" the problems they purport to measure? In developing my argument I shall first say more about the definition of indicators and the way they are used. I shall then move on to consider the criticisms of indicators that are touched on in the various contributions. I end by considering the problems of regulating indicators (the theme of the Rome workshop from which this book emerged), focusing in particular on the effort to make indicators more contestable.

DEFINING GLOBAL INDICATORS

The studies gathered here take their cue from the idea of indicators as "a named collection of rank-ordered data that purports to represent the past or projected performance of different units generated through a process that simplifies raw data about a complex social phenomenon." As the editors tell us, they are a crucial part of exercises "to compare units so as to evaluate their performance by reference to one or more standards" (Davis, Kingsbury, and Merry 2012a). But, helpful as this definition is, it leaves a number of issues open. Social indicators are commonly found in both social science explanation and policy evaluation contexts. Just as those using indicators for governance may rely on data gathered for more "scientific" purposes, so social scientists sometimes use indicators as part of their explanations (as when writing, e.g., about "fragile states").

What is important is to understand exactly what is new (if anything) when indicators are used as global technologies of governance. Indicators may be linked to the data either deductively by operationalizing a theory of what data need to be looked for so as to provide evidence for the phenomena, and/or they can be built up inductively working from already existing data or bodies of statistics.[4] What is at issue here, however, is the way using indicators for governance transforms "facts" (data), into norms and "standards" – as well as vice versa. Whether indicators are ontologically closer to "facts" or standards is a moot point. What is more, the "same" phenomena may count as "facts" for one group, or at one time, and as a standard for another group, or at another time. In any case, by destabilizing the line between the normal and the normative, indicators produce (and are intended to produce) pressure on their targets to come into line with common standards (or at least to succeed in "signaling" that they have done so).

In examining such indicators Merry and her collaborators are particularly interested in what are described as their "knowledge" and "governance" effects. As to the first, indicators, Merry tells us, are "performative"; naming produces knowledge by announcing categories to be measured as if they were self-evident, open to public scrutiny, simple in conception, and readily accessible, in a way that private opinions are not. But the labels thus chosen do not necessarily accurately reflect the data that produce the indicators (Merry 2011). These numerical measures, she says, "submerge local particularities and idiosyncrasies into universal categories to produce a world knowable without the detailed particulars of context and history." The second set of effects, by contrast, have more to do with the new systems of governance emerging in the postwar period, that seek to shape behavior "at a distance" through "governance of the soul" and self-management rather than command and control models. Through the use of this tool, individuals, organizations, and countries are made responsible for their own behaviour as they seek to comply with the measures of performance articulated in an indicator.

It is not entirely clear whether these "effects" should be treated as part of an extended definition of the phenomena in question. Arguably, they could also be seen as empirically contingent and variable features of only some indicators. Given that knowledge is often power, these "two effects" undoubtedly also overlap, perhaps especially so for the sort of indicators with which this book is concerned. The reports in this collection provide many illustrations of this. Uribe tells us that since the notion of development remains contested in the development field, indicators are concealing a specific commonsense of what constitutes development, which joins the ongoing debate on the promotion of development in the Global South. What is more, indicators played a role in winning the argument for the neoliberal approach to development.

But, in addition, she argues that, indicators have a normative effect in the promotion of development knowledge, because they produce the standards against which a societies' development ought to be measured and that determine the path that has to be followed to comply with those standards. Therefore, they send a message to the developing countries of what kind of society they ought to become and how to achieve that society. This knowledge effect in turn determines the governance effect produced by indicators in the development field, since the use of development indicators by the donor community for the allocation of aid creates an incentive for states in the Global South to accommodate their performance to receive a good ranking in the indicator. Thus, development indicators have a regulatory effect on receiving states. Development indicators have yet another effect on governance: they implicitly allocate responsibility for failure in the development process. Development indicators that measure state performance assign the responsibility to the developing states, because their failure to achieve the preestablished standard is seen as the prevailing reason for underdevelopment (see Uribe in this book).

It is obviously not possible to cover everything in a definition. Other features that arguably could have been included are the importance of publicity and dissemination of these comparative rankings via the media. On the other hand, the value of case studies of single indicators is the possibility they offer of bringing out differences as much as similarities. We could distinguish level of sophistication, as seen, for example, by the complexity of the "assemblages" in which they are embedded. Some indicators, such as those used for assessing progress in meeting targets for protecting refugees, can require filling out practical guides that can run to more than 300 pages. Or we might contrast indicators that base themselves on perceptions[5] by experts or the public, for example, in estimating levels of corruption or financial strength, from those that require information to be collected and collated by the agencies themselves. Indicators can be intended to play roles at different stages of an intervention. Or else they may have different supposed (and actual) users, and targets. It is true that the indicators described in this collection are all broadly about finding ways to promote economic and human development. But differences also matter. Measuring the level of the rule of law or the level of corruption may not be quite the same: indeed the point of Serban's case study of the application of the rule of law indicator in Romania is to demonstrate why one should not be reduced to the other.[6]

The global indicators described in this volume concern the role of states, intergovernmental organizations, nongovernmental organizations (NGOs), and private agencies responding to transnational problems and thereby helping to create the sinews of a new transnational order. Understanding their genealogy and evolution belongs to – and calls for analysis by – some of the most advanced forms of social science theorizing. Sally Merry and her colleagues note the relevance of writers such as Foucault and Latour.[7] Scholars of governmentality tell us that the concern with standardization and normalization can be traced back at least to the growth of social welfare, state insurance, and technical standardization.[8] Other relevant factors include the rise of consumerism and the increasing stress on branded goods as guaranteeing reliability (or fashionability). As will be seen, thinking about contestation as a means of taming indicators leads to consideration of the competing visions of social legitimation in the work of leading social theorists such as Habermas and Luhmann, and their followers.[9]

But although the authors in this collection do make reference to the larger context their main focus is on providing empirical specificity about the genealogy of particular indicators rather than on discussing the genealogy of indicators in general.[10] The contributors to this book (as well as the chapters in previous collections organized by the editors) seek above all to identify the needs[11] or goals that given indicators are supposed to fulfill and discover what in fact transpires. Indicators, we are told can serve a variety of purposes and provide many kinds of benefit. Most obviously, for their proponents, there is the assumption that (only) what is measured gets improved, and that "what is measured and reported improves exponentially" (attributed apocryphally to the statistician Karl Pearson). Indicators can be used to measure accountability to standards and norms; assess compliance with policies and targets; and evaluate performance with respect to stated objectives. They can also facilitate an efficient processing of information and reduce the costs and resources devoted to decision making. The appeal of indicators lies in their ability to translate phenomena such as respect for the rule of law into a numerical representation that is easy to understand and comparable across actors. Moreover, their simplicity enables more effective communication with those who are governed as well as the general public, thereby promoting ideals of transparency and accountability. They are particularly useful because donors require and value them and because they are seen as precise and have the legitimacy of science.

Indicators have other merits. They can promote horizontal accountability between governments and can form part of a delegation of autonomy or discretion in exchange for providing feedback on decisions taken. They promote collaboration at the domestic and international levels in dealing with transnational problems such as those to do with health needs or water supplies, and are especially useful where international law obligations are difficult to enforce. In addition, their use facilitates interaction between groups, organizations, or "regimes"[12] that otherwise would have difficulties in doing so. They bridge the different cultures represented, for example, by public health approaches and legal approaches and provide a working language for intersystem communication, as when they help development experts talk to human right lawyers. Indicators allow us to decide who gets what in a way that is transparent. Yet by providing evidence of self-regulation they help create space for maneuver for NGOs and intergovernmental organizations who need to gain independence from donors and beneficiaries. Indicators allow you to decide who gets what in a way that is transparent.

In describing – and evaluating – the effects of the indicators in question, the arguments used by contributors often comes very close to Merry's discussion of two kinds of effects. Thus Uribe explains that, indicators in the development field create not only realities, but also identities, as by promoting a determined development discourse they also promote the categories embedded in it. The establishment of identities, in turn, divides the development actors into a hierarchical order in which some of them are placed above the others. And Serban tells us that rule of law indicators are a technology of control used by the European Union through the Cooperation and Verification Mechanism. Its disciplinary effects include (re) defining the rule of law as anti-corruption and judicial reform. Second, rule of law indicators are a technology of reform deployed by state and civil society actors unevenly and within distinct reformation domains. This domestic mobilization depends upon indicators' value added and ability to deliver on promises of objectivity and impartiality.

But using descriptions of outcomes to decide whether or not an indicator has been "successful" turns out to be far from straightforward. The contributors do not always distinguish (nor see a reason to distinguish) between talking about the success of an indicator being adopted, in the competition for attention among indicators, from the different issue of whether it achieves its aims and the further question of whether these aims are worth achieving. Evaluating success involves making normative judgements. Who wanted a given indicator to "succeed"? How, when, where, and why? What some of the actors on the ground – or some observers – may see as success, others, especially those unsympathetic to the overall project to which a given indicator is linked, may well describe as failure. What observers claim to be the point of indicators may or may not correspond to what their makers or users seek to achieve, still less to the intentions of the targets being evaluated.[13] In the accounts of indicators in this collection some observers endorse actors' own criticisms of the weakness of given indicators. But others keep their distance. It is to be expected that countries or organizations given poor ratings will be unhappy with this and try to find fault with the assessment. But when those being evaluated get blamed for not meeting requirements it may also sometimes be reasonable for them to argue that the outcomes did not depend on them (though this point is less likely to be raised in cases where they are awarded credit!).

It is notoriously difficult to know what would have happened (counter-factually) had an indicator not existed given that other social changes are happening at the same time. We also need to distinguish intended from unintended outcomes. It is usually difficult for those who make indicators to control the outcomes of their use. Given that most of the matters being highlighted by global social indicators have, in one way or another, to do with what the sociological literature calls "social problems," success in any case has as much to do with imposing a given definition of problem and solution as it does with producing objective changes (Rubington and Weinberg 2010). What happens in practice therefore depends on how the various parties using them define or redefine them, and on how, when, and why they are used in the course of struggles over their very meaning. Bradley, for example, speaking about development indicators, tells us that the actors that participate in such a struggle are (1) the donor institutions, whether national or multinational; (2) the receiving States; (3) the elites of the developing countries; (4) the social movements from the South; (5) nongovernmental organizations; and (6) development experts. These actors battle to determine an ideal model of delivering development to a society that is labeled as underdeveloped.

The "natural history" of the different indicators described by our authors shows how often actors can have different agendas. We learn that, in Romania, state actors "work within a discourse of modernization and governmentality, both predicated on a technocratic logic that is inherently opposed to politics. Civil society actors are more concerned with state accountability and are deeply politicized" (Serban, this volume: 208). Other contributors explain how and why some forms of shared definition do emerge. Musaraj tells us that "looking into the various acts of displacement and translation – of forms of knowledge and political action –" can "make visible the complicated origins and movements of expertise involved in the making of the USAID/IDRA corruption perception survey." She argues that "the content of this survey's questionnaire came into existence through dispersed acts of sharing, negotiating, and transferring of knowledge across various nodes of knowledge production – the local research center in Albania, global private consultancies, American higher education institutions' opinion-polling centers, and USAID-sponsored polls in Latin America" (Musaraj, this volume: 224).

Indicators are made by, in, and for organizations and these have their own reasons for using indicators. Organizations that make indicators use them to bolster their image, by giving them visibility and credibility – even where these are only a small part of their activities and involve a small part of their resources (as shown by Bradley in this volume). Both financial and political considerations may matter to them. Bradley tells us that Freedom House considered "direct effects on world affairs' highly desirable" and that "influencing the flow of money to 'not free' or 'partly free' countries based on indicator scores has been an explicit pursuit." The same applies to the targets of indicators (who may not always be easily distinguishable from users) (Bradley, this volume: 53). Thus Sarfaty, in this volume, tells us that Global Reporting Initiative (GRI) indicators have become "the de facto international reporting standard" but that companies use the corporate responsibility indicator mainly because this is helpful for their own purposes[14] (Sarfaty, this volume: 110). The effects of "successful" indicators can even be otherwise counterproductive. For example, critics of the "better business" indicator argue that the use of this indicator is implicated in the "land grabs" that lead to the displacement of populations, impoverishment, and the loss of livelihoods. While promising to create work, what actually happens is that the best jobs go to foreigners and the dangerous, poorly paid jobs go to the locals. What is more, much of this development involves producing food for others when there is not enough locally and dependence on foreign economic interests increases.

CRITICIZING GLOBAL INDICATORS

Arguing that indicators have knowledge and governance effects (in general or in particular cases) may not always be meant to count as a criticism. Interestingly, some contributors consider valuable exactly those features that those critical of (given) indicators see as problematic. Thus while some applaud "a technology of producing readily accessible and standardized forms of knowledge that is able to convert complicated contextually variable phenomena into unambiguous, clear, and impersonal measures" (Dutta, this volume: 162), others see this as a path to objectionable oversimplification. But what if criticisms point to faults that cannot be remedied? Merry, Davis, and Kingsbury help us understand that indicators are interpretative "all the way down" – that they "constitute" the phenomena they seek to measure – even as they assert a claim that there is a measurable preexisting reality. They also have feedback effects, bringing to life what they purport to be measuring (and sometimes intending to do this) as with notions such as "better business," "corruption," and "fragile states." But then the same could also be applied to all concepts, including "progressive" goals such as "human development." In fact, some of those who are the most positive about the indicators they describe are not worried about indicators constituting reality. According to Urueña (this volume), for example, "it would be wrong to accuse WJP of mistaking perception with reality, when it is arguable that there is no reality beyond such perception. In the case of the rule of law, the indicator allows the WJP to see reality – in this very restricted sense, reality is being constructed by the indicator."[15]

Nonetheless, most contributors do find matters to criticize – and these range from matters of method and meaning (which we might see as referring to the knowledge effects) to more political concerns (more relevant to issues of governance). Do indicators rely on sound theories and concepts?[16] Because indicators always claim to be measuring something it is always possible to query whether they are doing so satisfactorily.[17] Are the indicators selected valid and reliable proxies for the phenomenon they are talking about? For example, is the fact that a state signs up to a commitment necessarily a measure of political will? Are the right things being measured- and are the right sources being used?[18] Do – and should – indicators try to measure underlying conditions or only people's perceptions of them?[19] Indicators focus too often only on what can be (easily) measured at the expense of what may be other more important matters. Sarfaty, with respect to indicators of corporate responsibility, tells us that

> In the case of the GRI, issues that are easy to quantify, such as greenhouse gas emissions, are prioritized. At the same time, issues such as human rights and community impact are subordinated or even diluted as they are translated into mere business risks. In this way, indicators may lead to better performance on certain issues by relying on the power of numbers, but may neglect those issues that are difficult to quantify. (Sarfaty, this volume: 121)

Many of the descriptions in this book point to problems in the way perceptions or opinions are turned into data. Authors worry about what is being left out – for instance, both chapters about Kenya (Akech, this volume) and Albania (Musaraj, this volume) criticize the stress on low-level rather than high-level corruption. Indicators are also stigmatized for what we might call "junk comparisons." This is in part because of the considerable differences in the kind and quality of information available in different places. But comparative exercises may also be shipwrecked when encountering a variety of less obvious obstacles in translating meaning and significance. Values such as the rule of law or judicial independence have different interpretations in different places – and are applied – or (need to be) applied differently in different circumstances.[20]

Objections that have more to do with governance effects, by contrast, commonly reflect judgments about the larger projects that indicators are seen to further. For many commentators the whole enterprise of indicators is seen as part of the turn to neoliberal politics.[21] Thus Collier and Benjamin object that

> Steeped in neoliberal ideology, the Executive Opinion Survey suggests to respondents that social policy interventions are problematic, in the same way that crime and corruption are problematic. In the opinion survey, respondents are asked to select the most "problematic" factors in their country – from a list of fifteen factors, in which "Tax rates" and "Restrictive labour regulations" are listed alongside factors such as "Corruption," and "Crime and theft"…

There is criticism moreover of the application of neoliberal recipes to particular contexts. Collier and Benjamin go on to tell us that

> WEF's standards and rankings are unhelpful and they establish an unrealistic expectation around the possibilities for deregulation. Political infeasibility aside, a free market approach to labor market regulation in South Africa would establish an inferior brand of efficiency and equity. In its current iteration, the WEF's norms do not resonate with existing domestic laws and are a catalyst for an increasingly polarized debate on labor market regulation in South Africa. (Collier and Benjamin, this volume: 298)

Neoliberalism may be seen as the villain of the piece even where indicators are not ostensibly about helping business, as, for example, where they deal with business responsibility or the protection of human rights. Thus Sarfaty tells us that

> The GRI's progression toward integrated reporting represents an effort to translate public values into financial terms and transform them into business risks. In the case of human rights, what is developing is a risk management approach that defines potential violations as strategic risks, which may damage a company's reputation, threaten its profits, and lead to possible litigation.[22] While risk management has become increasingly common in public and private governance (Power 2004), what are the implications for it being applied to more value-laden issues such as human rights? Translating rights into financial risks and indicators may emphasize

their regulatory dimension (including their instrumental, rule-oriented, and administrative qualities) but disregard their sovereignty dimension (which invokes their universal character, symbolic valence, and emancipatory power). (Sarfaty, this volume: 122)

Beyond the objection to the specific neoliberal agenda, the chief criticism of indicators is the way they de-politicize, replacing judgments on the basis of values with apparently more rational decision making on the basis of statistical information. They do not eliminate the role of private knowledge and elite power in decision making but represent it as technical, statistical expertise. In addition, the whole point of most indicators is to shift the burden of responsibility. This means that indicators rarely acknowledge how the donor community is to blame for poverty and underdevelopment, because it has continuously imposed structural adjustments with an imperfect knowledge of the local environment. Being identified as a fragile state or having a poorly functioning healthcare system may get you either more or less aid depending on the donor's political choices. But there may often be little that the targets of indicators can do to affect those circumstances. As Sarfaty again documents, imposing indicators encourages box ticking and superficial compliance. Some companies she studied complained that they were on a "reporting treadmill," where they spent so much time gathering data that they were left with few resources to implement changes in the organization.

On the other hand, the targets of indicators, those whose conduct is being measured, may sometimes be able to turn the tables and manipulate or "game" indicators. This is especially likely to happen when they are required to provide evidence about the outcomes that lenders, donors, or others are looking for. More, even where this is suspected, little may be done. Serban tells us that "it is rather unlikely the EU will expel Romania, and its deep unpopularity in the country raise questions of implementation. … Romanian authorities seem to have become very apt at mimicking progress in the areas they consider important for the EU with the consequence that changes are introduced not for the country's benefit in the long term but rather to please Brussels." One of her interviewees referred to the old socialist slogan – "we pretend to reform, they pretend to care" (Serban, this volume: 203–204).

But how are we to distinguish gaming on the one hand from resistance or contestation (which some authors see as improving and legitimating the operation of indicators), on the other? The case studies in this collection show us how local and international actors make pragmatic use of more parochial or more general standards according to a calculus of political advantages. They therefore remind us that the key issue – also for those involved – is whose standards are being assumed – and whose standards should be applied. Sometimes the standards being relied on are ones already existing favored by the most powerful groups involved in the making or monitoring of the indicators concerned. On the other hand, many exercises in governance through indicators involve a deliberate effort to schematize controversial issues explicitly.[23] And what might otherwise seem a mindless "one-size-fits–all" approach may sometimes be justified as the attempt to find applicable standards that do not belong to any given society. Indicators can encourage "a race to the bottom," for example, in seeking to attract investment. But it can sometimes be good that we apply "our" standards of health and security elsewhere if this counteracts the tendency of globalization to lead to lesser standards. Ideals may be "found" as well as "lost" in translation.

REGULATING GLOBAL INDICATORS

Do indicators need to be – and can they be – regulated? As Merry tells us, those who produce indicators (and perhaps some of those who use them too) govern through and with indicators So they may certainly be considered as examples of the exercising of power without responsibility. As Bradley puts it,

> If an indicator is to be used to make a public policy decision, then the making of the indicator merits all the scrutiny that the decision would have merited in the absence of the indicator. The fact that a judgment is made by an indicator producer instead of a policymaker should not, in itself, provide any comfort unless the scrutiny that would have been applied to the policy decision can be applied to the indicator. (Bradley, this volume: 60)

Likewise, it seems only fair that organizations that seek to judge the success of others in matters regarding corruption, good governance, and corporate responsibility do not fall short according to their own criteria. It can be sobering to discover that those who seek to make others accountable for what they are doing are happy with rough and ready impressions of whether they are fulfilling their mandate – and that they treat other peoples' perceptions of their success in this as conclusory.

This collection provides us with a valuable starting point for thinking about how to develop principles for judging indicators. Dutta, in his study of two exercises using indicators, one concerned with the disbursement of funds (the Millennium Challenge Corporation [MCC]), and the other with deciding on accession to the EU, asks not whether indicators succeed in the sense of successfully influencing the candidate nations being evaluated, but rather whether the process itself meets criteria of legitimacy (Dutta, this volume). He discovered a paradoxical relationship between accountability and participation and concluded that

> MCC's process was more legible than the EU's process, and that the EU did focus more assiduously on reason-giving than the MCC. In contravention of our predictions, however, we found that the EU's qualitative process did not provide

more genuine opportunities for participation than the MCC's quantitative
process."[24] (Dutta, this volume: 185)

Some of the contributors go further and examine the way some indicators already
try to make their own exercise transparent. According to Urueña in particular, "The
Index (of rule of law) and other similar indicators seem keen on measuring their
own influence by applying a yardstick situated in a middle point between the first
and second levels mentioned previously. More often than not, the Index will quote
a head of state, a minister of justice or a high level judge, praising the Index and its
possibilities" (Urueña, this volume: 94). He admits, however,

> It is worth noting, though, that there is currently no research available on the
> actual influence of the Rule of Law Index on decision making; and, as far as I have
> been able to gather, there are no plans to develop a methodology to test a pilot of
> such study. The WJP does publish media coverage of the Index in its webpage by
> country; however, most of the coverage is only marginally concerned with the rule
> of law and the Index, and makes passing references to it. (Urueña, this volume: 95)

Special attention was given in the workshop on which this book is based to the role
law can play in regulating indicators. The fact that indicators are usually (though
not always) made by private actors poses a challenge that administrative lawyers and
others are increasingly facing up to. What is more problematic is the fact that what
law is able to do by way of regulating indicators tells us more about how law works
than about what may be needed to get to grips with this form of governance. This
emerges clearly if we ask not when law is *entitled* to regulate the making or using of
indicators but what it has to do if it is to *succeed* in regulating indicators. Trying to
monitor the making of indicators according to legal values such as reasoned decision
making, accountability, participation, and so forth could deal with some of the
criticisms we have discussed so far. But there are limits to how far law is able to deal
with the substantive rather than the procedural aspects of decisions.

In fact, law is often criticized for many of the same faults as indicators – it is
seen as being too often used to promote ideological goals and agendas, while being
subject to manipulation by those who frame its meaning in actual practice and
subverted by those who game their responses. Law too swings between rules and
discretion, oversimplifies factual situations, invents and imposes categories, and so
on. And it is hard to see how substantive outcomes of regulating indicators can be
measured without again resorting to indicators. Indicators themselves are intended
to act as a form of law-like regulation (playing a role as an alternative or supplement
to law), especially when we are dealing with administrative actions outside of the
typical national context. Finally, even if indicators could be made (even) more
law-like through regulation, would we always want this? There could be drawbacks

to juridifying indicators if it serves, for example, to legitimate the larger project for which such indicators are being used.

Should we then leave indicators to be regulated by the criteria of social scientists? They would likely concede that indicators need to be made more accurate and progress made in overcoming errors that derive from superficial comparisons. But social scientists also have something to say about more specifically normative issues. For example, when it comes to policy evaluations they point to the need to consult different stakeholders and even see this as necessary to be sure that the indicator is salient – not just legitimate. But certainly, social science criteria are not the same as legal considerations. For example, from a sociological perspective the distinction between legally binding and voluntary indicators will often be irrelevant.

But we should also not forget the role that social science itself played in the emergence of indicators, and continues to play in their legitimation. Indeed, many of the criticisms of knowledge and governance effects can be related to methodological debates in the social sciences between supporters of more quantitative or more qualitative strategies of understanding. Qualitative approaches for their part certainly gain in validity in being closer to the experience of those they evoke. But what they gain in this they lose in reliability – which is essential to those who wish to use indicators across times and places. (It is also interesting that the study by Dutta finds quantitative methods more effective in terms of accountability.) Social scientists have their own good reasons for seeking to make certain that indicators as tools are fit for the task. But their reasons are neither necessary nor sufficient for deciding what to do about indicators as instruments of governmentality. As with law, we cannot be sure that our goal in regulation is to put indicators beyond scientific criticism. Merry's arguments about knowledge and governance effects suggest that, apart from being implausible, this "solution" might be worse than the problem.

In practice, social science arguments are used to make indicators scientifically legitimate and law gives its blessing to the enterprise of indicators by treating science as more capable of producing knowledge free from challenge than is really possible. Even if it is the supposed scientificity of given indicators that is the source of their normative and political legitimacy – and their power to persuade,[25] what purport to be scientific statements result from prior normative judgments or policy calculations. And, as the case studies reveal, those who actually produce indicators often feel little need to respond to methodological criticisms.[26] Supposed differences between law and indicators can thus be exploited in a sort of three-card trick aimed at providing legitimacy at all costs. But perhaps there are ways of dealing with criticisms of indicators that do not look to law or social science? Could the answer to their tendency to de-politicize lie in a determined effort to re-politicize them?

CONTESTING GLOBAL INDICATORS

When it comes to bringing politics back in the main proposal to be found in the literature has to do with finding ways of making indicators more contestable.[27] In a recent retrospective Rosga and Satterthwaite (2008), leading commentators on the role of indicators in the realm of human rights, argue as follows:

> Although there is much in our original, largely sceptical, analyses that we find well-worth retaining – the turn to indicators by human rights practitioners may actually present unique opportunities to initiate vital political contestation. We remain vigilantly watchful for signs that the seemingly quenchless thirst for more and better quantitative data will, ..., have largely negative effects: replacing substantive political debate with the techno-bureaucratic language of audits and/or attempting to disguise real differences in geopolitical power arrangements with the putative point-of- view-less-ness of social scientific statistics. Nevertheless, we believe that a careful study of what has actually occurred in the field of human rights indicators reveals that something considerably more complicated is going on. In brief, debates over numbers provide lively venues for discussion of one of the most enduring challenges of international human rights: its sources of authority and the role of judgment in assessing State compliance with its rules. Attempts to create standardized universal indicators with which to assess states' human rights performance, in their very concrete failure, we believe, may yet provide new opportunities to think through long unresolved issues of intergovernmental, transnational rule.

They go on to explain:

> Although it may be true that quantitative methods, in their very abstraction and stripping away of contextualizing information have particular – and especially high – risks for misuse by those with the power to mobilize them, they are tools like any other. All tools can be misused; all social actors with power can misuse that power. The key lies in knowing where – and how – human judgment and political contestation should enter. Rather than trusting in numbers alone, those using human rights compliance indicators should embrace the opportunities presented by this new project, finding ways to utilize human rights indicators as a tool of global governance that allow the governed to form strategic political alliances with global bodies in the task of holding their governors to account. Such contestation saves indicators from being mere tools of governmentality, as they tell us, 'Thus, the human rights community's efforts to use statistics as part of a larger project of holding governments accountable to their populations, while it partakes of the same technologies of governmentality, can arguably be said to aim at different ends.' (Rosga and Satterthwaite 2009: 256)

In a similar way, in this volume, those like Urueña, who are more positive about the indicators they describe, see it as one of their key virtues that they expose the issues they deal with to debate. As he puts it, "Rule of law indicators are veritable technologies of global governance and, as such, it is important to engage with them, as they open a space for contestation, intervention and for a policy debate on what it means to encourage the rule of law in the developing world." The good result, as he describes it, is that "A community emerges around the Index engaged in a particular practice that consists of debating a complex concept (and as such, the community converges around the Index and also interacts with other communities through the indicator)." This community is "involved in a normative undertaking, where the debate occurs with the purpose of achieving a goal shared by the community (the rule of law) which provides the normative criterion to evaluate the proposals."

For his part, Bradley suggests that, whatever is the case at present, organizations *should* be encouraged to use indicators for this purpose. The motivations of this organization (and other similarly situated indicator producers)

> could be harnessed to foster the production of more useful indicators. Most importantly, indicator producers should be encouraged to highlight – rather than obscure or understate – the contingent and contestable nature of their measurements, as a way of sparking active, inclusive, and locally informed policy dialogue. Such a move might begin to close persistent and deeply problematic gaps between the measurers and the measured. Freedom House, for example, could use its platform as an indicator producer to provoke policy dialogue, spark social organization, encourage local involvement, and educate communities, all with the goal of contributing to durable progress on otherwise intractable policy difficulties. (Bradley, this volume: 32)

But it is not entirely clear what is meant by contestation. Is it a program, or just a fact about indicators (or about some indicators) as compared to others? Arguably the indicators described in this volume, concerned as they are with human rights or development, are particularly appropriate candidates for contestation, as compared say to health strategies, the reduction of malaria or the rating of credit worthiness. (On the other hand, the idea that some indicators are inherently more "technical" than others could be a fallacy.) We also need to ask how if at all is contestation to be differentiated from "experimentation"[28] or "resistance"? Must contestability be somehow deliberately built in? But can contestation always be anticipated? Would we want to be able to do so? Would there not be same danger of blunting potential criticisms by such efforts? Or is it just something that should be allowed to happen through the cut and thrust of battle during the use of indicators (or resistance to their use)? Thought also needs to be given to the stage of indicators where contestation does or should take place. All indicators involve at least some level of discussion or negotiation in their formation. Is there anything different about the contestation that takes place once the indicator is fully formed?

Understanding exactly what (successful) contestation can achieve, and how far it is feasible and desirable, takes us to the heart of the question of "success" that we have been examining in this afterword. On the one hand, Merry's approach could make it seem that indicators that *avoid or overcome contestation* are the most successful. On the other hand, these are surely the ones most likely to be exerting questionable knowledge and governance effects (unless we assume that contestable indicators are exactly those most likely to be socially accepted.). Helpfully, the contributions in this collection provide us with the chance to think more about when indicators are likely to be contested, by whom, and why. They show us that in practice those involved in contestation tend to be nation states (see, e.g., Serban) or international organizations (see Collier and Benjamin). Weaker parties have more need and less ability to contest. In his case study of the Freedom House indicator Bradley sees the lack of contestation as a bad sign because it fails to stimulate more careful development of the indicator. The same goes for Sarfaty's study of corporate responsibility indicators.[29] What also emerges clearly from the case studies is that – as with other social interventions – even without contestation the shape and meaning of indicators over time evolve as they are put to various uses and as the wider context changes.

In his case study Urueña sees this process of change as an entirely positive one.

> Although the rule of law is still seen as instrumental for development, a new view seems to be emerging, according to which legal institutions are parts of development in themselves: law is, in this context, a developmental goal for its own sake (Santos and Trubek 2006). And, following the lessons learned from the use of indicators in the instrumental view of law, it became clear that indicators could also be a useful platform to implement this new developmental commonsense, in which the rule of law could be measured as a value, regardless of its direct impact on other variables of development. (Urueña, this volume: 80)

But, as we have seen, change is not necessarily always for the best. Sarfaty, for example, shows how the meaning of corporate responsibility has evolved over time from a way of limiting risk to a form of governance. Serban argues that the redefinition of the rule of law in Romania in terms of corruption was a step backwards.

This returns us to the question what contestation is for. Is it, for example, a way to produce better results or more about improving participation?[30] Put in Merry's terms, is it more about correcting knowledge defects or improper governance? Certainly, the legitimation of indicators could gain from either of these improvements – but we could just as easily imagine potential tension between these tasks. Does contestation always assume that an ideal indicator can be found? According to the Habermasian approach taken by Urueña, the role of indicators is more than justified if it helps the community learn to debate with essentially contested concepts. As he argues, "The problem here is that it is hard to reach a significant agreement on what the rule of law actually means. And if it is impossible to define the notion with any analytical clarity, it becomes impossible to measure – or, at the very least, any measurement always will be open to this definitional challenge: Why this definition, and not that one? Why include this aspect of the rule of law and not this other?" But, he goes on,

> This concern misses the point. Although it is certainly true that no clear-cut, generally accepted, definition of the rule of law is forthcoming, arguing that this eliminates the uses of the concept (or its measurement) overlooks some of its most important dimensions. Indicators do not (indeed, cannot) measure reality objectively, in the way a thermometer would measure temperature. Rather, they inject, as we have seen, a normative analysis to the reality they measure, and constitute it. That is the case of the Rule of Law Index. Despite the conceptual approach of the Index, the rule of law is not a checklist but rather, as Jeremy Waldron has suggested, an essentially contested concept. (Urueña, this volume: 89)

But is re-politicization (through contestation) really a viable solution? Many case studies seek to reveal the controversial political choices and governance strategies that are hidden when indicators are (re)presented as mere techniques of measurement. But often the same authors admit that their ability to do this is exactly their appeal, pointing out, for example, that once in use it does not matter (to its success) if what an indicator refers to corresponds to what is out there; it is enough that it corresponds with a porous set of acceptable uses and deployments. Likewise, they tell us that indicators are used to talk about complex social realities about which there is little agreement. From the point of view of Luhmannian systems theory the maintenance of social complexity produces and requires differentiation of codes and programs. On this view there is little to be gained by re-politicizing what law and indicators have depoliticized. Public consensus is a chimera at a time of increasing (and competing) types of expertise – nor are the resources available that would be needed to allow members of civil society to double check on indicators.

If targets could contest every evaluation, what would be left of their normative force? What of the danger of "regulation by the regulated"?[31] Law and development initiatives may typically serve to perpetuate Western hegemony or neoliberal ideas. But the results are not necessarily better when projects are captured by corrupt local elites. In their role as accountable interventions indicators may need to be just as counterfactual as law if they are to stabilize expectations. Too much contestation can have counterproductive effects.[32] The strongest argument against contestation, however, is the claim that, as with law, indicators need to have some means of imposing closure at some point if they are to be of practical use. Whether and when contestation be seen as sign of success – or of failure – will therefore depend on how far a given indicator needs to provide certainty to users and targets. Why would anyone want to use an indicator that put itself radically in doubt?

NOTES

1 Merry tells us that "Indicators are a special use of statistics to develop quantifiable ways of assessing and comparing characteristics among groups, organizations, or nations" (Merry 2011: s84. See also Davis, Kingsbury, and Merry 2012b, 73–74.)

2 In any future agenda for the study of indicators it could be important to identify differences between these kinds of indicators and others.

3 I shall not summarize the chapters, as this has already been done in the introduction.

4 Some scholars also speak of "abduction," a way of formulating indicators that takes into account the responses of those whose behavior and ideas are being measured (see, e.g., Bezzi, Cannavà, and Palumbo 2010). This issue is highly relevant to the concluding discussion in this chapter with regard to contesting indicators.

5 On perceptions and reality, see Baudrillard (1975, 1994). This is complicated by the fact that some indicators, of course, aim only at measuring perceptions.

6 Mia Serban (this volume), "Rule of Law Indicators as a Technology of Power in Romania."

7 According to Davis, Merry, and Kingsbury (2012b), the sources of work on global indicators and power include scholarship dealing with "new governance" and experimentalist learning models, theories of governmentality and networks, theoretical writings on quantification and indicators as social phenomena, and insights from science and technology studies (STS), including actor–network theory.

8 See especially Francois Ewald's stimulating writings on normalization, e.g., Ewald (1990).

9 For Habermas the problem posed by indicators would be connected to the need to get beyond what he calls systematically distorted communication (see, e.g., Boeder 2005). For Luhmann, on the other hand, the issue would be rather how indicators illustrate the necessary limits of communications in conditions of highly differentiated social systems (see, e.g., King and Thornhill 2006).

10 See, e.g., Uribe, in this volume, who set out to study the International Development Agency's performance indicator to understand the underlying commonsense of development that is being promoted by the institution. The history of the indicator is analyzed to track the changes and continuities that have shaped the development commonsense promoted through the use of this development indicator. Then, the specific knowledge and governance effects produced by IDA's performance indicators are discussed, to finally argue that the type of effects produced by this indicator reproduce hegemonic worldviews because of the lack of contestation and regulation in the use and production of the indicator. Or Seban, whose careful empirical account tells us that the civil society has been partially co-opted and politicized, and is internally divided. Indifference or resistance to indicators does not necessarily break down along government/ civil society lines, however, but along perceived technical/political lines, both within the government and civil society. This dividing line is also at the heart of the emerging indicators consciousness in the country.

11 At the same time, provision of this kind of data also *creates* the need, in the sense of demand for these indicators, as in the case of *U.S. News & World Report* and its publication of university rankings. An even clearer case is that of financial rating agencies.

12 According to Urueña, in this volume, the Rule of Law Index serves as the working language for interaction among regimes, both at the international level and in the interaction between national systems and international law (for instance with the use of internationally developed indicators by domestic courts).

13 Serban, in this volume, tells us that Romania does not itself make use of the statistics it collects about its compliance with required rule of law standards but just hands them on to the European Union.

14 Sarfaty, in this volume: 115, explains that in the United States, "although ESG disclosure remains on the SEC's long-term agenda, it has become less of a short-term priority given the resources needed to implement the Dodd–Frank Act."

15 In a particularly interesting passage, Urueña points to a paradox involved in measuring the rule of law. It is important, he argues, to measure the law in action and not only the law in books. On the other hand, he admits that doing this can easily lead to the conclusion that the rule of law is a myth and that only the rule of men/(and sometimes women) exists. The solution, he says, is that "(T)he indicator's mediation is both a descriptive and a normative exercise… It is descriptive, because it allows the WJPE to see what the respondents think of their own country's performance under each principle, factor, and subfactor. But it is also normative, as it reflects WPJ's set of deontological choices (the principles, factors, and subfactors) about what it means to adhere to the rule of law. The Rule of Law Index therefore can be read as both a technology of observation that facilitates the Realist ideal of going beyond "law on the books" (and is akin to statistics or demography), and a new layer that injects normative judgment where only disorganized facts existed. The Index thus embodies a particular way of defining the rule of law normatively and a theory about what the rule of law is. The Index then acts, in effect, to promote this theory" (Urueña, this volume: 89).

16 Bradley, in this volume, for example, criticizes the causal claims underlying Freedom House's indicator concerning the acceleration of economic growth, arguing that it is unsupported by any of the "findings" of the indicator, which does not engage in any of the statistical tests available in the social sciences to assess causation. These assumed – or, perhaps less charitably, presupposed – paths of causation can in fact do serious harm. For instance, they can become excuses for manipulation by government or corporate actors able to exploit performance on indicators to serve their own agendas without actually bringing any of the promised benefits.

17 For example, as Sarfaty (this volume: 111) says, "there is a general concern that the GRI ranks the quality of reports based on the amount of disclosure (e.g., the number of indicators that companies report on) rather than the quality and accuracy of a firm's actual performance. Critics have also questioned the credibility of third-party verification services (usually performed by private accounting and consulting firms), given that there are no uniform guidelines to ensure their reliability."

18 As opposed to being based on partial or self-interested ones, such as businessmen's ideas of ideal labor laws see, e.g., Collier and Benjamin (this volume).

19 Bradley (in his conference presentation) tells us that the Freedom House "indicator at all points remains one of perceptions, reliant on the accuracy of other analyses closer to actual data, and thus lagging or completely missing changes on the ground. If Chinese gender equality were in fact to change, Freedom House's score for it would change only if other observers brought it to public attention first."

20 As Musaraj (this volume: 230) argues, "transplantation of particular research frames from one place to another – in this case, from South America to Albania – ignore differences in the very meaning and definition of terms such as 'corruption' and 'transparency.' These transfers also conceal the historical origins of specific concepts while generating new forms of political action."

21 The ideology of neoliberalism can be detected in the popularity of this form of technology and the way it seeks to influence action, as much as in the substance of the goals single indicators seek to achieve.

22 A prominent example of this approach is the Voluntary Principles on Security and Human Rights, which promote human rights risk assessments in the extractive industries sector. *Introduction*, Voluntary Principles on Security & Human Rights, voluntaryprinciples.org/principles/introduction.

23 Uribe (this volume) explains, with respect to the Study on Governance Indicators promoted by the World Bank Institute, that their notion of governance encompassed six dimensions: (1) voice and accountability, (2) political instability and violence, (3) government effectiveness, (4) regulatory quality, (5) rule of law, and (6) control of corruption.

24 As Sarfaty (this volume: 105) tells us, "Private regulatory bodies have emerged as significant players in the production and enforcement of international law" but "the legitimacy of private actors is questionable given their lack of public accountability, an absence of oversight mechanisms, and possible manipulation by special interests."

25 As Rosga and Satterthwaite point out, "the treaty bodies seem to be hoping that the power of social science will have greater 'compliance pull' than well-reasoned General Comments or persuasive decisions in individual cases." (See Rosga and Satterthwaite 2009: 203)

26 See especially Bradley's chapter on the Freedom House indicators, in this volume.

27 The role of law and social science would then be to find ways to help keep open the possibility for such contestation.

28 Bradley (this volume) suggests that while some basic principles and parameters may already be clearly established and broadly applicable across all sites, many essential elements for success may be quite uncertain, or indeed unknown. It may therefore be very desirable to promote locally initiated experimentation at numerous sites. Enhancing 'freedom' would seem to be an example of where this sort of approach might be useful, as the specific developments and characteristics of freedom could differ based on available resources, history, and social and political structures.

29 Sarfaty (this volume: 119) tells us that "it is difficult for stakeholders to challenge the power of experts and their methodology and assumptions in producing the indicators. Because indicators carry scientific authority, they mask potential conflicts of interest among technical experts and leave little room for contestation. This is the case for the GRI, where accounting firms are heavily involved in both indicator production and data verification."

30 The issue of participation is a recurrent one in discussing indicators. As Uribe, for example, writes, "the lack of mechanisms for participation and ownership in the development field has prevented contestation by non-hegemonic development actors. The few existing mechanisms of ownership, such as the Poverty Reduction Strategy Paper in the World Bank, provide a limited space for participation, as receiving governments are expected to pick and choose development policies and goals from a set of accepted preestablished objectives that respond to the hegemonic theory promoted by the donor institution" (Uribe, this volume: 141).

31 Seban (this volume) tells us that once Romania won the EU-accession prize, all interest in the rule of law index almost disappeared.

32 According to an EU official interviewed by Seban, "politicians subject to constant reflection are more likely to focus on immediate results instead." (Serban, this volume: 213)

REFERENCES

Akech, Migai. 2015. "Evaluating the Impact of Corruption Indicators on Governance Discourses in Kenya." In Sally Engle Merry, Kevin Davis, and Benedict Kingsbury, eds., *The Quiet Power of Indicators: Measuring Governance, Corruption, and Rule of Law.* New York: Cambridge University Press.

Baudrillard, Jean. 1975. *The Mirror of Production.* New York: Telos Press.

1994. *Simulacra and Simulation*, Ann Arbor: University of Michigan Press.

Bezzi, Claudio, Leonardo Cannavà, and Maurizio Palumbo (eds.). 2010. *Costruire e usare indicatori nella ricerca sociale e nella valutazione*, Rome: Franco Angeli.

Boeder, Pieter. 2005. "Habermas' Heritage: The Future of the Public Sphere in the Network Society." *First Monday* 10: 9–5. http://firstmonday.org/ojs/index.php/fm/article/view/1280/1200.

Bradley, Christopher G. 2015. "International Organizations and the Production of Indicators: The Case of Freedom House." In Sally Engle Merry, Kevin Davis, and Benedict Kingsbury, eds., *The Quiet Power of Indicators: Measuring Governance, Corruption, and Rule of Law.* New York: Cambridge University Press.

Collier, Debbie, and Paul Benjamin. 2015. "Measuring Labor Market Efficiency: Indicators that Fuel an Ideological War and Undermine Social Concern and Trust in the South African Regulatory Process." In Sally Engle Merry, Kevin Davis, and Benedict Kingsbury, eds., *The Quiet Power of Indicators: Measuring Governance, Corruption, and Rule of Law.* New York: Cambridge University Press.

Davis, Kevin E., Benedict Kingsbury, and Sally Engle Merry (eds.). 2012a. *Governance by Indicators*, Oxford: Oxford University Press.

(eds.). 2012b. "Indicators as a Technology of Global Governance." *Law and Society Review* 46(1): 71–104.

Dutta, Nikhil. 2015. "Tradeoffs in Accountability: Conditionality Processes in the European Union and Millennium Challenge Corporation." In Sally Engle Merry, Kevin Davis, and Benedict Kingsbury, eds., *The Quiet Power of Indicators: Measuring Governance, Corruption, and Rule of Law.* New York: Cambridge University Press.

Ewald, Francis. 1990. "Norms, Discipline and the Law." *Representations*, No. 30, Special Issue: Law and the Order of Culture, 138–161.

Jacobsson, Bengt. 2000. "Standardization and Expert Knowledge." In Nils Brunsson and Bengt Jacobsson, eds., *A World of Standards.* Oxford: Oxford University Press.

King, Michael, and Chris Thornhill. 2006. *Niklas Luhmann's Theory of Politics and Law.* London: Palgrave Macmillan.

Kundera, Milan. 1991. *Immortality.* New York. Faber and Faber.

Merry, Susan Engle. 2011. "Measuring the World: Indicators, Human Rights, and Global Governance." *Current Anthropology* 52(Supplement 3): s83.

Musaraj, Smoki. 2015. "Indicators, Global Expertise, and a Local Political Drama: Producing and Deploying Corruption Perception Data in Post-Socialist Albania." In Sally Engle Merry, Kevin Davis, and Benedict Kingsbury, eds., *The Quiet Power of Indicators: Measuring Governance, Corruption, and Rule of Law.* New York: Cambridge University Press.

Power, Michael. 2004. *The Risk Management of Everything: Rethinking the Politics of Uncertainty.* London: Demos. http://www.demos.co.uk/files/riskmanagementofeverything.pdf.

Rosga, Ann Janette, and Margaret L. Satterthwaite. 2009. "The Trust in Indicators: Measuring Human Rights." *Berkeley Journal of International Law*, 253.

Rubington, Earl, and Martin Weinberg. 2010. *The Study of Social Problems: Seven Perspectives.* Oxford: Oxford University Press.

Santos, Alvaro, and David M. Trubek. 2006. "The Third Moment in Law and Development Theory and the Emergence of a New Critical Practice." In David M. Trubek and Alvaro Santos, eds., *The New Law and Economic Development: A Critical Appraisal*, 1–18. Cambridge: Cambridge University Press.

Sarfaty, Galit A. 2015. "Measuring Corporate Accountability through Global Indicators." In Sally Engle Merry, Kevin Davis, and Benedict Kingsbury, eds., *The Quiet Power of Indicators: Measuring Governance, Corruption, and Rule of Law*. New York: Cambridge University Press.

Uribe, María Angélica Prada. 2015. "The Quest for Measuring Development: The Role of the Indicator Bank." In Sally Engle Merry, Kevin Davis, and Benedict Kingsbury, eds., *The Quiet Power of Indicators: Measuring Governance, Corruption, and Rule of Law*. New York: Cambridge University Press.

Urueña, René. 2015. "Indicators and the Law: A Case Study of the Rule of Law Index." In Sally Engle Merry, Kevin Davis, and Benedict Kingsbury, eds., *The Quiet Power of Indicators: Measuring Governance, Corruption, and Rule of Law*. New York: Cambridge University Press.

Index

Puddington, Arch, 44, 51
purchasing power parity (PPP), 139

qualification, 4
quantification, 161–162, 171–172, 180
Quigley, Thomas E., 62

Raik, Kristi, 181
Rama, Ina, 222, 224, 230, 231, 232, 234,
    235–240, 241
Rapid Results Initiative (Kenya), 264
reason-giving
    defined, 171
    Millennium Challenge Corporation (MCC),
        172–174
reform
    accountability, 210–213
    business-friendly labor, 292, 306
    constitutional, 255
    global indicators, 18
    institutional, 78, 140, 248, 264, 266
        Kenya, 249
    judicial, 200, 236, 322
        Romania, 199, 200–204, 205, 208
    legal, 20, 77, 78, 79, 285, 289
    levels, 170
    objectives (EU), 160, 168
    political (rule of law), 208
    prioritizing, 169
    public sector, 275
    rule of law, 54, 77, 86, 200, 217
        Romania, 8
    shallow, 182
    state actors, 208–210
regulation, 149–150
    approaches, 3
    business, 79
    distance, 139
    domestic financial, 111–117
    ineffective, 255, 256
    information, 108
    international, of private persons, 19
    labor, 16
    labor market, 79, 284, 285, 290
        contextual, 287
    legal, 107
        human rights, 91
    self-, 103, 107, 120, 321
    Smart (World Bank/IFC), 80
    state, of financial entities, 20
    sustainability, 110
Rehn, Olli, 175

*Report on the Competitiveness of European
    Industry* (WEF), 293
reporting
    climate change, 109
    corporate sustainability, 107
    economic, social, and governance
        (ESG), 112
    Global Reporting Initiative principles, 107
    sustainability, 105, 112, 113
    treadmill, 111
reputation, 29
    cerebral versus objective, 51
    Freedom House, 48–52
    threats to, 51
research, 29
    Freedom House, 33, 34
responsibility, corporate social (CSR), 106
Rhineland (business) model, 294
rights
    civil (and personal autonomy, Freedom
        House), 38
    cultural, 37, 47
    economic, 37, 47
    human, 91, 104, 106, 122, 123, 330
    individual (and personal autonomy), 41
    labor, 106
    minimum statutory labour, 286
    negative, 41
    operating without undue governmental
        influence, 38
    political (Freedom House ratings), 37
    social, 37, 47
risk management (defined), 122
Romania, 17, 175, 205, 323, 326
    Cooperation and Verification Mechanism
        benchmarks, 201
    European Union accession era, 201
    Netherlands and, 204
    post-Communist periods, 201
    rule of law scrutiny, 201
Romanian Academic Society, 212
Roodman, David, 142
Roosevelt, Eleanor, 32
Rose, Nicholas, 8
Rosga, Ann Janette, 330
Ruggie, John, 107
rule of law (indicator), 331, 332
    benefits, 156, 199
    Bulgaria, 202
    characteristics, 85
    confusion surrounding, 206
    contested as concept, 204

Books in the Series

The Gacaca Courts and Post-Genocide Justice and Reconciliation in Rwanda: Justice without Lawyers
Phil Clark

Law, Society, and History: Themes in the Legal Sociology and Legal History of Lawrence M. Friedman
Robert W. Gordon and Morton J. Horwitz

After Abu Ghraib: Exploring Human Rights in America and the Middle East
Shadi Mokhtari

Adjudication in Religious Family Laws: Cultural Accommodation, Legal Pluralism, and Gender Equality in India
Gopika Solanki

Water On Tap: Rights and Regulation in the Transnational Governance of Urban Water Services
Bronwen Morgan

Elements of Moral Cognition: Rawls' Linguistic Analogy and the Cognitive Science of Moral and Legal Judgment
John Mikhail

A Sociology of Constitutions: Constitutions and State Legitimacy in Historical-Sociological Perspective
Chris Thornhill

Mitigation and Aggravation at Sentencing
Edited by Julian Roberts

Institutional Inequality and the Mobilization of the Family and Medical Leave Act: Rights on Leave
Catherine R. Albiston

Authoritarian Rule of Law: Legislation, Discourse and Legitimacy in Singapore
Jothie Rajah

Law and Development and the Global Discourses of Legal Transfers
Edited by John Gillespie and Pip Nicholson

Law against the State: Ethnographic Forays into Law's Transformations
Edited by Julia Eckert, Brian Donahoe, Christian Strümpell, and Zerrin Özlem Biner

Transnational Legal Process and State Change
Edited by Gregory C. Shaffer

Legal Mobilization under Authoritarianism: The Case of Post-Colonial Hong Kong
Edited by Waikeung Tam

Complementarity in the Line of Fire: The Catalysing Effect of the International Criminal Court in Uganda and Sudan
Sarah M. H. Nouwen

Political and Legal Transformations of an Indonesian Polity: The Nagari from Colonisation to Decentralisation
Franz von Benda-Beckmann and Keebet von Benda-Beckmann